THE NEW ASIAN CITY

T0338058

The New Asian City

*Three-Dimensional Fictions of
Space and Urban Form*

JINI KIM WATSON

UNIVERSITY OF MINNESOTA PRESS

MINNEAPOLIS • LONDON

Publication of this work has been supported in part through the generosity of the Abraham and Rebecca Stein Faculty Publication Fund of New York University.

An earlier version of chapter 3 was previously published as "Seoul and Singapore as 'New Asian Cities': Literature, Urban Transformation, and the Concentricity of Power," *positions: east asia cultures critique* 19, no. 1 (Spring 2011): 193–215. A version of chapter 5 has appeared previously as "The Way Ahead: The Politics and Poetics of Singapore's Developmental Landscape," *Contemporary Literature* 49, no. 4 (2008): 683–711; copyright 2008 by the Board of Regents of the University of Wisconsin System; reproduced courtesy of the University of Wisconsin Press.

"Catering for the People" and "The Way Ahead" from *Gods Can Die,* Heinemann Educational Books (Asia), 1977. "Island" from *Ulysses by the Merlion,* Heinemann Educational Books (Asia), 1979. Copyright Edwin Thumboo. Reproduced courtesy of the author.

All excerpts from Arthur Yap's poetry are reproduced courtesy of Jenny Yap.

Published by the University of Minnesota Press
111 Third Avenue South, Suite 290
Minneapolis, MN 55401-2520
http://www.upress.umn.edu

Library of Congress Cataloging-in-Publication Data

Watson, Jini Kim.
The new Asian city : three-dimensional fictions of space and urban form /
Jini Kim Watson.
p. cm.
Includes bibliographical references and index.
ISBN 978-0-8166-7572-2 (hc : alk. paper) — ISBN 978-0-8166-7573-9 (pbk. : alk. paper)
1. East Asian fiction—History and criticism. 2. Cities and towns in literature.
3. Urbanization in literature. 4. Space in literature. 5. Urbanization—East Asia—History.
6. Cities and towns—East Asia—Growth—History. I. Title.
PL493.W37 2011
809'.933585009732—dc22
2011003818

Printed in the United States of America on acid-free paper

The University of Minnesota is an equal-opportunity educator and employer.

18 17 16 15 14 13 12 11   10 9 8 7 6 5 4 3 2 1

To my parents,

TAISOO KIM *and* KEITH WATSON

As we gain perspective, from the long history of the literature of country and city, we see how much, at different times and in different places, it is a connecting process, in what has to be seen ultimately as a common history.

—RAYMOND WILLIAMS, *The Country and the City*

That space signifies is incontestable. But what it signifies is dos and don'ts—and this brings us back to power.

—HENRI LEFEBVRE, *The Production of Space*

Contents

Note on Romanization / xi

INTRODUCTION The Production of Space in
Singapore, Seoul, and Taipei / 1

PART I **Colonial Cities**

1   Imagining the Colonial City / 27

2   Orphans of Asia: Modernity and Colonial Literature / 53

    TRANSITION Export Production and the Blank Slate / 87

PART II **Postwar Urbanism**

3   Narratives of Human Growth versus Urban Renewal / 99

4   The Disappearing Woman, Interiority, and Private Space / 133

    TRANSITION Roads, Railways, and Bridges:
    Arteries of the Nation / 167

PART III **Industrializing Landscapes**

5   The Way Ahead: The Politics and Poetics of Singapore's
    Developmental Landscape / 179

6   Mobility and Migration in Taiwanese New Cinema / 203

7   The Redemptive Realism of Korean *Minjung* Literature / 227

CONCLUSION   Too Late, Too Soon: Globalization and
New Asian Cities / 251

Acknowledgments / 257

Notes / 259

Bibliography / 277

Index / 293

Note on Romanization

In general I used the Pinyin (for Chinese) and McCune-Reischauer (for Korean) Romanization systems. Exceptions are made for proper names more commonly known by other Romanization forms, for example, Park Chung Hee (not Pak Chŏng-hŭi). Similarly, I retained variant spellings of Chinese and Korean names, places, and terms (such as *hsiang-t'u*) if they have been commonly used or translated as such; in particular, many Taiwanese texts use the Wade-Giles system. Where needed for clarity, I indicated the Pinyin or McCune-Reischauer form in parentheses.

The Production of Space in Singapore, Seoul, and Taipei

In all these actual social relations and forms of consciousness, ideas of the country and the city, often of an older kind, continue to act as partial interpreters. But we do not always see that in their main bearings they are forms of response to a social system as a whole.

—RAYMOND WILLIAMS, *The Country and the City*

THE NEW ASIAN CITY

With the recent industrial rise of China and India, the postwar success of the so-called Asian Tiger economies seems to have blurred into the more general pattern of industrializing Asia. It is easy to forget, then, that an earlier generation of booming metropolises—including Seoul, Singapore, Hong Kong, and Taipei—were not always such gleaming beacons of development. They themselves went through enormous upheavals in urban space and populations. This book analyzes the histories and fictional representations of urban transformation in Singapore, South Korea, and Taiwan— three of the Pacific Rim's original "newly industrializing countries"—from the colonial period to the late 1980s. In the decades immediately after decolonization, these nations displayed incredible rates of economic growth and effectively led the way in industrial development outside the West, becoming the "good pupils," in Samir Amin's words, of third world development (80). Drawing partly on the economic and urban model of Tokyo, and precursors to the now-common signifiers of globalization that we see in dazzling Shanghai, Kuala Lumpur, or Bangalore, these three sites document a founding moment of third world industrialization that has been uniquely influential in terms of urban and industrial strategy, as well as the aesthetic responses to its results. In one sense, this book can be understood as a cultural and spatial history of the developmental state. More centrally,

1

it argues that the massive shift in urban forms produces a particular kind of fictional text, one that foregrounds the complex realities and conflicts of these transformations.

My title borrows from architectural critic Jeffrey Kipnis,[1] who has used the term "New Asian City" to describe the bustling metropolises of newly industrializing countries such as South Korea, Taiwan, Singapore, Malaysia, and, more recently, mainland China (169). In Kipnis's account, the New Asian City model is typified by Seoul's postwar development, which produced "an ugly, sprawling urban monster true enough, but a money machine that buried South Korea in cash" (169). Its essence is rapid construction and tabula rasa policy, and its urbanism occupies an uncanny place with regards to both discarded prewar modernisms ("Avant-Garde I," as Kipnis calls it) and French-inspired theories of postmodernism (or "Avant-Garde II"). In his words, "The New Asian City warps past any Marxist notion of 'formation' or 'construction'; it is an artifaction of Speed and Dominance, unholy and beyond history" (170). While it is clear that such Asian cities are neither new nor "beyond history," they have certainly become the "interpretive image" of Asia Pacific development.[2] Despite the hyperbole, Kipnis's comments contain the simple observation that there is a particular material configuration and corresponding aesthetic form to regions of postcolonial Asia.[3] This study argues that these cities evidence a new model of development in which the city is conceived first and foremost as a production platform—for the production of surplus values, laboring bodies, and national subjects—and less as a site of traditional civic, ceremonial, or economic transactions.[4] *The New Asian City* is concerned with the processes, conflicts and representations of this shift. In this introductory chapter, I give a brief historical background and rationale of my choice of these sites, as well as suggest how the New Asian City draws on and challenges traditional conceptions of postcolonial studies. I will also outline the transdisciplinary method—linking literature, architecture, urban studies, and film—at work in this book.

Postcolonialism and the East Asian Newly Industrializing Countries: Singapore, Taiwan, and South Korea

To understand the coherence of the New Asian City as category, we must consider, in broad strokes, the colonial and postcolonial histories of

Singapore, Taiwan, and South Korea, which are as different from each other as they are from the more usual regions examined by postcolonial studies.[5] Although the history of each site will be discussed in more detail as the book progresses, we may begin by briefly sketching their colonial histories.

Established in 1819 by the British East India Company on an island off the tip of the Malay peninsula, Singapore became a Chinese-majority trading post and was ruled as part of the British Straits settlements. After a brief period of Japanese rule during World War II and the return of the British, it passed bloodlessly to self-rule in 1959, and then into a short-lived federation with Malaya in 1963. Full independence of the city-state was only achieved after it separated from the Malaysian Federation in 1965, an event that followed tensions between Singapore's People's Action Party and the United Malayan National Organization.[6] Wishing to distance itself from communist China, the city-state maintained close strategic ties with Britain and the United States. Although its national language is Malay and its official languages are English, Chinese, and Tamil, it adopted the former colonizer's language as its language of state, trade, and communication. In other words, it did not so much reject its colonial formation as strive to update and nationalize its original function as a British trading entrepôt to become a successful global importer/exporter. One of the founding members of ASEAN (Association of Southeast Asian Nations), Singapore has prided itself on being a modern, multicultural, postcolonial city-state.

The other two countries under consideration were the two longtime colonies of Japan, Taiwan or "Formosa" (occupied 1895–1945) and Korea or "Chosen" (1910–45), both liberated at the end of the World War II with Japan's defeat. They too followed a successful export-led path of development and are now regional economic leaders. However, their status as postcolonial nations has been little recognized for several reasons. For a postcolonial territory such as Taiwan (as for the Philippines and Indonesia), the multiple colonizations by Europe, Japan, and (arguably) mainland China need to be considered.[7] After centuries of occupation by the Dutch, Spanish, Southern Chinese, and Japanese, the establishment in 1945 of the Republic of China government, led by Chiang Kai-shek's Kuomintang (Nationalist or KMT) party, has been viewed as another kind of colonialism. Although some scholars believe that this internal colonialism ended only in 1987 with the lifting of martial law and recognition of the Minnan and Hakka ethnic identities, from the aboriginal perspective, neither 1945 nor 1987 would properly signal the postcolonial. Taiwan remains an effective "state without nationhood" (Liao, "Postcolonial Studies," 210), even while its legitimacy as a state is much contended by mainland China. Liao notes the inadequacy of established postcolonial theories regarding Taiwan: "As the effects [of Chinese and Japanese imperial power] are very different from those of European colonialism, the dominant postcolonial theory can only partially describe what constitutes the 'postcolonial' condition in Taiwan" (210). The legacy of multiple imperialisms is echoed in the Korean situation, which may best be summed up as "a nation with two states." Debate over the validity of the term *postcolonial* here has centered on the implicit question of how such status can be granted to a nation still divided as a result of conflicting imperial forces. After the devastating civil war of 1950–53 and the implementation of what Paik Nak-chung calls the "division system," half arguably remains in a neocolonial relationship with the United States,[8] while the other is on the brink of either collapse or nuclear war. In a sense, Korea (and especially North Korea) remains decidedly "anti" rather than "post" colonial.

What all three sites—Singapore, Taiwan, and South Korea—point to are the many complexities and gradations that must fill out the concept of the *postcolonial.* Such a term is too often thought of as simply the condition following independence from European powers in the decades after World War II, with Anglophone Africa, India, and the Caribbean as its paradigmatic sites. Further, my project is not driven by the more standard postcolonial question of "'displacement' of indigenous cultures wrought by colonialism" (Kusno, 7)[9]—that is to say, the interest in British or Japanese identity versus Singaporean, Korean, or Taiwanese. Yet neither is the absence of this question, or the incongruousness of East Asia within postcolonial studies, what brings these three sites together as objects of analysis. Rather, I suggest we examine these Asian Tiger nations for their comparable postcolonial developmental paths within what Frübel et al. famously termed in 1980 "the New International Division of Labour."[10] All three were home to important colonial cities, and all three transformed themselves into the most successful of newly industrializing countries via a fundamental rearrangement of urban and national space that had begun in the colonial period. Along with Hong Kong, these four Asian "miracle economies" constitute the poster child of postcolonial industrialization. Let us note here that although the history of Hong Kong broadly shares the same economic path as the others, it is distinct thanks to the 1997 handover from British crown colony to mainland special administrative region. Because I am interested in the troubled articulations of postcolonial nationalism and modernity after independence, Hong Kong's unique case lies outside the scope of this project.

Outside postcolonial literary and cultural studies, my grouping of these sites is not especially new. Their remarkable career as Asian miracles has long constituted an exemplary object within modernization studies, a subfield of area studies. Along with architectural observations about the region's material forms, books such as Robert Wade's prize-winning *Governing the Market* (1992) are evidence of the sustained focus on this region within other disciplines. Wade's work, among many others, has helped to establish a regional characterization from the perspective of economic development of these New Asian Cities as both exceptions and models.[11] This book, then, offers an alternative narrative to the one we are used to within postcolonial studies, which has had little to say on the apparent success stories of the Asia Pacific, but goes beyond analyzing them as mere economic models. By focusing on how historical contradictions inform a particular configuration I am calling the New Asian City, I attempt to flesh out an idea of postcolonial space in its East and Southeast Asian manifestation.

ON THE POSTCOLONIAL

While this study pays attention to concrete spatial and economic histories, my task is not simply to shift the focus of postcolonial literary studies to these objects. I am interested in the *logic and form* of developmental spaces—accessed through the fictional text—rather than the sites or buildings themselves as empirical objects in space. Nor am I interested in an abstract use of spatial vocabulary. For anthropologists Akhil Gupta and James Ferguson, the recent overreliance on spatial metaphors in postcolonial theory—the global versus the local, diaspora, borders, and marginality—occlude what should be the primary focus: "the processes of *production* of difference in a world of culturally, socially and economically interconnected and interdependent spaces" (43). It is not simply a matter of tracking the ways cultural localities are imagined in a globalizing world, but of discerning the spatial processes that produced those differences in the first place. Postcolonial studies has been absorbed by questions of migration and diaspora, but less so by internal migration and the striking urban and industrial transformations reshaping many postindependent states. One of the ways we can understand the "shared historical processes that [differentiate] the world as it connects it" (46) is to trace the spatial differentiation produced internally by states under globalizing capital. Thus, although this book includes substantial literary and film analyses, I do not reproduce the common interpretive methodology of much post-colonial studies that relies on a politics of textuality. Such a strategy derives from Said's highly influential book *Orientalism* (1978) and his demonstra-tion of the "worldliness" of the cultural text, or how literature and art may serve as ideological underpinnings for the most unscrupulous of imperial deeds. Notwithstanding the undeniable import of his work, the primacy of this relationship has resulted in the reverse task of recovering resis-tance to imperialism and neoimperialism, especially in the recovery and validation of (post)colonial cultural texts. In its most typical form, such literary studies find progressive agency in the written expression of the oppressed or subaltern subject, and may depart from the important task of explicating anticolonial thought and culture to "the move which effec-tively replaces politics with textuality" (Gandhi, 156).[12] Such an approach has indeed become the trademark of a kind of postcolonial analysis that aims toward an ever more specific cultural politics of difference. More-over, the recuperating of occluded or oppressed cultures brings with it the associated problem of equating literary or other texts with an authen-tic expression of a particular culture's political resistance or identity.[13] As Peter Hallward notes, "unless we are prepared to equate creative expression with the direct reflection of a specified community, culture or some other underlying reality, we must find a way to account for the specific without recourse to the criteria of the *authentic* (as measured by fidelity to cultural origin or norm)" (39–40). Like Hallward, I see the problem with such approaches in that they figure autonomous cultures and identities as the only proper object of study, with literature as their vehicle of transparent expression. By bringing to the fore spatial realities, modes of production, and the shifting and contradictory figures of expression they give rise to, this book moves beyond both the emphasis on cultural production as identity and the metaphoric understanding of space.

To attend to the material and spatial (rather than cultural) and national (rather than transnational) aspects of postcolonial development involves a fundamental recognition of a basic asymmetry in global development. Aijaz Ahmad has called this arrangement the "gaps between the various layers of world capitalism" (316) or—as I would put it—the unevenly productive role of spatial relationships. In a pointed passage, Ahmad writes of India's postcolonial dilemma:

> European transition occurred when there were no external, imperialist, far more powerful capitalist countries to dominate and subjugate the European ones; when the world's resources—from minerals to agricultural raw materials to the unpaid labour of countless millions—could form the basis for Europe's accumulation; when vast reservoirs of European populations could simply be exported to other continents.... Where can India send the approximately five hundred million people for whom Indian capitalism simply cannot provide, and whose minerals is the Indian bourgeoisie to extract to fuel our economy and guarantee our balance of payments for the next two hundred years? It has only *its own* forests to ravage, *its own* mountains to denude, *its own* rivers to dam up and pollute, *its own* countryside to consign to generalized filth, *its own* cities to choke with carbonized air—in a subordinated partnership with imperialist capital. (315, emphasis added)

Among postcolonial studies' important, ethical examinations of the unequal conditions wrought by imperialism, we can pose Ahmad's specific question of uneven spatial development as the central concern of this book: what does it mean for a third world country to attempt to develop from the subordinate and constricted position he describes? As we will see, the postcolonial state's development under these asymmetrical conditions is particularly striking in the Asia Pacific, where national economic landscapes, political ideologies, imagined communities, and aesthetic responses all coalesce, overlap, or counteract each other in the decidedly limited spaces of New Asian Cities. This study, then, is devoted neither to cataloging the general conditions of late capitalism nor to examining textual resistance, subaltern traces, or hybridized cultural identities. I use literary

and cinematic texts not for their privileged access to any cultural or subjective truths, but as historical palimpsests that register the most profound
contradictions of postcolonial development. In other words, I explore a
particular strand of postcolonialism that can best be understood in terms
of the struggle over space rather than over culture or identity. I suggest
that there is a kind of postcolonial historical development whose primary process is spatial and architectural transformation, a process most
clearly registered in the figures and displacements taken up in various
fictional texts.

The New Asian City is therefore not about reevaluating the field of postcolonial studies to include a region or object of study previously excluded.
Rather, reading New Asian City literature and film can move us toward
a new way of thinking about colonialism and globalization; such texts render lucid, recreate, and reimagine the very production of (postcolonial)
space. Accordingly, my use of the term *postcolonial* must be understood in
this altered sense: I take it to describe aesthetic production arising within
the material, social, economic, and political configurations that obtained
during and after colonial occupation, *as well as* the spatial production of
those configurations. I am especially interested in the "code switching" of
power from the colonial regime to the postcolonial (Baucom, "Township,"
234) and how the working through of this transfer occurs in spatialized
aesthetic form.

To sum up, rather than take the colonial map as the defining limit of
my project (which would dictate that Korea and Taiwan be studied with
Manchuria, and Singapore with Malaysia), I use a regional material formation—the New Asian City—already acknowledged in both architectural
criticism and modernization studies as my point of departure. This project
approaches certain late twentieth-century Pacific Rim urban sites in a way
that complicates both standard postcolonial accounts of the region as well
as earlier—and still dominant—Western theorizations on modernity and
urbanization.[14]

Three-Dimensional Fictions: Contradiction, Figuration, and Spatial Form

In Cho Se-hŭi's 1978 novella "A Little Ball Launched by a Dwarf" ("Nanjangi
ka ssoaollin chagŭn kong"), the protoganists—three teenage children of a

squatter-dwelling family—face the harsh realities of South Korea's indus-trial push under dictator Park Chung Hee. The sparsely narrated story details the family's struggle to maintain their unregistered home, which is quite literally in the way of the country's development: an urban renewal ordinance announces the settlement is to be demolished and replaced with high-rise apartment buildings for middle-class residents. The closer they are to losing their home, the odder their father's (the dwarf of the title) behavior becomes; he takes to climbing the smokestacks of a nearby fac-tory and throwing small balls toward the moon. In this image alone, the interplay between bodies, buildings, social classes, and individual longing is succinctly evoked. While chapter 3 of this volume will look in detail at the historical processes behind the narrative, it is not the realism or accu-racy of "A Little Ball"—although it is significant in Korean literature—that is of primary interest. Rather, the questions that animate this book have to do with the way fictional arrangements of bodies, buildings, and urban forms stage a constellation of profoundly changing social and spatial rela-tionships. The image of the dwarf atop the smokestacks reveals a range of conflicts and struggles at different scales: the precarious physical and psychical state of the squatter family; the ruthlessness of Seoul's urban renewal; the emerging opposition between working and middle classes; the architectural replacement of low-rise squatter settlements by high-rise buildings; and—at the largest scale—the new global economic system in which postcolonial Korea competes as an export manufacturer. Such fic-tional representations must be read neither for a one-to-one, transparent relationship to the city's material spaces, nor as abstract, metaphorical tex-tual inventions. As Balshaw and Kennedy write, more than simply tracing historical processes, "literary and visual representations of urbanism map the fears and fantasies of urban living, within which—through practices of reading and seeing—we all dwell" (6). Let us look more closely at the way figures of urban form offer themselves up for analysis both in general terms and with the New Asian City as our particular focus.

Without doubt, studies of architecture and urban form have been cen-tral to understandings of modernity, capitalism, industrial development, political formations, and—not least—aesthetic theories of modernism. We need only think of Walter Benjamin's fascination with nineteenth-century Parisian life in *The Arcades Project;* Gramsci's tapping of history's

A new subway line intersects high-rise apartment complexes in Seoul's Chamsil district, 1979. Photograph by H. Edward Kim/National Geographic/Getty Images.

"fundamental motor forces" (98) through his analysis of the Italian city and countryside; Frantz Fanon's devastating critique of colonial life in the "divided city" of *The Wretched of the Earth* (discussed in chapter 1); and the dialectical development of capitalism traced by Raymond Williams in *The Country and the City*. More recently, theories of postmodernism and globalization have come just as much from urban analysis as from literary or other cultural studies (for example, the work of David Harvey, Fredric Jameson, and Saskia Sassen). Perhaps all these studies could be summed up by Im Hŏn-yŏng's claim that the city is "the cognitive object in the structure of conflict inherent in modern society" (Im 24). The wide range of disciplines these thinkers come from—literary studies, political theory, anthropology, social sciences—points to the way the city as object incites an endless multiplicity of ways of looking. Sarah Nuttall and Achille Mbembe put it well:

> A city (whether global or not) is not simply a string of infrastructures, technologies, and legal entities, however networked these are. It also comprises

actual bodies, images, forms, footprints and memories. The everyday human labor mobilized in building specific city forms is not only material. It is also artistic and aesthetic. ("Introduction," 8)

In other words, when looking at what Nuttall calls "city-ness," we are dealing at once with the material built environment and various lived experiences of its inhabitants, as well as the many "images, forms, footprints and memories" that surround these.

Yet at the core of many literary analyses of city-ness is an assumption that the role of fictional texts is simply to show the realities of urban spaces and characters through description, that is, the nonspatial literary form is the transparent presenter of material external realities. The text provides accounts of streets, crowds, factories, shops, or shantytowns, as well as the types of people that inhabit them—the dandies, orphans, colonialists, natives, prostitutes, workers, and gamblers; we might think here of how the adjective *Dickensian* connotes, above all, a particular kind of city scene. As Franco Moretti has put it, commenting on a range of twentieth-century city writers, "it is essentially through *description* that the city penetrates literature, and literature our perception and understanding of the city" (*Signs,* 111). Literary description is certainly one way to answer the question of what "gets made" in the "act of summoning the city . . . into words" (Nuttall, 215).[15] However, a more complex approach traces broader homologies between narrative form and urban environment, where, for example, the disjointed style of a novel echoes the fragmented status of a certain city. In this vein, Moretti traces how the essentials of modern urban experience have been taken up into narrative form along less descriptive lines. What Balzac's great Parisian novels present are not so much convincing descriptions of the city's spaces as the city's social mobility narrated through the social system's unexpected variables, twists of fate, and accompanying plot suspense and surprise (Moretti, *Signs,* 120). In this account, the result is that the physical city becomes not more perceptible, but less so: it "becomes the mere backdrop to the city as a network of developing social relationships" (112). The metropolis takes a backseat as mere setting, and the city (space) is subordinate to narrative (time). If indeed there is a multiplicity of ways of looking at urban form, what other ways can we understand the relationship between space and representation beyond either transparent description or as background to a plot? Throughout this book, I contend that the very distinction between material and literary, or physical and representational space, must be done away with.

To my thinking, the most helpful theorist to have moved to a more complex understanding of space is French Marxist philosopher Henri Lefebvre. His great insight, outlined in his seminal *The Production of Space,* is that we need to understand how space is produced socially, and that this production involves a number of different registers simultaneously. For him, space is not merely an empty container for things: "space is neither a 'subject' nor an 'object' but rather a social reality . . . a set of relations and forms" (116). Consequently, any analysis of space must take into account three registers, which Lefebvre terms "the lived" (correlating to spatial practice), "the conceived" (representations of space), and "the perceived" (representational space). The first category, *spatial practice,* includes buildings, squares, monuments, and streets and the associated practices and competencies of their users—for example, "the daily life of a tenant in a government-subsidized high-rise housing project" (38). The second category, *representations of space,* refers to "conceptualized space, the space of scientists, planners, urbanists, technocratic subdividers and social engineers" (38), the abstract, bureaucratic space of the drawing board and government office. Finally, *representational space* is that "directly *lived* through its associated images and symbols, and hence the space of 'inhabitants' and 'users,' but also of some artists and perhaps a few of those, such as a few writers and philosophers, who *describe* [it]" (39). Linking all three registers together is the "dialectical relationship which exists within the triad" (39). Lefebvre shows us that the essential reality of (social) space must exist at the material, practical, historical, ideological, and imaginative levels all at once. He thus helps dispel the simplistic opposition between material and imaginative spaces—as well as the arrow of determination from the former to the latter—allowing for a conception of representational or literary space as more than a descriptive window to the real world. His project is resolutely against the mental mapping of philosophical space (Cartesian, mathematical) on the one hand, and the study of things in space (architecture, urbanism, geography) on the other. As a result of the properly dialectical nature of Lefebvre's thinking, his conceptual framework resists static oppositions or mere dualities, positing instead "the triplicate" of "mental imaging, perceptions of built forms, and social practice" (Gottdiener, 131). M. Gottdiener summarizes how, like Marx's categories of money and commodities, Lefebvrian space is "both a material product of social relations (the concrete) and a manifestation of relations, a relation itself (the abstract)" (130). He thus notes the complex relationship between space, power, and the reproduction of social relations, the last of which, importantly, is reproduced primarily spatially under capitalism. Gottdiener goes on to note how Lefebvre's work revolutionized urban sociology by introducing the notion that "space is both a medium of social relations and a material product that can affect social relations" (132); in other words, space is a means of production and also a means of control. This study takes seriously Lefebvre's claim for the centrality of space in the production and reproduction of society, viewing it as an equally important topos for study as class, the commodity, or relations of production.

What exactly does this revolutionized way of thinking about space mean for literary and cultural analysis? One result is that it allows us to study space and built form simultaneously as discrete physical objects (a square, an apartment building, or a factory) and as concrete abstractions resulting from complex social and productive relations. *The New Asian City* makes use of Lefebvre's insights by insisting on the spatial reality of textual representations.[16] Indeed, Lefebvre shows us how both "representations of space" (conceptualized, abstract space) and "representational space" (lived, imagined space) trade in mental processes, ideas, and imaginaries. The former

> intervene in and modify spatial *textures* which are informed by effective knowledge and ideology. . . . Their intervention occurs by way of construction—in other words, by way of architecture, conceived of not as the building of a particular structure, palace or monument, but rather as a project embedded in a spatial context and a texture which call for "representations" that will not vanish into the symbolic or imaginary realms. (42)

"Representations of space" depend on acts of construction, but above all aim at a fixity of representation within certain ideological contexts and textures. Its most typical expression is the collusion of space and power under capitalism whereby space conceals (analogously to the commodity) the nature of its very production. "Representational space," by contrast, is alive: it speaks. It has an affective kernel or centre: Ego, bed, bedroom, dwelling, house; or: square, church, graveyard. It embraces the loci of passion, of action and of lived situations, and thus immediately implies time. Consequently it may be qualified in various ways: it may be directional, situational or relational, because it is essentially qualitative, fluid and dynamic. (42)

Although Lefebvre warns against reifying the two terms (and repeatedly asks "what occupies the interstices between [them]?" [43]), this book is principally concerned with the overlapping struggle between representations of space and representational space comprising the heterogeneous contours of the New Asian City. That is, to move beyond the false coherence or givenness of urban forms, we must pay attention to both the interventions and homogenizing forces that fix them, as well as to the temporalities, the "loci of passion, of action and of lived situations" that unfix them. This means we can view architecture and the built environment at once as products of historical processes and as integral *figural or narrative* elements in the ordering and telling of these histories.[17] Literary texts that foreground the built environment tell us not only about the immediate physical changes they explicitly narrate, but also about competing new and old relations, ideologies, and imaginaries deposited in architectural form. The story of our dwarf, for example, can be read as exploding the narrative of triumphant modernization into a variety of contested relations involving urban renewal, class exploitation, individual impoverishment, and postcolonial desires.

Another way to frame this inquiry is to appreciate more generally how three-dimensional changes in the social and urban system become registered in two-dimensional textual forms. Fredric Jameson has famously tackled the problem of connecting the inside and outside of the work in his widely influential book *The Political Unconscious*. He poses the question of how to open textual/literary analysis to the outside social world—for him, the "synchronic system of social relations as a whole"—without the work becoming merely a superstructural effect. In positing literature as a symbolic act, Jameson connects the fictional text to the *Umwelt* in such a manner that the latter is the "determinate situation, dilemma, contradiction, or subtext to which [the literary text] comes as a symbolic resolution or solution" (42). Developing Althusser's critique of mechanical expressive causality, Jameson's model is decidedly not one of homology, where one level (the material world) merely finds expression in another (the literary). Instead, the text has its own partial autonomy and acts, according to Macherey, as a mirror that does not "give a direct reproduction of any object" (134). Such a mirror is a necessarily broken mirror, revealing through "indirect figuration" some truth content of History (or the "absent cause" of the Real) to which we have no unmediated access. Jameson writes of this paradox: "the literary work or cultural object, as though for the first time, brings into being that very situation to which it is also, at one and the same time, a reaction" (*Political Unconscious,* 82).

This knotty concept becomes clearer when we recall that for Althusser, Macherey, and Jameson alike, History, the ultimate determining set of conditions, is nothing other than the prevailing mode of production—that Marxist term for both the means of production (machines, raw materials, and energy) and the relations of production (classes and the reproduction of class structures). The social ground for every text is the structuring mode of production, a totality that by definition can never be apprehended in itself or all at once, just as a given language cannot be apprehended all at once but only through selected utterances. The aesthetic whole of the text stands in for this totality, registering and picking up on aspects of its various structural contradictions and ideologies. What Jameson and Macherey articulate is the active role of literary representation as one system in a mutual relationship with other systems: it provides access to processes of the social world that otherwise could not be perceived. It is not therefore a text's accuracy or correlation to physical reality that interests me, but how the very contradictions of spatial formations are narrated and imagined in it. By seeing the text as a symbolic solution that reflects an invisible structure, we are able to tap into the elusive spatiality that defines any historical mode or production. In other words, while there is no unmediated, total view of all the processes and forces making up South Korea's new urban landscape, the dwarf's plight expresses a cluster of spatial ideologies, discourses, practices, and relations that are integral to Seoul as both physical and social fact.

Late Capitalism and Postcolonial Modernity

Now what of the New Asian City? Is there something specific to the forms of fictional representation that emerge in those nations embarking on independent modernity at such unprecedented speed? First we must note that the social and productive processes embedded in its built forms are determined in part by global processes; that is, as former colonies, they include the material and ideological differential of core–periphery in the development described above by Ahmad. To understand the etiology of this differential, let us recall in some detail Ernest Mandel's seminal account of *Late Capitalism* (1972, 1975), where the postwar era marks a third and fundamentally different stage of capitalism's career. Following the earlier periods of free competition (prior to 1880) and "classical" imperial capitalism (1880–1940), the 1960s and 1970s saw the beginnings of a new relationship between the metropolitan, or formerly imperial, countries and the periphery. The imperial period, while bringing the nonimperial countries into the sphere of the world market, had the general effect not of stimulating capitalist industrial development there, but of destroying native industries for the production of raw materials, foodstuffs, and cheap labor for the metropole's needs. In Mandel's words, capitalist economic growth is defined as "the juxtaposition and constant combination of development and under-development. *The accumulation of capital itself produces development and underdevelopment as mutually determining moments of the uneven and combined movement of capital*" (85, emphasis in original). In so-called late capitalism, following the period of decolonization, the simple extraction of colonial surplus profits is replaced by unequal exchange and the shift of investments in industrial production to certain of the newly decolonized countries.[18] With the rise of the multinational company, the production of surplus values (that is, profit) now takes place internationally, "in actual manufacturing industry, outside the domain of raw materials" (324). The differently valued labor-power of underdeveloped countries—"the fact that the labour of industrialized countries counts as more intensive" (351)—results in unequal exchange and a new means of the "transfer of value" to the multinational capitalist players. Evidence of such a shift is arguably played out most clearly in the Asia Pacific region, where Japanese and U.S. multinationals, along with military–strategic U.S. loans, ushered in the region's new industrialization. Mandel notes, for example, the shift in production of transistor devices, textiles, and watches for the U.S. and Japanese markets to South Korea, Formosa (Taiwan), Hong Kong, and Singapore, among others (373). Multinational firms are interested not only in new rates of profit, but in securing "*future* mastery of these markets" (347). *Late Capitalism* thus explains how the export of machines and technology to such locations expresses a new phase in global capitalism, which cannot be understood "merely as a 'tactical' response to the liberation movements in the colonies and semi-colonies" (347). Instead, we understand how the expansion of capitalism relies on development in selected parts of the third world and continued underdevelopment in others. That Mandel describes these transitions and shifts as "complementary movements of a single, worldwide process of capital accumulation" (363) need not prevent us from acknowledging the myriad of specific social, cultural, and spatial forms through which such apparently totalizing processes occur. The "single, worldwide process" of capital is paradoxically always made up of multiple movements, heterogeneous events, and contradictory tendencies.

At a basic level, then, we must recognize the complementary processes occurring between the metropole and certain regions of the periphery: the shift to postindustrial Western societies is predicated on the shift from colonial or semi-industrial modes of production toward industrial ones in these other regions. Processes of development and industrialization are therefore emphatically not mere imitations or belated versions of those occurring in the metropole, but internally linked.[19] This book's focus on New Asian City aesthetic production of the 1960s to 1980s corresponds to the consolidating moment of Mandel's third stage, or late capitalism, and my analysis is invested in tracing these local forms and responses to a larger, uneven force field of global capitalism. As Jameson glosses, this stage of capitalism is actually "the purest form of capital yet to have emerged" because it "eliminates the enclaves of precapitalist organization it had hitherto tolerated and exploited in a tributary way" (*Postmodernism,* 36). Part of the New Asian City's elusive spatiality, therefore, must be accounted for by its role in the process Mandel describes. Otherwise, in the celebratory discourse of the Pacific Rim, "the United States, Japan, the East Asian NICs [newly industrializing countries], and the second tier of developing Pacific Rim nations (Thailand, Malaysia, Indonesia, coastal China) are linked in a Rim that is an imagining of transnational capital, a co-prosperity sphere" (Connery, 36).[20] Rob Wilson and Arif Dirlik have challenged the boosterlike logic of this expansion by examining the people and places in the Pacific that get left out of this geopolitical imaginary.[21]

My own approach, complementary to theirs, looks critically at the spatial contradictions and connections within a kind of development whose historical specificity must move beyond invocations of third world miracles and tigers.

Thus, one goal of this book is to enable, for the Asia Pacific, a "cross-scalar synthesis" (Soja, "Socio-Spatial Dialectic," 211) of the sociospatial dialectic that Lefebvre's work opens up for us. Soja, like Mandel and Manuel Castells, is interested in how vertical spatial relations of urban classes are overlaid with a second, horizontal spatial system of center–periphery relations. Glossing Lefebvre, Soja argues that the dominant relations in capitalist production

> are not reproduced in society as a whole but in space as a whole, a concretized and produced space which has been progressively occupied by advanced capitalism, fragmented into parcels, homogenized into discrete commodities, organized into the locations of control, and extended to the global scale. (215)

What *The New Asian City* does, via analyses of literature and film, is trace the way built forms, taken up into textual form, are informed by both local relations of production and the broader "center-periphery structure" (209). Examining fictions that deal with the Asia Pacific at a particular historical moment is one way to investigate the "cross-scalar" nature of the production of space.

If I have used Lefebvre, Jameson, and Mandel to think about ways of reading imbrications of the social, architectural, and the global, I turn to Walter Benjamin to consider how moments of massive technical, industrial, and urban change are conceived and imagined as processes of modernity. Benjamin's fascination with Second Empire Paris in *The Arcades Project* may be explained by the technological—rather than political—revolution of that historical moment that followed the failure of the 1848 uprisings. Advances in steel and glass manufacturing as well as the mass production of commodities transformed the way Parisians occupied buildings, went shopping, consumed goods, and moved through the city's spaces. Developing his own distinct philosophy of historical materialism, Benjamin regards the innovations of nineteenth-century industrial capitalism as potentially harboring within them the seeds of a revolutionary new social order. He describes how the new technologies function as something like a text: on their very surfaces are written conflicting and competing images. For example, new iron technology—the first "artificial building material" to appear—is at first cast into the familiar load-bearing form of classical columns, and only later used in ways more expressive of its construction in structures like arcades or railway stations. New building materials elicit multiple expressive possibilities and interpretations that correspond to "images in the collective consciousness in which the old and new interpenetrate" (4). Crucially, this very moment of conflicting images arising with new architectural forms also releases the desire to move beyond them:

> These images are wish images; in them the collective seeks both to overcome and to transfigure the immaturity of the social product and the inadequacies in the social organization of production. At the same time, what emerges in these wish images is the resolute effort to distance oneself from all that is antiquated—which includes, however, the recent past. These tendencies deflect the imagination (which is given impetus by the new) back upon the primal past. In the dream in which each epoch entertains images of its successor, the latter appears wedded to elements of primal history "*Urgeschichte*"—that is, to elements of a classless society. And the experiences of such a society—as stored in the unconscious of the collective—engender, through interpenetration with what is new, the utopia that has left its trace in a thousand configurations of life, from enduring edifices to passing fashions. (4–5)

If such passages, along with Benjamin's studies of Baudelaire, are among the most influential theorizations of European modernity—"the resolute effort to distance oneself from all that is antiquated" as it is summarized here—how might we read the distinctively postcolonial moment of massive technological advancement and its attendant desires? There is, I argue, a curious parallel between the twentieth-century New Asian City and the Second Empire Paris Benjamin describes: both are moments of incredible modernization that were not, however, socially revolutionary periods. Nineteenth-century France witnessed the momentous introduction of new technologies under Louis Napoleon's reactionary Second Empire, while in the New Asian City we see the shift from colonial territory to independent nation along with the consolidation of neocolonial authoritarian rule. Where the temporality of modernity paradoxically rejects the past yet leaps back to the "primal past" or *Urgeschichte,* we might think of the similarly paradoxical invocation of precolonial pasts made by many postcolonial nations striving for modernity. This primal past is not a dateable, historical past but is imagined as the moment of utopia before colonial time, invasion, and its technologies, and it has as its correlate an as yet unrealized version of the modern postcolonial nation.[22] For this reason, postcolonial modernity can also be understood as "seek[ing] both to overcome and to transfigure the immaturity of the social product and the inadequacies in the social organization of production." In this moment of old–new interpenetration, we can similarly detect "the utopia that has left its trace in a thousand configurations of life."

Yet I contend the technological and spatial shifts of the New Asian City go beyond the extent of those in Second Empire Paris. As Kipnis and other architectural theorists have described with their own vocabulary, the primacy of new urban forms and relations characterize the New Asian Cities' mode of production as that in which space itself must be produced anew: "we have passed from the *production of things in space* to the *production of space itself*" (Lefebvre qtd. in Elden, 94). For the works I examine in this book, contradictions around the mode of production and its symbolic expressions—those competing "wish images"—are primarily to do with the effort to create new space. Struggles over the creation of new urban and national spaces constitute the social, material, and ideological world that is imperfectly incorporated by fictional texts. Such texts of the New Asian City thus invoke and rearrange images and ideologies of space—both old and new—into a state of temporary turmoil, where the reconciliation of such images, and the possible surpassing of them, are the very tasks of the aesthetic impulse. Three-dimensional forms are not merely narrativized into static descriptions of types or shapes of buildings, people, or things; they become the curiously shifting three-dimensional fictions that use built spaces as simultaneously literal and figurative objects. As we have seen above, the built environment is a prime locus for the lodging of desires and fantasies, both individual and collective. At the same time, these forms bear an indexical relationship to the absent social and political forces that go into their making. To evoke Cho's story once more, the scene on the smokestack constellates individual, classed, gendered, national, and even international relations with reference to a single urban image: the stunted figure atop a factory building. Such textualizations reveal a complexity far beyond the use of built forms as flat description such that the text itself, when tapped for these layers, becomes three-dimensional. Urban forms and their textualizations both reflect our desires and show us our history.

I have argued that what is specific to the New Asian City's mode of production is its dramatic spatial transformation enabled partly by its position in the global economy. We will see that what is common to many New Asian City texts is the foregrounding of urban and architectural processes as the principal social forces in which these works are produced. Accordingly, I read such fictions for the way they stage and work through a range of contradictions specific to the New Asian City, especially the antinomies between colony/metropole, country/city, body/building, public/private, and nation/globe. In other words, this book traces the spatialized processes of Asia Pacific development that constitute just some of the many historical transitions from colony to postcolony.

The Chapters

As expected, not every text will take on all, or even just a few, of the many codes and historical contradictions that constitute the social reality of these cities. Rather, each chapter groups together several texts that share a logic of space in terms of a determinate literary strategy. My goal is not to provide an exhaustive survey of all cultural production from these three sites in the period (an impossible task for one book) but to bring together selected texts—novels, short stories, poetry, films—that foreground spatial and urban transformation in the most provocative and illuminating ways. In doing so, this study is firmly indebted to a transdisciplinary methodology: it moves back and forth between empirical histories of urban developments on the one hand, and textual analyses of fiction, poetry, and film on the other.

The book is organized into three parts, each with a different scalar focus: "Colonial Cities," "Postwar Urbanism," and "Industrializing Landscapes." Part 1's chapter 1, "Imagining the Colonial City," sets up a conceptual base for the following analyses by tracing colonial urban development in historical and theoretical terms. How have colonial cities been theorized in terms of global modernity, capitalism, and imperialism? What can a postcolonial perspective bring to the existing debates, and how does bringing East and Southeast Asia to these debates challenge existing theories? Chapter 2 examines literary representations of the Manichean spaces of the colonial capital and explores how such logic is activated in both new realist narrative styles and the abstract description of early modernist texts. Rather than arguing for the inaugural moment of either realism or modernism in Taiwanese and Korean colonial literature, I am interested in how the blatant discrepancy between metropolitan and colonial spaces is staged in colonial writing, especially in Wu Zhuoliu's *Orphan of Asia,* Yŏm Sang-sŏp's *Mansejŏn,* and Yi Sang's *The Wings.*

I use two short transitions to contextualize the literary and cinematic analyses of the book. The first Transition, moving to the period immediately following decolonization, offers a more in-depth account of uneven development and underdevelopment (Amin, Frank, and others), export production, and its economic and spatial shaping of these countries. Part 2, "Postwar Urbanism," then deals with the newly rationalized spatial logic of the city expressed in urban renewal processes, high-rise apartment living, and the production and reproduction of labor forms that accompanied the shift to export-oriented production. The analysis is taken from two perspectives, the exterior and interior, respectively. Chapter 3 traces the literary assimilation of the high-rise building as a metonymical device for government and global capitalist alliances. It examines short fiction by Goh Poh Seng, Cho Se-hŭi, and Huang Chunming. Chapter 4 examines the role of the privatized interior in framing the disappearing female subject in works by Kang Sŏk-kyŏng, Su Weizhen, and Su-chen Christine Lim. Together, these two chapters explore the way urban systems and the modes of labor they require actively produce, via distinct narrative tropes and strategies, ways of imagining individual subjectivities.

The second Transition briefly examines the implications of a developmentalist orientation for both official and alternative nationalisms via theorizations of the postcolonial nation (Castells, Cheah, Fanon, and Anderson). Following this, the three chapters constituting part 3, "Industrializing Landscapes," each explore in detail one New Asian City site and a representative aesthetic genre. Here I am less interested in a symmetrical account of cultural production in each country than in a sustained analysis of the interactions between local political and economic conditions and a particular aesthetic form, which I choose for its unique resonance with the discourses of official nationalism. If part 2 is concerned with how individuals are reimagined against the background of the new production-oriented city, part 3 is interested in how collectivities are figured in terms of the nation-space as a newly productive space, where regions are linked for the fluid transportation of goods and laboring bodies. Chapter 5 analyses the political discourse of Lee Kuan Yew in contrast to the (anti)nationalistic poetics of Edwin Thumboo and Arthur Yap, while chapter 6 examines tropes of migration and transportation in Taiwanese New Cinema and the early work of Hou Hsiao-Hsien. Finally, in chapter 7, I look at Korean popular *minjung* literature and the work of Hwang Sŏk-yŏng as a response to dictator Park Chung Hee's prescriptions for national productivity and growth. In all three of the chapters of part 3, I argue that official nationalist discourses and fictional forms struggle over the appropriate relationship between new spaces and human communities.

Again and again, this book will show that the discordant spaces of the New Asian City encode other histories, struggles, and desires that make up what we call modernity.

PART I

COLONIAL CITIES

1

Imagining the Colonial City

> At some very basic level, imperialism means thinking about, settling on, controlling land that you do not possess, that is distant, that is lived on and owned by others.
>
> —EDWARD SAID, *Culture and Imperialism*

> In the name of the imperial project, space is evaluated and overlain with desire: creating homely landscapes out of "alien" territories, drawing distant lands into the maps of empire, establishing ordered grids of occupation.
>
> —JANE M. JACOBS, *Edge of Empire: Postcolonialism and the City*

ALGIERS AND THE "CROUCHING VILLAGE"

Where does one begin a spatial history of a city? Although Seoul, Taipei, and Singapore have had varying careers as major urban settlements, this chapter is devoted to excavating their spatial developments under colonial rule. If the Introduction posed the question of how a postcolonial country attempts to develop from a subordinate position, how exactly is that subordinate position effected in the first place, and by what spatial mechanisms? How has this process been understood in postcolonial and urban theory, and what can Western-oriented urban histories learn from colonial cities? A good place to begin is Frantz Fanon's much-discussed passage from *The Wretched of the Earth,* in which he presents one of the most fertile descriptions we have of the colonial city. For Fanon, the problem of the colonial world is precisely its Manicheanism, the psychic effects of which are well described in his earlier book *Black Skin, White Masks.* In the colonized world, it is the spatial form of a bifurcated system that comes to bear the greatest resonance. To quote Fanon at length,

> The colonial world is a world cut in two. The dividing line, the frontiers are shown by barracks and police stations. . . .

The zone where the natives live is not complementary to the zone inhabited by the settlers. The two zones are opposed, but not in the service of a higher unity. Obedient to the rules of pure Aristotelian logic, they both follow the principle of reciprocal exclusivity. No conciliation is possible, for of the two terms, one is superfluous. The settlers' town is a strongly built town, all made of stone and steel. It is a brightly lit town; the streets are covered with asphalt, and the garbage cans swallow all the leavings, unseen, unknown and hardly thought about. The settler's feet . . . are protected by strong shoes although the streets of his town are clean and even, with no holes or stones. The settlers' town is a well-fed town, an easy-going town; its belly is always full of good things. The settler's town is a town of white people, of foreigners.

The town belonging to the colonized people, or at least the native town, the Negro village, the medina, the reservation, is a place of ill fame, peopled by men of evil repute. They are born there, it matters little where or how; they die there, it matters not where, nor how. It is a world without spaciousness; men live there on top of each other, and their huts are built one on top of the other. The native town is a hungry town, starved of bread, of meat, of shoes, of coal, of light. The native town is a crouching village, a town on its knees, a town wallowing in the mire. It is a town of niggers and dirty Arabs. The look that the native turns on the settler's town is a look of lust, a look of envy; it expresses his dreams of possession—all manner of possession: to sit at the settler's table, to sleep in the settler's bed, with his wife if possible. The colonized man is an envious man. And this the settler knows very well; when their glances meet he ascertains bitterly, always on the defensive, "They want to take our place." It is true, for there is no native who does not dream at least once a day of setting himself up in the settler's place. (38–39)

What is striking in this account is not that it ends with the murderous desire of the colonized toward the colonizer—this is, after all, from the famous section "On Violence." What is surprising is the centrality of the description of the colonial city, placed only a few pages into the book's clarion call for decolonization. Fanon offers us a way to think through the consequences of the daily, bodily, lived experience of the "crouching village," where the contrasts in spaces and lives are obvious: brightness, health, spaciousness, and abundance on the one hand, and hunger, darkness, poverty, and congestion on the other. In other words, he shows us how the moral and political imperatives of decolonization are produced, and felt, most keenly in the spaces of the Manichean city.

A number of urban and postcolonial theorists have commented on Fanon's passage, each with slightly different emphasis. For Ian Baucom, Fanon's piece describes that "spatial policing" that is "the first business of empire" (*Out of Place,* 102) and confirms that "all imperial cultures exist in large part to erect and guard those internal frontiers which mark the limits of colonial intimacy" (103). In this sense, colonial space operates explicitly to prescribe behavior, an observation confirmed by Lefebvre's point that space inevitably signifies "dos and don'ts" (142). With a slightly different emphasis, Zeynap Çelik understands Fanon's passage as providing the archetypal image of the colonial city and, drawing from Kevin Lynch's work, highlights the importance of the "imageability" or legibility of a space (2).[1] Unlike the mere facts of geographer's or planner's space, images are contingent on place, context, and perceiver, in something like a play of Lefebvre's representational space: "The same urban image . . . has the potential to signify different messages. Because a form—even a seemingly crystalline one—can be viewed from a myriad of perspectives, focusing on physical aspects alone does not allow for a meaningful analysis of the city" (4). Çelik's study of colonial Algiers examines the writings and documents of French planning authorities, where the city is both the source and object of competing spatial and social discourses.

Urban historian Anthony King is equally interested in architecture and planning as a tool of colonial domination, but he reads Fanon's passage as a warning of the way Manichean urban forms persist into the postcolonial period. He writes of the longevity of the "world divided into compartments": "In the immediate post-independence years, despite modifications, in most cities the basic pattern has often remained," with native elites simply "flow-[ing] into the expanded area of the old colonial settlement" (283). Finally, Ranjana Khanna has written of the passage with regard to Pontecorvo's classic anticolonial film *The Battle of Algiers,* which depicts the Algerian resistance struggle against the backdrop of this infamously divided city. Khanna's emphasis also touches on the problem of futurity: "the very structure of the divisive colonial city for Fanon shapes the temporality of colonial and postcolonial life"—that is, Fanon's city is one of those "remainders [that] will insist upon the future" ("Post-Palliative," 10).

Despite the variances among these commentators, there is an important unity in these interpretations. From the question of "spatial policing" to competing urban images, to the futurity of the postcolony—what all these analyses imply is that the burden of producing, maintaining, and managing the contradictions of capitalist–colonial relations falls on the colonial city. My goal here is not simply to somehow lay bare the truth of such cities, but to show how the most fundamental processes of capitalism and colonialism include the struggle over space, manifested most clearly in the colonial city. Such embedded processes, in turn, have a bearing on the postcolonial urban forms analyzed in the later parts of this volume. This chapter examines the phenomenon of the colonial city across several scales; beginning from the psychic, lived intimacy of Fanon's description, we move to the world-scale approach of Marxist thinkers and to urban history. In linking these different approaches, I posit the colonial city as the bridge—or nodal point—that at once links and constitutes the discrepant ends of the modernity/coloniality system. If this book is concerned with the kinds of space that allow for the (re)production of imperial social and political relations, the point is not to gain access to some "true," precolonial Korean, Taiwanese, or Singaporean space underlying the colonial imposition and analyze it in contrast to imperial space. Rather, I am interested in how the territorialization of the colonial/capitalist system actively renders various spaces metropole, colony, or native territory, thereby creating the conditions for the reproduction of certain social forms and not others. This chapter explores the distinct spatial logics that produce, and are produced within, colonial territories. In chapter 2, I will then examine the textualization of such colonial spaces in detail, as well as the psychoaffective dimensions that result.

IMPERIAL SPACE

Fanon's passage above evocatively reveals the contradictory nature of colonial space as a space that must be misrecognized in order to function. That is, despite the two distinct worlds that seem to negate each other, it is the medina—that "town of niggers and dirty Arabs"—that politically, economically, and morally shores up the "brightly lit town" of whites. Formally separated, the two parts of the city are actually components in a single, functioning system. Further, such space is not a neutral container of human

actions, but rather is the matrix for both political and ideological production, where "production . . . means both the strictly economic production of things, but also the larger philosophical concept, 'the production
of *oeuvres,* the production of knowledge, of institutions, of all that constitutes society'" (Elden, 94). The divided city is an effect of material colonial policy—it is a "hungry town"—and simultaneously reinforces social
categories—it is a "town of niggers and dirty Arabs." Indeed, the study of
colonial space can shed light on the larger nature of imperialism itself.

We have already seen that the problematic of space uniquely stretches
across differing scales because, following Lefebvre, space "subsumes the
problems of the urban sphere . . . and of everyday life." It raises not just
the question of social relations under a particular mode of production, but
"the problem of their *reproduction*" (89, emphasis in original). Space links
political rule—the arrangement of social relations—with the individual's
daily experience and the futurity of such social relations. What Fanon's
passage indicates is that colonial urban construction and planning signify
much more than mere changes in the material environment: they carry
with them ideological functions crucial to the operation of the most abstract political and economic systems. Jane M. Jacobs describes how the
colonial city is an "important component in the spatiality of imperialism. It
was in outpost cities that the spatial order of imperial imaginings was rapidly and deftly realised. And it was through these cities that the resources
of colonised lands were harnessed and reconnected to cities in imperial
heartlands" (4). At the seemingly other end of the spectrum of analytical
approaches from the intimate spaces of Fanon's Algiers is the discipline of
critical geography dealing with what Jacobs has called "an international
framework of accumulation based on corporate monopoly capital and an
international division of labour" (16). This Marxian tradition deserves our
brief attention and, moreover, can be seen as altogether complementary
to the Fanonian divided city. These accounts posit that the discrepancy
between town and country is the originary spatial differential that capitalist development is predicated on,[2] and they tackle the riddle at the heart of
capitalist expansion: the twin tendencies toward homogeneity/universal-
ism on the one hand, and differentiation/unevenness on the other.[3]

As Marx observed, the most obvious tendency of capitalism is to central-
ize and accumulate. Thus, "Capital proper does nothing but bring together

the mass of hands and instruments which it finds on hand. It agglomerates them under its command. That is its real stockpiling; the stockpiling of workers, along with their instruments, at particular points" (Marx qtd. in Smith, 122). Building on natural topography and geographic differentiation—rivers, valleys, harbors, and so on—that determined the location of medieval towns, capitalism gradually stockpiles labor, capital, infrastructure, and services into the spatial form of cities, that, with their political exceptionality (discussed below), become more and more opposed to the countryside as mere provider of labor and cheap food. Yet globally, despite capitalism's universalizing tendency, which moves "toward the equalization of the conditions of production and the level . . . of the productive forces" (114), differentiation occurs with regard to the role of colonies, resulting in "the specialization in early colonial economies whose major function was the production of raw materials for the European colonizer" (111). Simply put, the spread of capitalist relations results not in the expected repetition of the city–country distinction in new territories, but the subordination of colonial territories to a role as raw materials provider. David Harvey has famously theorized colonialism as capitalism's "spatial fix." He notes that while the initial form of capitalist production typically demands the agglomeration of capital, workers, and misery in the industrialization process, when such a process reaches the limits of spatial infrastructure and becomes both materially and politically unsustainable, "spatial dispersal begins to look increasingly attractive" (418).[4] This results in the necessarily contradictory form of capitalist space:

> the space economy of capitalism is beset by counterposed and contradictory
> tendencies. On the one hand spatial barriers and regional distinctions must
> be broken down. Yet the means to achieve that end entail the production
> of new geographical differentiations which form new spatial barriers to be
> overcome. The geographical organization of capitalism internalizes the con
> tradictions within the value form. This is what is meant by the concept of the
> inevitable uneven development of capitalism. (417)

Paradoxically, as we saw outlined by Mandel in the Introduction, capitalism's development relies on the necessary underdevelopment of certain regions of the world. Such necessary unevenness was early observed and theorized by V. I. Lenin. In his "Imperialism, Highest Stage of Capitalism" (1916), the logic of capital is understood to have spread through the spatial mechanism of the colony, turning vast areas of the world into servile surplus labor pools and ready markets for the manufactured goods of the metropolis.[5] Here, the main colonizing countries—France, Britain, Germany, the United States, Japan, and Russia—are something like a world bourgeoisie, exploiting the colonial countries as their proletariat. The apparatus of modern colonialism has the effect of reproducing on global terms the subordination of Europe's rural areas to the productive capabilities of its manufacturing cities. Along these lines, Raymond Williams urges us to take the labeling of imperial as "metropolitan" seriously:

> We find that what is meant is an extension to the whole world of that division of functions which in the nineteenth century was a division of functions within a single state. . . . Thus a model of city and country, in economic and political relationships, has gone beyond the boundaries of the nation-state, and is seen but also challenged as a model of the world. (*Country*, 279)

Even more radical than the view of capitalism temporarily overcoming its crises through outside spatial fixes, Rosa Luxemburg sees capitalism's inherent will to expansion as a result of its prior dependency on these noncapitalist outside territories. Luxemburg shows how the process of "primitive accumulation," which Marx posits in *Capital* as the genesis of capitalism, is actually an ongoing requirement of which one form is colonial policy: "From the very beginning, the forms and laws of capitalist production aim to comprise the entire globe as a store of productive forces" (55–56). Here, the relationship between the capitalist and noncapitalist world—she calls the latter "natural economies"—is one of necessary engagement and transformation and not merely an external space that relieves internal tensions: "Capitalism must therefore always and everywhere fight a battle of annihilation against every historical form of natural economy that it encounters, whether this is slave economy, feudalism, primitive communism, or patriarchal peasant economy" (62–63). We thus arrive at an inverse relation-ship of dependency between metropole and colony: colonial policy is simply the political form necessary for effecting this "annihilation" that sustains capitalist processes. The analyses of Smith, Lenin, Harvey, and Luxemburg allow us to recognize the expansion of the town–country dichotomy through imperialism as the manifestation of a central contradiction inherent to capitalism, rather than as an auxiliary complement to it.

While these larger frameworks have been enormously useful, we need to understand how the global workings of capitalist expansion become territorialized in Fanon's crouching village and a myriad other forms. What must follow is to examine colonial territories as complex entities in themselves, beyond their function merely as producers of raw materials, natural economies, and the external expression of capitalism's contradictions. Williams has recognized the global scale of the "penetration, transformation and subjugation of 'the country' by 'the city'" (*Country,* 286) through worldwide imperialism. Yet he also notes the complicated internal implications of this process: "one of the effects of imperialist dominance was the initiation, within the dominated societies, of processes which then follow, internally, the lines of the alien development. An internal history of country and city occurs, often very dramatically, within the colonial and neo-colonial societies" (286). Nezar AlSayyad has discussed the specificities of a range of colonial practices and the resulting urban forms. In the Spanish Philippines, for example, there was "no urban legacy prior to Spanish conquest," although the imperial rulers had a clear "blueprint" from Latin America that "consisted of a single European administrative capital surrounded by a smaller number of regional capitals, presidios, mining towns, and host of missions" ("Urbanism," 7). The British, in New Delhi, emphasized the "hierarchy of roles and spaces, this division between 'us' and 'other,' 'new' and 'traditional'" at the level of the city itself, to produce, in Hosagrahar Jyoti's phrase, an "imperial theatre and a theatre for imperialism" (qtd. in AlSayyad, "Urbanism," 8). The French, as we have seen, stressed the strict separation of native town and settler's town, resulting in the "effective creation of a *cordon sanitaire*" (8). There are many other models of colonial urbanism, such as the unique international "concessions" that were set up in colonial Shanghai and the more laissez-faire urban arrangements of various port cities.[6] What ties all these developments together is, as AlSayyad puts it, that today's urban form "can only be understood in the context of the colonial past" and that it is "socially produced and is consequently a product of global processes" (4).

We have now sketched a broad model of the way internal histories of city and country unfold inside a larger framework of the geopolitical subordination of colonial territory as rural to Europe's metropole. Moving beyond a perspective that sees colonial spaces as external territories, dependent on metropolitan development, we see how the problematic of colonial space intersects multiple levels of analysis at once. It includes the psychoaffective dimensions of the racialized colonial subject, the role of the city in a world-systems framework of capitalism, and internal development in regard to its own hinterland. It is to this internal history of urban development in the East Asian context, and especially the expression of colonial power through urban imagery and symbolism, that we now turn. At the same time, this history will question Western urbanism as the universal, normative model of development.

THE ADMINISTRATIVE CITY, EAST AND WEST

Castells has made the productive distinction between two basic kinds of colonial cities: one is the colonial-type settlement "characterized by a function that is above all administrative," and the other is a business center or "gateway city" directly linked to the home country (*Urban Question*, 45). Using this typology, we find that Korea and Taiwan, developed as colonial hinterlands to provide raw materials and defensive territory to imperial Japan, exhibit cities that exemplify the definition of "administrative city." Seoul (known then as Kyŏngsŏng, or Keijo in Japanese) and Taipei (Taihoku in Japanese) are spatial extensions of the metropolitan government at the same time they are growing urban centers in relation to their own countryside. The administrative colonial city thus functions as a node in the larger empire as seat of centralized colonial power, as well as the locus of new native urban populations and—not surprisingly—potential site of anticolonial movements. In contrast, Castell's second category describes "the urban form of a trade economy, the beginning of a close conjunction between the local trading bureaucracy and the imperialist businessmen and their protective apparatus" (45). Typifying this urban category are Singapore and Hong Kong, centers that were never conceived as spaces of colonial productivity but as entrepôt stations for trade between Southeast Asia, China, India, and Europe. Growing from a small fishing village in an area controlled by local Malay sultans, Singapore is imagined as a completely blank slate: "Singapore represented what a foreign creation, sited on an island, and without an economic hinterland in the early years, could accomplish with private enterprise which was free from indigenous customs or government interference in trade" (Dale, 10). A typical gateway city, it handles the exchange of goods by way of its intermediary location and intermediary population—the immigrant Chinese—and becomes a transfer point between British global trade and raw materials (mostly rubber and tin) produced in the Malay hinterland. We will return to the question of trading ports later in the chapter; this section looks closely at the spatial logic required in the transformation to administrative cities. As a point of comparison, we begin with the development of European imperial administrative centers.

The European urban settlement of the Middle Ages, forerunner to the modern city, had a social and legal status that distinguished it from many other urban traditions: it was a corporate entity whose citizens enjoyed a legal status outside serfdom's ties to the feudal manor. Political and legal separation of towns from the feudal lord gave their inhabitants a distinct level of autonomy, as urban historian Lewis Mumford explains:

> The liberation of towns was a step toward the efficient ordering of economic life: the replacement of barter by money, and of life-service by urban piece-work or seasonal hire: in short, the transition . . . from status to contract. . . . For the corporate town was in fact based upon a social contract between the landed proprietor and the settlers or inhabitants. (24)

This distinction between Western categories of urban versus rural spheres was unlike that which produced cities in the Chinese ecumene. The latter, in contrast, "possessed no government distinct from that of the surrounding countryside and thus no corporate identity that set it apart from the rural areas" (Xu, 82). In China, cities "existed for the sake of the country and not vice versa" (Joseph Needham qtd. in Xu, 79), just as feudal Korean cities were merely "the place of residence and the place of consumption for the class of bureaucracy" (Im, 24). Although Chinese or Korean cities were often walled, this was a symbol of imperial organization rather than the legal separation between country and city.

In the seventeenth and eighteenth centuries in Europe, however, the nature of the distinction began to change. Foucault notes how the European "city was no longer perceived as a place of privilege, as an exception in a territory of fields, forests and roads" (368) and eventually became reintegrated with its surrounding territory. This shift was linked to the rise of mercantilist capitalism and its new political framework "of a centralized despotism or oligarchy, usually focused in a national state" (Mumford, 75). Replacing the sovereign city-states, the capital city developed as the locus of a powerful bureaucracy needed to administer growing populations and territories. Unlike the defensively walled medieval town, what Mumford terms the "baroque city" expresses the standardization, formal planning, and principles of scale needed for political and economic centralization, as well as for the passage of new national armies. The history of the Western city is thus intricately bound up with the development of capitalism and the nation-state. Mumford writes, "it was one of the great triumphs of the baroque mind to organize space, make it continuous, reduce it to measure and order, to extend the limits of magnitude, embracing the *extremely distant and the extremely minute*" (91, emphasis added). In a similar observation, Foucault notes that medieval "localization was replaced by extension" (350), whereby the rationality and governmentality first developed for the city was now enlarged to the scale of the state:

> There is an entire series of utopias or projects for governing territory that developed on the premise that a state is like a large city; the capital is like its main square; the roads are like its streets. A state will be well organized when a system of policing as tight and efficient as that of the cities extends over the entire territory. . . . The model of the city became the matrix for the regulations that apply to a whole state. (369)

Note that here, the state territory functions metaphorically like a city: "the capital is like its main square; the roads are like its streets." Surprisingly, both Mumford and Foucault omit the role that colonial space—the epitome of the "extremely distant" territories to be administered and policed—played in the development of the home country's urban forms. Note too that the expandable metaphoricity of the city as the "matrix" for governing distant territories is the inverse of the city concept in the Chinese-centered world where cities were spatially distinct, but not politically or legally differentiated. They were not—and could not be—in any sense microcosms of the structure of territorial power as they came to be in the West. Although imperialism had certainly existed in the East, it did not require the imagined even and homogenous penetration of political sovereignty across foreign territories. For modern, Western-style colonialism to be effected in these regions, this particular relationship of city to territory had to be imported. Thus, one of the first tasks of imperialism was to dramatically reconstruct or build new colonial cities. Such a process is clearly seen in East Asia, one of the last regions of the world to be incorporated into the modern imperialist world system.

To understand these processes in Seoul and Taipei, the specific history of the Japanese empire must be taken into account. After the 1868 Meiji Restoration's program of modernization and adoption of the principles of "civilization and enlightenment" *(bunmei kaika),* only the means and methods that were used for the creation of a modern, European industrial nation-state were considered most effective. As a result of its unique chronology, the construction of Meiji Japan (1868–1912) as a modern, industrial nation-state depended on the simultaneous spatial transformation of both Japan and its colonial territories. That is, in Japan's case, what Foucault describes as the extension of the city model over the nation-state is instituted at the very same time that Japan accedes to the logic of modern colonialism. Understanding the imperial stakes of the modern state, the Japanese prudently set up a chair of colonial studies at Tokyo University alongside academic departments devoted to studies in Western technologies and sciences. The Meiji period policy of employing foreign experts *(oyatoi)* brought to Japan some 3,000 European and American professionals trained in law, finance, military, science and culture. Yet, "by far the greatest number of *oyatoi* were associated with the Ministry of Construction and were specialists in the fields of engineering and architecture, itself an indication of the importance of building to the state" (Coaldrake, 216–17). The new building sciences were first and foremost used to transform and modernize the metropole. The newly designated capital, Tokyo, replaced the Shogunal center of Edo and was reconstructed "for the conduct of the affairs of state and the development of modern industry, commerce and education" (208). Along with grand government buildings designed in European classical revival styles, Japan's new imperial center boasted the neobaroque Tokyo train station (1914), which was linked to the Imperial Palace by a new processional boulevard. At seventy meters wide, this avenue "reflected the dramatic vista-planning in contemporary European cities—notably Baron Haussmann's Paris of the Second Empire" (227).

The opening of Japanese space to the expediencies of modern institutions—not least to the institution of its national army—was simultaneously effected in the major colonial capitals. Because Japanese-style planning and public architecture were not thought appropriate to the Western-led colonial endeavor, Japanese imperialism was not created in the image of the colonizer's traditional styles but of Europe's, blurring the assumed boundary between an original modernity and colonial derivation.[7] In both Seoul and Taipei, the two most important cities of the empire, one of the first acts undertaken by the colonial government was the removal of the city walls. The walled city, in traditional Chinese planning, was one of the great symbols of Chinese imperial rule. In Taipei, a wall had been erected under the auspices of the Qing dynasty (1644–1911), which in 1875 made Taiwan a prefecture of Fujian province (it was promoted to its own province in 1895 just before the Japanese takeover). After Chen Hsin-chu was sent as the first magistrate to administer the island, construction began in 1878 on a 5,000-meter-long, six-meter-high wall, enclosing what would be the heart of modern Taipei (Selya, 22). In Korea, centuries of tributary connections to Chinese politics and culture meant that a Chinese-style wall had long enclosed the Chosŏn dynasty (1392–1910) capital city (then known as Hansŏng). Both Taipei's and Seoul's walls were anchored by prominent directional gates, which the Japanese usually spared, and which are today almost the only remnants of the former walled city. Along with the destruction of the city temples (primarily in Taiwan), the Japanese reorganized space in accord with the accepted tenets of Western rational planning, straightening and widening streets and creating uniform city blocks. The historical contrast between precolonial, Sino-influenced planning and Japanese-controlled space can thus be attributed to the expediencies of Western-style colonialism.

Architecturally, in both Korea and Taiwan, enormous neobaroque colonial administration buildings were built to tower over the newly dominated land and disrupt traditional axes of architectural power based on geomantic principles (*fengshui* in Chinese or *p'ungsu* in Korean). In Korea, the governor general's building was designed in 1912 by French architect Georg de Lalande with Nomuru Ichiro and was constructed in the very front yard of the Korean royal palace, Kyŏngbokgung, effectively blocking the latter from the city and its landmark Kanghwamun Gate. The structures of the Qing administration in Taiwan had similarly been planned following the principles of *fengshui*, which dictated that important buildings be located in the north and face the south. Urban historian Hsia Chu-Joe describes how "the Japanese colonizers violently changed the directions of the buildings into facing east, i.e. worshipping the 'rising sun,' a very Japanese symbol. They not only reformulated the directions of the roads within the city but also eliminated and decomposed the traditional buildings" (11). New and monumental public buildings in neoclassical and neobaroque styles concretized the authority of the Japanese as well as symbolized the modernity of the state's new institutions: railway stations, banks, trade offices, and city halls stood for pan-empire rail links, modern finance, trade systems, and a bureaucratized, colonial government. For the colonizing Japanese, just as for the colonizing French and British, spatial planning both actively intervened in everyday life and symbolically authorized colonial power. However, even more than other empires, with Japan we see the extent to which colonial modernization was linked to that at home: the conscious modernization of Tokyo only makes sense in its new role as center of empire.

As exemplars of Castells's first kind of city, Seoul and Taipei effectively become, somewhat oxymoronically, colonial metropoles: zones for the operations of imperial power and authority. Such a city exhibits a Fanonian duality of urban forms correlating to the colonizer/colonized, echoing and stabilizing the geographic hierarchy of Japanese home country and colonial Korean or Taiwanese territory. In his analysis of the preeminent Indian administrative city, Delhi, King has described the general tendencies of colonial society. Under the city's new organization and the general redistribution of land by the colonial authorities, it undergoes a "partial break-down of a traditional, territorial-based social structure associated with religious, ethnic, caste and socio-occupational criteria (in the old city) and the building up of a new, territorial-based system of class linked to

Taiwan Tobacco and Wine Monopoly Bureau, Taipei, built by the Japanese Central Government, 1912–22. Reproduced courtesy of Little Grass Art School.

occupational, socio-economic and racial groupings" (31). While this may be superficially similar to the shift from premodern to modern industrial societies in the West, there are fundamental differences. In contrast to the politically autonomous settlements, there is no conflict of interest between the minority who wish to influence urban forms for profit and the controls of the planning authority, because under colonialism they are the very same institutions. Thus, there was a freedom and license in colonial city planning not often found in the metropolis.[8] Further, Castells notes that whereas urbanization in the West was predominantly linked to its industrialization, the colonies themselves initially saw very little increase in secondary industries. Rather, the "impact of the western process of industrialization" (*Urban Question,* 46, emphasis altered) conditions colonial urbanization; more than the draw of jobs toward the city, the disruptive reorganization of the rural economy in the service of the metropole's development pushes migration from the countryside.

At the everyday level, too, such a program produced multiple spatial contradictions. Reproducing the forms of Western public space while maintaining colonial domination is an inherently conflicted project, so that the

Japanese contributed to new civic spaces in Taipei at the same time the hierarchical structure of colonialism prevented "any autonomous civil society and public space for citizens" (Hsia, 12). Unlike traditional Chinese planning, in which courtyards attached to temples or other institutions constituted the only public space (Xu, 199), Taipei's Public Hall was built adjoining an open, European-style square. Yet, Hsia argues, the public appearance of the square was negated by the presence of the police head-quarters on its other side. The "public sphere, a sphere controlled by the state, was an irony of the colonial dependent city, symbolizing the absence of a public sphere" (12). The presence yet absence of the public sphere is precisely due to the colonial city's role as the articulation point of colonial power relations. The city embodies the contradictory processes and structures through which both the larger colonial and metropolitan spaces make sense. The colonial city, located at the juncture between native populations, colonial settlers, and administrators, is therefore a vital, if turbulent, site for the production of the global capitalist system. Useful here is King's understanding of colonial cities as neither derivative of, nor deviation from, the Western city, but as "unique entities" (31) in themselves—objects that are the very nodes through which the functioning of the modernity/coloniality dyad occurs. King considers the colonial city a "laboratory for cross-cultural research," the examination of which "can tell us of inherent, core characteristics of the metropolitan society which . . . a study of that society alone would never make apparent" (13). He also theorizes, in the spirit of Homi Bhabha before the letter, a "third culture" or sphere of hybridity: "It is a culture which emerges not simply as a result of interaction with a second culture in a 'neutral' diffusion situation, but necessarily, as a result of colonialism" (59). In Delhi, colonial third culture is understood as the combination of British and Indian spaces that encode an "institutional system which comprehends ideational systems, meanings and symbols, social structure, systems of social relations and patterns of behaviour" (65). The Japanese case is similarly hybrid: the urban system exported to Korea and Taiwan was in no way simply Japanese. Despite his term "third culture," I argue that King's concept be understood primarily as a spatial rather than cultural configuration; it is not simply a matter of adding British (or Japanese) and native culture to create a third iteration, but of tracing the active and complex interpenetrations of colonial spatial forms—the colonial settlement, administrative section, and cantonment—with local dwelling patterns to produce the colonial encounter itself.[9] As we will see in the next chapter, it is precisely in the colonial city that such a paradoxical system of connections and disconnections is most evident.

Worlding the Gateway City

Our second urban type, Castells's trading or gateway city, must also be understood as neither a deformed version of metropolitan urbanization nor as a simple object of dependency, but rather as crucial node in the production and daily reproduction of global capitalist space. Here, Martin Heidegger's fertile work is useful in offering a rethinking of the third space of colonial cities in a more philosophical mode. Like those of Lefebvre, Fanon, and King, his writings on space connect everyday lived places with larger questions of being, power, and (in the way I read his work) geopolitics. His 1951 essay "Building, Dwelling, Thinking" is relevant in that it demonstrates the nodal qualities of the urban forms I have been describing. In Khanna's gloss of Heidegger's theory of art, "art objects do the work of opening up the world so that one can imagine a way of being in it." In this sense, the art of "worlding performs the 'unconcealedness of being' because it brings a new way of being in the world, along with the attendant concealedness of the earth that occurs simultaneously" (*Dark Continents*, 3). An "essential strife" of being occurs between the tendency toward the light and open—associated for Heidegger with the world—and that toward the concealed, hidden, and dark—associated with the earth. Developing Spivak's "analogy [of] substituting colonized space as phantasmatic 'earth'" ("Rani," 253n18), Khanna sees the latent resources of the earth opposed to the thoroughly realized social and political space of the world. This creative but always violent process of worlding is useful for understanding the project of global colonialism, where "the passage from earth to world [means] the establishment of colonial control of space through mapping, land appropriation, and the transformation of the raw materials of the earth into the politico-economic and geographical category of 'world'" (*Dark Continents*, 4). What must remain concealed or repressed in this process are the dark continents of the colonial world—women and the primitive. Drawing from such provocative notions, I interrogate the explicitly spatial mechanisms by which the urban or metropolitan is worlded while the rural or colonial earth is subordinated and concealed.

In Heidegger's understanding, neither locations nor spaces simply exist, but the act of building, "by virtue of constructing locales, is a founding and joining of spaces" (360). The produced nature of space is made explicit: "Space is in essence that for which room has been made, that which is let into its bounds. That for which room is made is always granted and hence is joined, that is, gathered, by virtue of a locale, that is, by such a thing as the bridge. *Accordingly spaces receive their essential being from locales and not from 'space'*" (356, emphasis in original). Heidegger's thinking invites us to consider built form as precisely the site, "bridge," or location that gathers, joins, and gives being to the opposing spaces of metropole and colony. Note that Heidegger's concept of dwelling/building is based on the idea of a "place that is freed for settlement and lodging," as "that for which room has been made" (356). These concepts contain the defining gestures of colonizing logic: to destroy natural economies, clear hitherto "unoccupied" land, and install one's own settlement. Heidegger's understanding of truth/presencing *(alethia)* is a process that at once discloses certain ways of being while concealing or closing down others.[10] What happens in the clearing (or rebuilding) of colonial space is the emergence or unconcealedness of the land as appropriable territory, and the simultaneous concealment of those natural economies and social systems of the precolony. To return to Foucault, we see that a precondition of the imperial capital's dominance over a territory like a city over a state is the revealing of the world into cleared spaces to be dominated and inscribed by that city: the Japanese imperial constructions in Taipei and Seoul arrogate themselves to symbols of the subordination of Taiwanese and Korean space as colonies, retroactively achieved through the very constructive acts of colonization. The subaltern role of the entire colony is thus given reality by the worlded political/social form of the administrative city. We see how the colonial city is the crucial, interstitial location that gives the global/colonial system its being.

Our second kind of colonial settlement similarly operates through a curious spatial tautology. In the Japanese empire, ties between Japan and its colonial ports, Taiwan's Keelung (Jeelong) or Korea's Pusan, "[become] even stronger than those within [the colony's] own territory" (Hsia, 9) such that Keelung and Pusan are more integrated with Japan than to the rest of the colonial territory. Singapore, as exemplar of the colonial port city, is a site whose strategic location literally allowed for a reinvigoration of the colonial system. The "founding" of Singapore was motivated by the British East India Company's need for a safe port along the China route and an access point to the Malay Archipelago (Dale, 2). After Sir Stamford Raffles secured ownership of the island through treaties with local Malay rulers, Singapore became a trading outpost run by the company until 1858, when it passed to the India Office in London (4). With few resources of its own, Singapore initially was almost purely a trading entrepôt: "it was trade between India and China—raw cotton and opium one way and tea the other—that guaranteed most of the profit for the East India Company" (7). Histories of Singapore inevitably begin at the year 1819 and the arrival of Raffles; there is supposedly nothing there until he and his men begin clearing the vegetation, draining the Singapore River, and allocating land (13). In a different configuration, Singapore again demonstrates the way the colonial city operates as a node in global trade, helping to organize Southeast Asia, India, and China into their roles as producers of raw materials while strengthening British imperial power as the arbiter and profiteer of these trade flows. The establishment of Singapore is thus a crucial moment for the worlding of India and China into compatible and profitable (for the British) trading blocs, and the fresh revealing of Malaya and the Dutch East Indies as suppliers of much of the world's tin and rubber by the early twentieth century.[11] With a majority immigrant labor force, however, the operation of space differs from that seen in the Japanese administrative cities, which actively use architecture and rezoning to transform natives into colonial subjects.

While both kinds of cities are fundamentally ordered by ethnic separation, in Singapore, this was "based on both expediency and the belief that each community was so different that close integration would create conflict" (Dale, 15). The majority of the population was Chinese, who were used by the British as middlemen to "[liaise] between the European merchants who imported Western goods and the South-East Asian producers who bartered their produce for manufactured goods" (8). This racial division of labor was echoed in the planned spatial division of races. Dale writes of the early city:

The European quarter occupied an extensive site on the Rochor Plain between the government sector and the Arab quarter to the north. The latter was given land adjoining a 20-hectare site of Kampong Glam allotted to Sultan Hussein while the Bugis, a seafaring people, were moved further east along the coast. The entire area west of the river, adjoining the commercial sector, was allocated to the Chinese communities. Indians or Chulias were allotted land further up-river. (14–15)

The constant influx of Chinese migrants to Singapore fleeing war and famine in China peaked at an unmanageable 242,000 per year in 1930 (21) and contributed to the chronic overcrowding of shophouses in the Chinese district. Unlike the highly orchestrated administrative/symbolic colonial roles of Seoul or Taipei, Singapore might best be understood as the physical embodiment of the trading entrepôt ideology: different areas were simply allotted to different ethnic groups in the assumption that each would find its position in the harmonious global trading business.

Yet the contradictions of colonial Singapore, with its racially segregated quarters correlating with different political forms and labor patterns, are no less a result of the worlding required by the imperial system. Revealed as mere human energy source, the urban form associated with the Chinese workers is necessarily the antithesis of the luxurious British residential sections and grandiose government offices. Even as the overcrowded and squalid conditions of the Chinese quarters were an affront to British senses of decency and hygiene, they were, in a sense, the required form of this colonial trading system. Yeoh writes of the shophouse system—narrow two-story structures combining businesses on the ground floor and innumerable dwelling cubicles on the upper floor—and its suitability to the colonial economy:

The physical integration of productive work and consumption not only minimized transport costs by abolishing the journey to work, but also allowed a large proportion (at least 100,000 or over 30 percent according to 1921 figures) of the Chinese population who were either dependent on casual work or engaged in service sector jobs to remain in central locations (or near the harbour) within easy reach of potential employers and customers. . . .

Singapore's government district, 1930s. Victoria Memorial Hall is in the foreground, the Supreme Court to the right, and Fort Canning military headquarters on the hill in the background. Photograph by Popperfoto/ Getty Images.

> The system of subdividing living space into this cubicle form functioned as a mechanism by which subtenants could live within the central area of the city on urban space which commanded high rents. The cubicle system allowed the labouring classes to occupy minimal accommodation at rents which although high, could be reckoned within their means, as houses or even complete rooms could not. (144)

We recognize here the familiar tendency of capitalism to stockpile productive forces, but Singapore's colonial urban system adds to this tendency the complication of racial segregation and intermediary laboring populations necessary for the imperialist trading system. Colonial urban squalor, unlike that of early European industrial centers, could not be addressed as an object for planning reform since it was plainly at one with the economic raison d'être of Singapore. Consequently, without overhauling the race-based labor system—which imperial sense could not allow—the filthy conditions of the laboring classes were simply attributed to the Asiatic's general preference for darkness, and unsanitary Chinatown was little changed by half-hearted British housing ordinances. As one British doctor commented, "The Asiatic does not like air in his dwelling-house. It does not matter how many windows or ventilation openings there are, he always endeavours to close them up.... [Neither] does it matter how much room you give [Asiatics], they will huddle together" (Dr. Glennie qtd. in Yeoh, 142). Indeed, by 1918, attempts at outlawing cubicle housing were simply abandoned (148). The Chinese riots in the 1850s caused the British government to build new forts protecting the city, not from foreign ships or invasion, but from further unrest in Chinatown (17). These military fortifications were the ultimate guarantor of this inherently contradictory spatial system. As Dale writes:

> On the surface, life had never been so pleasant for the prosperous and the well-to-do, particularly the European community. It was an era of gracious living in beautiful houses surrounded by green lawns and tended by a retinue of servants. Singapore was an exceptionally clean city by Asian standards, and the city centre and the fashionable residential areas were kept in meticulous condition. However, the mass of the population lived in squalor. Malnutrition and child mortality were high. But in the 1930s, most Europeans could lead a life oblivious to the poverty, slums, and crime of the more crowded sectors of the city. (21)

We return here to the fundamental spatial discrepancy produced by the colonial system. In revealing one part of the world as master, profiteer, and consumer, and inscribing the other as reserve of natural or labor resources, the Heideggerian struggle between presencing and concealing manifests itself on the urban level in the striking contrast between quarters of light and dark. Such differences are then conveniently explained by the association between darker races and darker environments. Like the contradictory spaces of the colonial administrative city, racially segregated Singaporean urban space is both result and justification of the exploitation inherent to colonialism.

Such blatant duality is to be found to some degree in all colonial cities. King comes to a similar conclusion in describing the distinct divisions within the colonial city of Delhi. Like Singapore, the colonial urban settlement—that part of the city inhabited by the colonizing society—is an area "one might mistakenly compare to an early twentieth-century upper, or middle-class European suburb," and is characterized by large residential plots, open spaces and the modern amenities of water, sewers, telephone, and electricity (33). In contrast, permanent in-migration to the indigenous town, like Singapore's Chinatown, results in extremely dense housing and squatter settlements without modern amenities or transport systems (33–34). Although King is merely elaborating the "socio-spatial structure in the colonial city," like both Dale's Singapore and Fanon's Algiers, his description belies a necessary *misrecognition* that the coexistence of two such worlds produces: arriving in the colonial urban settlement part of town, one will probably mistake one's location for an upper middle-class European

Singapore boat quay and shophouses, circa 1930. Photograph by Popperfoto/ Getty Images.

suburb rather than the colonial capital of India. Equally, the "gracious living" of Singapore's European community necessarily requires oblivion to the shophouse slums of Chinatown. The very perceptual experience of the city demands that one aspect of it be foreclosed. Such a paradox results, of course, from the impossible demand put to the colonial earth to yield only its resources and labor, while other indigenous, precolonial, or immigrant ways of being—colonialism's necessary excesses—are blocked.

Both our two categories of colonial city—the administrative centers and port cities—are founded and operated through the contradictory forms of colonialism. At first, colonial urbanisms may seem incongruent to accounts of metropolitan city development—Fanon's town of "niggers" or Singapore's dingy Chinatown are outside the progressive history of urbanization, civilization, and trade. Yet an examination from both a larger, world-systems perspective and the specific history of such cities demonstrates their essential function to imperialism and modernity. As bridges between the colony and the metropole, they are crucial in producing these territorial distinctions themselves. Both internally and externally, such spaces are rich with paradox, division, exclusion, and contradiction. We find ourselves inexorably back at Fanon's Manichean description with which we began: "the two zones are opposed, but not in the sense of higher unity." Within the heterogeneous forms of the colonial city we must reckon with the ongoing microprocesses of such a worlding: of the way in which some—and not other—material, economic, cultural, and even psychological ways of being are revealed and ordered by the urban system. We have seen how the unconcealing of the colonial administrative cities Seoul and Taipei involved the shift from traditional geomantic conceptions of space to those informed by rationalized Western–Japanese urbanism. The administrative city, linked metonymically to the imperial center, both replicates parts of the metropolitan center (state buildings, banks, businesses, settler-residential areas) and contains the means by which the native territory is ordered and controlled (cantonments, police stations, trade monopolies). Similarly, the cosmopolitan and global functions of gateway cities, as Yeoh notes, "cannot be understood apart from their pivotal role in establishing, systemizing, and maintaining colonial rule" (1).

The next chapter changes our focus, exploring the way colonial literature assimilates and responds to such modern urban forms. As Baucom has argued in his concept of "township modernism," such cities are not outside modernity, because "modernity is not a thing but a system, a system of connections and active disconnections, of accumulation and exploitation, of development and abjection" ("Township," 237). As the nexus of such complex forces, colonial urban forms come to the fore in literary expressions of modernity and anticolonialism.

2

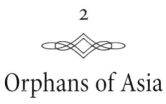

Orphans of Asia

Modernity and Colonial Literature

> Modernity was generated by a distinct mode of production condensed in the
> life of the cities and inflected throughout the industrializing world, especially
> in the semiperiphery and colonial realms of Asia.
>
> —HARRY D. HAROOTUNIAN, *History's Disquiet*

DISCREPANT MODERNITY

In Yŏm Sang-sŏp's 1924 novel *Mansejŏn (Before the March 1st Movement)*[1]—
arguably the most complete representation of colonial Korea (or Chosŏn,
as it was then known)—narrator Yi In-hwa is called back from his studies
in Japan by his wife's serious illness. With little actual concern for his wife,
he recounts his train trip south from Tokyo, the ferry ride to Pusan, and
then further rail trips up the Korean peninsula to Kyŏngsŏng (Seoul). The
novel describes In-hwa's passage along new transport systems and through
rapidly modernizing cities with an overriding sense of melancholy, death,
and decay. On the train to Seoul, he meets a traveling salesman who, eager
to talk to this refined and Japanified student, immediately questions him
on the colonial government's insistence on urban, public cemeteries in
opposition to traditional Korean mountain tombs. Before being taken away
by the military police, the salesman asks incredulously, "Are there really
public cemeteries *[kongdong myoji]* in Japan?" (105).[2] Thinking of a recent
conversation with his brother on his wife's burial, the narrator wryly notes,
"Unexpectedly, this salesman was also bringing up graves" (104). In the
novel's most frequently discussed scene, the protagonist observes the cruel
treatment of a Korean woman prisoner and notes how the local youths
have "faces like rotting cabbage leaves." He has the urge to yell, "Is this living? Everyone's dead! . . . It's a grave! A maggot-infested grave!" (111). For

the erudite and philosophical literature student who has been enjoying the cosmopolitan amenities of Tokyo (and the attentions of a Japanese bar-girl), his journey through Korea's urbanizing landscape does nothing less than render visible the morbidity of colonial society. What is striking, of course, is how the very modernity of Korea's spaces is experienced by the protagonist as something deathly and moribund. Interrogating representations of the colonial territory in Korean and Taiwanese texts from the mid-1920s until just before independence in 1945,[3] this chapter is concerned with the problem of colonial dwelling. The key trope throughout is the *discrepant*: the contrapuntal perspective described by Edward Said as a way of making connections and relationships that are unavailable to the univalent view. For Said, thinking by way of the discrepant experience is a necessary, critical task: "we must be able to think through and interpret together experiences that are discrepant, each with its particular agenda and pace of development, its own internal formulations, its internal coherence and system of external relationships, all of them co-existing and interacting with others" (32). Yi In-hwa's unsettling experience of Seoul may be described as a quintessential experience of discrepancy.

Building on the previous chapter's spatial history of colonial East Asia, we can now explore the conceptual frames made available by such modernizing colonial urban spaces, and the way they are activated in realist and modernist literary modes. The question of modernity—that key concept that encompasses an array of processes, forces, and desires—is raised in a two-way comparative manner: first, as a concept that provokes the literary strategies of realist description and modernist abstraction; and second, in comparison with broader Western notions of urban modernity as canonized by writers such as Charles Baudelaire and Georg Simmel. In setting up this multivalent inquiry, I take as my starting point Tani E. Barlow's statement that "the modernity of non-European colonies is as indisputable as the colonial core of European modernity" (1).[4] The colonial urban centers of Taipei and Seoul are thus examined for the way they reveal at the micro-, everyday level existential contradictions of modernity that in turn put new demands on literary forms. Recall from the previous chapter that the colonial city is in essence a nodal contradiction, neither metropolitan nor colonial but rather what produces the distinction. Here, literary analysis of three texts addresses this discrepancy to reflect on the imbrications of capitalism, colonialism, and modernity. What the several narratives have in common, I will demonstrate, is the city as the prime mediator of this contradictory modernity, in both its form and content. In Yŏm's novel, for example, the stark discrepancies between Yi In-hwa's carefree life in Tokyo and the grim realities of Korea require a new kind of conceptual frame—and narrative strategy—to carry the close observations, detailed descriptions, and philosophical reflections that ultimately coalesce in a sustained anticolonial critique.

In the first part of the chapter, I consider how the experience of urban discrepancy structures realist anticolonial literature by examining Yŏm Sang-sŏp's *Mansejŏn* alongside *Orphan of Asia* (*Aija no koji* in Japanese or *Yaxiya de guer* in Chinese) (1945) by Taiwanese writer Wu Zhuoliu (Wu Chou-liu). In the second section, I consider the appearance of strikingly modernist literature in the colonial periphery of Seoul with a close reading of Yi Sang's *The Wings (Nalgae)* (1937). If coloniality is the indisputable, but invisible, core of European or Japanese modernity, the Fanonian duality of the colonial city not only incites anticolonial thought, but also offers a unique epistemic perspective that connects and condenses aspects of that diffuse system. The questions motivating this chapter can be summarized thus: How does the particular geopolitical situation at the end of the nineteenth and beginning of the twentieth century—the demise of the China-centered world and the "modernization movement that swept East Asia" (Fulton, "Historical," 620)—inflect the literary modernities of that region? How are the well-studied questions of modern urban life, consumption, travel, gender, and everydayness articulated differently in the colonial territory? And how are the discrepant spaces of the colonial world figured and imagined as tools, gateways, organs of power, places of freedom, or prisons? In short, what kind of modernity was experienced in them?

Overseas Students, Orphans, and the Realism of Urban Form

As the brief scene above from *Mansejŏn* indicates, the trope of Korea's negative comparison with the outside was strong in the colonial period. Indeed, early narrations depicting the experiences of overseas Korean students *(yuhaksaeng)* shared much with late nineteenth-century reform discourses that sought to modernize Korea along Western/Japanese lines as a way to avoid being colonized. We can think of the beginnings of Korean modern literature—the genre commonly known as *sinsosŏl* ("new fiction")—as precisely the linguistic vehicle required for such comparative, reform-oriented theories. Yi In-jik's *Hyŏl ŭi nu (Tears of Blood),* published serially from 1906, was groundbreaking for departing from the Chinese-influenced literary genres of tales of wonder, biographical fictions, and unofficial histories. Its use of the vernacular Korean script *(hangŭl)* and its focus on social reality were new, as was its sustained portrayal of the development of an individual against the conditions of contemporary reality.[5] Further, in *Tears of Blood,* realist descriptions of modern Japan or America function as clear spatial contrasts to backward Korea, giving physical shape and content to the hierarchy of development among nations. Realism cannot therefore be understood simply as the Eastern equivalent to the European genre that developed over the eighteenth and nineteenth centuries. In Asian literatures, the genre was not linked to the rise of a capitalist middle class and secular outlook, but rather was one of a variety of modes through which Western- and Japanese-influenced modernity was appropriated and opposed to traditional culture and society. In Korea, after the disillusionment of the failed March 1st independence movement, there were several options open to writers: "they could be escapist like the symbolist poets; they could be propagandist like the nationalists; or they could be Marxist" (O'Rourke, 651). Literary realism was associated with the latter mode, seeking to depict life "as it was";[6] it was formalized in the short-lived movement of proletarian literature *(nodong munhak),* unified under the banner of KAPF (Korea Artista Proletaria Federacio, 1925–35). These writers viewed literature as a means to raise class consciousness and workers' solidarity "and fashioned workers as the central subject of art and politics" (Barraclough, 347), blending a critique of industrialization with Japanese anticolonialism. Writers such as Yŏm, Kim Tong-in, and Hyŏn Ching-ŏn were also influenced by European naturalism and "saw man as living in an oppressive society, a prey to forces such as sex, anger, poverty, the marriage system, and the political system. These forces led to inevitable defeat and destruction" (O'Rourke, 652).[7] Yŏm, as one of the few Korean writers to deliberately use the naturalist mode, nevertheless does not ignore the political consciousness-raising function of literature. Thus realism in Korea—unlike its Western development—was closely linked to both the leftist task of describing systemic oppression and a naturalist interest in the individual within the laboratory of society. [8] *Mansejŏn* is no workers' novel, nor is it solely a study of the effects of environment on the individual; what distinguishes it from both these typical realist modes is the particular way that modern urban spaces of Japan and Korea are experienced, described, and marked by hierarchy and contradiction.

The very narrative tone of *Mansejŏn* is informed by the contrasting experiences of urban spaces. While in Tokyo, the narrator is oddly incapable of focusing on or naming his unease after receiving the telegram calling him home. Wandering in the cold after leaving a brothel, he muses, "I couldn't say how my mind felt . . . I felt so anxious I almost couldn't stand it. I was unable to know clearly if it was a reflection on myself, or a reflection on something else; moreover . . . something like unfounded pent-up anger and ill will surged inside of me" (21). And a moment later, "I couldn't stand it anymore and jumped on a tram in front of the artillery ironworks" (21–22). Once on the tram, he nonchalantly surveys the workers commuting to Japan's new factories: "aside from twisted faces with skin shriveled by labor, nothing caught my eye" (22). In this scene, Tokyo's urban modernity displays all too clearly its militaristic and exploitative side (the artillery works; the twisted, shriveled workers), yet the protagonist is stubbornly unaware of what might be causing his anxiety. While feeling only disgust and pity at the sight of the (Japanese) proletariat, he ruminates loftily on human desires and pursuits: "On trams and on the streets, perhaps the most pure and beautiful thing is the young men and women who instinctively search for the beauty of the opposite sex" (23). His return to Korea is what focuses his anxiety into a concrete and critical view. Not only is he stopped and searched at the ferry station and deprived of his seat among the crowds of third-class passengers on the ferry, but the constant military police surveillance puts him in a state of identifiable tension throughout his trip. As An Ji-na notes, "his experience of the ferry forces In-hwa to recognize his position of coloniality rather than modernity," and it is through this repeated narrative mechanism that "from individual frustration a sense of nationalist resistance is raised up" (183, my translation). Despite his pride and confidence at being one of the "foreign students in Japan [who] were pioneers of the new age and new knowledge" (Yŏm, 102)—the ones leading the nation into the modern age—the shocking disparity between Japan and Korea as sites of modernity forces him into a new awareness of the contradictions and inequalities embodied by colonial modernization. In short, his consciousness becomes politicized through the experience of discrepant spaces.

The panoramic description of metropolitan and colonial spaces thus becomes the novel's true narrative object. For the protagonist, newly arrived back in Korea after his studies in Japan, the urban forms infiltrating Korean space indicate seduction by the cosmopolitan, but immoral, forms of the colonizers. Arriving in Pusan from the overnight boat from Japan, he surveys the rapidly transforming cityscape:

> Leaving the harbor behind, I walked west following the tracks of the tramway. All along both sides of the wide street, however, I saw only two-story houses standing one next to another in straight lines but not one Korean house. . . .
>
> . . . One house and then two houses went and ten houses changed faces and then one hundred houses. Old houses were pulled down and in no time new houses stood up. One-story houses turned into two-story houses and *ondol*[9] was replaced by *tatami* (Japanese straw flooring), kerosene-oil lamp giving way to electric lighting.
>
> "Did you hear, X's house is going to be pulled down to make the new road?"
>
> But the old man who had made this gossiping remark while filling his long pipe woke up, would hear the noise of the picks and the shovels busy at work coming from the direction of X's house and in no time, there would be tramways, running automobiles spitting dirt and hooting. The sound of Japanese wooden sandals would become louder daily and there would be the new post office. Old military buildings would be pulled down to make room for the new M.P. station and the brothel with its music of *shamisen* (Japanese string instrument) would quickly replace Korean inns and taverns. . . . The world becomes so convenient.
>
> "We have electric lights and tramcars now in our village. Come and see. There are a couple of nice cozy eating houses, too . . . I bet you never saw a Japanese whore, did you? I will show you one." (Yŏm qtd. in Im, 27–28)

The colonial system is implemented through the gradual destruction and replacement of Korean space: traditional Korean houses are demolished to make way for modern two-story dwellings, their faces literally changing.

Moreover, the material changes in the urban environment alter the phe-nomenological experience of these spaces: construction noises and hoots of cars now fill the air, as does the sound of Japanese sandals, which "become louder daily." Brothels and police stations are just as much institutions of this colonial modernity as electric lights and tramcars. Most striking in this description is the way the critical viewpoint of the protagonist Yi In-hwa—so scornful of the excited voices welcoming the new buildings and lights—is generated through the differential experience of metropolitan structures in colonial space. While the bar, restaurant, and tram are simply evidence of modernity in Tokyo, their transplantation to the colony enables an understanding of the problems of Korea unavailable to either the domestic or metropolitan view alone. Indeed, the discussion of graves and burial practices indicates a parallel, macabre side to urbanization: the movement of the dead from rural family burial sites to mass urban graves mimics the displacement of the rural population into the cities.

As the plot already suggests, the numerous detailed descriptions of altered spaces in Korea correlate with a sickness in colonial society that especially implicates women. Searching in vain for the remaining Korean neighborhood of Pusan, the protagonist ends up in a shabby area of more two-story Japanese houses inhabited by Koreans (65–66). This is followed by his visit to a Japanese noodle shop, where he meets a half-Japanese, half-Korean serving girl who has rejected her Korean mother and dreams only of finding her estranged Japanese father. Like the Koreans who so readily give up their houses for Japanese-style dwellings, the servant girl shows her evident Korean self-loathing: "even though she was raised by a Korean, she spoke Japanese rather than Korean, wore Japanese clothes rather than Korean, and even though she was born a girl, she wanted to find her Japanese father rather than be with her Korean mother" (73). For the serving girl, the supposed experience of hybridity only confirms the binary of Korean versus Japanese identities. At his next stop at Kimchŏn to visit his brother's house, the physical changes of the city again preface the social regression he finds inside.

> We walked in silence for a little way, and then reached the approach leading to my brother's house; there was a Japanese store I'd never seen before on the side of the road, and entering the laneway I saw two houses with Japanese

nameplates stuck on the doors. "Things have really changed while I was away!" I said and stared at my brother. He looked as if this wasn't a bit strange and calmly nodded his head. (80)

After noting that the front door of his brother's house is more dilapidated than the previous year, the narrator subsequently reveals that his brother has engaged in an old Korean traditional practice of taking a second wife (*yuchŏjuichŏ*) because the first wife did not bear a son, and the new wife's destitute family wanted to marry her off. In observing the awkward household scene with his two sisters-in-law, the motifs of foreign dwelling, colonized nation, and backward gender relations become oddly yet deeply entwined: "As I looked out through the partially glass-fitted window at the small and old mistress [the first sister-in-law] with her uncombed hair as she went back and forth to the edge of the room, the thought that she was like a strong country now withering [*sidŏrŏganŭn kangguk*] came to my mind. Somehow, she looked pathetic" (82). As An has commented, "at each part of the text, after an event or serious observation, there follows an observation regarding women" (179, my translation). Far from being an indication of advancement, the architectural shift to two-story houses, Japanese-style stores, and glazed windows are actually signs of Korea's regression into older social forms, especially gender relations. The promising surface of colonial modernity—made up of booming (Japanese) businesses, trams, ongoing construction, and increasing property values—has the reverse effect on the everyday lives of the Koreans whose livelihoods are squeezed by this very development. The use of realist, concrete description thus plays a crucial role in this narrative, because it is through the process of documenting discrepant urbanisms that the narrator arrives at this awareness.

　　Finally, the narrator understands how the reverse logic of "modernizing" spaces parallels the obtuse logic of the Koreans. The young salesman he encounters on the train explains why he refuses to cut his long, traditional-style hair or wear Western clothing as the protagonist does. Rather than signify a willingness to accept "enlightenment" (*kaehwa*) through such dress, he recognizes he would receive even worse treatment from the Japanese for daring to assume the accoutrements of modernity while unable to speak the colonial language (*naeji ŏ*, literally "inner land language"). It is therefore safer to pretend to be a completely ignorant *yobo* (derogatory term for Koreans). By means of this logic, the narrator reflects that "the wisest life conduct for the Korean people is to hide behind all things: fear, caution, making do, dissembling, submission, secrecy and servility—these are the most beneficial ways of life" (104). Awareness of the divergent logics behind the same forms of modernity in turn produces the crucial shift in the narrator: from nonchalant foreign student to critical anticolonial, from individual anomie to nationalist outrage.

Considered from his perspective, the reverse logic of the salesman posits a different understanding of modernity. Paradigmatic models of Western urban subjectivities, characterized by consumerism and individualistic self-reinvention, have been famously epitomized by Baudelaire's dandy or Benjamin's *flâneur*, figures joyfully ensconced in the new nineteenth-century European modernity of shopping arcades, crowds, and gas lamps. I invoke Jennifer Robinson, who argues for a broader meaning of modernity that

> appreciates that people in many different places invent new ways of urban life and are enchanted by the production and circulation of novelty, innovation and new fashions; a concept that explores the wide diversity of ways in which, in Marshall Berman's phrase, people make themselves "at home" in a changing, perhaps modernising world. (66)

Looking at examples of urban cultural practices in the United States, Zambia, Brazil, and Malaysia, Robinson argues for an approach to urban modernity that "frame[s] the city as a site for the constant reinvention of (already inventive) traditional practices" (90). To this way of thinking, we cannot assume that the Korean *yobo* is the antimodern, excluded remainder outside Japanified Western modernity. Rather, his actions—wearing traditional clothes and hairstyle as a way to mitigate Japanese prejudice—are negotiations with and reinnovations of certain Korean ways and mark him and the other Koreans in the novel as quintessentially modern subjects. What both In-hwa and the reader understand by the end of the novel is that, occurring within the unique frame of the colonial city, the single process of modernity/coloniality produces radically different experiences and responses across classes, races, and genders. This is one way of understanding the meaning of discrepant. For the refined, educated protagonist, despite his criticisms of Koreans as backward and nonmodern, modernity and coloniality cannot be separated and, ultimately, "modernity is precisely his rational choice to support [Korean] nationalism" (An, 184, my translation). This is not to say, however, that *Mansejŏn* satisfies with a recognizable course of action corresponding to In-hwa's newly found anticolonial stance. Despite the title, there is in fact no narrative lead-up to the events of the actual March 1st movement. In the end, our protagonist buries his wife in a public grave site and returns to Japan to continue studying, although he feels remorse over her death. Nevertheless, what the novel achieves is a strategy for viewing the central forms of colonial modernity—its urbanism, architecture, gender relations, and everyday practices—through the "internal coherence and system of external relationships" (Said, 32)—that is, through a discrepant, critical mode.

Compared with *Mansejŏn,* Wu Zhuoliu's *The Orphan of Asia* offers even less of a clear-cut narrative of political awakening.[10] Completed in 1945 and originally written in Japanese, *Orphan* is a curious text. Overtly autobiographical and meandering in its plot, it has been hailed as a pioneering examination of Taiwanese identity and a pathbreaking Taiwanese novel. *Orphan* follows the life of Hu Taiming, son of a wealthy farmer, and recounts his upbringing in rural Taiwan and his education and travels in both the imperial center, Japan, and the site of anti-imperial resistance, China. Its titular trope, of course, is that of Taiwan as orphan: belonging to neither Japan nor China, it is that "unpropitiously situated island" (Wu, 98)[11] stuck between two powerful and ancient nations. Simultaneously regarded as an uncivilized barbarian by the Japanese colonizers and as a possible Japanese spy by the mainlanders, Taiming is uniquely caught up in the maelstrom of world events. He grows up and becomes a schoolteacher in Japanese Taiwan; becomes one of the first Taiwanese to gain a degree (in physics) from a Japanese university; lives in Nanjing just as the Japanese begin their assault on Chinese territory; is later drafted to work as a translator for the Japanese imperial army; and finally, witnesses Taiwan's descent into barbarous military rule with the onset of World War II. His shuttling back and forth between the three territories—China, Japan, and Taiwan— leads Leo Ching to theorize the novel as an exemplary portrayal of "triple consciousness" (177) and demonstration of the way such "identity struggles [are] a historically induced colonial condition" (185–86).

As with *Mansejŏn,* we must place the question of Wu's realism into historical context. While the genre was prevalent in the broadly leftist anticolonial literature of Taiwan that produced accurate descriptions of the poverty and despair of colonial life, the very difficulty in choosing or developing a literary language was perhaps even more complicated for the Taiwanese. Denton describes how the mainland's May Fourth Movement—"the necessary tool with which to discuss literary modernity in China"—absorbed and developed literary styles in a much less sequential or developmental fashion than in the West. "Exposing a reality that traditional ideology concealed" (291) was crucial, and the prominent May Fourth writer Mao Dun, for example, "promoted 'naturalism,' wrote realistic novels and short stories about, for instance, the economic hardship of peasants or the inner workings of capitalism in Shanghai" (294). Many May Fourth writers, however, were equally concerned with the creation of new literary languages and aesthetic forms: "All writers in this early period were participating in the formation of the new national literary language—a mélange of premodern vernacular, Liang Qichao's 'new style,' Western and Japanese grammatical forms, foreign loanwords, and even remnants of classical Chinese" (292). Further, Kleeman relates how there were competing factors surrounding language choice in colonial Taiwan, including the vast difference between the hitherto use of classical Chinese and actual spoken Chinese; the influence of the May Fourth Movement, which advocated a vernacular literature based on spoken northern Mandarin, unintelligible to most Taiwanese who spoke Minnan and Hakka; and, perceived by many, the modernizing/Westernizing character of Japanese. In Kleeman's account, "the result in Taiwan was a fourfold contestation: between classical Chinese and vernacular Mandarin; between vernacular Mandarin and vernacular Taiwanese; between classical Chinese and modern Japanese; and between vernacular Taiwanese and modern Japanese" (146–47). Like Yŏm, Wu also read European writers in Japanese translation and, like many of his generation, wrote in Japanese. By the 1930s in Taiwan, a pessimistic naturalism that described the oppression and powerlessness of the natives under Japanese rule came to dominate, even though leftist writers like Yang Kui, known for his optimistic and explicitly Leninist 1932 story "Paperboy," wrote in opposition to this kind of literature (though also in Japanese).[12] Wu's realism, therefore, has not only to do with a perceived transparency of language, but the influence from the West through Japan as well as responses to the mainland's May Fourth Movement. This mix results in an exceedingly complex politics of language, genre, and style.[13]

We do know that under the strict censorship laws of the final years of Japanese rule, Wu risked his life to write *Orphan,* such that the novel represents "the definitive act and symbol of resistance against Japanese colonialism" (Ching, 178). In contrast to such bold action, however, Wu's protagonist Taiming is a surprisingly passive and ineffectual agent, not unlike Yŏm's In-hwa. Stubbornly holding on to a belief in pure knowledge over politics, he repeatedly finds himself a political sideliner. As a student, he stands uncomfortably by as his Taiwanese friends in Japan agitate for equality; later, he watches mutely as his mainlander wife speaks out at an anti-Japanese rally in Nanjing. Imprisoned in China because he is Taiwanese and therefore a "Japanese citizen," he must wait for rescue by former students from the girls' middle school he teaches at, and after a short stint in the Japanese army, he is discharged because of his weak nerves. Finally, at the end of the novel, he receives an exemption for the military defense draft, thanks to his Japanese friend Sato's influence. If Wu's novel does not actively anticipate anticolonial resistance, like *Mansejŏn,* it succeeds in portraying the deep psychological confusion resulting from the hypocrisies of colonialism. Young Taiming works first as a teacher for a colonial school near his native village in Taiwan, where his reverence for the modernity and refinement of Japanese ways (made clear in his affections for a young Japanese teacher, Hisako) is undermined by the police violence against peaceful Taiwanese and the blatantly unjust relationship between Japanese and Taiwanese teachers (99). The novel is best, perhaps, in its stinging depictions of the sychophantic Taiwanese who readily adopt Japanese language, manners, and names in an attempt to curry favor and status with their colonial masters. At the same time, however, Taiming himself does not escape or actively resist the system in any way. Despite his hatred for the increasingly despotic Japanese rule in Taiwan, he firmly remains a product of its system. Over the course of the novel, he works not only for a colonial school and as a translator for the Japanese army's interrogations and torture, but for a corrupt bureaucratic government department and, finally, for an intellectual journal that publishes slogans "made at the request of the Propaganda Bureau" (226).

Despite the marked difference in narrative tenor to Yi In-hwa's obsessively morbid journey along the Korean peninsula, Taiming's most profound moments of clarity about the larger geopolitical and imperial systems also come about through the experience of discrepant spaces. At a superficial level, the novel reads like a travelogue, and as Ping-hui Liao has pointed out, the China section closely follows Wu's journal *Nanking Chagan (Nanking Journals,* or *Mixed Feelings toward Nanking)* of 1942–43. Liao surmises that both Wu's journal and *The Orphan of Asia* owe much to the writings of Japanese colonial intellectuals and artists Akutagawa Ryunosuke and Ishikawa Kinichiro, who wrote on China and Taiwan, respectively (Liao, "Travel," 285). Quite fittingly for a travelogue, what one finds in the descriptions of Tokyo or Shanghai is the urge to compare and ascertain national characters, while delineating the homeland or Taiwan in the same stroke. Yet the task is made uniquely difficult for Wu because "his hermeneutical codes were paradoxically supplied by two metropolitan centers—Japan and China—to which he had no relation" (Liao, 294) or, perhaps, had only a subaltern relation. Consider Taiming's experiences of the Japanese and Chinese metropolises. First, Tokyo: "The traffic was frightening—the masses of people and the busy machines, streetcars and automobiles—moving aggressively in an endless stream.... To the swimming eyes of the young man from Taiwan, [the pedestrians] seemed not so much to be walking but trotting. He wondered why so many people in Tokyo were busy" (Wu, 54). And now Shanghai:

A piece of the real, living China, the city demolished the shallow, dated notions he had had of the country. The modern, Western atmosphere of its French settlement drove home to the young Taiwanese that he was, after all, a country bumpkin. The modern clothes of the quite visible young women did not succeed in concealing the aura of a mature culture, five thousand years old. (98)

In both the above passages, the third national culture implicitly described is that of Taiwan, defined negatively by what it is not—"the swimming eyes of the young man from Taiwan" and the "country bumpkin" indicate a subject whose senses can barely keep pace with the intensity of the metropolis. While there is an interest in defining Japanese and Chinese civilizations against each other, it is the comparative spatial presentations of colonial Taiwan in the rest of the novel that are the most revealing. The detailed descriptions of changing towns, streets, and buildings in the colony give rise not merely to further comparative musings on national character and modernity, but also to the peculiarly discrepant perspective so central to *Mansejŏn*. In other words, Taiwanese space, read against the spaces of the metropole, contains and crystallizes the larger contradictions of the modernizing, imperial project.

At first, hints of altered spaces in Taiming's homeland appear subtly. After his escape from the Nanjing prison via Shanghai, he arrives back to the "gloomy homeland" to find his village had "changed a lot and felt new and more alive. The main street was much wider and flanked by full-grown eucalyptus trees. Down this avenue, a bus—a beaten-down old model but nevertheless a bus—bumped along four or five times a day, leaving the scent of civilization in its wake" (157). In an apparent discard of old for new, his family home's main ceremonial hall is now covered in cobwebs, the letters on its shrine peeling with age (157). Civilization and traditional Chinese customs appear, rather predictably, to be at odds. But not long after he is welcomed home by his family and the villagers, he realizes it is the accelerated war effort rather than the blessings of modernity that Japan ruthlessly bestows upon Taiwan, its oldest and most loyal colony. Cash "donations," "voluntary" enlistment, metal drives, rice rationing, and the ever-menacing presence of corrupt Japanese officials make the final two chapters of *Orphan* increasingly harrowing reading. Seemingly less interested in questions of national identity or character, the narrative becomes a litany of these hardships, largely provided through villagers' anecdotes told to Taiming.

Taiming's greedy brother, Zhigang, literally brings home the contradictions of Japanese rule. A greedy and corrupt government arbitrator, he is emblematic of the downward shift in both Taiwanese morals and architecture: "Also upon becoming an arbitrator, Zhigang had remodeled his house into a Japanese-style abode, constructing a household Shinto altar, and even a tatami-mat room, which was very unusual in the countryside" (164). Indeed, no part of Zhigang's house is beyond Japanification: "For him the new regime meant installing a new bathroom containing a bathtub made of cedar that emanated a strong woody smell. Furthermore . . .

he even had it repainted in more typically Japanese colors. The toilet had also been remodeled into a Japanese-style one" (167). While this description seems narratively to function as satirical evidence of Taiming's brother's excesses, the fusing of architectural and national/political fate is familiar. It is not simply that the architectural shift is metaphorical of a deeper shift in political identification; rather, such a shift becomes conceptually available through the very narration of Zhigang's newly Japanified toilet: "the new regime *meant* installing a new bathroom" (emphasis added). Two further scenes involving architecture and urbanism finally precipitate a stronger narrative voice.

The first follows a protracted dispute between Taiming's family and the irrigation association, who, on noticing Taiming's mother's meager banana plantation, insist on taxing them for the water used. When Taiming objects, the authority declares that they must pay tax on the pond or it will be removed. Furious, Taiming goes to talk with an officer at the authority itself to argue his case: "The Irrigation Association occupied a majestic two-story building, more splendid than the local district headquarters. The entire facility had undoubtedly been funded with the unjust taxes exacted from the sweat and blood of the masses. With trepidation, Taiming pushed open the door and entered" (183–84). The encounter goes badly, and Taiming leaves even more frustrated and disgusted. Yet the most shocking thing is what he sees on his way out:

> When he left the Irrigation Association building, he noticed a row of seven or eight attractive apartment buildings at the back. They were the lodgings for the Irrigation Association employees. From the interior of the complex, a phonograph record was blaring a vulgar, Japanese pop song that was current in the cafés. So this was what became of the money culled from the blood and sweat of the people—all in the name of irrigation! (185)

The hypocrisy and injustice of the colonial system are perceived nowhere more sharply than in its most modern forms: the new apartment buildings "blaring" current Japanese music. It is one of the few moments the reader thinks Taiming may actually act against the colonial system: "Taiming felt an undefined indignation well up in him with the thought, and when he raised his eyes, flaring with that indignation, he saw white clouds" that "appeared full of turbulence" (185). Here, the descriptive verisimilitude of spatial reality produces not merely a believable background to the plot, but rather becomes the plot itself; it is what allows Taiming both a visceral and intellectual understanding of injustice.

Ching has written of the importance of space and movement to the novel, and suggests that Taiming's travel between the three countries "underscores the very contradictions of these places." He goes on to note:

> Locations are not only populated with people, buildings and landscapes; they are also invested with feelings, sentiments, and emotions. Taiming comes to perceive the incommensurability in each locale in terms of the similar schematization of contradictions within colonialism (between assimilation and discrimination), modernization (between metropolitan center and colonial periphery), and nationalism (between the imaginary and the real). (197)

More than simple locations, the colonial built forms and spaces in the narrative elicit a powerful sense of incommensurability and discrepancy. In a passage close to the end of the novel, Taiming and his Japanese friend, Sato, are walking the streets of Taipei. Up to this point, the colonial capital has played little role in the novel, because Taiming's travels are always from his village to the port city of Jeelung and then on to Japan or China. In this scene, however, the dire contradictions of the wartime colony flare up unbidden from the city streets:

> The summer sunlight glistened on the baking hot asphalt. They heard a chorus of voices coming up behind them, singing a Pacific War marching song: an Imperial Training Squad made up of young Taiwanese cadets was passing through. Because the two men were walking slowly, the squad quickly caught up with and passed them. They were marching in four orderly columns, but their uniforms were in tatters and their appearance in general was almost pathetic. As he watched them march past, Sato remarked, "Just look at that. They look like the battered leftovers of a defeated army. And those women!"
>
> He was referring to a group of Japanese women walking along the road in their finest kimono. "What a contrast, eh?" he said to Taiming. No further words were necessary for them to know that they were thinking the same thing. (224)

The shabby Taiwanese troops, of course, are a stark juxtaposition to the well-dressed Japanese ladies. A paragraph later, Sato comments grimly that "the long, winding lines of finely dressed Japanese housewives and pompous gentlemen in front of the sweet shops and restaurants would soon ... come to feel the same misery as did the Taiwanese themselves" (224). What should be the epitome of Japanese-ordered modernity—the neat columns of soldiers, alongside the urbane Japanese and their prosperous businesses—turns out to be evidence of the unsustainable contradictions of the Japanese empire. The two line formations of the shabby soldiers and the Japanese elite conjure up symmetrical yet opposed architectural figures, one symbolizing the refinement of colonial civilization and the other the military means by which it is maintained.[14] The growing pressure on the Taiwanese to sacrifice themselves for the war effort becomes too much to conceal. Taiming describes how, after the American invasion of Leyte in the Philippines, "the Japanese started looking hounded by fate. Even the building of the governor-general, the symbol of Japanese imperialism, appeared to be dressed in doleful mourning clothes" (232). By the end of the novel, the defeat of the Japanese empire is imminent but comes too late for Taiming and his family. His mother dies, and his younger half-brother, Zhinan, returns home close to death after suffering appalling conditions at an imperial service construction site. The novel ends with Taiming losing his sanity, wandering about and mindlessly screaming accusatory verses at both the Japanese "daylight bandit" and the Taiwanese "imperial errand-boy" (246).

What may not be clear from the above is the oddness of *Orphan*'s narrative form. Characters appear and disappear without subsequent effect on the plot; not only do we never hear of Taiming's wife and daughter after he leaves them on the mainland, but their absence warrants only a couple of lines in the remainder of the novel. Other characters are described, disappear, and need to be described all over again when they reappear many pages later. Thus, while certain aspects of society are portrayed according to what we now recognize as the conventions of realism, there is little narrative buildup or coherent protagonist development outside well-known historical events. I suggest that what takes the place of realist plotlines, and what enables interior subjective development, is precisely architectural and urban experience, apprehended in certain epiphanic moments—the moment outside the irrigation association apartments, the scene of the shabby soldiers marching down Taipei's streets, the pathetic facade of the governor-general's building. Indeed, the novel's political and emotional insights have less to do with Taiming's own adventures or interactions with individual Japanese (who are never pilloried as individuals) and more to do with the experiences of discrepant colonial spaces and the inherent contradictions they embody. If *Mansejŏn* works by positing a literal and metaphorical underside of morbidity to the surface modernity of colonial Chosŏn, *Orphan* affords glimpses into a larger system through momentary apprehensions of the exploitation built into modern forms of colonialism. Although the hermeneutical code of Taiwan was yet to exist, the major spatial figure and critical apparatus of the novel is that of the orphan island. Described through its built spaces, the territory is the interstitial space across which the narrator shuttles back and forth in uneasy desire and mistrust for Japan and China.

Although the two novels discussed work via different narrative affect and registers of interiority, both achieve their primary moral, political, and narrative momentum from the discrepant spaces their protagonists inhabit and describe. Such descriptions function not to immerse the reader in a social reality in order to directly show the oppression of the colonial milieu, or to study the individual's responses to such an environment. Rather, the realistic presentations of colonial urban and architectural forms are crucial for their role in working through the core problem of anticolonialism: for conceptualizing and articulating the violent and exploitative substrate on which the system rests. At the same time, urban forms also operate as the contested locus of modern desires and perceptions. Even as Japanese colonial modernity is shown to be untenable, the old forms of village or traditional life are equated with the superstitious and feminine (In-hwa's dying wife, Taiming's incomprehension of the backward village women), which must be denied in order to access the new and the rational. If the city, like woman, is a major signifier of relative civilization and progress, the discrepancies between colonial and metropolitan spaces are equally sources of colonial angst and self-critique. For Yŏm Sang-sŏp, the replication of the Japanese modern city in Korea allows him to decry the colonized's forced subservience; for Wu Zhuoliu, we see the stirrings of an outrage against both colonial injustice and Taiwanese passivity. For the former, colonial urbanization is the material and visual counterpart of the very structure of inequality inherent in the modern project: it posits a back-ward, unenlightened space to be brought into the present through indus-trialization and exploitation. For the latter, such inequalities are perceived via moments of epiphany in certain spaces of the colonial territory. Nei-ther native nor metropolitan itself, the colonial city is the spatial form from which these distinctions are put into currency; it is both the shiny beacon of modernity and repressive mechanism of authority. In its trans-position into literary form, the unique spatial mode of production that colonialism demands emerges as both preeminent object for literary real-ism and object of critique.

INTRANSITIVE MODERNISM AND *THE WINGS*

But what of modernist literature and subjectivity formed not through the contrapuntal viewpoint, but within the hermetic spaces of the discrepant city itself? Rather than focus solely on the construction of an anticolonial-ist position through the discrepant experience, I am also interested in the psychological and existential implications of that very spatial incoherence. Again, my discussion assumes the pivotal role of architecture and urban-ism as both the built forms mediating colonial power systems and the physical envelope of everyday life. The following analysis traces another means by which the physical contours of the colonial city are given "rep-resentational space" (Lefebvre) by the contours of literature. In turning here to the way the demand for misrecognition produces an alternative lit-erary modernism, I consider Yi Sang's 1936 *The Wings* as another exem-plary work of colonial literature.

In the previous chapter we discussed how the transformation of colo-nial space is tied to changes in the metropolitan industrial system. The his-tory of Korea's earliest urbanization and growth of the working class may be understood within this framework. By 1920, a rural exodus, resulting from the disintegration·of the traditional feudal system, was drawn toward "factory, mining, and construction work sites in the fast-rising industrial centers of Kyŏngsŏng [Seoul], P'yŏngyang, Pusan, Inchŏn" and other cities, increasing the urbanized population to 13.2 percent by 1944 (Soon-won Park, 135).[15] Unlike the rest of the country—and more like Tokyo—Seoul was reducing its food industries and expanding consumer goods pro-duction, primarily in the cotton textile industry and machine industries

(Soon-won Park, 138); new legislation simultaneously limited domestic food production in the effort to introduce a money economy (Chulwoo Lee, 40–41). The Japanese residents in Korea, numbering three-quarters of a million by the end of the colonial period, were mostly located in the large metropolitan areas and contributed to consumption demands. Yet despite the apparent rise in urbanization and shift in industries, a 1928 government census of wage earners in the nonagricultural sector revealed that "most of the 1.16 million urban workers recorded . . . were 'miscellaneous workers,' who were composed mainly of free day-laborers, domestic household workers, and factory and mining workers"—that is, workers in the informal economy (Soon-won Park, 134). This confirms Castells's point that "the rush towards the towns is, in general, regarded much more as the result of a rural *push* than of an urban *pull,* that is to say, much more as a decomposition of rural society than as an expression of the dynamism of urban society" (*Urban Question,* 46). The incongruity of a burgeoning consumer society, patronized by the local elite and expatriate Japanese community, and an ever-swelling population of underemployed natives are the very conditions of Fanon's bifurcated colonial world. To evoke the Heideggerian vocabulary once more, it results from the struggle occurring between space cleared or "worlded" for the colonial bureaucracy and metropolitan consumers, and that remaining for the colonial "earth."

Written against this background, Yi Sang's 1936 novella is often regarded as the pinnacle of modernist Korean fiction. It noticeably departs from the realist literary movements outlined in the previous section of this chapter, which sought to describe and document the crushing poverty of urban dwellers, for a highly stylized modernism. Yet as with realism, literary modernism in colonial East Asia cannot simply be understood in the developmental terms accorded to European modernism—typically the rejection of dominant, nineteenth-century representational modes. Only ten years after Yŏm Sang-sŏp's realist breakthrough with *Mansejŏn,* the mid-1930s witnessed the forced breakup of leftist movements that was the political impetus for many practitioners of realist literature. In all of Japan's territories, the gentler period of "cultural rule" gave way to military buildup in anticipation of a second Sino-Japanese war. Reacting to the newly tightened censorship, writers were naturally inclined to use more abstract literary techniques to deal with their new surroundings. Without the long Western genealogy or entrenched realist literary styles, "the mid-1930s witnessed an early high point of modern Korean fiction" (Fulton, "Historical," 631).

Indeed, what has struck many critics about *The Wings* is its astonishing modernism: it is narrated entirely through the interior monologue of the protagonist, and it shares with many of the great Western modernist texts a bored yet anxious subjectivity through which the world is ordered and perceived. The petulant tone is reminiscent of Dostoevsky's *Notes from the Underground,* and the few proper names in the text include Dostoevsky, Hugo, and Marx. One could very well surmise that Yi Sang, an architect educated in Japanese colonial schools and working for the governor-general's office of architecture, is portraying the paralyzing experience of the colonial intellectual: educated but barred from civic participation or meaningful employment by Japanese rule, he is just one of the many "miscellaneous workers" of the colonial urban population. To push beyond this reading, I want to draw connections between the distinct spaces of the colonial city and the experimental narrative space of the text.

Immediately, one notices the protagonist's curious relationship to the space he dwells in. He begins by declaring the utter satisfactoriness of his environment:

> My room—it is not a house, because we never had one—suited me, by all means. The temperature of the room pleased me, and the duskiness of the room comforted my eyes. I did not want any other room cooler or warmer than my own, nor a room darker or more comfortable. I thanked my room all the time because it seemed to maintain itself to please me, and I was glad that I might have been born to the world for that particular room. (11)[16]

The story has little action, no dialogue, and no character development. The narrative tension of the novella is produced by the gap between what the reader understands quite clearly and what the narrator disavows: the fact he is living with his wife in a brothel compound in colonial Seoul, conveniently ignoring her business and the visits by her "guests," and is, moreover, living by virtue of her labor. He ponders naively, "Did she have a job *[chigŏp]?* I could not tell what her occupation was. If she did not have a job, she not have to go out, as I did not have to—but she did. She not only went out but entertained many guests at home. When she had many guests *[raegaek],* I had to stay under the bedding quilt in my room all the time she was with them" (16). The narrator's hermetically sealed mental life and the contracted spatiality of his world echo each other: his room becomes a living universe "maintaining itself" for him and fitting him like a "well-tailored suit," while he remains defiantly untainted by the exchange relations going on in the next room. The two main characters in *The Wings* thus seem to be the protagonist and the space he occupies.

Initially, the existential reach of the narrator is limited to the subtle differences in the environment of his room-universe. The events of the first half of the novella are nothing more than his waking up, determining whether the sun is coming in through the window or not, whether his wife is in or out, whether the electric light is on or off, appreciating the way his wife's cosmetics look in the light, eating, feeling tired, and sleeping. The claustrophobia of this text is both psychological and spatial, yet it is not clear which is determining of which. On the one hand, the subjectivity of the self-absorbed, skeptical, modern individual is apparently sequestered into a tiny box; on the other, the restrictiveness of the environment may be what produces such a subjectivity. In either case, a plot development spoils this self-sufficient existence: the mysterious and tiresome appearance of coins at the head of his sleeping mat—coins left for him regularly by his wife. As the pile grows, she eventually gives him a cash box to deposit them in, prompting him, from bed, to naively conduct research into the money's origin: "I found out. I realized that the money she spent was given by the strange visitors, whom I considered very silly. However, I could not understand the ethics *[yeŭi]* of the guests leaving the money and my wife taking it" (18). Furthermore,

> The reason why my wife had to leave me silver coins was as much a mystery to me as the reason why the visitors offered her money. Though I did not disapprove her of tipping me the coins, it offered me no more pleasure than the short happiness *[jjalbŭn ch'ogak i choatdal bbun]* lasting from the moment my fingers touched the coin until it disappeared into the miniature coffer's slot. (19–20)

The narrator adamantly denies any notion of the exchange value of money—and what services are being performed for it—by repudiating all but the materiality of the coins. Through this attitude (he later tips the cash box into the outhouse) and his petulant wish that his wife would "manage the savings business herself" (20), we understand the narrator to be rejecting the interdependent relationships between labor, money, and commodities—the very relationships currently restructuring all of colonial Korea and its gender roles. Not only is the narrator feminized in receiving money from his working wife, but also this role reversal is signified in the spatial arrangement of their dwelling. He occupies the inner room, or *anbang,* traditionally the protected space of the woman, while his wife lives in the *sarangbang,* or outer men's quarters.[17]

The story soon develops into an odd battle of wills: the narrator desires to go out in the evenings, but he repeatedly fails to heed his wife's injunction not to return until after midnight, when we presume her last guest will leave. The narrator's wandering of the streets contains a strange echo of Benjamin's *flâneur.* He is, like this figure, both a part of the crowd and a threshold observer of it—not because of the *flâneur's* financial independence and leisure, however, but precisely the reverse. He is unemployed, and he does not seem to know how to spend money. Taking his five *won,* he finds a kind of freedom loitering around the streets, but "I did not spend a penny, of course. I could not even think of spending any. It seemed I had a long time ago completely lost the faculty of spending money" (21–22, translation modified). After being reprimanded for coming home too early when his wife is still with a guest, he laments his own consumer incompetence: "If I had known how to spend that five *wǒn,* I certainly did not need to return home before midnight. But the streets were too crowded, and there were too many of them. I could not point out a single person out of the crowd, the one to whom I was supposed to give that money away. Eventually, I tired myself out" (24–25). Like modernists around the world, the narrator displays an ambivalent relationship to the crowded streets. For theorists of the modern such as Marshall Berman, the fragmentary, influx experience of the city is celebrated for the way it captures "the interfusion of [modern life's] material and spiritual forces, the intimate unity of the modern self and the modern environment" (Berman, 132). We must note, however, a fundamental obstacle to such a unity in the colonial context. With regard to another of Yi Sang's stories, Choi Won-shik notes that despite the ease with which others may dive into the alluring city, "for [Yi

Sang's] 'I' the streets mean terror" (131). Unlike Baudelaire's Paris, "the streets of colonized Seoul, caught in a dense net of taboo, are streets where the possibility of creative dynamism has been blocked at its source" (131). The inability to accept the function of money prevents the protagonist from fully exploring the space of the modern city, which then becomes mere exhausting confusion. In giving back a few *wŏn* to his wife, the narrator thinks he discovers some of the pleasure of money: "I simply could not describe the joy I had felt when . . . I thrust the money into her hand. I was enthralled that I understood, to some extent, the psychology of the visitors leaving money to my wife" (26–27). Refusing its symbolic exchange value, however, he insists on presenting the money as a gift, precisely removing it from circulation.

The misunderstood relationship between money and space deeply structures Yi Sang's text. Following the general rules of colonialism, we see how local production is replaced by the metropole-dictated logic of a money economy, which, as famously theorized by Simmel, "reduces all quality and individuality to a purely quantitative level." This results in both a new spatial and social form: "the modern city . . . is supplied almost exclusively by production for the market, that is, for entirely unknown purchasers who never appear in the actual field of vision of the producers themselves" (71). Simmel shows how the absolute flattening effect of money, as "what is common to all," alone connects unknown individuals to each other in the absence of knowable production and consumption communities. Despite having long preexisted capitalism, money in the colonial system now becomes the integrating tool of the new institutions of trade, commodity exchange, and imperial economics. Yet because the colonial city facilitates the circulation of commodities from the metropole without allowing for their general purchase, money alienates the colonial subject even more acutely than in Simmel's theorization. The protagonist's naive solution is simply to remain untouched by both urban spaces and the circulation of money. Yi Sang's narrator, novice of the metropolis and excluded from its mode of production, cannot accept even the basic function of money under capitalist organization and fails as a consumer by not knowing "to whom I was supposed to give that money away." *The Wings* thus dramatizes the peculiarly colonial-modern predicament of a man unable to enter either the spaces, or relations, of exchange of the modern city. Unlike Berman's ideal modern subject, he cannot interfuse the material and spiritual forces of his life. His wife, on the other hand, has fused them all too well by arrogating herself to the very level of the commodity.[18]

Harootunian has written on the great importance of the city in the worldwide experience of modernity. He writes,

> In modernity, during the epoch of industrialization and the establishment of mass society, the places of history are the cities, the expanding industrial sites, and their experiences are the everyday. It is thus the cities, not anymore the countryside in general, that make up the contemporary scene, the now of the present. This scene is the stage that both figures the experience of the everyday and provides the space on which it is enacted.... The modernity of everydayness is the streets, the buildings, the new institutions and constant movement, the ceaseless interrelationship between public and private that register large and small events alike. (19)

For Harootunian, the everydayness of the modern city is the unifying frame of the "ceaseless interrelationship[s]" that structure it. The category of the everyday allows for a convergence of the new buildings, vehicles, and objects of the colonial city as the "the now of the present," and an understanding of the self through the small relationships with objects and spaces of everyday experience. Similarly, for Kristin Ross, the everyday is "what remains when all specialized activities have been eliminated" and what bridges the subjective and the objective (9). Yi Sang's text, however, attempts such an everydayness of existence while disavowing the mode of production that has engendered such spaces. From the colonized's point of view, the urban experiences produced by colonial modernity are emphatically not unifying but rather dislocating. We might see Yi Sang's modernist approach as an alternative formation of the critical subjectivity produced in *Mansejŏn* and *The Orphan of Asia* that works its ways through colonialism by describing and rationally understanding the (il)logic of its discrepant spaces. With Yi Sang, instead of presenting everyday urban objects as the privileged bearers of meaning, there is a partial retreat *within* certain spaces to avoid the reality of the city's relationships and systems. Hence the fixation on the surface materiality of things: of coins, his self-sufficient room, his wife's ever-fascinating cosmetics. These are modes of experience that precisely deny money's exchange value—at work both in the brothel compound and the disposable commodity—and produce a very different structure of feeling from the gritty celebration of modern cities inaugurated by Baudelaire.

Waking from a nap one day, just before discovering that his wife is trying to kill him with a gradual overdose of sleeping pills, the protagonist stretches out on his wife's bed and "wanted to brag to God that my life was so comfortable and pleasant. I maintained no relations with anything in the world. Not even God perhaps could praise or punish me" (34). The figure, or "spatial alibi" (after Benjamin), for this fantasy of complete independence is his cell-like room, seemingly detached from the rest of Seoul, in which he has been able to find minimal food, comfort, and entertainment. His desire to leave this safe space produces a crisis: in other spaces of the city, such an alibi protecting him from the actual connected everydayness of the colonial city is untenable. After his earlier failed wanderings on the street, the narrator makes a wonderful discovery in Seoul Station: a tearoom that appeals to him because of its anonymity and its large, accurate clock, which would save him from the "misfortune of returning home too early, mistaken by stupid clock" (31). Sitting in a booth, his understanding of the space is, again, unsuited to the bustling atmosphere of a railway station cafeteria:

> I sat with nothingness in a booth and sipped a cup of hot coffee. Amid their busy hours, the passengers seemed to enjoy a cup of coffee with relish. They would gaze at a wall as if in deep thought, sipping the coffee in a hurry, and then would leave. It was sad. But I truly loved that sadness about the place, something I cherished more than the burdensome atmosphere of other streetside tea rooms. The occasional shrill screaming of the train hoots sounded more familiar and intimate to me than Mozart. (31, translation modified)

Words like *bench, tearoom, hall,* and *box* (meaning booth) are all in transliterated English in the text, underlining the entrance of these new structures into both space and language. Counterintuitively, it is in the most anonymous and colonial of architectural spaces that he finally feels intimacy and connection with others. The warm humanity he finds in the very transience of the tearoom is simply the reverse of his disavowal of the intimacy taking place in his wife's room. We thus find an aesthetic reversal in the space of everydayness, which is inscribed in the delinking rather than unification of the subject and environment, the material and spiritual, the public and private.

I want to contrast the presentation of everyday spaces in *The Wings* to that of Yi Sang's more conventionally modernist piece "Tokyo," published posthumously in 1939. Here, in the metropolitan capital, the narrator delights in the new ecosystem of the modern city, where gasoline fumes replace air, tall buildings become the "occupants" of the city, "cars function as shoes," and the landscape is made up of neon signs, coffee shops, balloon ads, and department stores (97). The entire globe is brought into a simultaneity of time and space through the varied everyday activities of the city

The neobaroque Seoul Station (architect Sukamoto Yasusi), built 1922–25. This image was taken in 1945, just after liberation from Japan. Photograph by George Silk/Time & Life Pictures/Getty Images.

dweller: drinking at the French Mansion café, going to see "The Japanese New Theater Movement" (97), pondering the existence of Brazilian coffee, and reciting the poetic names of Japanese department stores: "Mitsukoshi, Matsuzakaya, Itoya, Shirokiya, Matsuya" (99). The text is peppered with transliterated English words denoting places, brand names, and such universally modern institutions as *shop girls, apartment, neon, promenade, taxi,* and, indeed, the adjective *modern* (presented as *moden*). The cosmopolitan modernity of Tokyo is thus a frenzied and fantastic mixture of international ideas, objects, styles and subjectivities that make present the rest of the world's urban centers, allowing the narrator to complain nonchalantly that "if I went to Broadway in New York, I might feel the same disappointment" (96). Unlike this phantasmagoric world of international consumer culture, I argue that the everydayness in *The Wings* is completely intransitive. Rather than being a space into which the rest of the world enters, the colonial city is primarily the social and material mechanism for transmitting metropolitan power relations and selected goods to the colony, while extending the logic of imperial control. Rather than the joyful heterogeneity of Tokyo's whirlwind spaces, its logic is manifested in contradictory and opposing urban components that demand misrecognition.

In chapter 1 we saw that for Fanon's Algiers, the opposing components within the colonial city are the "crouching village" and the "town of steel and stone"; for Yi Sang's Seoul, they are the seedy brothel district on the one hand, and the bustling downtown streets with its Japanese-built train station and department stores on the other. Unlike Fanon's colonial subject, who, faced with the urban discrepancy of the colonial city, is seized by a violent desire for the colonizer's house, bed, and wife, in Yi Sang's story, there is no mention or thought of the Japanese; it is his own wife and bed that he does not have access to. In both cases, woman is merely seen as the material good that the male subject does or does not possess. Further, as in Wu's depiction of Japanese imperialism, the structure of colonial spaces is such that they do not actually need the immediate presence of the colonizers to wield their power. Fanon's *Wretched of the Earth* passage amply demonstrated how the material difference between the two zones is enough to produce an immense psychic reaction in the native. The psychological turmoil of Yi Sang's narrator is similarly less a function of character or plot and more of the unbearable social relations frozen in spatial form. Choi Won-shik comments on this aesthetic: "[his] modernism, as his writing name 'Sang' (literally, box) suggests, is not a 'modernism of the streets' but a pathetic 'backroom modernism.'" Isolated from any "residual rural sensations in the city" by the pavement and modern buildings (137) but denied the possibilities of cosmopolitan culture evident in Tokyo, the narrator's world is a sequence of spatial refuges from his wife's business, the pseudo public spaces, and increasing consumerism of Seoul. The structure devoted to the latter—the department store—becomes the very setting of the story's climax.

According to Manfredo Tafuri, the history of the department store is linked to its role in the self-education of the masses. In it, the crowd is taught to see itself as a spectacle alongside the goods. The function of modern cities as productive organizations is precisely "why the ideology of consumption ... must be offered to the public as the ideology of the correct use of the city" (83–84). In the colonial city, the spectacularization of goods from the metropole has an even more important ideological role.[19] In colonial Seoul, Japan's commodity culture was definitively introduced through the Mitsukoshi department store (built 1930), the grandest and most upscale of stores catering mostly to Japanese or high-ranking Korean customers. Designed by one of Yi Sang's alumni Oh Seumi, this four-story monument to consumption was a major attraction in downtown Seoul and is now the site of the Shinsegye department store in fashionable Myŏng-dong. Having accidentally witnessed his wife's economic activities with a customer, the narrator heads for the familiar tearoom of the Seoul station in desperation. But forgetting to bring cash with him, he must wander further afield, and he ends up atop the fashionable roof garden of the Mitsukoshi department store surveying the total view of the city. From here, he contemplates his life and the strange world around him:

> I looked down at the littered street below. Down there, the tired life swayed heavily like the fins of the gold fish. They could not free themselves from the glue—the invisible tangles of threads *[nun e poiji annŭn ggŭnjŏk ggŭnjŏkhan chul]* shackling them. I realized that I could not but mingle into that littered street, dragging my body suffering from fatigue and hunger. (38–39)

For the protagonist, these "invisible tangles of threads"—those relations of economic dependence defining the colonial system—are precisely what he has been disavowing, but they are what his wife's occupation and the spaces of the city no longer allow him to do. In the moment before he rediscovers his wings, the tenuous physical unity of the city seems to disintegrate into its component parts:

> The siren wailed, announcing noon. It was a glorious noon, people vigorously whirling around amid the commotion of glass, steel, marble, banknotes and ink.
>
> My armpits suddenly itched. Ah, it was where my imitation wings had split out. The wings that I had no longer; the deleted phantasms of hope and ambition flashed in my mind like the flipping pages of a pocket dictionary. (39–40, translation modified)

In this epiphanic moment, the city is recognized as satisfactory on its own terms—as an agglomeration of people, building materials, and money—but as an organization against which the protagonist recognizes his fundamental alienation. This realization prompts him to finally free himself from the swirling life by means of the quintessentially modern method of suicide: the leap from a tall building. [20]

Tafuri has argued that the modern city as structured by international capitalistic relations typically exhibits the characteristics of "improbability, multifunctionality, multiplicity, and lack of organic structure" (124). It might be argued that it produces equal effects of alienation, as well as the possibilities for aesthetic modernism, for both its European and colonial city dwellers. However, the structural contradictions between different sectors of the colonial city—the settlers' residential zone, colonial administration buildings, and the new spectacles devoted to trade and commodity alongside a marginalized native society—make the modernity of the colonial city unique. Unlike the sense of urban modernity described by critics from Baudelaire to Harootunian and Berman, everyday lived experience of the colonial city does not unify either the past or present, or the here and there, but tends rather to confirm the subordinated status of the colonized. The existence of the Mitsukoshi department store in downtown Seoul or upscale stores in colonial Taipei are precise concretizations of modern colonial spatiality: they are structures that both provide for the education in exchange values and consumerism *and* legitimize the actual impoverishment of the native society.

If the modernity of the colonial city is structurally different from other modernities, what can we make of the exemplary modernism of Yi Sang's literary style? In his essay on "Modernism and Imperialism," Jameson describes how for modern European national literatures, "a significant structural segment of the economic system as a whole is now located elsewhere, beyond the metropolis, outside of the daily life and existential experience of the home country," such that that experience "can now no longer be grasped immanently" (50–51). Conversely, at the other end of this system, "the colonial subject will be unable to register the peculiar transformations of First World or metropolitan life which accompany the imperial relationship" (60). While Jameson posits Ireland as the exceptional case distinguished by the existence of the "two incommensurable realities . . . those of the metropolis and of the colony simultaneously" (60), it seems that the colonial city, and especially the highly developed colonial cities of Seoul and Taipei, also share in this exceptional structure of "both-and." We might posit that Jameson's "incommensurate realities" parallel what we have been describing as "discrepant" throughout this chapter. Jameson shows how, at the level of representation, the response of metropolitan literature to its incomplete access to totality is "a new spatial language, therefore— modernist 'style'—now becomes the marker and the substitute . . . of the unrepresentable totality" (58). In other words, the spatiality necessarily repressed from the daily life of the metropole reappears at the level of the text.[21] I argue that the urban colonized, interpellated both as subject of foreign domination and of new consumer-based identities and forms of life, is in a position of unexpected epistemic privilege and actually witnesses both sides of the imperial economic and political system. Yet as Jameson points out—and as *The Wings* demonstrates—these are incommensurable: their effect on the individual psyche is ultimately destructive. What this means for the modernist colonial text is, then, not a new textual spatiality that stands in for the absent world, but a flooding of the text with too much world, precipitating a necessary misreading or closing down of those psychologically untenable spaces. The Manichean, discrepant urban realities of the colonial city shape the hermetic form of the text and the hyperinteriorized modern subject, giving us an alternative genealogy of literary modernism.

(Colonial) Modernism

In both European and Japanese imperialisms, controlling and replacing traditional spatial forms of the native society is not only a primary function of the colonial city, but is also the way the colonial system unfolds, or worlds, itself across time and space. Yet the city itself, being at once object, tool, environment, and experience, is also the perceptual lens through which to comprehend this very process, whether it is through the returning overseas student, the visit to the colonial or metropolitan capital, or the everyday experience of its claustrophobic spaces. In Georg Lukács's theorization, the novel is the art form proper to a society "in which the extensive totality of life is no longer directly given" (*Theory,* 56). In his account, an artfully organized fiction based on an individual's development takes the place of the original unity of being and community in the epic. A key indication of the new nonorganic literature is its "architectural construction" (67), and in Dante—the transitional figure between the pure epic and the novel— "we see the architectural clearly conquering the organic" (68). We could say that in both *Mansejŏn* and *The Orphan of Asia,* that transitional moment when the architectural takes over from the vernacular occurs not only in the organizing logic of literary form, but also at the level of the modern landscape. For Yŏm Sang-sŏp's and Wu Zhuoliu's protagonists, the nature of colonial development is understood and ultimately critiqued by narratively working through and describing contrasting metropolitan and colonial spaces. As we have seen, the global spatial system finds its most (in)coherent expression in the colonial city itself—an urban form that is at once modern and cosmopolitan, indigenous and premodern. As demonstrated by the bitterness of *Mansejŏn*'s In-hwa at the Japanified urban conveniences, the scorn of *Orphan*'s Taiming for his brother's new house, or Yi Sang's protagonist who ends his life among the Japanese commodities, the discordant spatial and material experience of the colonial city is fundamentally alienating and destabilizing. We discover, then, that the spatial organization of colonialism simultaneously produces both realist narratives—Lukács's "architectural" novel replacing unmediated life worlds—and modernist stylistics as compensation for a structurally impossible perspective.

Let us keep in mind that at the level of experience, each separate building or square cannot be consciously registered as an imperial or native space. As has been said of Korean colonial modernity, such encounters "cannot be broken into discrete Japanese, Western or Korean parts" (Shin and Robinson, 12). At the same time, however, such spatial reality does not tend toward a creative modernity of corresponding to a "now" informed by international flows of culture and commodities. Rather, from the colonized's perspective, the colonial city stubbornly foregrounds its own disjunctive and restrictive spatiality. Although this could be termed a kind of "blocked modernism," I prefer to see it as the legitimate counterpart to other, already cataloged, modernisms of Europe and the colonizing world. Berman contends that "modern life has a distinctive and authentic beauty, which, however, is inseparable from its innate misery and anxiety" (141). He fails to note that these two sides to modernity have, to a large extent, been separated—the beauty accumulating in the growing metropolises of imperial nations, and the misery systematically exported to the colonies. The only site, then, of their actual inseparability is the colonial city, the very location from which both are founded. We can thus finally make the claim that all the discrepancies, longings, confusions, and hopes found to circulate through and around the colonial city would actually be the most authentic expression of so-called modern life.

This section of the book has examined global capitalism's territorialization through specific colonial urban forms and their incorporation into literature. In moving to part 2, "Postwar Urbanism," we are faced with new, but related questions: How are such territorializing forces and responses reconfigured after the "liberation" of Taiwan, Korea, and Singapore from their Japanese and British colonizers? Does the attempt to build an independent modernity negate or resolve the spatial contradictions apparent in the colonial period? In the next two chapters, I analyze literary constructions of spaces and subjectivities produced under the new pressures of national industrial transformation, urban renewal, population growth, and renewed patriarchy.

Export Production and the Blank Slate

> After regaining their political independence, the peripheries embarked on industrialization, although on unequal terms, to the point that apparent homogeneity previously induced by a shared lack of industry gave way to increasing differentiation between a semi-industrialized third world and a fourth world that had not begun to industrialize.
>
> —SAMIR AMIN, *Re-Reading the Postwar Period*

Part 1, "Colonial Cities," showed us how colonial urbanism was important both for the production and maintenance of the imperial system and for perceiving and unmasking its contradictions. The remaining two sections of the book deal with the postwar period, especially the mid-1960s to mid-1980s, the period of intense industrialization and urbanization of the Asian Tigers. Unlike many single-country studies of East or Southeast Asia, I do not dwell in detail on the important in-between years from the end of World War II to the beginning of the economic take-off years. Instead, this short interlude will serve as a transition from the colonial era to the later period, as well as introduce the theoretical and thematic foci of part 2, "Postwar Urbanism."

For all three countries, the beginning of the postwar period was marked by liberation from Japanese occupation in 1945 by the Allied Forces. In Taiwan, this was termed *retrocession,* or return to mainland China's Republic of China (ROC) government, led by the Nationalist (Kuomintang) Party's Chiang Kai-shek, and was initially cause for celebration. Under the rule of provincial governor Chen Yi, however, the ROC quickly took control of the power structures and national industries the Japanese had vacated. Tensions erupted in the "2.28" massacre of 1947, in which up to 30,000 Taiwanese were killed after a marketplace scuffle between mainlander officials and a local cigarette seller. In 1949, mainlander domination of the island was consolidated with Chiang Kai-shek and the Kuomintang's retreat to Taiwan after losing the civil war with Mao Zedong's Communist Party. In Korea, 1945 saw both liberation from Japan and the division of the peninsula into two halves, with the Soviet Union in control in the north and the United States in the south. By 1948 each side had proclaimed it was the legitimate Korean state, setting the stage for the northern attempt to reunify the peninsula by invasion in 1950. The war lasted for three years, involved the United States, its allies, and the Chinese, and claimed hundreds of thousands, if not upward of a million, casualties. The end of the Japanese colonial period thus ushered in a tumultuous period for its two main colonies: in Taiwan, retrocession and the Kuomintang's arrival would result in the world's longest period of martial law, while the Korean War would constitute the first "hot war" of the cold war period and result in one of its last front lines.

In contrast to these abrupt endings to the colonial period, for the Straits Settlements, the end of Japanese occupation (1942–45) saw the return of the British and the drawn-out Malayan Emergency (1948–60), a guerrilla war in which the British fought the largely ethnically Chinese, Communist-inspired Malayan National Liberation Army. Partly due to this struggle, and partly as a consequence of the larger wave of decolonization in the 1950s and 1960s, Malaya won its independence in 1957. Singapore, which had been administered as a separate crown colony since 1946, achieved home rule in 1959; the delay was arguably caused by British concern about Chinese communism. Singapore gained full independence from Britain when it joined the Federation of Malaysia in 1963, but it seceded two years later to become the city-state it is today.[1] Although Lee Kuan Yew's left-leaning People's Action Party (PAP) won the first home rule election in 1959 partly on its tough anticolonial stance, it would later become increasingly authoritarian and anticommunist. While each of these national scenes warrants a book-length study in itself—and each will be revisited in more detail in the final three chapters—let us note for now that a major factor of postcoloniality in these locations is the ongoing question of political legitimacy within the context of the cold war.

In terms of the larger political overview of this period, the key features of the decade to 1958, in Samir Amin's summary, were the consolidation of U.S. hegemony, the importance of the Soviet bloc in the east, and the latter's alliance with the third world liberation movements of Asia and Africa. He writes: "For the first time in history the system of sovereign states was extended to the entire globe" (28–29) under three broad political formulations: "Fordism in the Western countries, Sovietism in the East European countries, and developmentalism in the third world" (11). While postcolonial studies has rightly been concerned with the anticolonial liberation movement and the rewriting of cultural politics from indigenous perspectives, it has been less interested in the developmental theory and policy that fundamentally shaped the third world in the years immediately after independence. In my understanding, postcoloniality does not refer exclusively to the cultural legacy of Japanese or British rule, but to the complex effort of postindependent states to transform their political economies under the newly minted banners of nationalism.

Beginning in the late 1960s, Andre Gunder Frank, Samir Amin, and other so-called dependency thinkers importantly theorized the difficulties concerning this effort. They explain how the conditions of third world *under*development (structural and prolonged pauperization) as opposed to simple *un*development (untapped resources) was linked not to their exclusion from the history of capitalist development, but to their very inclusion in it or, in Frank's term, their "satellization." Thus, "When we examine this metropolis-satellite structure, we find that each of the satellites . . . serves as an instrument to suck capital or economic surplus out of its own satellite and to channel part of this surplus to the world metropolis of which all are satellites" ("Development of Underdevelopment," 6).[2] In the economic wisdom of the postwar period, many third world countries were encouraged to industrialize along import substitution lines. They were to slough off their colonial economic character as raw material producers, trading ports, and consumers of imported metropolitan goods—those "instruments to suck capital"—to become autonomous, well-balanced economies, replacing dependence on foreign imports with the buildup of selected manufacturing industries for domestic consumption. Like Fordism in the West, this would require the increased purchasing power of local workers and promote a better-distributed income structure (Frank, *Crisis,* 4). By the mid-1950s, however, the drop in raw materials prices had reduced these countries' foreign exchange rates, while it became clear that small domestic markets would make the West's efficient economies of scale impossible to replicate. After this false start, import substitution was largely discarded as the golden ticket out of third world stagnation (Frank, *Crisis,* 4).

In the logic of modernization theory through which East and Southeast Asian development has primarily been understood, the Asian Tiger nations have been uniquely successful in following Japan's model of export-oriented industrialization and capitalist development.[3] Japan's paradoxical position in the postwar global economic landscape must be duly noted: as former colonial occupier of Korea and Taiwan, it was in turn occupied by the United States. With massive loans from the superpower, it was encouraged to be a regional economic motor and anticommunist stronghold. Despite its fraught relationship with its former colonies and wartime territories— South Korea, for example, did not normalize diplomatic relations until 1965—it nevertheless became a model of development and an indirect investor for several of the region's developing economies. By the 1970s, moreover, Japan's cost of labor and exports had risen, allowing some of its neighboring countries entry into the world market, especially in the production of cheap electronic goods and textiles.

This story, however, is less straightforward than it sounds. Production for export departs from the principles of import substitution in several important ways and constitutes a new model of modernization altogether— one that has become unquestioned for today's developing countries, but whose origins deserve revisiting. Ernst Utrecht notes a major factor for its rise was that the late 1950s and early 1960s saw a "sudden, huge outflow of corporate activities from developed to developing countries" (140). This outflow coincided, of course, with a large number of newly independent postcolonial states, all looking for ways to manage unemployment and social unrest, especially of the communist kind then sweeping the world (141). Beyond the social appeal, "a second aim was to generate through participation in foreign capital operations [their] own domestic capital, which would in the first place strengthen the economic, social and political position of a rising national comprador bourgeoisie" (141). This model of industrialization usually begins with light consumer items such as textiles, shoes, toys, wigs, leather, and electrical goods. Unlike import substitution, it is directed not at internal consumption but at the world market, which effectively means the large first world markets of the United States and Europe, to which typically 75 to 90 percent of goods are destined (Utrecht, 143). More so than import substitution, it is likely to be financed by multinational enterprises looking for cheaper labor, or undertaken in a partnership with the local government. Although many exporting countries had some import-substituting industries, by the early 1970s, it was clear which countries had definitively chosen the export route. By 1972, the leading manufacturing exporters were Hong Kong, Yugoslavia, South Korea, Singapore, India, Brazil, and Mexico (Frank, *Crisis,* 98); indeed, fully 50 percent of Singapore's exports were produced by local labor working for multinationals (99). One is immediately struck by the incongruity of tiny Hong Kong, Singapore, and South Korea on this list, especially given the assumptions in the early 1960s that the main candidates for rising third world modernization were Brazil, Mexico, and the oil-producing Middle East (6)—countries thought to have enough labor, resources, and land to be successful.

One of the ways small states climbed their way onto this list was through the Export Production Zone (EPZ), also known as Free Trade Zone or industrial park, the ultimate expression of export-driven industrialization. First invented in Ireland in 1959 to revive the ailing Shannon Airport district, the first true EPZ was established in Kaohsiung, southern Taiwan, in 1966. It subsequently set the model for Korea's important Masan EPZ (1970) and many other such zones around the world, including Iri in South Korea, Jurong in Singapore, and Nanzih in Taiwan. In 1987, the International Labour Organisation described the novelty of the EPZ in contrast to the colonial character of ports like Singapore and Hong Kong, which "were geared essentially to the storage, trans-shipment and re-export of goods produced elsewhere, and were to be found along existing trade routes. The essence of the EPZ lies in the idea of developing such a zone for manufacturing purposes, and not just for storage or trade" (ILO, 1). The beauty of the EPZ is that it can be located anywhere infrastructure and transport can be laid out, and its success in attracting foreign manufacturing firms has been a worldwide phenomenon. In 1970 there were only ten countries with EPZs, with a total of 20 zones; by 1986, forty-six countries had 175 zones, with many more in the works (ILO, 2). Moreover, there is a very high correlation between the success of third world industrialization and the proportion of manufacturing labor in EPZs: in 1986 the five highest

EPZ-employing countries were Mexico (predominantly due to the maquila-dora industry on the U.S. border); Singapore, the Republic of Korea, Hong Kong, Malaysia, and Taiwan (ILO, 8). Typically, one sees economic growth rates of 7 to 18 percent advertised for countries engaged in intense export-oriented development (Utrecht, 150).

In terms of shaking off their dependent economies, however, the gains of EPZs and export production are not quite so clear. According to Frank, such development skews resource distribution away from internal development toward providing EPZs attractive to foreign transnational companies, and it promotes foreign debt because these countries have to borrow to set up infrastructure (South Korea, for example, had a $7 billion debt in 1976). It also encourages the lowest wages and unskilled labor, especially favoring young female labor—often 70 to 90 percent of labor in EPZs—and inhibits technology transfer because production is "broken down into partially mechanized operations and partially simple, repetitive manual operations" (Frank, *Crisis,* 104). The International Labor Organisation notes that the EPZs may encourage backward technological linkages with the rest of the domestic economy because the indirect employment generated by multinational enterprises is often limited to supply of raw materials, subcomponent parts, and basic services (74). Further, Utrecht argues that the real, integrated economic growth—as distinguished from production for export—should be recalculated at only approximately 1 to 3 percent per year (150), and that this kind of development, at best, concentrates wealth in the hands of a tiny comprador elite (153).

The history of EPZs is especially of interest to us in that, as Zhu Ying has commented, such development is a political as much as an economic process (62). Both Korea and Taiwan, for example, turned to export-led production at moments when the United States was threatening to withdraw aid, and the import-substitution policies they had begun had reached their potential (117–19). Both countries had large, newly urban populations; Korea required massive rebuilding after the devastating civil war. Singapore, in the wake of its separation from Malaysia and the race riots of 1964, needed to reinvent its role from that of a colonial trading port, turning outward as a labor exporter. In short, all three countries, poor in natural resources, needed massive new industries to absorb and stabilize populations. Amin further notes that Korea and Taiwan, along with Israel, "received the bulk of U.S. aid throughout the postwar period" (109). The relative success of export production for the Asian Tigers must therefore be weighed against recognition of their specific internal conditions, colonial legacies, and alliances in the postwar decades.[4] Frank writes:

> The "models" for the development of "export-led growth" were South Korea, Taiwan and the city-states of Hong Kong and Singapore in the 1960s. In each of these cases political support of existing regimes (in the first three instances as bulwarks against socialism) would seem to have played a part in creating a growth model that would be economically "viable" and politically "stable." (*Crisis*, 100)

In other words, what we see expressed in the seemingly purely economic character of this development are the center–periphery relations of the colonial period giving way to a new relationship of unequal exchange that exploits, rather than resists, the neocolonial arrangement of global capitalism. In this manner, to recall the discussion of Mandel in the Introduction, certain postcolonies begin to differentiate themselves from others. Giovanni Arrighi has noted how the cold war project of U.S. military and economic hegemony was "highly successful in launching one of the greatest system-wide expansions in capitalist history" (58). This expansion, however, is a complicated process involving the reorganization and mobilization of labor, cold war politics, and struggles over various visions for the postcolonial nation.

For this study, the most critical aspect of export-led development and the EPZ is the *logic of space* underwriting them. Again, it is useful to distinguish it from the earlier import substitution models:

> To some extent, this manufacturing export is simply the extension of industrial production originally developed for import substitution. Yet more often the promotion of industrial exports starts from what is literally a *tabula rasa*. A flat piece of land is supplied with the necessary infrastructure (factory buildings and productive equipment) and the materials that are to be processed are brought in from afar (often the other side of the globe). The labor to process these materials is supplied from the surrounding rural or urban areas. The archetype of this "new industrial development" is the "free

production" or "export promotion" zone, which specializes in producing textiles and electronics components for export to the "world market." (Frank,
Crisis, 97)

The International Labor Organisation concurs that the appeal of the EPZ
lies in its blank slate character—"the EPZ as a planner's dream"—that
avoids traditional obstacles, local histories, and poorly functioning infrastructure by literally starting from scratch (3). What is important to recognize is how the spatial logic of the blank slate has informed the broader
nature of urban growth and renewal in the New Asian Cities, those very
mechanisms by which "the labor to process these materials is supplied
from the surrounding rural or urban areas." Moreover, as we saw in chapter 1, treatment of these cities as tabula rasa spaces is emphatically not
new: the Japanese already fundamentally reorganized Seoul and Taipei
along Western, rationalist planning principles, while the British effectively
erased any trace of the Malay-inhabited island that preceded Singapore. If
we have noted the way in which export promotion came to be a novel,
defining feature of the immediate postwar decades, we should not be surprised that it was adopted most readily in postcolonies that were already
efficiently reorganized as productive spaces by imperial powers.

   Our focus in the next two chapters is the nature of dwelling in such a
profoundly reshaped urban environment, both directly and indirectly
influenced by the logic of the EPZs, industrial parks, or smaller factory
spaces. As the economists note, export production does not just result in
isolated EPZs, but these zones "must form part of an overall country-wide
export-oriented development strategy" (Zhu, 91). Such reorganization of
energies entails a myriad of social and spatial transformations including
massive country-to-city migration (with the exception of already-urban
Singapore), government urban renewal schemes, the prevalence of factory
labor, the mass mobilization of women into the workforce, as well as the
introduction of high-rise apartment dwelling and new domestic arrangements of space. In other words, if in part 1 we saw the colonial city as the
node that "worlds" global imperialism, in part 2 we are interested in postindependent cities as nodes in a new kind of global system. Again, it is
through literature that we can ask those questions beyond empirical economic analyses: How is the individual reimagined both against and in

terms of the new export-oriented industrializing city? How does this complicate the simple narrative of postcolonial success stories? And how do
certain fictional forms adapt, assimilate, or resolve these problems and
contradictions? More centrally, the next two chapters will return to Lefebvre's question of the role of space in the production and reproduction of
social relationships. Recall that "any space implies, contains and dissimulates social relationships—and this despite the fact that a space is not a
thing but rather a set of relations between things (objects and products)"
(82–83). The problematic of space revolves around its tendency to mask
configurations of power as inert and fixed forms ("representations of
space"), and its potential to disrupt by fluid imaginaries and interpretations ("representational space"). But note that this is not a simple process
of identifying good or bad spatial forms or representations. For Lefebvre,
the idea of a straightforward readability of values in space must be replaced by a more complex understanding of its ideological and material
functioning:

> The impression of intelligibility conceals far more than it reveals. It conceals,
> precisely, what the visible/readable "is," and what traps it holds; [for example]
> it conceals what the vertical "is"—namely, arrogance, the will to power, a dis-
> play of military and police-like machismo, a reference to the phallus and a
> spatial analogue of masculine brutality.... In produced space, acts reproduce
> "meanings" even if no "one" gives an account of them. (144)

The task of the next section is precisely to "[give] an account of" produced
space through the heterogeneous acts, experiences, and perspectives that
constitute it.

The following chapters thus deal with a set of questions and texts that
broadly challenge the monolithic logic of the production-oriented New
Asian City. In chapter 3, I examine the conflation of body and building
in New Asian City stories that deal with the new proletariat inhabiting the
factories, apartment blocks, and construction sites of the city. I analyze
these texts in light of their loose bildungsroman fictional form, the literary
genre that in Western modernity simultaneously problematized youth and
demanded its incorporation into the fixity of the social world. At the same
time, in a sort of bildungsroman of space itself, I am interested in the

historical development of the New Asian City urban aesthetic.[5] In chapter 4, the focus turns inward to the interior, feminized spaces of the New Asian City dwelling spaces and examines contradictions surrounding domesticity, changing gender roles, and female labor. At the very moment when working-class women played a crucial role in providing cheap labor for the growth of Asian Tiger economies, new forms of dwelling were making different demands on them. The texts I look at resolve this dilemma by figuring the woman as absent and the city spaces as the mise-en-scène that both can and cannot accommodate her.

PART II

POSTWAR URBANISM

3

Narratives of Human Growth versus Urban Renewal

It is exactly this "new" density—the high-rise explosion of which the HDB housing blocks were only the beginning—that will be the sign of the Asian.

—REM KOOLHAAS, "Singapore Songlines"

GROWTH AND SEPARATION:
THE DIMENSIONALITY OF THE NEW ASIAN CITY

In related but distinct ways, expanding Seoul, Singapore, and Taiwan of the 1960s and 1970s share an urban aesthetic that owes much to the logic of the export-oriented production that fueled their economies. To examine this aesthetic, I use two conceptual frames that deal with urban and literary transformation, respectively. First, I address the question of dimensionality of the postcolonial New Asian City: in contrast to the metropolitan experience of horizontally expanding industrial cities, growth in the geographically and resource-limited New Asian City is typified by height, density, and constant reconstruction. Where European metropolitan residents might have been overwhelmed by the city's endless extension, subjects of the New Asian City are alienated by its decisive qualities of newness, repetition, and ominous compression. Second, in terms of the literary reworking of such spatial realities, I use the model of the European bildungsroman as discussed by Franco Moretti to consider Korean, Singaporean, and Taiwanese short fictions that present youth as a distinctive problem against the new and shifting postcolonial cityscape. Again, we must make the assertion that not only have such cities been a fundamental component of global modernity, but that this modernity looks somewhat different from their Western counterparts. Just as we saw with colonial cities and

99

their discrepant spaces, postcolonial cities will manifest an aesthetic and dimensionality of development corresponding neither to the prewar modernisms of Europe (of which they would be belated versions) nor to the postwar Fordist, consumerist societies (or postmodernism in the West).[1] This chapter is thus framed as an interrogation of the interlinked concept of *growth* across human, urban, and economic terms.

A paradox that immediately demands our attention is that while growth—of GNP, labor power, agricultural productivity, exports, and urbanization—unarguably remains central to discourses of third world development, the most astounding growth has occurred in the geographically smallest and most resource-poor territories of Asia, earning for these nations the epithets "economic wonders" or "man-made miracles."[2] Indeed, we can think of the question of postcolonial development in these cities in terms of how human growth is controlled, ordered, and transformed into growth of production.[3] In contrast, Moretti's well-known account of bildungsroman literature deals with growth in terms of the relationship between individual and society. The "novel of formation" appears in the West with the shift away from traditional apprenticeship models of learning, corresponding to a new mobility that is characteristic of modernity. In the classic bildungsroman, the education, moral growth, or development of the young individual is problematized but must eventually coincide with and internalize the larger imperatives of the social world. Moretti describes how the novel stages the conflict between individual and social desires, to arrive at the paradoxical formulation: "I *desire* to do what I in any case *should* have done" (*Way of the World,* 21). If, as Moretti suggests, "the structure of the bildungsroman will of necessity be *intrinsically contradictory*" (6), how might we read New Asian City fictions as working through a homologous set of tensions between youth and stability, individual and world, but set against a wholly different notion of growth? In other words, what can we make of both modern urban and literary forms in which urban growth, the separation from traditional communities, and individual formation mean vastly different things than they did for the development of the imperial powers? I suggest that the postwar international division of labor described in the first Transition, in which peripheries embarked on industrialization under unequal terms, requires a reappraisal of the assumed symbolic dimensions of both youth and urban modernity.

Building on the comparative historical accounts of chapter 1, we must recount the broad changes to the urban environment that occurred in the three sites, and how they relate to the fictional texts I examine. Consider post-1945 Seoul, which saw the massive repatriation of Koreans who had been living in colonial Manchuria and Japan, followed at the end of the Korean War by the influx of displaced rural dwellers and refugees from the north. The 1960s and 1970s industrial push initiated yet another surge in rural to urban migration. At each of these stages, lack of affordable housing resulted in the construction of squatter housing, which by the 1960s was a dominant physical feature of Seoul, accounting for some 30 percent of its buildings (Li, 43). By the late 1960s, the government had responded to the crisis by sponsoring slum clearance projects and high-rise public housing, often using for-profit private construction contracts rather than public funds. Kim and Choe report that one of the earliest high-rise public apartment buildings collapsed in 1970, killing thirty-two people—a traumatic introduction to this new architecture (113). The resulting large-scale urban redevelopment of squatter settlements can be considered a defining, if painful, aspect of Seoul's industrial modernity. It may be for this reason alone that Cho Se-hŭi's "A Little Ball Launched by a Dwarf" ("Nanjangi ka ssoaollin chagŭn kong"), the title story of a 1978 collection that deals with urban redevelopment, made such an impression and became unofficial required reading for the following generation of college students and labor activists. Kim Yoon-shik writes that, at a time when little dissent about the nation's prospects was tolerated, it was Cho Se-hŭi who bravely posed the question of "what there would be at the other side of the seemingly bright future promised by industrialization" (98).

The case of Singapore's dramatic transformation—from an overcongested, poor, and unstable commercial city of Britain at midcentury to a sophisticated, wealthy, and efficient independent city-state—has attracted many outside cultural commentators, perhaps the best known being architect Rem Koolhaas. He notes that there is something uncanny, and perhaps illegitimate, about the way the discredited "prewar urbanism of the modernist heroes" (1034) finds its unlikely home in the postcolonial Asian city.[4] For Koolhaas, "the mystery" of Singapore's success is left unsatisfactorily "suspended between the assumption of greater authoritarianism and the inscrutable nature of the Asian mentality" (1037). From the perspective of

1950s Singapore, however, there is little mysterious about the adaptation of an urban planning scheme that most resembles Le Corbusier's infamous plan for a "City of Three Million" of 1922. William Lim reminds us of the squalid conditions of a city recently reclaimed from the Japanese by the British: "the poor were packed into cubicles in dilapidated shophouses in which living conditions were very close to being intolerable," and "squatter settlements constructed out of wood and attap were multiplying all over the island" (168). In 1961, the independent Singapore parliament received the help of the U.N. Technical Assistance Administration, which advocated "a ring of high-density public housing residential areas around the central water catchment area" that would fill in most of the island (Chua, *Political Legitimacy*, 36). Established just before this in 1960, the Housing and Development Board (HDB) would build over 600,000 public housing dwelling units in the next three decades to eventually house around 90 percent of the population (Chua, *Political Legitimacy*, 139). Although implemented with less social conflict produced in cases of mass migration like Korea's, urban renewal in Singapore must also be understood as a central feature of the country's modernity. At the time of Goh Poh Seng's 1972 *If We Dream Too Long*, usually considered the first Singaporean novel to be written in English,[5] the remarkably durable People's Action Party (PAP) was implementing its second five-year plan and in the process of relocating a large proportion of Singapore's population into HDB flats. After the traumas of the 1964 race riots and the 1965 separation from Malaysia, the novel is set during the consolidating years of PAP-directed modernity. If "A Little Ball" is notable for its representation of the bureaucratic and political violence wrought by urbanization, *If We Dream* focuses on the psychological complexity involved in such modernization processes. Goh's novel won the National Book Development Council of Singapore award in 1976 and has since been widely translated and taught as a staple of Anglophone postcolonial literature.

Turning to Taiwan, with the communist takeover on mainland China, it is estimated that "over 1.5 million Kuomintang soldiers and refugees flooded into Taiwan increasing the total population from 5 million to over 6.5 million" (Li, 33). As in Korea, this postwar migration was exacerbated by substantial rural to urban migration in the industrializing 1960s, a decade in which Taipei's population, a mere 270,000 in 1946, surged to over two million (Li, 35). Despite squatter settlement rates of 25 percent in 1960 for the urban population, the KMT government—who well into the decade was devoting as much as 75 percent of expenditures on military defense (Li, 34)—did not adopt public housing as a major policy until the 1980s. Although similar to South Korea and Singapore in its dependence on export manufacturing, public housing here did not become another profit-making industry for large conglomerates; nor was it was part of a "national building plan as a production related development" (Li, 55), as in Singapore. In another paradox of New Asian City growth, we see that while on one level, Taiwan's cities were the motor behind manufacturing-led national growth; on another, they remained profoundly at odds with the organizing logic of capital. In any survey of Taiwanese literature from this period, the category of *hsiang-t'u wen-hsueh*⁶ (nativist; literally, "homeland soil literature") is soon mentioned. Partially a reaction against the Western-inspired, hermetic, modernist literature favored by the urban-educated postwar writers, the *hsiang-t'u* movement is usually claimed as a regional, or nationalistic, literature written about the "ordinary people of the local region" (Faurot, 3) and "depict[ing] rural life with unaffected realism" (Chang, "Modernism," 151). Huang Chunming's late 1960s and early 1970s short works were foundational of the *hsiang-t'u* literary movement and grapple with precisely the growing contradictions between urban and rural lifeways.

Before moving on to the individual texts in more detail, we must also briefly review the discourses around emerging Western industrial cities to help frame the comparative analysis of modern urbanism. In Max Weber's influential understanding of the emergence of the modern city, traditional concepts of space and dwelling no longer obtain; "dwelling" and the city are simply incompatible. As Dal Co explains, "For Weber, the city, ever since its initial emergence, represents a severance of man's organic, telluric bond with nature and the environment, since it arises as a collective settlement of *people previously foreign to the place*" (34, emphasis in original), such that the city is, by definition, a city of foreigners. The consequences of the severed, migratory character of modern dwelling are most fearfully explored by Oswald Spengler in his essay "The Soul of the City" from *The Decline of the West (Der Untergang des Abendlandes)* of 1922. For this early urban theorist, separation from the land is not only the moment when the countryside is henceforth subordinated to the city—"all great Cultures are town-Cultures" (65)—but also the point at which the civilization begins its decline. For Spengler, the replacement of traditional land-bound interactions by money as "the pure form of economic intercourse . . . not more limited in potential scope by actuality than are the quantities of the mathematical and logical world" (74), marks a fundamental shift in the dimensionality of the modern world, most discernable in the built environment. With horror, Spengler imagines the view of an old city undergoing this modernization of space:

> Now the old mature cities . . . begin to overflow in all directions in formless masses, to eat into the decaying countryside with their multiplied barrack-tenements and utility buildings, and to destroy the noble aspect of the old time by clearances and rebuildings. Looking down from one of the old towers upon the sea of houses, we perceive in this petrification of a historic being the exact epoch that marks the end of organic growth and the beginning of an inorganic and therefore *unrestrained process of massing without limit.* (76–77, emphasis added)

The directionality of the endless massing is decidedly horizontal—"our suburbs and garden cities, invading the wide countryside" (78). In short, "Not now Destiny, but Causality, not now living Direction, but Extension, rules" (85). Modern dwelling, if it can still be called that, becomes subordinated to abstract rationality and "the dimensions of extension and quantity" (Dal Co, 27).[7] Yet not only does the process of modernity result in a metropolitan "aesthetics of purely *horizontal* space" (Rosario Assunto qtd. in Dal Co, 27); it also assumes a commensurate, empty space across the rest of the country and indeed the world—"the provinces" for Spengler—which corresponds neatly to Lefebvre's concept of abstract "global space." According to Lefebvre, by around 1920 "space opened up to perception" (125), resulting in three things: a new spatial consciousness involving the breakup and rotation of planes in art, the disappearance of the facade as privileged aspect in architecture, and the discovery of "global space," which "established itself in the abstract as a void waiting to be filled, as a medium waiting to be colonized" (125). While both Spengler's and Lefebvre's periodization comes several decades after the usual recognition of global colonial space—the 1884 Berlin Conference and the "scramble for Africa"—

Spengler's "unlimited extension" nevertheless describes this aesthetic and social fact: the possibility of endless extension into global space coincides with the rise of mass production, urbanization, and industrialization.[8]

For Weber, the ascendancy of the modern market economy further results in a split between production and consumption, where the dominance of either activity results in a specific typology of city. The "consumer city" is characterized by "large consumers of special economic character" (27) who support the activities of tradesmen and merchants. In contrast, the "producer city" may be home to "factories, manufactures, or homework industries supplying outside territories—thus representing the modern type" (27). A third category is the "commercial city," which supports international banking, trade, and shipping (28). Weber's observation of a new kind of city appropriate to the modern period—the producer city—underlines the imbrications between industrialization, imperial divisions of space, and city form. Yet where Weber's characterization of the producer city was, we assume, modeled on the European manufacturing metropolises that provided commodities to both domestic and colonial markets, the export-oriented postwar New Asian City raises the producer city to a whole new level, one in which the split between production and consumption falls along national lines and reinforces the division of the colonial period in a new way.[9] This brings us to the following questions: How do the specific developmental patterns of postwar Seoul, Singapore, and Taipei constitute their *own* typology, and how does the analytic of postcoloniality qualify previous accounts of industrial cities beyond the "city of foreigners" or its newly massified aesthetics? And, not least, what new strategies arise for bringing such complex urban, state, and global forces into representation? In what follows, I show how such literary strategies rely especially on architectural figuration. Following Raymond Williams, I understand the personified representations of physical forms as working to bring into perception "those social institutions and consequences which are not accessible to ordinary physical observation" (*Country,* 156). Such strategies in coming-of-age stories connect the embodied subjectivities to both the structures in which they dwell as well as to the logic behind their construction. The literary confusion between the human and the architectural presents us with a new figuring of individual and world peculiar to the New Asian City.

COMPRESSION, GROWTH, AND THE APARTMENT BLOCK:
CHO SE-HŬI'S "A LITTLE BALL LAUNCHED BY A DWARF"

It is important to understand Korean literature of the 1970s—the very early days of South Korea's spectacular economic rise—within the specific context of military dictator Park Chung Hee's 1972 *Yusin* ("revitalizing") reforms. As Cho Nam-hyun writes, "political regression and giddy economic growth were the twin realities Koreans had to cope with in the 70s" (45). During the years of martial law and "relentless [government] pressure to attain production or export targets" (Woronoff, 100), it is no wonder that Cho Se-hŭi's dwarf became the archetypal "small man" figure, alienated by the forced progress of his country. Cho's stories were originally published in serial form in several different magazines: "Knifeblade" ("K'allal") appeared in *Literature and Thought (Munhak sasang)* in 1975 and "A Little Ball" in *Literature and Intellect (Munhak kwa chisŏng)* in 1976. The 1978 published collection is an interlinked series of stories with many of the same plots told from different characters' perspectives and in varying narrative styles. It was immediately met with both popular and critical acclaim, receiving the Dongin Literary Award in 1979.

Born in 1942, Cho was one of the so-called Hangŭl Generation—the first generation of Korean writers to be educated in Korean rather than in colonial Japanese or classical Chinese. Differing from other social realist works of the period (such as the workers' literature of Hwang Sŏk-yŏng, to be discussed in chapter 7), Cho's stories are characterized formally by their disjointed perspectives and frequent shifts in tone and voice. The plot is not the sole focus; rather, events are diffused and accumulate into a larger narrative picture only in the connections between the stories. For example, we only know of the brothers' violence that ensues after the end of the "A Little Ball" from events in other stories. In theme, however, they deal with the most pressing social changes and conflicts of the 1970s, including class struggle and housing disputes ("A Little Ball"), environmental pollution ("City of Machines"), and the militarization of society ("Moebius Strip"). Taken as a whole, the collection is among the foremost of postwar Korean works in the larger tradition of proletarian literature *(nodong munhak)*. Cho's title story deals firmly with the new postcolonial realities yet includes dreamlike sequences and is composed of a three-way narrative voice, with each chapter told from the perspective of a different child from the same family. Structuring the story is a finely rendered "oppositional worldview and aesthetics" ("daeryŏpjŏk segyegwan kwa mihak"; Kim Byŏng-ik, 277) that is predicated not only on the growing intellectual awareness of class differences, but on a more visceral understanding of growth and shrinkage. In this story, Cho presents the conflicting forces of modernization through a dialectic of the small and the large, the human and the architectural.

"A Little Ball" revolves around the family of dwarf protagonist Kim Pul-i as the marginalized human remainder left over from the nation's rush to modernize. At the most obvious level, this is the story of the literal compression of a certain section of society, the urban poor, who—like much of Seoul's population at the time—exist day to day on factory work and odd jobs, and occupy an unregistered *(muhŏga)* shack in a squatter settlement. Presumably located on the outskirts of Seoul, "Felicity Precinct, Eden District" lies in the shadow of a brick factory and is anything but heavenly. With the help of interspersed flashbacks, we are told the story of the imminent demolition of the family's home by the city government for the construction of new high-rise apartment complexes. Urban historians Kim and Choe have described how, in the procedure of urban renewal, displaced squatter families were issued with occupancy rights *(ipjugwŏn)* to the new apartments. However, because rental and moving-in costs were prohibitively high for most squatters, their only option was to sell their housing rights (sometimes illegally) to middle-class purchasers or brokers and relocate even further from the city center (Kim and Choe, 140–45). Aside from narrating the blatant injustice of this process, "A Little Ball" can be read as an attempt to render these new spaces and structures legible in terms of larger economic and social transformations. At the same time, we recognize the familiar bildungsroman problems of youth, development, and mobility such that the interior, psychological conflicts of the three children are crucial narrative features. Unlike the bourgeois Western novel of formation, however, Cho's narrative of growth has a decidedly more literal aspect.

A flashback in the first chapter marks the event of the family constructing their shanty house with intense nostalgia: "That was the happiest time for us" and "Every day was fun" (Cho Se-hŭi, 133). [10] The remainder of the novella is preoccupied, however, with structures that limit and negate life. In contrast to the "fun" work of building their house, the factory work into

New public housing apartments in Geumhwa District, Seoul, 1969. Courtesy of Chosun Ilbo.

which brothers Yŏng-su and Yŏng-ho are forced after quitting school is nothing but a zero-sum game between the growth of the company and that of the individual. Written in a deceptively simple, rhythmic Korean, the language itself seems stunted or incomplete, echoing the diminished status of the slum dwellers' lives:

> We were limited to thirty minutes for lunch. We worked in the same factory but led an isolated existence there. Everyone in the factory worked in isolation. . . . They kept us at a distance from each other—no socializing—and all we did was drip with sweat. . . . We worked into the middle of the night in a stuffy, noisy environment. . . . And so although we were still growing, we exhibited growth deficiencies. (143–44)

Quite literally, the energy that is needed for the workers' own growth is siphoned off into economic growth for the company and the larger imperatives of the national economy. They are physically "reduced" by the continued "increases" in work hours, their growth stunted for the maximization of productivity. The word used by the company president to instill fear and discipline in the workers is "recession" *(pulhwang),* highlighting the opposing criteria for human and economic growth. Despite the shared situation of the employees ("we," "us"), the work spaces keep them working "in isolation"; the factory's growth, while essential for the nation's development, is thus antithetical to that of the workers. When the two boys manage to form a labor union and organize a strike, they are betrayed by the other workers and fired (150).

Daughter Yŏng-hŭi is the character who most directly confronts the contradictions of the growing economy, largely driven by big state-backed conglomerates or *chaebols*.[11] As the family nervously monitors the illegal market for the best time to sell their housing rights, a man in a sedan appears at the squatter settlement's district office and buys up all the remaining titles. Though never named, he is evidently the son of a wealthy family who runs a real estate and construction company, most likely a *chaebol* conglomerate. While his main business is selling apartments on the affluent south side of the Han River, he picks up extra profits by illegally brokering urban renewal occupancy rights. Noticing his interest in her, Yŏng-hŭi agrees to prostitute herself to him in order to steal back the family's housing rights. Living with him for several days as his sexual servant, she comes to understand the social system that has determined her life: her weakness is in direct proportion to his strength, such that even the sexual encounter with him is motivated by this binary:

> He and I were different from the day we were born. Mother said that my first cry was a scream. Perhaps my first breath was hot as hellfire. I had insufficient nourishment in my mother's womb. His birth was a thing of warmth. My first breath was the pain of acid flowing over a wound; his was comfortable and sweet. The foundation of our growth *[sŏngjang kiban]* was different as well. Many choices were available to him. I remember nothing but what was given to my two brothers and me. Mother had dressed us in clothes without pockets. He had become stronger as he grew, but we were the opposite—we weakened. He wanted me. Wanted me, then wanted me again. (160)

Like the logic of the factory, the *chaebol* son's healthy growth is a direct, even causal, corollary to Yŏng-hŭi's weakness: "He became stronger . . . we weakened," even more clearly rendered in Korean with the linguistic equivalence of the two parts of the sentence, *"kŭnŭn . . . dŏ'uk kanghaejyŏssŏyo"* and *"urinŭn . . . pandaero yakhaejyŏssŏyo"* (*Nanjangi*, 113). From their very first spatial residence in the womb,[12] their two lives are presented as gendered inversions: one of masculinity, happiness, strength, and growth, and the other of femininity, pain, and lack of nourishment. The differences in their lives are most directly signified through the biological and material reproduction of social classes in terms of dwelling: their contrasting prenatal homes predict and determine the later forms of high-rise apartment and squatter shack. The function of contrasting urban forms for Cho's novella is thus twofold. It is both the etiology of current class inequalities—the dispossession of the dwarf's shack being the primary event of class violence in the story—and the novella's chief hermeneutical device: architectural forms give representation to otherwise unperceivable social structures.

After secretly securing the housing right documents along with cash and a knife, Yŏng-hŭi must register her family's occupancy at the site office of the *chaebol* company's apartment buildings on the newly developing south side of the Han River. Cho's breathless and disjunctive narrative is again pared down to the bare minimum of syntax and vocabulary:

> After emerging from the Namsan Tunnel I crossed the Third Han River bridge. His apartment building, standing in an open field, came into sight. I opened my handbag and felt his knife inside. At the top of the ivory handle was a small metal attachment the size of a bead. Press it and the blade shot out. I had the taxi stop in front of the Housing Affairs office. Numerous people were walking toward the entrance. I hurriedly worked my way among them. And then I was carried forward. Carried by the people to the plaza in front of the building. The white building reflected the sunlight, dazzling my eyes. (166)

At the scene of Yŏng-hŭi's final heroic action, "his apartment building" stands in for the *chaebol* son himself. Its phallic posture is enough to cause Yŏng-hŭi to finger the knife in a potentially castrating gesture, while it threateningly "stand[s] in an open field." In stark contrast to the shadowy squatter village, the building throws out a blinding glare to all who approach. Yŏng-hŭi's relationship with the *chaebol* son is thus repeated metonymically through the apprehension of the apartment building itself as the most tangible physical expression of state and *chaebol*-led development. In the schema of "A Little Ball," the two classes of people exhibit a metonymic relationship to two kinds of dwellings and to two architectural aesthetics: the gleaming, modern apartment building dominates an open field like the *chaebols* dominate the national economy, while the shabby, hand-constructed house is, like the squatter community, finally reduced to dust. The connection between inhabitant's body and house is confirmed when Yŏng-hŭi returns to Eden District to find both the family house demolished and her father dead. Having fallen (or jumped) while climbing the brick factory smokestacks, he is found by the demolition workers, his broken body literally merging with the rubble of his own house.

The social conditions behind such a narrative are readily determined. We have seen how the burden of a developing postcolonial society such as South Korea is precisely the forced pursuit of economic independence and growth through a reliance on its subaltern position within the conditions of late capitalism. Imperial cities and nations experienced growth partly on the basis of the productive power of the invisible colonies, resulting in a perceived aesthetic of expansion and horizontality. In contrast, in Cho Se-hŭi's novella, the absorption of this entire political and productive apparatus to the interior of the nation space effects a concentricity of power expressed through the geometries of height and compression. The extraordinary discrepancy between national and individual growth in this period is resolved at the narrative level by the figure of the looming high-rise apartment building: it is the massive architectural body that both destroys the dwarf's home and adds wealth to the *chaebol* economy. Considering the bildungsroman dilemma of individual will versus social formation, the question left unanswered in "A Little Ball" is to what extent the smallest people of the nation can expect things to change for the better, or whether the nation's continual growth will simply mean their continued shrinkage.

At various moments in the text, for example, the irrevocable shrinkage of the subject into oblivion is imagined simply as death. For Yŏng-hŭi, the image of death as a gray horizon necessarily leads to a meditation on the scale of her family:

> Our life is grayness. Not until I left our house could I observe it from the outside. Our gray-coated house and our gray-coated family were revealed to me in miniature. The people in our family ate with their foreheads touching,

talked with their foreheads touching. They spoke softly and I couldn't understand them. Mother, reduced to a size even smaller than Father's, stopped on her way into the kitchen and looked up at the sky. (157)

Not only do the family members shrink to less than the size of the dwarf father, but the house too is "revealed . . . in miniature." Similarly, for Yŏng-ho, "to imagine the day I would close my eyes for the last time" would imply that "my body had become smaller than Father's" (149). In other words, Cho Se-hŭi's oppositional aesthetic between the strong and the weak, the tall and the dwarfed, is more than a dramatic rendering with which to extract readerly compassion or to ask what is waiting at the other side of industrialization for the young workers. It is also a more literal—or tragic—reworking of the bildungsroman's concern for individual growth and reconciliation with the social world; here, the impossibility of reconciling individual and society is given solution through the blurring of body and architecture. That is, the question of individual versus state/*chaebol* growth is raised most evocatively through the image of the multiplying high-rise apartments that, through a nationalized and masculinist mode of reproduction, literally replaces the dwarf's family and community. The characters—and readers—arrive at the understanding that the concentric structure of nationalized exploitation means that the growth of one section of society is predicated on the shrinkage of another; there is no typical bildungsroman reconciliation of the individual with his or her environment. For those whose labor the nation is built on, youth merges into dwarfhood, which is not a biological aberration or chronological stage but the structuring dimension of life.

Standardization, Seriality, and the HDB Flat: Goh Poh Seng's *If We Dream Too Long*

Before considering Goh Poh Seng's *If We Dream Too Long,* we similarly need to recall the political and social situation of early postcolonial Singapore. Chua explains how the left-leaning PAP was first elected in 1959 by "a society craving for a new future" and a population that "strongly support[ed] a development-oriented government" (*Political Legitimacy,* 160). The almost total rationalization of Singapore's urban space necessitated strong government leadership and the authority to expropriate private land when needed, a power realized through the remarkable Housing and Development Board. While the British had equipped Singapore with an excellent "entrepôt infrastructure," including world-class ports and financial, trade, and communications facilities, they had typically ignored basic social needs like health, education, and housing (Ho, 216). Beginning in the early 1960s, the central ideological concern of Lee Kuan Yew's PAP was material development and "the survival of an independent island nation" (Chua, *Political Legitimacy,* 130). As in South Korea, this survival rhetoric armed the government with a philosophy of pragmatism, which translated into the aggressive development of export-oriented industries and services. If Cho Se-hŭi was the first to give literary representation to the new section of society being steamrolled by South Korea's rapid industrial development, Goh Poh Seng delivers a more familiar postcolonial sensibility with his melancholic protagonist Kwang Meng, a figure who "drifts through both the Singapore of the colonial past and the postcolonial present without being able to relate his own condition imaginatively to either" (Koh Tai Ann, "Intertextual Selves," 178). In part, these differences speak to the discrepancies between the two authors regarding both their literary and political environments. Cho is one of the new generation of postwar Korean writers, and his work reflects a coming to terms not only with a lack of literary tradition in the Korean vernacular, but also with the country's brutal domestic dictatorship that followed the devastation of both the Korean War and Japanese occupation; it is therefore more overtly concerned with domestic struggles over labor and political culture. Goh Poh Seng, on the other hand, born slightly earlier in 1936, was a British colonial subject of Chinese descent and educated in Kuala Lumpur before receiving his medical degree from University College, Dublin. His novel is consequently more focused on a different set of contradictions: how to write a Chinese Singaporean novel in English that reflects the more cosmopolitan history of the port city and its transformation under the authoritarian, but not dictatorial, PAP. While tracing common literary strategies and figures, we must also keep in mind the different meanings of *postcolonial* in these two contexts, which will differ again in the case of Taiwan.

Regarded as "the first serious attempt to represent critically contemporary Singaporean experience," as well as to create a "national cultural identity, ... an indigenous linguistic idiom and expressions of a local sensibility"

(Koh, "Telling Stories," 131, 137), Goh's novel is a window onto the smooth-running early years of the PAP's ascendancy, where the average citizen has little to do but observe the nation's rapid progress. Indeed, Goh's work is perhaps best understood as the portrayal of an average citizen's forced passivity in the face of remarkable state activity. As in the classic bildungs-roman, in which mobility and interiority define the subject of capitalist modernity, Kwang Meng is a youth yearning for freedom from the social structure he is placed in, a yearning expressed through his individual personality. The novel thus follows the "conflict between the ideal of *self-determination* and the equally imperious demands of *socialization*" (Moretti, *Way of the World,* 15). The typical resolution of the bildungsroman novel—epitomized, for example, in the Bennet–Darcy marriage of Jane Austen's *Pride and Prejudice*—comes when the individual's desires coincide with the larger rationality of the social world; that is, "when the logic of social integration has been interiorized, turning into a desire that the individual perceives as his 'own'" (*Way of the World,* 67). Again, we will see such a reconciliation takes different form for the New Asian City subject.

Described by Koh Tai Ann as an "internal exile," Goh's Kwang Meng is a lowly clerk in a shipping company, not bright or rich enough for university, and trained only for the dwindling number of white-collar jobs associated with the former colonial economy. His existence consists of the drudgery of office work, family life in a small HDB flat, and a listless affair with a bar-girl. The narrative takes place in what Moretti would identify as the novel's proper location: "'in the middle,' where it discovers, or perhaps creates, the typically modern feeling and enjoyment of 'everyday life' and 'ordinary administration'" (Moretti, *Way of the World,* 12). In other words, Kwang Meng is an appropriately unremarkable protagonist whose personal desires are nevertheless at odds with social reality. His life is given spatial expression through the dull physical surroundings of "mundane modern Singapore" (Goh, 75) where nothing seems uniquely his own: his daily routine is dominated by long queues for the bus, his seventh-floor flat is indistinguishable from countless others, and his thoughts are frequently infiltrated by the generic language of advertising slogans—"So they slaked with Tiger beer. Be a Tiger man" (64). And yet, as in every novel, there is something singular about this ordinariness. While Kwang Meng complains that "his days have no spaciousness" (24), the novel's accounts of the city inform us that it is the overwhelming standardization of the abstract, functional space that produces Kwang Meng's unique feelings of claustrophobia; the density of the city was actually much reduced through urban renewal. The rationalization of space is less a signifier of violent urban renewal than it is an indication of the way the new nation-state's orientation toward productivity permeates all aspects of life. Here, a slightly different version of the concentricity of power—where production is directed toward the international market in the name of national survival—results in claustrophobia at the psychospatial level.

In addition to spatial alienation, the acute temporal dissonance produced by the rapid urban transformation troubles Kwang Meng's most personal perceptions. Performing the daily task of taking the bus to work with his father, Kwang Meng prefers to remember the father of his colonial childhood more than to see the one in his immediate present. "He sat next to his father, not looking at him" (Goh, 29), while fondly recalling the Chinatown shophouse in which they used to live and their evening bicycle rides together. "Now," he notices, "there were hardly any cyclists on the roads, the roads long abandoned to the ever-increasing motor-cars. Singapore, a city without bicycles" (29). The mental return to Chinatown is also a return to the British colonial urban system of ethnic enclaves where Malays, Indians, and Chinese were concentrated in cramped districts away from the spacious British residential section.[13] Yet even as the PAP's urban renewal program eases congestion and removes segregation, it is not perceived as a move toward more physical or psychological freedom. In contrast to the metropolitan sense of an opening up of the world brought by industrialization, postcolonial Singapore—despite the fact that it utilizes the very same urban forms—is characterized by a peculiar aesthetic of displacement: the increasing presence of mass-produced buildings and commodities indicates rather the total erasure of a previous urban system by another. William Lim writes, "Within the span of the working life of one single generation the physical environment has developed, altering almost beyond visual recognition," adding that such rapid change is potentially "psychologically disturbing to those who live within the country" (169). Thus, the rapid modernization of one's immediate surroundings produces a strong sense of the negative spatiality of the city. It is a city replacing the Chinatown way of life by wiping out Chinatown itself: "Singapore, a city

without bicycles." The dissonance between interior and exterior development we see in the bildungsroman must here reckon with a different
degree of spatial and temporal dislocation.

Kwang Meng's anomie may further be understood in terms of the seriality symptomatic of industrialized society. In Fredric Jameson's discussion of this Sartrean concept, seriality is the condition in which "my basic
relationship to other people is something that might be described as sta-
tistical anonymity." In other words, "when performing most of the acts
characteristic of industrial civilization—waiting for a bus, reading a newspaper, pausing at a traffic light—I seem alone, but am in reality simply
doing exactly what everyone else does in the same situation; and this is
not an external, but an internal identity" (*Marxism and Form,* 248). A precondition to seriality is a certain relationship to objects that stand in for
the very institutions of the modern metropolis. Termed objects of the
"practico-inert" by Sartre, they include such things as "subway, policeman's
uniform, checkbook, sidewalk, calendar . . . [an object] which functions
like an institution, which replaces direct human relationships with something more ordered and more indirect" (245). For Singaporeans of the late
1960s, the HDB flat is precisely such an object of the practico-inert, an
institution of the state that actively replaces old community forms, values,
and relationships with housing estates and industrial "new towns."[14] Struggling to summon his pre-HDB life from "the dreamy murkiness of memory," Kwang Meng recalls the saturated sights, smells, and sounds of the
provisions store above which he once lived:

> Dried salted fish, strings of reddish-brown Chinese sausages hanging from
> wire hooks, sacks of rice, tins of coconut oil, dishes of bean curd, bottles of
> black soya sauce, boxes of salted ducks' eggs preserved in black ash, candles
> of a vermilion red, joss-sticks, dried oiled ducks . . .; all those smells mingling
> with the smells of the often rubbish-choked monsoon gutters. (Goh, 40)

This pungent cornucopia is remembered in precisely that most serial of
spaces, the elevator, where Kwang Meng can only do "what everyone else
does in the same situation." Thus, lurking beneath the monotonous surface
of his life is a vague yearning for differentiation tied to his nostalgia for
an intensely colorful and scented Singapore. Escaping from work to go

swimming, Kwang Meng feels both an alienation from, and a tedious familiarity with, the city:

> Suddenly, everything had become strange, almost weird. The busy people on the street, involved with something he could not now comprehend; the traffic; the lamp posts; the traffic lights blinking, changing; the sound of his own footsteps: all remote to him. He was like a somnambulator in a daylight world. He felt a compulsion to get away from the town, from the noise and the crowds. Oh for the rivers of blue and green water, oh for the really foreign cities. How inaccessible! (80)

Singapore, in the midst of its striking urban transformation, embodies all the awkwardness of postcolonial modernity. To all appearances, it now *is* a foreign city boasting the accoutrements of any industrialized society—"the traffic; the lampposts; the traffic lights blinking." And yet it refuses to satisfy: "oh for the really foreign cities." Neither does the unease over Singapore's growth follow the logic of Weber's "city of foreigners" where urban centers are made foreign by the influx of rural migrants. Rather, Goh describes the abrupt appearance of a foreign city from the perspective of a stationary subject. The affective result of this predicament is the claustrophobic, uncanny feeling of being in, and yet still desiring, a foreign city.

From the government's point of view, the repackaging of the colonial entrepôt into an "export platform for manufacturing by multinational operations" (Ho, 219) simply necessitated the massive reorganization of the built environment. Furthermore, the housing of the population in standardized "high-rise containers" was not just a response to the immediate crowding problem but can be seen as a way of training people to become an efficient and attractive workforce by tying residents to regular rental payments and encouraging them to enter the formal economy (Chua, *Political Legitimacy,* 135). Thus, what may seem for Koolhaas evidence of an incongruent tropical modernity is a far more complicated process involving the demands of the global market and the various forms of domestic modernization these precipitate. As with Cho's "Little Ball," we remain with the question of the individual's ability to fathom these processes through the very forms of the city and its qualities of compression and seriality. From Kwang Meng's point of view, it seems there can be no personal reconciliation with the ordered spaces produced by the hunger for development: the initial, national urgency to survive is now in the process of being buried, leaving behind only the pure, rational forms of their solutions. Yet for a brief time, Kwang Meng befriends his neighbor, teacher Boon Teik, who appears to offer the possibility of a spatially reconnected and meaningful existence. Boon Teik's "tastefully furnished" HDB flat—with its local batiks, prints of Van Gogh, and Japanese ikebana arrangements—is instructively cosmopolitan, as are his reading recommendations comprising Dostoevsky, Hemingway, and Narayan (Goh, 134). It is at this moment that we see a potential bildungsroman-type reconciliation between individual and society. However, at the very moment Kwang Meng graduates to reading Jean-Paul Sartre's *The Reprieve,* this just-opening world is abruptly and firmly closed. His father suffers a stroke, rendering him unable to work and making Kwang Meng the family breadwinner. From now on, Kwang Meng cannot afford the daydream of a better life, even along the lines of Boon Teik's (or the PAP's) prescriptive vision of cosmopolitan modernity. Instead, he must cling to his dreary job until his younger siblings finish their schooling.

At stake here is to see that the relationship between Kwang Meng and the new urban environment is not simply one of alienation symbolized by the repetitive, sterile descriptions of the architecture, though these have their own significance in Singaporean literature. Nor is this environment to blame for the failed bildungsroman plot, where education and experience fall short of bringing the individual in line with his proper place in society. Rather, the novel uses the form of the HDB flats to figure a multitude of contradictory relationships that contribute to Kwang Meng's postcolonial anomie. Kwang Meng's subjectivity, figured in opposition to the city, brings into expression a range of different spatial, psychic, and economic relations: between the individual and larger, serialized society; between father and son; between Singapore's colonial past and the present; between the existing city and its negative spaces. At the two extreme ends of the scale—the citywide scope of urban renewal and the microcosm of Boon-Teik's apartment—the housing blocks signal, respectively, the new global economic system in which postcolonial Singapore must compete and the individual's appropriate relation to it. The range of narrative layers this relationship produces can be rightly described as three-dimensional. At the end of the novel, Kwang Meng has neither succeeded nor failed in formation through a typical bildungsroman plot; his route is a wholly other one where he must simply progress along, or spiral through, a range of figurative relationships to the spaces of the city.

At the end of the novel, Kwang Meng returns to the pleasures appropriate to a serialized life, revisiting the Happy Bar, where "he drank and saw the sailors dance with the hostesses, he heard that girl with the burning eyes sing, and his being seemed to throb in time with the mad crazy beat of the drums" (Goh, 176). No longer able to entertain thoughts of going somewhere "really foreign," Kwang Meng remains at home contemplating his life through the landscape of repetitive housing blocks: "He was surprised on looking up to find a nearly full moon overhead. Kwang Meng looked out of the balcony across the blocks of flats to the distant glow in the sky due to the thousands of lights in the city, and at the neighboring identical block next to theirs, standing silhouetted in the bright, silver light" (175). Here, Kwang Meng finally becomes aware of the strange beauty of the mirrored blocks, "in the bright, silver light." It is only at this point, when he understands that his life will be "identical" to his father's and will reproduce the muted urgency his father lived under, that he is able to reconcile the exterior form of the flats with his own interiority, albeit in a defeated, sterile mode. In this final scene, as at the end of "A Little Ball," the exchangeability between inhabitant and building is complete, mediated by a spatial–literary operation specific to the New Asian City's status. If Cho's dwarf revealed the unresolvable antagonism between state-led and individual growth in Park Chung Hee's Korea, Goh's novel depicts the less violent but sweeping logic of PAP-driven Singaporean modernization. Not merely the "new density" that Koolhaas sees as "the sign of the Asian" (1057), Singapore is the monumentally modern, the embodiment of rationalized growth in the New Asian City.

HSIANG-T'U LITERATURE, HUANG CHUNMING, AND THE ARCHITECTURE OF ILLUSION

Jing Wang has written that the *hsiang-t'u* movement traces its origins back to the "native Taiwanese literature of the Occupation period" (60), and that its resurgence in popularity in the 1970s "gratified the public's thirst for nationalism" (44). Following the pattern of many peripheral industrializing societies, it was the agricultural sector that both provided much of the cheap labor for the cities and—by setting the price of rice at below-market levels—cheap fuel for its human growth (Woronoff, 76). The official KMT economic policy of the 1960s acknowledged, in somewhat reversed logic, the interdependency of the different spheres and advocated "developing agriculture by virtue of industry and fostering industry by virtue of foreign trade" (Woronoff, 83). It is no wonder then that most of Huang Chunming's works, like those of the genre's other major writers such as Wang T'o and Ch'en Ying-chen,[15] are firmly based in the countryside and usually depict the struggle against Westernization and industrialization as "the moral victory of the enduring underdog in a changing society" (Wang, 54). The literary landscape in Taiwan, like its urban one, is thus slightly different from that of South Korea and Singapore in its early emphasis on the countryside. Sung-Sheng Yvonne Chang recounts the two main camps of literary practice that dominated the 1960s and 1970s: the first was the so-called modernists, grouped around the journal *Modern Literature (Hsien-tai wen-hsueh)* and National Taiwan University, and which grappled with liberal, existentialist questions of morality, humanism, and alienation in the Chinese idiom. In contrast, the nativists, with the journal *Literary Quarterly (Wen-chi)* as their base, aligned their literary practice to political activism, "believ[ing] that the socioeconomic system of Taiwan must be changed" (Chang, *Modernism,* 150). Chang shows that such polar characterizations did not always obtain, and it is also not the case that nativists wrote exclusively about the rural sphere: what was occurring across Taiwan was precisely a shifting relationship between city and country.

The *hsiang-t'u* movement was nevertheless attacked in terms of the accepted tropes of the modernist versus nativist debate in 1971 at the well-known KMT-convened National Symposium of Art and Literary Workers. At this conference, the movement was accused of being leftist and (contradictorily) of promoting localism and even separatism (Hsiau, 71). A-chin Hsiau notes that it was not until the 1979 Kaohsiung incident, in which a rally organized by the political magazine *Formosa (Meilitao)* ended in violence and large-scale arrests, that a political opposition to the KMT coalesced under the banner of the *tang-wai (dang wai,* or "outside [the KMT] party"). The result of the Kaohsiung incident was a general politicization of Taiwanese society, which forced writers "to address various sensitive socio-political issues, such as the '2.28' massacre, life under martial law, and the problem of national identity" (Hsiau, 96). By this account, Taiwanese cultural nationalism did not, or could not, precede political nationalism. Furthermore, although the *hsiang-t'u* literary movement has often been understood as commensurate with the separate Taiwanese identity movement, Hsiau suggests that its writers were primarily responding to neocolonial structures of postwar Taiwan's capitalist development, and that their localism was not necessarily "incompatible with Chinese nationalism" (72). Indeed, Huang Chunming was able to argue that "because Taiwan is part of China, Taiwan's problems are also China's problems" (Hsiau, 72).[16] More than attempting to represent a distinct Taiwanese nation, *hsiang-t'u* writers were consciously pitted against the modernist group of urban, Western-influenced Taiwanese writers and their hermetic poetry and literature. In Wang's understanding, *hsiang-t'u* literature simply became the medium through which many of the antagonisms over national sovereignty, mainlander domination, Americanization, and class conflicts surfaced. What many of the debates boiled down to was the struggle between two existing modes of production—the agricultural and the industrial—that, through a malleable "principle of opposition," could mobilize multiple opposing-pair terms such as farmers and workers, the exploited and capitalists, Taiwanese and mainlanders, the indigenous and Chinese. "All of these classified binaries," Wang notes, "primarily revolved around the axis of village versus city" (48). Thus, "city and village form one dialectic couple, not only in their opposing modes of production and their corresponding effect on Chinese consciousness, but in the complementary opposition between the sectors of the economy which they represent" (56). We must therefore read Huang's *hsiang-t'u* literature as principally concerned with the articulation of new social contradictions, focused around the distinction between rural and urban rather than as a Taiwanese nativist movement. Again, we will see how the bildungsroman concerns around youth and mobility are articulated in a unique fashion that takes account of the specific forms of urban growth. Huang's bildungsroman themes will also be discussed in their adaptation to film in chapter 6.

Huang Chunming was born in Ilan in 1939, graduated from P'ingtung Normal College, and during the 1960s became one of the prominent contributors to the journal *Literature Quarterly*. His two collections, *His Son's Big Doll (Erzi de da wan'ou)* and *Sayonara, Goodbye (Shayonala zaijian),*

from 1969 and 1974, respectively, portray nonurban moral victories without glorifying the countryside; indeed, they are "written in a mocking tone
with a touch of commiseration" (Chi, 24). In examining the metonymic
function of architecture in his works, I argue that because the Taiwanese
city of the 1960s and 1970s has a more uneven spatial distribution than
our other sites, Huang's literary mode casts modern architecture as at once
more anomalous and more seductive. The urbanization of Taiwan recalls
Spengler's understanding of the metropolis's irrevocable split from, and
subordination of, the land: for him, modernity means "the *city-as-world,*
which suffers nothing beside itself and sets about *annihilating* the country
picture" (70). Spengler assumes that the "country picture" is to be erased
by a totalizing and apparently unified "city picture," corresponding to
broader (usually national) development in industrial and mass-production
technologies. In general, this has been the case: modern cultures are almost
always urban cultures. In the case of Taiwan, however, despite strong state
control over certain industries and basic utilities[17] and the invention and
establishment of export processing zones, there were few large-scale,
capital-intensive endeavors with their profound tendency to restructure
the countryside. After U.S. aid ended in the early 1960s, the Taiwanese
economy was partly driven by investment from transnational corporations and overseas Chinese, while other domestic capital came largely
"from the people" (Woronoff, 75) through small-scale entrepreneurship.
Taiwan's manufacturing economy thus never relied on a select group of
state-favored conglomerates as in Korea, or state–multinational partnerships as in Singapore. Rather, it consisted of "some 10,000 trading companies, 36,000 exporters and 27,000 manufacturers" (Woronoff, 87). Many of
these small companies focused on textiles and light industries, using
labor-intensive methods to produce cheap articles or subcomponents for
American manufacturers (Woronoff, 72). In terms of spatial development,
this indicates the partial transformation to modern industrial practices
and technologies, and the persistence of perspectives other than the dominant "city picture." We can note, then, that urban domination over the
countryside—the world as city—does not always follow the same trajectory. Even though Taiwanese cities were exceedingly successful in connecting the nation's economy to the global market, the existing spatial logic of
the city was largely retained—the shophouse form lasted much longer here

than in Singapore—and existing work relations were not dramatically restructured.[18] In short, this is an arrangement of uneven urban development, whereby "some small space in a make-shift factory or . . . living quarters" and "rudimentary" machinery (Woronoff, 72) comprise the basic units of this most successful export economy. In such a situation, the city grows, but without the evenly increasing rationality the early social theorists of the West had imagined; instead, the urban system penetrates the countryside, and vice versa. Accordingly, in the 1970s, the government, unable to provide substantial public housing and faced with critical housing shortages, actually responded by "deregulat[ing] building restrictions and legalis[ing] self-constructed buildings"; in 1983 it even legislated for the construction of "huts on the roofs of apartments and on public use areas" (Li, 39). In looking at Huang's exemplary *hsiang-t'u* literature, we

Shops on Chung-hwa Road, Taipei, 1955. The taller buildings on the right date from the Japanese period. Photograph by Three Lions/Hulton Archive/ Getty Images.

see how these contradictory modes of production and multiple spatial logics of the city result in a particularly disjunctive aesthetic of modern architecture. In the following, I look closely at two of Huang's stories from his translated collection *The Taste of Apples* that deal with the troubling arrival of modern architectural forms and their effect on individuals.

The central image of "The Two Sign Painters" ("Liang ge youqi jiang") (1974) is a striking visual contrast between small people and large structures, not dissimilar to that in Cho's "A Little Ball." Two sign painters, rural migrants Ah-li and Monkey, have the job of painting an enormous advertising billboard on the side of the newly built tallest structure in Qishan, the twenty-four-story Silver Star Hotel.[19] This new structure is an unwelcome intrusion into both the town's landscape and the residents' spatial understanding. Not only does the sight of the hotel's massive gray wall put passing motorists into a "momentary panic," but its white base coat turns the building into a monstrous mirror, so that "three-hundred-plus families who lived opposite the wall had signed a petition, complaining that once the wall turned white . . . they were blinded by the early morning glare of the sun's rays off the wall" (184). One family even sues the sign-painting company, claiming their grandfather suffered a seizure while "pointing his cane at the wall and swearing" at what "seemed to be a living object" (184). Huang thus parodies the new, unevenly spreading economy through the building's preternatural size and austerity; for the residents of Qishan, the evil forces of modernization and Westernization literally come to life in the facade of the new architecture. For Ah-li and Monkey, contracted to paint a seminude mural of popular starlet VV for the Jishi Cola Company, the building is no less tormenting. Having been awarded the dubious honor of painting the starlet's huge breasts, they struggle with the inhumanity of both the working conditions and the mural's ridiculous scale.

> The heat of the sun beat down on their backs, its glare reflecting off the painted wall into their eyes; not a drop remained in their water bottles, and the water in their bodies oozed out through their pores, dripping to the ground below or evaporating in the air. Getting another drink of water was not going to be easy. In the three days since they'd been applying the color, they'd lost their appetites for everything but guzzling down tea and water. Their bodies had turned dark in the sun, the pounds melting away.

What distressed Ah-li the most was the job before him. They were supposed to be painting VV's breasts, but who could tell? The breasts alone were several stories tall; the two men were plastered up against the wall endlessly slapping on paint, until finally they began to wonder just what they were doing up there. (184–85)

Like Cho's factory workers, the painters' bodies are literally reduced by the process of work; the more flesh they add to the starlet's body, the more their own pounds melt away. Paralleling the rationalized factory assembly line of meaningless components, the starlet's breasts are so large that the two workers cannot know their whole form, let alone the total picture of the mural. The advertiser's desire to bring the building to profit-making life therefore comes at the expense of the mental and physical well-being of both painters and observers.

The remainder of the story asserts the metonymic relationship between bodies, buildings, and economies. The two workers, having survived another grueling shift, decide to climb to the top of the unfinished building and survey the world from a dangling mesh construction basket (190). Daring each other until they are both inside it, they look back, spatially and temporally, to the train station and their arrival in Qishan some three years ago, when they were lured away from their mountain hometown by the promise of the big city. They are stuck in dangerous, underpaid jobs but unwilling to return home until they have "made some money" (196), and their position in society is spatially expressed by the dangling basket at the top of the new skyscraper: at the summit of the city's greatest symbol of development, they are among its poorest, most precarious residents. The scene, however, turns from nostalgic to tragic when they are noticed by pedestrians on the street below. Before long, police, journalists, and camera crews are crowding the edge of the building pleading with them not to add to the number of recent suicides, which have been growing "ever since they started putting up high-rises" (203). The media circus and police "counseling" eventually precipitate Monkey's suicidal leap from the basket, fulfilling the media's desire for spectacular news items. The unnatural view from the hotel's roof—the city as worldview—proves fatal. Modern architecture is the flashy form that dissimulates the corruption at industrialized society's core: the brightness of the city attracts country migrants, only to use up their labor and let them fall. With remarkable efficiency, Huang evokes the plight of the young rural migrants through their relationship to the twenty-four-story hotel; the building is at once site of the Taylorized labor processes of the factory, the seductive viewpoint of city as worldview, and object of mass media spectacularization. What takes the place of bildungsroman individual development and resolution is a narrative densely packed with different metonymic relationships between worker and building/world. If we have seen the literal and metaphoric shrinkage of the youthful characters in Cho's text and the merging of self and urban scene in Goh's, in Huang's, we witness a more cynical view of the individual's relationship to this rapidly changing world.

While not a bildungsroman as such, the title story, "The Taste of Apples" ("Pingguo de ziwei") (1974), also deserves brief mention for its complex figuring of modern built forms, through which Huang offers no less negative a view of modern architecture and the city. Compared to "The Two Sign Painters," it is narrated with less sympathy for the protagonist, unfortunate rural migrant Ah-fa, who is run down by an American's car while bicycling to work. In demonstrating the way that the first world literally collides with the third, "The Taste of Apples" brings into sharp relief the uncomfortable fit between the two modes of production, the neocolonial and the postcolonial, which coexist and depend on each other in the space of the city. Its primary literary strategy is the ironic juxtaposition of characters and the building types to which they do not belong. These juxtapositions are clearly rendered in two complementary scenes: in the first, the American, accompanied by a local policeman, visits the squatter settlement where Ah-fa's family lives to deliver an apology for the accident. In the second, extended, scene, Ah-fa's six family members—wife Ah-gui, oldest daughter Ah-zhu, the nameless mute daughter, two sons Ah-ji and Ah-song, and the baby—visit the American hospital in which Ah-fa is recovering from two broken legs.

In the scene subtitled "The Labyrinth," the policeman escorts the American through the "capricious disorder" of "tiny illegal shacks made of wooden crates and sheet metal" (136). Sensing the impropriety of the foreigner's witnessing the squatter settlement, the policemen assures him that "'Their new homes are nearly completed—those apartments by the river. Once they've moved these people out, they're going to put up a high-rise here.' He felt pleased with himself about his alert reaction but at the same time was uneasy about lying" (137). In a reversal of the person-building proportions we have seen thus far, the American literally dwarfs these buildings: "The foreigner was a head taller than any of the shacks in the area, so all he could see was a mass of rooftops thrown together with sheet metal and plastic covers, plus some old tires and bricks to hold them down. Some of the roofs also sported an array of wooden crates, birdcages, and the like" (136–37). From the American's point of view, these homes appear only as a landscape of rubbish, and the top-down view of the shacks obscures their even more insignificant and undersized inhabitants. As in Cho's story, the dialectic of the high and the low is again mapped on to a class antagonism, which is now also a geopolitical one; the foreigner's towering height necessarily involves the dehumanization of the local Taiwanese. More so than the behavior of individual characters, the figuring and contrasting of bodies and architecture are what reveal underlying social, political, and labor relationships.

In the second important scene, Ah-fa's family is comically juxtaposed against the white surfaces and rationality of the American hospital. Like the scene in the squatter village with the policeman, the outsider is unable to perceive the inhabitants of the other's building form, so that the architecture itself takes on these characterizations. At the hospital, the building is perceived only as an object of curious, aesthetic regularity—parked cars, fences, and dazzling grass. Most striking is the hospital's whiteness, which extends from its facade to its interior: "A clean, white, medium-sized hospital stood on the scenic mountaintop. Although the parking lot was filled with cars, no people were out walking. Some white sedans and ambulances were parked among the cars, and there was a short white fence surrounding a patch of Korean grass made dazzling by recent rainfall" (145). To the children, the uniform color of the building itself is puzzling:

> "Hey, everything in the place is white," Ah-song noted with amazement.
>
> "It's an American hospital."
>
> "Their clothes are white, so are their hats and shoes."
>
> "So is the room." Ah-ji looked around. "The sheets are white, the blankets, even the bed. So are the windows and the walls. . . . (147)

A few minutes later, their father—a mass of bandages—is wheeled in, pro-voking the reasonable question from one child, "Brother, is that white thing our daddy?" (148). Awed by the cleanliness and brightness of the building, Ah-fa's wife and children temporarily forget the unfortunate cir-cumstances in which they have come. In a stroke of luck, however, it turns out that Ah-fa has in fact been run over by Colonel Grant of the U.S. Army, whose generous compensation transforms the accident into a family for-tune. Forced to be grateful to the colonel for running him over, Ah-fa can only address his assailant with "Thank you! Thank you! I'm sorry, I'm so sorry . . . " (154). Huang's obvious point is the undignified capitulation of the Taiwanese in the face of American material wealth, the very sym-bol of which (the car) caused the accident in the first place. In narrative terms, however, this subordination takes place through the architectural subsumption of Ah-fa's body into "that white thing"—the hospital. By implying such confusion and contrast between bodies and architecture, Huang's story denounces the seduction of the Taiwanese by American material comforts—the hospital's impressive whiteness, its "terrific toilet paper" (147)—and the colonel's financial compensation. In his unflattering portrayal of Ah-fa's family's readiness to reap material benefits from his tragedy, Taiwan's independence, Huang suggests, is irrevocably ceded to capitalist and neocolonial forces.

The American hospital is simultaneously the space that seduces the family and begins to train them in the spatiality of modern, Western living (the hospital scene is tellingly titled "The White House"). Although the family members are naturally "frightened by the strange, new environ-ment" (146) when they arrive, by the time Ah-fa is wheeled out, they have negotiated the codes of conduct required by the waiting room, the gender-specific bathrooms, and even the Western-style toilet ("'How did you pee?' 'Aren't you supposed to sit on it?'" they ask each other [147]). Huang's narrative, therefore, is equally invested in describing the troubled inter-action between rural and modern spatiality as it is in describing Taiwanese and American (or Taiwanese and mainlander) ethnic–national relations. Echoing the way modern architectural forms are inserted piecemeal into the Taiwanese city, older ways of life negotiate modern, rational ones not in terms of large-scale urban renewal projects, but over the mere threshold of a building. It is precisely the uneven infiltration of capitalist industry that is Huang's object of critique, and the localized appearance of modern architecture functions as both its concrete expression and duplicitous signage. In the two stories, we see how the downfall of rural migrants comes about precisely through the seduction by the towering, white, and gleaming modern building. In an economic system that allows, and indeed relies on, the juxtaposition of peripheral forms of life—the rural villages and the squatter settlements—with American-style advertising, capitalism, and material goods, the experience of modern architecture is dramatized as the illusionary, dissimulating, and potentially lethal encounter with such a system.

STORIES OF NEW ASIAN CITY GROWTH

Williams has noted that although the West certainly led the historical shift to urbanization, it is in the post- and neocolonial world that the most spectacular urban and population growth has occurred: "the last image of the city . . . is the [postcolonial] political capital or the trading port surrounded by the shanty towns, the barriadas, which often grow at incredible speed" (*Country,* 287). Yet the modern industrial city's apparent translatability beyond the West is not evidence of the simple outward spread of capitalist development. Rather, the postcolonial world's historical lack of resources, infrastructure, and possibility for colonies of its own—in short, the structural asymmetries of global development in which the postcolony only has "its own cities to choke with carbonized air" (Ahmad, 315)—mean that the processes and forms of urban growth here cannot simply replicate those of the imperial center. As we have seen, primary among such determining conditions of New Asian Cities is the hurried development, often enforced by strong, sometimes military, states, which retain much of the colonial regime's instrumentalist view of cities and populations, updated for the cold war and new international division of labor. From the perspectives of these new, postcolonial producer cities, industrial society seems less a shift to mass production, consumption, and urban expansion than a way for labor power to be produced and consumed by the developing nation; external demand for labor or goods by the former metropolitan is now replaced by the internal rule of the authoritarian postcolonial nation-state in a concentric arrangement of power. Oriented toward the world market, the nation's gap in production and consumption is now justified in terms of GNP rates and the nation's future prosperity. Chua writes, "in an industrialized society, the demands of the economy take precedence over those of the people. First, the economy must be fed its human resource, then the people can consume the products of economy" (*Political Legitimacy,* 161).

Just as we have identified the asymmetries of postcolonial industrial modernity, we have found asymmetries in terms of the classic bildungsroman literary models. While we may not be surprised to find fictions that dramatize the problem of youth against an entropic world of market economies and urbanization, the narrative of formation here finds unique expression. The growth period of the New Asian City economy paradoxically requires contraction at the level of the workers themselves, curtailing and limiting the very possibilities of "formation." In Korea, the new multistory building is figured dialectically against the individual as the physical correlate of a social sector that extracts surplus labor—the elite local business class in a state–*chaebol* partnership, backed by U.S. and Japanese loans. In the case of Singapore, the nation's mastering of modernity's technologies may better be understood as the mastering of people by the city, symbolized by Kwang Meng's eventual merging with the HDB flats. In Taiwan, the uneven penetration of industrialization into the city fabric produces anxiety around individual encounters with its architectural forms. If, in Moretti's terms, the typical bildungsroman must, in order to complete the plot sequence, find the youthful protagonist a "homeland" by necessarily "'merging' . . . the protagonist with his new world" (*Way of the World,* 26), the New Asian City texts take this imperative to its most literal, and troubling, level.

We must be wary, however, of giving a one-way deterministic reading of the built environment in which certain psychological realities necessarily follow changes in urban form. Because we are dealing with the logic of space rather than an empirical study of subjectivities, we must resist the temptation to psychologize fictional characters or, in an equally misguided gesture, to attribute positive political value to, say, Yŏng-hŭi's resistance to the *chaebol* son and negative value to Kwang Meng's or Monkey's apparent submission. What is most important about these texts is not their portrayal (or lack of portrayal) of revolutionary subjectivities, but their provocative use of built form to signal and work through a range of historical processes and contradictions. In analyzing and comparing them, we can again conclude that urban transformations are a primary mediator of struggles over modernity, industrialization, and the place of the individual subject. In the New Asian City, processes of construction and demolition, urban renewal, and export-oriented development are among the most formidable forces shaping both social reality and literary forms. While the state- or corporate-directed forces that connect the nation's economy to the world market are largely indiscernible to the individual, the built forms arising from these linkages, operating as textual actors, become tangible evidence of them. The repeated confusion between the human and the architectural is therefore the narrative means by which to make sense of the nation's dramatic leap into postcolonial modernity.

If we have here examined the exterior, public forms and dimensions of urban development, what can be said about its internal spaces? How, specifically, does the changing role of women in the New Asian City workforce become figured in relation to new conceptions of private and public, feminine and masculine space? It is to these questions that we turn in the next chapter.

4

The Disappearing Woman,
Interiority, and Private Space

It is hard to tell now which became more private first, the room or the soul.
Certainly, their histories are entwined.

—ROBIN EVANS, "Figures, Doors and Passages"

PUBLIC AND PRIVATE IN THE NEW ASIAN CITY

In Kang Sŏk-kyŏng's 1985 novella "A Room in the Woods" ("Supsok ŭi Pang"), soon-to-be-married Mi-yang attempts to break through the apparent wall that encases her younger sister, So-yang. Written in the thick of South Korea's democratizing movement, which challenged military rule in 1987, it may be read as the tragic story of So-yang, whose failure "to find a place in the student movements and activism of the era" (Ch'oe Yun, 492) leads to her eventual suicide. Of more interest, however, is its unique narrative construction whereby one character's search for another is the unifying structure.[1] In short, the novella is formally organized as a detective story, with Mi-yang as the tireless investigator seeking the truth of her sister's behavior.

The Yi sisters live comfortably in their middle-class home in Seoul with their extended family, which includes their industrialist father, dutiful mother, third sister Hye-yang, youngest brother Chŏng-u, grandmother, and half-uncle Hyŏk. Enjoying the material benefits of their father's successful sweater factory, the sisters are intelligent, well-off, and well educated. All three are destined for good marriages, attested to by Mi-yang's approaching union with a bank supervisor. The story begins, however, with the alarming news that So-yang has dropped out of her prestigious university, is refusing to obey her parents' wishes to reenroll, and is staying out at night. Narrator Mi-yang, having just quit her job in the bank in readiness for marriage—"I thought it natural to resign before getting married" (50)—uses her newfound free time to investigate her sister's private life. She calls So-yang's university department, secretly meets with her college friends and boyfriend, and sneaks into her room to read her diary. In actuality, the novel is less about So-yang's character and more about Mi-yang's detective work on the trail of her sister's ever-elusive interiority—work that consists not only of phone calls, interviews, and diary reading, but also the frequent study of her sister's room.

If the last chapter explored the problem of (male) youth against the changing dimensions of the city, this chapter explores the textual and spatial production of the postcolonial New Asian City woman who appears at the threshold of public and private spaces. I am interested here in the question of both psychic and architectural interiors as revealed in "A Room in the Woods," along with "Missing" ("Li jia chu zou," literally, "leaving home, deserting family")[2] (1988) by Su Weizhen and *Rice Bowl* (1984) by Su-chen Christine Lim, from Taiwan and Singapore, respectively. What does the literary search for the absent woman in the new interior of the private room indicate? Why is the figure of the individual room so important in these fictional representations of women? What does the changing relationship between public and private spaces tell us about the conception of femininity, and how do material advances in the welfare of some women square with their symbolic and economic role in developmental nationalism? As in the previous chapter, I deal with the way literature figures architectural transformation and narrates spatial neologisms. While the previous chapter may be summarized by the question, "How do I avoid becoming one with the logic of the city?" this chapter asks, "Where is it that I belong in the city?" To continue my emphasis on the asymmetry with Western urban and social forms of modernity, I argue that the shift to new spatial arrangements—nuclear families, individual bedrooms, and private spaces—does not produce the same kind of individualized feminist consciousness seen in the earlier industrializing Euro-American context.[3] Rather than finding solace, security, or creative autonomy in the individual room, the New Asian City woman is caught uneasily at its edges.

The question of interior, private, domestic space and its opposing realm of exterior, public, and civic space has long been important to feminist

analyses. Jane Rendell summarizes how the latter realm is valued as patriarchy's positive term, involving the concepts of "production, public, male,
city," while the former is its inverse and associated with "reproduction, private, female, home" ("Introduction," 104). This duality not only determines
the city's divided physical organization, but its material processes leave
traces on the subjects' corporeality. According to Elizabeth Grosz, "the city
orients and organizes family, sexual, and social relations insofar as the city
divides cultural life into public and private domains, geographically dividi-
ing and defining the particular social positions and locations occupied by
individuals and groups" (250). Insofar as these are general descriptions
of spatial hierarchies, they hold true for traditional Western as for many
Asian patriarchal systems. In her account of feminism and nationalism in
the colonial world, Kumari Jayawardena notes that the contradictions of
third world industrialization are, to some extent, prefigured in the West,
where two broad objectives characterized nationalist reformers: to edu-
cate women for employment in new capitalist forms of production, and to
make them the repository of traditional values. Non-Western nationalisms
therefore echoed

> earlier events in Europe where the development of the factory system dur-
> ing the Industrial Revolution had changed the nature of the home and the
> family which, in pre-capitalist times, had been a centre of production. Capi-
> talism had drawn women of the poor from the home into the factory as
> wage labour, while the women of the bourgeoisie were confined to the home
> as housewives and the family was idealized in all the propaganda of the
> bourgeois media. The bourgeoisies of the Third World, as part of their strat-
> egy for achieving economic growth, "civilization" and reform, also began to
> propagate the concept of a family system based on strict monogamy for
> women, monogamy in theory (if not in practice) for men, and the abolition
> of "feudal" extended family relationships. (15)

Arguably, these two contradictory shifts concerning women—the move
outward to industrial workplaces and the move inward to the bourgeois
family—take on sharper and more conflicted contours in postcolonial
nations. As Partha Chatterjee has controversially theorized, in accepting and
emulating the development of the West, the postcolonial nation typically

separates the material and spiritual spheres, reserving the expression of national identity for the latter. In opposition to the technologically (and therefore Western) dominated public sphere, the home becomes the repository of untouched indigenous values: "The home in its essence must remain unaffected by the profane activities of the material world—and woman is its representation" (*Nation*, 120). In East Asia, this split had already been conceptualized by the Meiji Japanese in the formula of "Eastern morality, Western technology" (*tongdo sŏgi* in Korean).[4] Expressions of public and private and the changing architectural arrangements of domestic space are thus crucial to our understanding of postcolonial nationalisms and gendered subjects.

As we might expect, the extraordinary level of development and modernization of the New Asian City profoundly affects the distinction between public and private. The industrializing 1970s and 1980s especially saw huge changes in educational and job opportunities, including material gains, for women in all three countries under consideration.[5] Cho Nam-Hyŏn has described the social background to the development of feminism in South Korea, a process broadly repeated in Taiwan and Singapore:

> In the case of Korea, especially in the 1970s and 80s as industrialization accelerated, society changed in several different aspects. Industrialization and urbanization were like two sides of the same coin: urbanization overturned the existing family system and brought about changes in the reorganization of the social and class system. As the extended family system was replaced by the nuclear family, high school education was universalized, and economic growth achieved, femininity, masculinity and the relationship between the two began to change. ("1970–80 Nyŏndae Sosŏl," my translation, 166)

Such shifts in industrial and family organizations, however, do not necessarily replicate Western women's movements based on increased access to the public sphere, sexual equality, and individual rights. As Hampson notes, "industrialisation has reinforced, rather than challenged, the sexual division of labour in Korean families" (172). Indeed, in the New Asian City context, feminist movements seem conspicuously late, largely arising after the transformation from agricultural to industrial productive modes. Yet we are mistaken both in labeling such movements tardy and expecting them to conform to the West's liberal-style feminism. In the first place, the lack of general political freedom under authoritarian governments must be considered. For example, despite its introduction (in American form) in 1971 by Lu Hsiu-lien,[6] feminist movements could not take root in Taiwan as a result of the Kuomintang's "wartime non-governmental organization law," which limited all kinds of political activity. Lu was jailed for her views in the 1970s, and a visible independent women's movement began only after martial law was lifted in 1987 (Lan-Hung Nora Chiang, 240). The anticommunism directed toward North Korea by the Park Chung Hee regime similarly suppressed almost all civil rights, such that "the national partition and the terrors of the ideological war surrounding it created a long hiatus in the development of Korean feminism that lasted until the 1980s" (Kim and Choi, 3).[7] In Singapore, although the People's Action Party afforded some women's rights relating to marriage, divorce, custody, and inheritance in their 1961 Women's Charter, a women's movement was not fully articulated until the late 1970s and early 1980s, partly in response to the government's becoming more patriarchal in its official orientations.

In addition to these teleological narratives of liberal feminism, however, we must reckon with the entirely different questions and preoccupations relating to gender in these contexts. We must explore, in other words, how the New Asian Cities exemplify one of the great paradoxes of postcolonial modernity: how modernization and industrialization proceed without altering hierarchal gender relations. Seungsook Moon explains that in South Korea, "gender hierarchy has been recomposed in modern forms. As a result, more and more women face the contradiction that they carry the socially ascribed [inferior] status of female gender in industrializing Korea which espouses, in principle, individual equality and achievement" (58). The fictions of Kang, Su, and Lim address precisely the question of the recomposition of "gender hierarchy . . . in modern forms" and do so, I argue, through the vexed shift to new spatial arrangements of public and private space. The architectural neologism of the privatized interior conceived against the public sphere is the spatial analogue of the private subject, seeming to promise the "individual equality and achievement" of modernity's general category of citizen. Yet we will see how this new interiority conflicts with patriarchal expectations for woman to remain simply the "mother, moulder of the nation" (Young, 368).[8] This irreconcilability results in the texts' *hovering over* the location of woman as a subject position unable to fully occupy either public or private space.

The interior thus takes center stage in both the literature and my analysis. Let us note that while its development has been well theorized in terms of capitalist production and commodity relations, gender must constitute one of its core analytics. Writing in regard to Euro-American modernity, Victoria Rosner defines interiority as the realm that folds together material space, psychic interiority, and gendered bodies: "By 'interiority' I refer to a cluster of interdependent concepts that extend from the representation of consciousness to the reorganization of home life; revised definitions of personal privacy, intimacy, and space; and new assessments of the sexualized and gendered body" (11). Beatriz Colomina has similarly stressed domestic architecture's generative role in private subjectivities: "Architecture is not simply a platform that accommodates the viewing subject. It is a viewing mechanism that produces the subject. It precedes and frames its occupant" (250). While Rosner and Colomina's studies examine private space and gender in a different context, their observations are useful starting points for our examination of both private spaces and the gendered body within the New Asian City.[9]

Film still from Hou Hsiao-hsien's *Dust in the Wind* (1986, discussed in chapter 6). A female figure contemplates Taipei.

WOMAN AS TRACE

Kang Sŏk-kyŏng, one of the major Korean writers of the 1980s, has explored many pressing feminist themes in her work and is perhaps best known for her 1983 short story "Days and Dreams" ("Nat kwa kkum"), which describes the lives of prostitutes on a U.S. military base.[10] While 1970s Korean women's fiction "expresse[d] disharmony with society" by creating new literary spaces outside oppressive value systems and focusing on inner realities and love relations (Ch'oe Yun, 488), 1980s literature more directly linked fiction and feminist issues. Writers such as Kang Sŏk-kyŏng and the second generation of postwar women writers such as Yi Kyŏng-ja, Kim Ch'ae-won, and Yang Kwi-ja have dealt explicitly with issues of neocolonialism, patriarchy, and postcolonial authoritarianism from a feminist perspective.[11] However, rather than its themes or events, it is the formal innovation of Kang's "A Room in the Woods" that marks it as a feminist text.

"A Room in the Woods" repeatedly invokes the figure of the inaccessible woman sealed off behind a "castle wall." In questioning why her sister "had cut herself off from everyone," Mi-yang blames the individualism of her family members, an individualism "made possible by the fact that each of us had a separate room" (Kang, 39). Whereas the two younger sisters shared a room before moving to their spacious two-story house, each child now had a room of her own to decorate as she pleased. Mi-yang narrates: "I remember vividly how happy So-yang was with her new room, and Hye-yang with hers. The first thing So-yang did was hang a poster of the Beatles on her wall" (40). So-yang's Beatles poster—and later, flowers, candles, and a music collection—denotes the shift to a distinctly Western mode of individualism drawing from American youth culture of the 1960s. Confirming this new individualized sense of space, Mi-yang complains about her mother's overdeveloped sense of privacy in not letting her daughter use the master bedroom's bathroom: "I realized of course, that this was the bathroom Mother and Father used" (44). The architecture itself demands a new privatized relationship to space, and Mi-yang suspects the move to the new house is to blame for the rifts in this otherwise happy family.

The designation of private spaces according to the individual (private bedrooms) or the generation (children's versus parents' bathrooms) reveals a stark departure from previous notions of Korean domestic space, which may be briefly described. In that system, the *anbang*, or master bedroom, was conceived not as the private conjugal space of the couple but rather as the women's and children's quarter, which only at night was converted into a bedroom for the married couple. This opposed the *sarangbang,* the male quarter, open to guests and usually located on the edge of the house. The pervasive influence of Confucian thinking in the Chosŏn period (1392–1910) rendered the greatest distinction within Korean domestic space between the sexes, not generations.[12] Accordingly, the *anbang* could function without contradiction as the most intimate space of the couple (at night) and as the area for raising children, an arrangement not easily translated into the Western concept of "master bedroom."[13]

Moreover, in such traditional planning, all rooms and spaces opened out to a common courtyard space, "eliminat[ing] the need for an entrance porch or entrance hall and corridors" (Sang-hae Lee, 384). Bathing was (and still is to some extent) done in public bathhouses segregated by gender. While such arrangements were already changing in the colonial era (evident in chapter 2's discussion of Yi Sang's *The Wings*), it was not until the 1970s and 1980s that Western planning for the nuclear family household came to predominance. The Yi household epitomizes the new domestic space embraced by the industrial middle class: a two-story Western-style house with separate, lockable bedrooms and bathrooms accessed by corridors and defined against a shared, more public living area. Such private spaces are what simultaneously enable So-yang's individualism and produce familial and social isolation: her troubling relationship to her room operates as a spatial allegory for the broader, ambivalent position of women in industrializing societies, which both demand and refute individualism. In her diary, she writes lines such as, *"I'm a castle now. I've broken off all relations with others"* (64), and *"I don't want to walk barefoot anywhere outside my room, even in the hallway"* (65). Mi-yang recalls a night when she was drawn to So-yang's room by a song by Leonard Cohen, "a folk singer I liked."

> I decided to pay a visit. The room was lit by a dozen or so candles that looked like little spirits, and the shadows of the flowers that covered the ceiling gave the effect of frost on a window.
>
> I entered the cavelike room cautiously and discovered So-yang lying toward the wall, her back to the candlelight. Something resembling a bat was huddled above her head. It was a black umbrella. The sight of So-yang

lying under that umbrella was grotesque, but it also seemed mystical, perhaps because of the candles.

The light from the flames glanced off the black cloth of the umbrella and scattered. So-yang was motionless, her eyes closed. Having lapsed into a world of her own, she was unaware I had entered her room. But that's it—a world of her own! Only now has the right expression come to mind. (40)

Transformed by the teenager's decoration, So-yang's room is a world away from the rest of the household: it is a sealed-off, cavelike interior, which locks in So-yang's own presence. With its occupant "motionless, her eyes closed," the room, rather than the character, speaks of her bleak and morbid interiority. On closer reading, it is not certain whether she is even asleep, or whether her body, "lying toward the wall," has simply become another object in the room. As Maeda Ai has elegantly commented with regard to the Japanese domestic novel, "To this extent . . . living space and . . . body language [saturate] each other" (340). The monadic space of the private interior produces a new kind of sealed-off subjectivity at the same time it produces narrator Mi-yang's need to search for her.

We may further understand this scene in terms of the rise of the bourgeois interior, as analyzed by Frankfurt School thinkers. In Theodor Adorno's study of Kierkegaardian philosophy, the obsession with inwardness is a function of the disavowed exploitative relations of production on which bourgeois existence depends. Both the interior of the room and the bourgeois subject are defined as "objectless interior[s] vis-à-vis space. Space does not enter the *intèrieur*; it is only its boundary" (43).[14] In disavowing the rest of the world, the commodity-filled interior comes to take its place. As with the Kierkegaardian bourgeois subject, So-yang must explicitly deny her relationship to the means of production supporting her existence. Viewing herself from the perspective of her student–labor activist friend, Myŏng-ju, she writes in her diary:

> *Granted, up till now I've been able to live materialistically, free of inconveniences, thanks to Father. But if I look at this through Myŏng-ju's eyes, I owe it all to the blood and sweat of the workers. . . .*
>
> *But as long as I'm living like a petit-bourgeois [ppŭtti purŭjua] thanks to Father's Yudo Trading Company, I'm afraid to look at how the workers live*

in the factory dorms. I'd like to put this problem aside for the time being.
Even thinking about it gives me a headache. (66)

So-yang acknowledges, but ultimately banishes from thought, the contrast between her well-appointed bedroom and the (undoubtedly female) workers' dormitories at her father's textile factory. For Adorno, the commodity is what dissimulates bourgeois reliance on alienated labor, allegorized in the obsession with the psychic and spatial interior. The Yi girls' bedrooms are indeed filled with shoes, clothes, books, posters, and records (Mi-yang's even accommodates her own piano), objects necessary to flesh out their individual personalities. The alienated form of the commodity is thus, paradoxically, what permits "authentic" individualism, "the concentration of selfhood specific to modernity [that] is also self-alienation" (Pensky, 170). Or, in Robin Evans's phrase, the bourgeois interior is now but the "emanations of an exquisite psyche" (52). Like So-yang's castle, the interior's appearance in the world is monadological: it has no history, is indivisible and exists purely independently from all others. In this sense, we can view So-yang's room as the airless and spaceless chamber replacing the entire world with "a world of her own."[15]

The structural account of the interior also seems to explain the organization of "A Room in the Woods" as a detective story. To compensate for the commodity's lack of trace of production, the bourgeois subject tends to leave her personal trace on all possessions: "The trace is appearance of a nearness, however far removed the thing that left it behind may be" (Benjamin, 447). For Benjamin, the shell is the "original form of all dwelling" that "bears the impression of its occupant" (220), and explains the nineteenth-century proliferation of plush surfaces, carpets, and cases: "pocket watches, slippers, egg cups, thermometers, playing cards—and, in lieu of cases, there were jackets, carpets, wrappers, and covers" (221). As we see in the cavelike atmosphere of So-yang's room, personalized ownership generates reversion to prehistorical modes of dwelling—the shell, the skin, and the case. As the interior calls up this exquisite psyche, it simultaneously interpellates the figure of the detective: "the traces of the inhabitant are imprinted on the interior. Enter the detective story, which pursues these traces" (Benjamin, 9).[16] Mi-yang's pursuit of So-yang's interiority may thus be explained as the narrative form demanded by this shift to individualized, imprinted space.

Yet while Benjamin provocatively connects the spatial/psychological inno-vation of the interior with the appearance of the detective story, both his encased bourgeois subject and his pursuer are implicitly male. What can we make of the strikingly parallel interior configuration in an example of postcolonial women's writing?

As the story progresses, we discover the Yi household to be a less mod-ern architectural arrangement than expected. Recall that, in the Confucian tradition of extended families, Mi-yang's grandmother lives with the fam-ily. But even more incongruous with modern bourgeois living is the pres-ence of Hyŏk, the girls' half-uncle born of their grandfather and a *kisaeng* (a female entertainer/prostitute), whose room in the "half basement of our house" echoes his marginal status in the family. Mi-yang explains: "Although I considered him my uncle, he was younger than So-yang. He had also failed the college entrance exam. We didn't like him because of the wild drumming that came from his room and because his clothing always had a strong odor. This boy's existence seemed a dark shadow over our family" (66). This sole mention of the family's "dark shadow" indicates how tradi-tional kinship structures, where wealthy men often had other families with concubines or *kisaengs,* haunt the project of the new and modern nuclear family. The Yi family's American-style consumerism, dwelling, and indi-vidualism are literally built over the remnants of a previous kinship struc-ture, the residue of which must be accommodated in the private space of the home. The difficulty of reconciling new spaces of domesticity with older kinship relations thus complicates the neat story of the rise of bour-geois individuality recounted above. Rather than a confirmation of the bourgeois interior's demand for individuality, the text dwells on private space because it is the place where modern woman should, but cannot, fully appear. It follows that because woman properly belongs nowhere, the search for her must take place everywhere.

Given that women's labor was foundational for Korea's leap into export industry, especially through textiles and electronics,[17] how was it that there was little accompanying change in the role of women vis-à-vis public and private arenas? An examination of contemporary Korean political discourse reveals how pressures to industrialize actually reinvigorated traditional conceptions of womanhood. In the 1970s, for example, the state launched the *ch'ung hyo* ("loyalty to the state and filial piety") campaign emphasizing

collective life over individual rights, while government publications especially sought to redefine modern Koreanness through the figure of the
women. One 1974 text

> explicitly states that although social service is important, it is absurd for a
> woman who cannot raise her child and respect her husband and the elderly
> (at home) to participate in social activities. Women's exemption from social
> service due to domestic duties illustrates the extent to which women are
> marginalized in the community of male citizens. (Moon, 51)

Surprisingly, the huge numbers of women entering factory work did not
affect such notions. Because young women workers were only seen as filling in time until they got married, when, like Mi-yang, they would quit
work, women's contribution to the national economy failed to disrupt traditional narratives of femininity and their position in the domestic sphere.
While earning only about half the salary of men in equivalent jobs, women
factory workers were often saving for their dowry or paying for the education of their brothers. Seung-kyung Kim describes how the state's need
for quiescent workers and cheaper exports dovetailed nicely with traditional Confucianist roles for women as dutiful and altruistic (8). This fit
also managed the decidedly untraditional movement of unmarried daughters out of the home.

The factory dormitory (the Singaporean version of which appears in
Lim's *Rice Bowl*), commonly attached to large factories, was the architectural solution to the problem of unmarried women working outside the
home. It offered minimal space—typically, a shared sleeping room for six
to eight people, with space only to roll out a sleeping mat at night—and
subsidized rent and meals. Women's activities were strictly supervised:
"The dormitory, in effect, extended family control to the factory environment" (Seung-kyung Kim, 26).[18] Surveillance on behalf of absent parents effectively preserves the fundamental idea—valid across all classes—
that women do not belong in public spaces of work and production. The
postcolonial developing state, built on cheap manufacturing labor, relies
heavily on both youthful female labor and the kinship systems that keep
their working careers short and interest in labor conditions minimal.
Under the banner of "collective life" and "Korean values," the state utilizes

both underpaid female factory labor and the unpaid labor of women in the home as child rearers and carers. Even for middle-class women like the Yi girls, receiving a more or less equal education can thus only lead to better marriage opportunities, and then "confine[ment] to the home as housewives" (Jayawardena, 15).[19] In "A Room in the Woods," the girls' father is the domestic representative of the modernizing state. In one of his many tirades against So-yang's behavior, the self-made industrialist reminds his daughters that a college education for women is simply the application of economic competition to the domestic sphere: "Why do you think I sent you kids to college? It's so you'll have a better marriage than others, a better job than others" (91) ("namdul poda dŏ choŭn de sijip kago namdul poda dŏ choŭn chikjang ŏtge"; "Supsok," 77). In this formula, it is not clear whether the two clauses "a better . . . a better . . . " are alternatives or simply paraphrases of each other. That a woman's job remains unquestionably that of mother and wife clashes with the reality of this period's unprecedented female access to industrial and educational spaces. The result is a spatial stammering over where to situate the female subject.

Over and again, Mi-yang finds evidence of So-yang's irreducible place-lessness in the world. Her diary (the objectless interior par excellence) is the only place where So-yang seems to truly reside, though it speaks incessantly of So-yang's spatial dislocation: *"This room of mine isn't a room. I need a room that will make this little bleeding sheep sleep, that will ease the heart of this startled deer, that will caress the steel-blue blade of this dagger"* (100). So-yang's suicide is foregrounded not only in the image of the "bleeding sheep" and "dagger" (she later slashes her wrists), but also in terms of lack of space. In one of Mi-yang's attempts to question So-yang directly, their conversation hinges on this problem of occupying space—both internal and external:

"Where have you been hiding these days?" I tried to sound as nonchalant as possible.

"I feel like I'm suffocating when I'm home. So I try to find myself outside." She didn't appear to suspect anything.

"Aren't people supposed to look inside to find themselves?"

"You sound just like Confucius." (84)

In her reference to Confucius, So-yang shows her disdain for traditional patriarchal thought at the same time she deliberately confuses "inside" and "outside" as psychological and spatial categories. Kang's text precisely maps out the complexities of psychological interiority—women's subjective constitution in industrial modernity—through descriptions of architectural interiority. The space of the interior can thus be contrasted with the space of the individual. Where the latter is, following Adorno and Benjamin, the sustaining alibi the modern subject adopts toward consolidating self-ownership, the postcolonial woman's interior is a psychic space that cannot find a direct spatial correlative.

In the final scene after Mi-yang discovers her sister's suicide, the dead girl's diary again speaks of the inability to properly occupy space:

> *A world in which people fight for the sake of business is alien to me, a scene in a bell jar.*
> *The glittering slogans are for someone else.*
> *I'm an island, an island that traps me and touches nowhere.* (146)

In this last line, So-yang figures herself as both an island and trapped by the island ("nanŭn sŏmiya ŏdiwado tachi annŭn hamjŏng kaťŭn sŏmiya" ["Supsok," 184]), invoking a completely sealed-off interiority that has no corresponding exterior. The unstable positioning of woman—neither wholly in public nor private, traditional nor modern space—results in her textual construction as trace. So-yang's "truth" is the missing object both for her own consciousness and for the narrator.

"A Room in the Woods" not only critiques gendered hierarchy in relation to labor practices and physical and psychological space. As mentioned above, its background is the 1980s student-led democracy movement, and it is into this emerging civic space that So-yang ventures when she leaves her room. The two main physical settings of "A Room in the Woods" are, in fact, the family house—unspecifically located somewhere in Seoul—and the streets of Chongno, an actual downtown district and Mecca for college activists, students repeating college entrance exams, and other disaffected youth. Its bars, discos, coffee shops, and crowded streets function as spaces of freedom and desire outside the regulatory codes of home, school, military, or work. In this sense, Chongno is a kind of heterotopia—

those other, but localizable spaces of utopia described by Foucault—outside the regimented ordering of military-ruled Korea. Like other young people, the Yi girls go there day or night to drink, smoke cigarettes (highly proscribed for Korean women), and meet strangers. Mi-yang, attempting to learn more by following So-yang's footsteps, takes her other sister, Hye-yang, to the Chongno bar So-yang frequents. They survey a typical scene:

> Sitting in front of a watch shop, on the steps of a building that had closed for the evening, or at the entrance to a beer hall, or eating hot dogs on the sidewalk, or going here and there in groups—the young people commanded the streets in this area. They were a mass unto themselves, an extraterritorial enclave that rejected the establishment.
>
> Two busloads of riot police had been posted at the entrance to a side street, but no one paid any attention to them. Not far away a group of people stood in a circle shouting their high school song. (Kang, 92)

Chongno is the very site of confrontation between the establishment and democracy movements and therefore is "the forest of youth; . . . at the same time it is a maze, it is the outlet for youth's radiating excitement" (Kwŏn T'aek-yŏng, 593, my translation). After making their way through the crowds, Mi-yang and Hye-yang drink beer at the "Something" bar and meet a group of college boys. Despite the apparent freedom of this counterculture, described by one youth as "a mess, but . . . also a lifeline" (97), So-yang is unable to find a place here either. Her friend, Kyŏng-ok, when interviewed by Mi-yang, reveals that So-yang had at first joined in the student demonstration movement but then quit: "After that she felt mixed up whenever there was a demonstration" (71). In another interview session, So-yang's boyfriend Hŭi-jung demonstrates the inconsistencies of the radical student movement. Hŭi-jung, a student activist waging battle with the riot police in the name of democracy, cannot countenance So-yang's acting "like a feminist." Mi-yang summarizes Hŭi-jung's account: "So-yang was acting like a feminist [yŏgwŏnjuŭija] but this was Korea with its Confucian society. These days women were making a big fuss over women's liberation and blaming men as if they were their enemies, but the union of men and women was the beginning and end of everything. Such was Hŭi-jung's pet theory" (115). Alienated by the narrow focus of the democracy movement, So-yang is similarly unable to join the labor movement, which at this period was tightly allied with the student movement. Seung-kyung Kim has noted that by the mid-1980s, some 3,000 politically active college students were working as disguised factory workers, an illegal activity that could bring both imprisonment and torture (132–35). Yet, "[d]espite their daily experiences with discrimination based on gender, women student activists saw gender issues as of secondary importance compared to class. . . . women who did bring up gender problems were generally dismissed by male students as not taking class issues seriously enough" (Kim, 141).

Mi-yang interviews Myŏng-ju, a caricature of the enlightened student activist who poses as a worker in order to "educat[e] the oppressed classes in the contradictions of the social system" (59). When they meet at a Western-style restaurant, Myŏng-ju performs both her political and national consciousness with the critical remark, "You know, it feels funny using a knife [and not chopsticks] like a bourgeois in a place like this" (59). Unlike Myŏng-ju's easy condemnation of what is bourgeois and Western, So-yang's acute awareness of gender oppression prevents her from following the student activist path. Instead, she attempts to move beyond her privileged class position by taking jobs that precisely involve both gender and class subordination: a waitress in a coffee shop and a hostess (prostitute) in a bar. In her diary, Mi-yang discovers an account of So-yang's one and only night working at the hostess bar: *"In any event, it's terrible that women can become objects, dehumanized things, through sex. A creep put his hands inside my blouse to give me a tip. I took out the money right there and ripped it up"* (68). Near the end of the story, moreover, through a deal brokered by the very college students Mi-yang has befriended at Chongno, So-yang is about to prostitute herself to an older businessman. Despite all the freedoms and challenges presented by the student democracy movement, an unaccompanied woman on the streets still only signifies as a prostitute, recalling Rendell's observation: "in patriarchal relations of exchange, men move through space as subjects of exchange; whereas women are moved through space between men as sexual commodities— as objects of exchange" ("Ramblers and Cyprians," 143). Like the home space, then, Chongno fails to provide So-yang with an occupiable place. Her inability to find herself either on the inside or the outside, in the domestic or in the public sphere, is a result of overlapping political and economic contradictions: the patriarchal state requires only women's cheap factory or maternal labor, while the nation's counterculture does not question its own participation in gender oppression.

Beyond confirming social and political conditions with textual evidence, we need to analyze further how the text apprehends and reworks these psychological, material, and ideological conditions. As Spivak writes, "the discourse of the literary text is part of a general configuration of textuality, a placing forth of the solution as the unavailability of a unified solution to a unified or homogeneous, generating or receiving, consciousness" (*In Other Worlds,* 78). The "unavailability of a unified solution"—here, the figuring of a particular feminism—is precisely what is given forth in "A Room in the Woods." Less concerned with thematically representing women's struggles of the day (although these are not absent), Kang's novella problematizes the very subject position of women. Nelly Richard's distinction between literature by women and feminine writing is relevant here. The former is concerned with "a representational conception of literature, according to which the text is called on to express realistically the experiential content of certain life situations, thereby portraying the 'authenticity' of the female condition" (19). Feminine writing, in contrast, points to the more fundamental role that writing plays in the construction—and not just representation—of femininity, that is, the very production of woman in the "linguistic–symbolic remodelling of writing" (20). In "A Room in the Woods," So-yang's "experiential content" is precisely not represented: her subject position is literally unavailable. Rather, the text's production of her in absentia foregrounds the conflicted "linguistic–symbolic remodelling" of woman around the threshold of private–public space. As So-yang's diary indicates, she refuses both the limited individualism offered by patriarchal, bourgeoisie society (the domestic role/spaces of the individual consumer) and the democracy movement (the masculinist labor movement and libidinized spaces of Chongno). So-yang's dilemma is that in rejecting the coordinates that patriarchy and capitalist forces ascribe to her, her interiority can only reveal itself in the spacelessness of the diary, or in death.

In the context of the New Asian City, a new nationalized regime of production recalibrates the symbolic and spatial system that traditionally marked off feminine from masculine. The (failed) search for So-yang's interiority and her "exquisite psyche" leads Mi-yang outward to pursue her traces in her friends, hobbies, school life, and streets of Chongno. The search for feminine psychic interiority and the text's incessant circling around architectural interiors leads us, finally, to the recognition of its absence. Formally, the surface tension of these competing logics of power is expressed through the operation of detecting. If woman cannot be self-evidently present, only the traces and tracks of her existence—traversing traditional patriarchy, exploitative industrialization, the democracy strug-gle, and countercultural movements—indicate her location. The end of the story, however, renders the work of detecting (and reading) void. We are led nowhere except back to So-yang's cave/castle/island room and her dead body. Woman's lack of space, her objectless interior, block the reso-lution of plot promised by the detective tale and by Mi-yang's desire to help her sister. And it is precisely in its failure that we understand the real work of the text.

Femininity and the Problem of Location

We can understand the remaining two texts under discussion as deal-ing with the domestic sphere's lack of the feminine in related ways. In Su Weizhen's (Su Wei-chen's) 1988 story "Missing," ordinary Taipei business-man and husband Chu Yongjian wakes up one morning to find his wife, Shuangwen, missing. As with "A Room in the Woods," the story cedes plot for the procedure of detection as Yongjian attempts to understand his wife's sudden absence by examining her room, desk, office space, and address book, by interviewing family and friends, and by retracing her youth in Tainan. In contrast, Su-chen Christine Lim's *Rice Bowl* (1984) presents a panoramic view of developing Singapore in an effort to place the feminine in a series of spaces that she can never occupy. Despite these differing narrative structures, Wu's and Lim's texts share (with Kang's) the disjunction of women and domestic space that demands a three-dimen-sional reading: spaces are at once figural and literal, symbolic and material. For Yongjian, his wife's disappearance leaves him nothing but her spaces to ponder—spaces, however, that refuse to yield any sort of trace or clue. In *Rice Bowl,* women appear to be active in the public arenas of university and work, yet are inexorably reinscribed back into domestic spaces and plots. These two texts again delineate how the material translation of older tial arrangements with and against a modernizing public sphere conditions the emergence of local feminisms.

Su Weizhen's "Missing" follows on the heels of an earlier generation of Taiwanese women writers who explored women's struggles without necessarily arriving at a recognizably Western feminist position. As Ying-ying Chien recounts, earlier women's fiction such as Yuan Ch'iung-ch'iung's "A Sky of One's Own" ("Ziji de tiankong"), clearly influenced by Virginia Woolf, shows "partial feminist consciousness," where "feminist" stands for "Western feminist." Typically, in those stories, female protagonists achieve some level of autonomy, such as financial independence after divorce, but remain dependent on and defined by the patriarchal system (632). Yang Chao adds that "the rising female novelists were once derided . . . because of their treatment of basic domestic issues and details of love affairs, which appear to male readers as womanishly fussy" (107), earning such work the moniker of "boudoir literature." In contrast, the generation of 1980s writers engaged more specifically with the themes of Western feminism. "Travel and contact with Western feminism appear to have affected the political consciousness or 'vision' of the women writers of [this] group" (Chien, 631), a vision exemplified by Li Ang's 1982 novel *The Butcher's Wife (Shafu),* in which a traditional peasant woman retaliates against her husband's brutality by murdering him. My choice in writing about Su Weizhen is again less determined by the presence of recognizably feminist issues such as financial autonomy, abuse, polygamy, or prostitution, and more by the formal and symbolic construction of woman within the material spaces of this particular social context—precisely a literal and symbolic focus on the boudoir. Note that like both Huang Chunming and Hou Hsiao-hsien (to be discussed in chapter 6), we should not consider Su the voice of native Taiwanese resistance: she is part of the "group of second-generation [mainland] writers who had grown up in military dependents' compounds" (Chi, 19). Further, the text's material and subjective negotiations with public and private space prevent a simplistic reading of cultural "resistance" as well as a "too quickly shared feminist notion of accessibility" (Spivak, "Politics of Translation," 407). We read Su's work not for an essential Taiwanese-ness, but for what her figuring of Taiwanese space reveals.

In "Missing," after Shuangwen's disappearance, her "typical civilized" husband (101), Yongjian, has trouble telling whether the room his wife occupied reveals any clues about her or not:

> The room was clean as always. There was a very thin layer of dust on the desk by the window. Pens were in the penholder, the plants had been watered, and the ash tray was clean. These were all the clues there were. It gave the impression of someone carefully preparing for her final departure, with everything meticulously arranged. But again Shuangwen was tidy in her habits, so maybe it was just in character for her to have everything neat and tidy? (93)[20]

Echoing Mi-yang's frustrated search for So-yang's traces, Yongjian fails to find any definite evidence of his wife's motive for leaving—or, indeed, even of her former presence. We switch here, of course, to the traditionally male figure of the detective and also to the more conventional temporality of a crime or event that precedes the story's opening (rather than concluding it, as with "A Room in the Woods"). Yongjian's more conventional role, however, does not make him any more capable a detective. He decides to visit Tainan, the southern city and premodern capital of Taiwan, where Shuangwen lived and attended university for six years. There, she rented a room from a family and tutored their son. Yongjian diligently studies the room in which she lived:

> Her room was occupied by a new lodger, and the door was unlocked; Chu Yongjian pushed the door open and stood at the threshold for some time. The room had been repainted. It was blue when Shuangwen lived there, and grey was her favourite colour. Now the room was painted white. The rent had gone up several times. The Chens' youngest son was at university and no longer needed a tutor. (94)

Despite not having "the faintest idea how she lived and studied" (95) in Tainan, Yongjian nevertheless decides "this could be a lead" (95) and believes he "felt her presence strongly, as if this was an old path and she might return to it yet" (95). Yet the room has, in fact, offered no information regarding his wife. Yongjian notes it had been blue, but this was no reflection of his wife's personality, as she had preferred gray. As the story progresses, the reader comes to understand that there are simply no leads to his wife's mysterious disappearance: Shuangwen's dwelling spaces yield nothing about the interiority of the woman. As in "A Room in the Woods," the narrative progression of the search, rather than leading toward a resolution, remains in a holding pattern around the woman's spaces. Similarly, the expectation of a feminism arising in tandem with industrialized society is suspended at the threshold of the new Western-style domestic space. The question of a local feminism is thus transposed to the question of whether women can enter and occupy these new spaces or not.

Returning to their modern Taipei apartment after a weekend of false leads in Tainan—"he followed every twist and turn, and it seemed to have taken him through the six years" (97)—Yongjian finds this space equally unforthcoming with information, and himself no closer to an explanation: "What reason had Shuangwen for doing this? They had a home, a house which would be paid up in a few years' time, jobs with good prospects, and although they did not have children, their home was as near to perfection as it could be" (100). Indeed, the Taipei apartment seems to have completely satisfied Shuangwen:

> He threw open the French windows, and the prosperity of Taipei was right there before his eyes. Their apartment was at the heart of downtown Taipei. They had spent all they could when they decided to buy it, mainly because living here would forestall any need for changing apartments in the future. The building was conveniently located for everything: schools for kids, places of work and shopping centres. The best thing was that it was quiet despite its convenient location. Shuangwen very much enjoyed leaning on the railing watching bustling Taipei. (106)

The apartment here is figured as something of a blank space in the center of the city: strangely quiet despite its downtown location, it bears no private or domestic content of its own, but functions merely as the viewing point from where "Shuangwen very much enjoyed . . . watching bustling Taipei." Like Shuangwen herself, it is an isolated space with no organic relationship to the objects around it. We can briefly recall that, in contrast, established Chinese notions of domestic space emphasize the interconnectedness of extended family over individuality. Although space was not strictly segregated according to gender, as in Korea, Chinese domestic space was similarly not organized around individual privacy; the central common room of the house *(tangwu, zhengwu,* or *gongting)* functioned as the symbolic link to extended family members and their patrilineal past (Knapp, 43): "The individual is essentially disregarded in the layout of a Chinese dwelling. Space is defined in terms of family rather than personal needs" (Knapp, 36). [21] In moving away from the extended family structure and anchoring space of the *tangwu,* it appears that the Taipei apartment offers no other way to accommodate femininity.

We sense that, spatially, there is something stubbornly disjunctive about Shuangwen's life. Her successful career in a news agency and her professed wish never to have children are at odds with the apartment's deliberate location near schools and shops, the usual locations of the housewife. Her husband admits to his wife's confusion over her public and private roles:

> Shuangwen could not distinguish between her roles as a housewife and as a junior section-head in her office.... She thought that one ought to be good at every role one took up. During the weekend or on holidays, she would don working clothes and go through the routines of scrubbing, washing and shopping. When it was done, she would sit at the desk, with her face in her hands, her back the very image of a woman fixated by housework. (101)

This description puzzles the reader by its figure of the housewife sitting at a desk, head in hands, and, the narrator adds, listening to Mozart. Rather than "the very image of a woman fixated by housework," it is the image of a private individual, alone with her thoughts at a place of intellectual work and contemplation (the desk). If Shuangwen is ill at ease as a working woman doing home duties, she is equally uneasy being a working woman with a family. Yongjian's examination of her office space also suggests an inability to reconcile public with domestic roles: "Things were neatly laid out in the drawers: stationery, index cards, books. There was nothing superfluous. There was none of the habitual photographic display of husband, children, family and pets most working women go in for. The impeccably neat drawers sent a chill down his spine" (103). Shuangwen's life at both private and public ends is thus strangely emptied out of content. Again, we need to understand this apparent vacuum as the textual solution to the "unavailability of a unified solution" with regard to Taiwan's specific social and political context.

While the 1980s saw greater numbers of women in the Taiwanese workforce than ever, especially in white-collar jobs, again we cannot assume the trajectory of Western feminism. As with Korea's and Singapore's industrialization, women supplied crucial cheap labor for Taiwan's burgeoning national economy. Uniquely, however, the international subcontracting system resulted here in the proliferation of small family-owned factories, where women's labor was less distinguished from women's traditional role as unpaid domestic workers. Because of their flexibility and willingness to work for little or no wages, women became extremely valuable to the family:

> They [Taiwanese manufacturers] are efficient and flexible. . . . To accomplish this, however, manufacturers need to have the cooperation of a workforce willing to work cheaply around the production cycle, that is, working overtime for days or even weeks to meet deadlines and taking unpaid time off when the market is slow. Who could be more likely to satisfy these needs than a manufacturer's own family? (Anru Lee, 108)

In these circumstances, women's participation in the workforce did not produce calls for equality with men's wages, rights, and legal protection, but actually renewed traditional gender hierarchies. As in many traditional societies, sons—the future heirs—run the family businesses, and daughters—who will be married out—work in them.

Moreover, in terms of gender ideology, Taiwanese feminism does not simply operate around the semantic binary between men and women, as it does in the West. Hwei-Syin Lu explains how, rather than the biological distinction between genders, Chinese feminist thought has considered woman's position within a network of relationships: *woman* is not a "unitary category" but is defined primarily in her kinship roles as mother, daughter, wife, sister, or in-law (225). Taiwan's mainstream woman's groups of the 1980s, Lu contends, focused less on opposition to patriarchy and more on better situating themselves within kinship networks.[22] In this sense, Shuangwen's apparent Western-style individuality as childless career woman diverges from these paths of Taiwanese feminism. Yet in defining

herself outside the traditional roles of kinship-organized femininity, Shuangwen simply disappears. Her blanked-out subjectivity finds expression
in the detached city apartment, her tidy bedroom, and her sterile office
space. "Missing" narrates how these modern, private spaces are not, on
their own, enough to sustain the newly individualized subjectivity that
they seem to promise. Shuangwen attempts to be both career woman and
housewife—a modern, individualized citizen and traditionally defined
wife—but fills neither role convincingly.

The only clue Yongjian eventually finds is an office file labeled "The
Chen Qiaogao Case," detailing the case of an elderly radio broadcaster
who also went missing without a trace. As with Shuangwen's disappearance, the man had simply vanished one day: "Chen Qiaogao was missing.
All the data were there, except the conclusion. It was clear that Shuangwen's interest was focused on the process of his disappearance" (104).
Yongjian visits Chen's family to interview them, only to discover they have
given up searching for the old man, who, they conclude, "must have his
own reason" (111). "Missing," like the "Chen Qiaogao Case," lacks a conclusion and focuses only on the "process of disappearance." Yet the woman,
it seems, has been missing all along, unable to fully occupy space either
at home or at work. The peculiar detective's trail of "Missing" is thus
woven around a completely black hole, an unoccupied and unoccupiable
female space.

In contrast to the previous two texts, Su-chen Christine Lim's novel
Rice Bowl seems to offer a female protagonist who is refreshingly present.
Revolving around the charismatic Marie-Therese Wang (or "Sis"), a young
Catholic novice and university student, the story is set in Singapore of the
late 1960s to early 1970s and deals with a group of student activists attend-
ing Temasek University (presumably Singapore National University) and
their involvement with workers at Jurong Industrial Estate. *Rice Bowl*,
Lim's first and most interesting novel, attempts to depict both the specificity of women's lives as well as the larger social whole of Singapore in the
early years of independence, from the slums of Chinatown to the brand
new estate towns and factories. The central metaphor of the novel is the
rice bowl, indicating satisfaction with a full stomach and material wealth,
whereby "individuals hesitate to break the existing order which guaran-
tees prosperity for the members of that larger family, the all-providing

patriarchal state" (Koh, "Self, Family," 280–81). Marie's youth and idealism are pitted against a city run by "the diligence of workers who day after day push the grains of white rice into their mouths busily manipulating chopsticks or fingers with no other thought in their head except that the rice bowls be full and the rice grains fluffy" (Lim, 250–51). The primary antinomy of values—rice bowl materialism versus political idealism—is fleshed out in the conflicts between different sections of Singaporean society. While the English-educated (Ang Mo) Chinese students take center stage, their faith in activism and progress is contrasted with Paul Tan, Marie's former boyfriend and a People's Action Party bureaucrat who believes exclusively in state-directed, rational progress. Other groups include the Chinese-educated students from Yuan Tung and Nan Hai Universities—young men "more serious than those from Bukit Temasek who were only good at recounting soccer games" (242)—and, at the extreme end of the political spectrum, Mak, a hard-line communist and Mandarin speaker who constantly speaks in Maoist clichés. There is also a diverse cast of Catholic nuns—English, Irish, Malay, and Tamil—as well as the expat lecturer, Dr. Jones; the American missionaries Reverend James and Hans (Marie's love interest); and the migrant female factory laborers, Pai Tan and Ah Huat, who join the Student Worker Alliance. Providing an overview of the fractured nature of Singaporean society, this ambitious novel explores an array of issues including the privilege of the English-educated Chinese, Singapore's role in the Vietnam War, the plight of migrants from Malaysia, the politics of Mandarin versus other Chinese dialects, the controversy over foreigners and missionaries, multinational operations in Singapore, and—not least—the changing city as it succumbs to rationalized, developmentalist planning logic.

In considering *Rice Bowl* alongside two other contemporary Singapore novels in English by women—*The Serpent's Tooth* (1982) by Catherine Lim and *The Scholar and the Dragon* (1986) by Stella Kon—Ruth Morse has categorized them as "novels of national identity" ("Case," 131). All three "offer the solid and seductive outlines of binary polarities: materialism vs. spiritual value, ethnocentricity vs. multiculturalism . . . , conservatism vs. progress, or authoritarianism vs. participatory democracy, or traditional family structures vs. individualism" (135). For Morse, these novels ask what it means to be Singaporean by fictionalizing "the same kinds of issues raised by the newspapers and magazines of the area, the educational establishments, and no doubt the papers of government policymakers" (142). Although for Morse the too-obvious thematization of such issues marks these novels' aesthetic failures, Koh Tai Ann commends their ability to "interpret or see their [the reading public's] society in terms of the important concerns and values of the time" ("Self, Family," 277), especially as they relate to the position of women. In her survey of six major Singaporean novels since 1972, Koh finds the experience of "Chinese family and filial piety" (280) in the context of modernizing Singapore to be a deep and recurring concern. Considering Prime Minister Lee Kuan Yew's frequent exhortations about traditional "Asian families"—where presumably this means traditional Asian women—it is no surprise that in addition to the other issues it raises, *Rice Bowl* is deeply concerned with new forms of family, women's labor, and feminine subjectivity.

In terms of the treatment of space, what distinguishes this novel is the presence of the convent: rather than figuring woman between the binary of domestic space and public arenas of the city, *Rice Bowl* opens with Marie as the adored high school teacher within the all-female confines of the convent. Indeed, we never see her at home, and her family barely plays any role; Morse rightly observes that there is an odd "suppression of Marie's father's role ("Novels," 69). While the convent extends the basic categories of spatial analysis we have been using to a tripartite system—public, private, and religious—it is also a way for the public (and sexualized) emergence of Marie from a controlled, feminine space to be presented even more dramatically and contentiously.[23] Two other characters, meanwhile, provide us with accounts of feminized domestic space in more familiar terms. The first is the tragic case of Ser Mei, a student at the convent who ends up part of Marie's group at the university. Quiet and reserved, Ser Mei is the only character after whom one of the four sections of the novel is named; they are "Convent," "Ser Mei," "University," and "Jurong," with the other three obviously denoting locations. The naming system is consistent if we understand "Ser Mei" to denote domestic–familial space, thereby completing the standard list of major social institutions: religion, family, education, and work. Ser Mei's home life, however, is far from typical. Her mother, we discover, is a prostitute who receives clients at her home in the upscale, formerly British neighborhood of Mountbatten Park to support her daughter. Despite her daughter's exclusive education—and rather implausibly—the mother recruits Ser Mei into the business for the one-time purpose of selling her virginity to an elderly Cantonese customer. Ser Mei reluctantly agrees, providing the first scene in which interior domestic space is described in detail: "The air-conditioner in the room hummed softly. The bedroom was hushed, cool and new. Thick maroon velvet curtains blocked out the street lights and muffled all sounds coming from the outside" (90). Recalling descriptions from "A Room in the Woods," the private bedroom is a world unto itself, cut off from the outside and literally imprisoning Ser Mei as she is tied to the bed and repeatedly penetrated, since the client "would get his money's worth" (94). In true melodramatic style, the old man collapses from a heart attack during the encounter, sending Ser Mei "running toward the new blocks of flats as heedlessly as the cars whizzing past her in the night" (96). We later learn she commits suicide by jumping from one of the recently constructed high-rise blocks. While certainly sensationalist and melodramatic, what is noticeable is the extreme negativity of modern private space: the seclusion of the private interior and the height of the new housing blocks seem to conspire in the young woman's death.

Contrasted with the sinister British-style home, the Chinatown scene immediately following the rape and suicide offers no more salutary a version of interior space. After hearing of her death, Marie's group gathers at a death house, a cramped loft space in the thick of Chinatown's gritty hawker neighborhood that houses both corpses and the almost dead. Its location on Kwan Koong Road is decidedly not the well-known Chinatown commercial area with "the bight lights, and the hustle and bustle of shoppers and diners" (97). Rather, it is the stubbornly unmodern space of Singapore's back rooms and used-up people, where "old men and women sat on the verandahs among abandoned boxes and cartons, fanning away the evening heat with palm leaf fans" (97). Because of Ser Mei's suicide, her family refuses to follow the traditional Chinese funeral rites, leaving the burial business to outsiders who won't be tainted by her bad luck. The coffin sits among those who are waiting for death:

> Along the walls in the semi-darkness were rows of beds upon which lay the
> shadows of the dying—old men and women—wheezing out the breath of

slow decay in the twilight world of Chinatown's death houses. Yean and Marie watched spellbound as an emaciated old man struggled to sit up. He got up, coughing a dry racking cough, cleared his throat loudly and spat into the spittoon by his bed. . . .

Yean turned away and studied the black coffin squatting in the centre of this room where the dead and the dying met. (98)

At the most obvious level, Ser Mei's life is a tragic parable about the ills of social climbing—her mother's funding of an upper-middle-class life with prostitution. Yet on another, it indicates the threshold status of woman in Singapore's postcolonial context. Ser Mei's and her mother's existence at home in the Western-style domestic spaces of Mountbatten is predicated on sexual subordination, while in traditional Chinatown, her body only finds a place in the cramped, leftover corners of the death house.

The novel's only other depiction of private space is of the comfortably upper class. Siew Yean, another of Marie's group, is from a well-to-do business family yet detests her luxurious life under the rule of her tyrant father, who openly takes mistresses and dictates every movement of the family (232–33). Her bedroom is portrayed as something between a refuge and a cell:

Yean retreated into the seclusion of her bedroom, closed the door and windows, drew the curtains and switched on the air-conditioner. Its comforting hum flooded the room as she lay stretched on her bed with head resting on the back of her hands; one lone lanky body. And she clung all the more to this sense of an aloneness which for the time being would have to be her sole protection against the discordant voices of aunties, uncles, parents and anyone with any familial link to her pouring their unwanted filth into her ears. (230–31)

For Yean, university and the political activism of Marie's group are a welcome antidote to the patriarchy and superstitions of home life: "She was determined not to be drawn into her parent's sordid affairs with female foxes, mediums and deities! With great agility Yean's mind fled home and family into the university where rationality claimed existence" (205). In this case, the precious aloneness of the bedroom allows her an escape to the public sphere's comforting rationality. Morse comments that *Rice Bowl,* obsessed with the theme of education, is ultimately didactic in purpose with an echo of the moralism of Confucian literature ("Case," 142). Yet the more relevant explanation for this tone may be less traditional Confucian values than the prominent, public debate over woman's appropriate level of education and consequently her appropriate location, which surfaced in the early 1980s.

After a successful 1970s government campaign encouraging women to enter the workforce and two decades of universal educational rights, Singapore's leaders soon faced the problem of how to ensure women did not forget their primary role as mothers and wives. Shored up by government-promoted values like "nation before community" and "family as a basic unit of society," Lee Kuan Yew explicitly spelled out the limits of gender equality in a newspaper article from 1983: "Equal opportunities, yes, but we shouldn't get women into jobs where they cannot, at the same time, be mothers. . . . You just can't be doing a full-time job heavy job [*sic*] like a doctor or engineer and run a home and bring up children" (Lee qtd. in Jasmine Chan, 51). In the same year, this evolved into what became known as the Great Marriage Debate, which followed the government's controversial new policies around maternity. Alarmed by low birthrates of university-educated women and higher rates for working-class women—and influenced by the theory of inherited intelligence from the mother—Prime Minister Lee tried to encourage "graduate mothers" to reproduce at higher rates. Otherwise, he feared "the quality of Singapore's population would measurably decline, with a tiny majority of intelligent persons being increasingly swamped by a seething, proliferating mass of the unintelligent, untalented, and genetically inferior" (Heng and Devan, 345). Heng and Devan rightly analyze Lee's anxiety as equally to do with race and class: the majority of those less educated were women of the Malay and Indian minorities, sparking in Lee and his ministers a fear of the Chinese eventually being outnumbered. Government policy went so far as to offer a payment of S$10,000 to working-class women to "volunteer" for a tubal ligation, while giving graduate mothers tax incentives and priority places at schools (Heng and Devan, 347–48). At the base of these astonishing policies, as Heng and Devan note, was the attempt to control a femininity that had—through the socialist policies of the early PAP days—been allowed to venture too far into the public realm. Along with the reintroduction of Confucianism and Mandarin classes into school curricula as ways to rebuild Asian values, these policies point not to an essential or traditional "Chineseness" but to "the efficient management of local capitalism" (Heng and Devan, 356). The management occurs, of course, through the attempted control of woman as productive in the private rather than public sphere.

Given that these debates were raging the year before *Rice Bowl* was published, we might assume Lim's negative portrayal of families, motherhood, and domestic spaces are rejoinders to such state fatherhood. Yet the novel, ultimately, does not argue for the emergence of its female protagonists into the public arena or question the definition of patriotic mothers and wives. This is even more surprising considering that the plot hinges on the Student Worker Alliance at Jurong Industrial Estate, where Marie's group is determined to improve conditions for its immigrant women workers employed by a U.S. company. The first scene of the section "Jurong" has Marie surveying the desolate landscape of the new town and its assault on her sensibility; it seems that Jurong is something to be resisted and opposed in both human and natural terms, and that Marie's energy and idealism will be employed to such an end:

> Marie shut her eyes; its newness was painful to see. Its mantle of green had been stripped off leaving the raw wound of red brown laterite. The land had been dug up, churned over and bulldozed so that piles of earth rose like painful boils all along the sides of the road, stretching inland as far as the new blocks of twenty-storey flats—the only landmark for miles around. (156)

Yet it is merely Marie's aesthetic sensitivity that is offended by Jurong, and we begin to suspect—against the grain of the novel's own presentation of its protagonist—that she is not quite the committed political activist and student leader she seems to be. Although Marie's group and the workers eventually form an alliance, the plot undermines any value to their solidarity. Indeed, the tough, brash women factory workers employed there are initially suspicious of the group of English-speaking, Christian activists: "Talk to us for what?" asks one of the workers when the group arrives. "We are all Buddhists, not Christian. Not interested" (161).[24] In a climactic scene near the end of the novel, a demonstration at the U.S. embassy is organized to demand better working conditions and to protest the Vietnam War. All goes horribly wrong, however, when Mak, the hard-line activist, loses control, strips naked, and turns the peaceful demonstration into an ugly farce, effectively destroying the coalition. The message appears to be that politics is pointless, vulgar, and misguided.

What is most perplexing about *Rice Bowl* is thus its duplicity. While engaging substantially with many social, political, and gendered issues of early independent Singapore through the main character of Marie, it ultimately eschews all the ideas of feminist or class action that it has spent several hundred pages describing. By the end of the novel, Ser Mei's death is all but forgotten, Yean is to be shipped off to California at her father's order, the Jurong workers Pei Lan and Ah Huat are deported back to Malaysia for their participation in the demonstration, and—as the novel's real climax—Marie leaves the convent to joyously marry Hans and follow him back to a life in America. She leaves unresolved her passionate critiques of Singaporean modernity and simply muses, "At least America would be a freer society. There she could follow her conscience and her will" (257). As Koh notes, "at the end, contrary to the earlier impressions given, Marie Wang's acts of political protest are also exposed by the author as hypocritical pretensions" ("Self, Family," 285). Reading the novel at face value, we can only conclude that *Rice Bowl* is a deeply reactionary and antifeminist text. Morse concurs: "[Marie's] choice of the private over the even moderately public life of the teacher is once again a rejection of political engagement for concern for a more limited sphere" ("Case," 141).

An alternative reading, however, of the novel's disavowal of action links it to the two texts discussed above. Although Marie is not literally absent from narrative space, as are So-yang and Shuangwen, neither is she simply present. She is, rather, emphatically produced by a "conflicted linguistic–symbolic remodelling of writing," to reuse Richard's term. She occupies the novel's center of gravity because she is the object of desire and admiration within a number of recognizable social and literary discourses of femininity. To her fellow students, she is the charismatic, sensitive group leader and teacher; to Paul, Mak, and Hans, she is a love interest; and to the senior figures in the novel, she is a young and attractive idealist. The disappointing end of the novel indicates less an authorial reactionism than the way that Marie all along has been constituted solely by these different discursive forms—teacher, novice, leader, potential lover—while her own interiority has been troublingly absent. The conclusion of the novel appears to make up for her prior lack of private interiority by endowing her with an exclusively privatized identity as Hans's wife. More importantly, the very confusion of the novel's genre stages a familiar uneasiness over femininity's appropriate location. *Rice Bowl* is a text torn in two generic directions: between a novel that attempts to "represent realistically to a growing, self-aware reading public the lives of individuals" and their values (Koh, "Self, Family," 277) on the one hand, and on the other, a romance novel or literature of the boudoir, structured by a love plot and ending in marriage. Its textual indecision—and strangeness—is produced by these two genres rubbing up against each other: the novel suddenly moves, for example, from a pointed critique of developmentalist logic and the way it particularly affects women, to a cloying description of Marie and Hans's kiss that comes straight from the pages of a Mills & Boon pulp romance. Similar problems around the literary production of the New Asian City woman thus inform *Rice Bowl* as they do "A Room in the Woods" and "Missing," but at the level of genre: it does not succeed in moving to the public realm proper, nor is it content to remain within the confines of the romance novel. Its troubled descriptions of women occupying private spaces are thus analogous to the novel's difficulty situating itself. Both in content and form, *Rice Bowl* remains stuck at the threshold between the public world of work and politics and woman's private domain.

Concluding the novel with Marie's and Hans's elaborate wedding would seem to confirm the priority of the love plot all along. Yet the wedding is told from the viewpoint of Paul Tan, Marie's former boyfriend and government bureaucrat. To him, the wedding is a farce and a mere popularity contest: "Showy! Beige and gold! How ridiculous Hans looked in his *dhoti!* An American in Indian garb!" (267). And, a little later, "He was disgusted to see the sacred moment of a whole life's commitment reduced to a performance of the hour to please the vulgar crowd" (269). Because there is no counterdescription of the wedding from Marie's perspective, the reader is inclined to agree that it simply *is* showy and ridiculous. Thus, although the narrative has also clearly mocked Paul Tan and his utilitarian views, it also refuses to provide a straightforward marriage-as-conclusion plot.

The novel's ambivalent ending seems rather to conclude that Marie—along with the other female characters—are simply better off leaving Singapore altogether. Indeed, by the end of the novel, all the main female characters have departed: Marie to marriage and the United States, Ser Mei in suicide, Yean to California, and the factory workers deported back to Malaysia. Exiting Singapore seems the only spatial solution to the problems of women's position. Neither domesticity—with its newly recomposed patriarchy and superstitions—nor the modern, public spaces of university, street protest, or industrial park are available as sustainable locations for women. Unable to decide just where the textualized production of women should take place, the novel simply evacuates them from the literary field.

As in the West, an essential aspect of New Asian City modernity is the shifting relationship between public and private, masculine and feminine, exterior and interior. For Lefebvre, the modern bourgeois apartment represses daily reproductive functions (sleeping, eating, lovemaking); "in the outside–inside relationship, it is the outside that predominates" (315). We have seen, however, that the general contradictions of Western industrialization—the confinement of bourgeois women to the interior as wives and mothers while working-class women enter the workforce—occur in the New Asian City in a more pronounced fashion. At the same time the postcolonial nation-state encourages general education and elicits women to join the workforce, it continues to rely heavily on women's underpaid labor in both industry and home in the name of independent modernization. In the above, I have traced the way this paradox is expressed in the literary treatment of private versus public space. The detective narrative form seems to arise—as it did in the West—in tandem with bourgeois interiority and the private room. Yet the resolution promised by the detective's search is never fulfilled; the woman's traces never lead to a determinate location, while spatial reflexivity takes the place of plots. Unlike the Western feminist path to individual rights and increased access to the public sphere, the New Asian City woman traverses the bedroom, living room, university, streets, and offices with equal unease.

According to Sita Ranchod-Nilsson and Mary Ann Tetreault, we typically understand the nation as a horizontal concept: it is the primordial signifier that includes all Americans, Koreans, or Singaporeans equally. In contrast, the state operates along a vertical axis and is constituted by state-versus-people power relations (5). These works demonstrate the way that the domestic sphere participates in both these social structures and is crucial to their organization and reproduction; in Lefebvrian terms, the problematic of industrialization is subsumed by the spatialized reproduction of social relationships (89). What upsets So-yang's family, Shuangwen's husband, and Paul Tan is a woman using her educational, political, or other energies on something other than those causes which would straightforwardly reproduce the nation, namely, other than taking underpaid jobs, marrying, and having children. In Heng and Devan's description of Singaporean state patriarchy,

> The demand that women serve the nation biologically, with their bodies—that they take on themselves, and submit themselves to, the public reproduction of nationalism in the most private medium possible, forcefully reveals the anxious relationship, in the fantasies obsessing state patriarchy, between reproducing power and the power to reproduce: the efficacy of one being expressly contingent on the containment and subsumption of the other. (349)

These fictions do not attempt to represent women's typical struggles within these industrializing postcolonial states. Rather, the textual effort to search for, contain, and locate woman in the public/private disjuncture both reveals and destabilizes the very concept of femininity.

Part 2's focus on "Postwar Urbanism" has allowed us to assess the constitutive relationship between localized architectural forms and the contested (re)production of bodies and subjectivities. In order to continue our research into postcolonial modernity, we now follow the broader inquiry into the constitution of the nation space and the collectivities that occupy it. How does the apparent liberation from colonialism play into ideas of national modernization and development? What happens to ideas of nation or nativism when their assumed place of origin—the countryside—is also brought under the modernizing logic of capitalism? The third and final part of our analysis requires us to leave the space of the city proper and consider the larger imaginings surrounding the rapidly changing national landscape.

Roads, Railways, and Bridges

Arteries of the Nation

> The objective of national liberation is, therefore, to reclaim the right, usurped by imperialist domination, namely: the liberation of the process of development of national productive forces.
>
> —AMILCAR CABRAL, "National Liberation and Culture"

As the last section has shown, the rise of the much-applauded Asia Pacific miracle economies cannot be understood without acknowledging the ways they reorganized their productive systems through urbanization and the effects this had on laboring and gendered subjectivities. Moving away from the question of individual reconciliation with the spatial logic of tabula rasa development, the next three chapters consider the developmental state as the site of the deliberate expansion of the images, values, and logic of cold war–defined, export-led capitalism in terms of a *national* project. In this brief introduction to part 3, "Industrializing Landscapes," I suggest we need to adjust well-known postcolonial theorizations of national culture for the New Asian City context and think through developmentalism as a contested expression of nationalist desires. In the era initiating the international flow of goods and capital we now call globalization, we will see how highly orchestrated and nationalized images of anticommunism and material wealth shaped the political and spatial forms of postcolonial Singapore, Taiwan, and South Korea. At the same time, we must ask, what are the implications of this emphasis on material progress for postcolonial theory, which has developed more often in response to the lack of such development? In particular, I investigate how the production of a modernized national space—arguably *the* preoccupation of these postcolonial developmental regimes—is narrated as the country's future path to freedom. In this Transition, then, my objects of study include the official national discourses of political speeches and government policies as well as the refiguring and imagining of the nation in various cultural texts. The topic of emphasis throughout is the concrete and metaphoric road, railway, or bridge—infrastructure that simultaneously turns national space into a free passage for goods, materials, labor, and commodities, and symbolizes the way chosen by the countries' leaders toward successful development.

I argue that nationalist sentiment in these three sites—at the level of official discourse, to begin with—turns on the question of economic nationalism. While conventional thought may see the essence of the nation in opposition to material progress (see my discussion of Chatterjee in the previous chapter), postcolonial Marxist-oriented thinkers have not opposed the two categories as such. African liberationist Amilcar Cabral, for example, writes of the armed revolution against colonialism creating "a veritable forced march along the road to cultural progress" (64); he assumes cultural progress to be a corollary of militarized struggle and the material development this requires. With a slight rewriting of this formula, we might think of certain Pacific Rim postcolonies as evincing a developmental revolution creating a forced march along the road to material progress, positing a statist version of Cabral's goal of national liberation as the "liberation of the process of development of national productive forces" (56). In the New Asian City context, physical infrastructural improvements and export levels themselves become the very terms of the national project: to produce or perish. This final section of the book interrogates the nature of this forced march—undertheorized as simply the Asian economic miracle—and its role in constructions of the nation.

It is necessary, then, to consider the remarkable physical form that political power has taken in the modernizing regimes of Singapore's Lee Kuan Yew, the Republic of China's Chiang Kai-shek, and South Korea's Park Chung Hee, in comparison with each other and with other postcolonies. The physical trappings of political power associated with grand architectural monuments were not (with some exception for Chiang Kai-shek) the goal of these postcolonial leaders. Lee remarks how he and his colleagues had no intention of memorializing their power in the usual manner of "renaming streets or buildings or putting our faces on postage stamps or currency notes" (*From Third World,* 50). Rather, political power attains the more far-reaching physical imprint in the roads, highways, industrial zones, bridges, and airports built by these regimes. In terms of the differentiation across third world sites alluded to in the first Transition, the obsession with infrastructure may be one way of understanding certain Asian versus African postcolonial modalities of sovereignty. Achille Mbembe has described Cameroon in terms of its "aesthetics of vulgarity," a political power defined by the grotesque, obscene, and "phallocratic" (103, 110). In his account, postcolonial rule "must be extravagant . . . ; it must furnish public proof of its prestige and glory by sumptuous (yet burdensome) presentation of its symbols of status, displaying the heights of luxury in dress and lifestyle, turning prodigal acts of generosity into grand theatre" (109). State power is characterized by "the obsession with orifices" (109) and lecherous living, such that "the unconditional subordination of women . . . remains one pillar upholding the reproduction of the phallocratic system" (110). In these Asia Pacific sites, however, the solidity—perhaps the hardness—of the built environment replaces the need for such a vocabulary of masculinist power, while the submission of women, as we have just seen, takes other forms.

The attempt to explain the variety of widespread post- and neocolonial conditions dates to the early moments of decolonization. With reference to African postcolonies, Frantz Fanon famously diagnosed the postcolonial problem as the historical and current weakness of the "national bourgeoisie," who become profiteering intermediaries between the nation and global capitalism. For Fanon, facilitating this "transmission line" (152) excludes the masses, inhibits the development of productive forces, and results in the stagnation of modern industry. In other words, without the intellectual—and not just muscular—participation of the masses, the "national bourgeoisie . . . reveals itself incapable of simply bringing national unity into being, or of building up the nation on a stable and productive basis" (159). He illustrates this nicely in the following:

> If the building of bridge does not enrich the awareness of those who work on it, then that bridge ought not to be built and the citizens can go on swimming across the river or going by boat. The bridge should not be "parachuted down" from above . . . ; on the contrary it should come from the muscles and the brains of the citizens. (200–201)

In arguing that under no circumstances should development be "parachuted down" by the state, Fanon underlines the productive and political activity required of all members of the independent nation: although material progress is a prerequisite for cultural development à la Cabral, too much state-directed progress inhibits real nation building. Pheng Cheah has more recently argued that the failure of nationalism has not been due to unfortunate historic factors—most typically where the neocolonial bourgeois state takes over the national liberation project. Rather, it fails because of a "more original susceptibility" (*Spectral,* 229) inherent in the actualization of national freedoms. This is "the irreducible susceptibility of life to *techne* that afflicts political organicism" (227), where *techne* is an Aristotelian term understood through the lens of Kant's moral philosophy. For Cheah, the basic assumption of postcolonial nationalism— tracing its conceptual origins in German idealist thought—is that people organized into an organically conceived nation is the best way to actualize political freedom; in other words, that political activity "finds its truth in culture" (7). Culture, conceived as "the product and self-conscious reflection of a society's life, its economic and political activities, . . . enables a society to rationally grasp and regulate its own historical progress" (216– 17). Not surprisingly, such ability explains the nation-form's appeal to postcolonial movements. Yet Cheah goes on to show how the very positing of a national culture, which would overcome individual finitude and project society into the future, necessarily carries with it the risk of "contamination," a problem inherent in all attempts to "incarnate ideals in the external world" (224). Drawing on Cabral and Fanon's condemnation of the neocolonial state, Cheah defines the danger of *techne* as the alien, externalizing mechanism of the state, which is deadly to, but inherent in, the nation as organic metaphor.

Cheah's study thus shares Fanon's unease about the genuine constitution of the nation: "Can the social or political body transcend finitude and assimilate the artificial prostheses that threaten to contaminate it, or is it irreducibly exposed to an inhuman and nonorganicizable *techne?*" (224). What interests me is the way Fanon's understanding of the precariousness of postcolonial nationalism is theorized as an inherent risk of contamination by Cheah: while its "economic and political activities" make the new nation viable, a materialism externalized in statist forms is fatal to national culture. As we saw in the discussion of export-oriented production, the New Asian City countries enjoyed exceptional status precisely in eventually having built up a relatively "stable and productive basis," and thereby accumulating capital. If this did not occur autonomously through the model of independent development and import substitution, it was nevertheless achieved with some kind of participation of the masses. In contrast to Cheah's ultimately pessimistic pronouncement on the possibility for the organic nation, I suggest that in the cases of the New Asian Cities, we need to consider how the material operations of *techne* do not always oppose the emergence of a postcolonial nationalism, but may actually constitute it. In other words, state apparatuses direct development toward international markets in a neocolonial manner, yet do so under the banner of popular nationalism. To flesh out my claim, let us consider further the relationship between *techne,* the state, and nationalist sentiment.

In the well-known configuration traced by Benedict Anderson, the combination of vernacular languages and empty, homogenous time, ratified through the daily plebiscite of print culture, allows for the horizontally and spatially uniform imagined community of the nation. Anderson notes that by the late twentieth century, modern nationalism had become modular and extended to every contemporary society. In *Imagined Communities,* one of the important questions Anderson asks is how official—state or imperial—nationalism "enters post-revolutionary leadership styles" (160), that is, how a popular revolutionary or anticolonial struggle is coopted by a nationalism "serving the interests of the state first and foremost" (159). He is especially interested in how revolutionary postcolonial states such as Vietnam succumb to what he calls the "wiring of the [old] colonial state": "Like the complex electrical system in any large mansion when the owner has fled, the state awaits the new owner's hand at the switch to be very much its old brilliant self again" (160).[1] Anderson identifies three important mechanisms for this ghostly inhabiting of existing state structures (or *techne,* to use Cheah's term): the colonial practices of census, map, and museum. Underwritten by the new currency of ethnonationalism, these practices produce a grammar of colonial ideologies and policies, which have become surprisingly useful for postcolonial state-building activities (163). As always, Anderson is exceedingly good at accounting for how the most abstract of national identities gets expressed in bureaucracies, schools, legal systems, and clinics and in time give "real social life to the state's ear-lier fantasies" (169). Of particular interest to us is the way the physical form of the colonial map functions as a model for what it "purported to repre-sent" (Thongchai Winichakul, qtd. in Anderson,173); the unity of the map belies the often haphazard setting down of territorial boundaries as natu-ralized containers of certain ethnic and religious groups. Similarly, colonial monuments or ruins were crucial to the construction of Malay, Chinese, or Javanese identities and acted as "regalia for a *secular* colonial state" (182). The map, along with educational and touristic publications surrounding colonial monuments and archaeological studies, were all guaranteed by an "infinite reproducibility" (182) newly enabled by print capitalism. Archae-ological objects, monuments, and native flora and fauna become fodder for schoolbooks, postcards, and eventually tourism sanctioned by the col-onizers. Anderson writes, "It was precisely the infinite quotidian reproduci-bility of its regalia that revealed the real power of the state" (183).

For the Singaporean, Taiwanese, and South Korean postcolonial states, the British and Japanese colonial "wiring" has been both reused and elab-orated. The colonial practices of ethnic categorization and museumization are vigorously retained, for example, in Singapore's neat tripartite racial breakdown of the population into Chinese, Malay, and Indian, and the zeal with which Korea adopted the national archaeological system intro-duced by Japan. In addition to such cultural identities and regalia, I argue that trading facilities and incipient manufacturing industries were built upon to create efficient economies, and it is the real and imagined forms of these—enhanced by new productive technologies—that can also provide an imaginable map and give real social life to postcolonial nationalisms. Like other forms of visual and symbolic culture, infrastructural technol-ogies give rise to certain representations that "[offer] legibility through the reproduction of what is seen" (Balshaw and Kennedy, 7). Narratives and images of roads and transportation networks—the very *techne* that fills in and connects the horizontal space of the nation—thus give us a way of viewing nationalism that works analogously to the temporal sleight of hand of the newly redrawn colonial map: the unity of the productive nation as both mechanism and image of the future.

There is one more important implication of the hyperproductive post-colonial nation. In his article on the rapid development of the Asia Pacific

Tiger economies, Castells gives a definition of the developmental state: *"A state is developmental when it establishes as its principle of legitimacy its ability to promote and sustain development, understanding by development the combination of steady high rates of economic growth and structural change in the productive system, both domestically and in its relationship to the international economy"* ("Four Asian Tigers," 56, emphasis in original). What this definition reveals is precisely that a form of legitimacy—one that arises not from civil society's consensual basis but that is coherent nevertheless—is fundamental to developmental states. To clarify, Castells gives the example of revolutionary states "which never pretended to be legitimate in terms of the acquiescence of the subjects, but in terms of the historical project they embodied, as avant-gardes of the classes and nations that were not yet fully aware of their destiny and interests" (57). In the revolutionary moment, the state "substitutes itself for society in the definition of societal goals" which include "the fundamental reorganization of the social order." Similarly,

> When the societal project respects the broader parameters of social order (although not necessarily the specific social structure) but aims at a fundamental transformation of the economic order . . . I propose the hypothesis that we are in the presence of what we call the *developmental state*. The historical expression of such a societal project generally takes the form (and such was the case in most of the East Asian experience) of the building or rebuilding of national identity, affirming the national presence of a given society or a given culture in the world, although not necessarily coinciding with the territorial limits under the control of the developmental state. (57)

In other words, despite obvious political and ideological differences, Castells tracks a basic structural similarity between revolutionary states and the repressive governments of the Asia Pacific. The latter enact an economic rather than political transformation but nevertheless see themselves in the business of rebuilding the national identity. Aside from abstract facts and figures (export earnings, growth rates) of the state's nation-building discourse, the economic and structural change in the productive system is, I contend, most clearly perceived in the concrete achievements of *urbanism and infrastructure*. We will see how such forms are able to signify future success to the outside (Lee Kuan Yew), become objects of national competitive development (Park Chung Hee), or showcase the operation of a model provincial economy in the face of political exclusion (the Kuomintang). In all cases, the shift to a modern built environment is the leap into the future that legitimizes the national project of development. Complicating narratives of simple authoritarian repression, Castells observes that "the fundamental element in the ability of developmental states to fulfill their project was their political capacity to impose *and internalize* their logic on the civil societies" ("Four Asian Tigers," 64, emphasis altered). Even though the forms of development promoted usually replaced local building methods and structures with generic layers of concrete or asphalt, when combined with the rhetoric of crisis and survival, they confirm that the most urgent national task is none other than accelerated economic development.

We thus arrive back at a strange reformulation of Cabral's notion of the national liberation of productive forces. In the context of the New Asian City, the object of postcolonial independence is shifted away from the freedom of a people to the setting free of the national industries' productive power. In other words, the subject of freedom moves from living societies to the dead labor of commodity production, and the mediating links between them are the fluid, nationalized transportation networks. National culture may be then defined as that in the name of which the shift in mode of production is undertaken. The nation is produced, paradoxically, as the unchanging term that organizes and directs the transformation of the rest of society; it must carry and bear the weight of this process while never losing its own (mythical) status of continuity. If the historic destiny of developmentalism is narrated by the state through its inscription onto the nation's physical spaces, it should not be surprising if literary and cinematic narratives of this period also explicitly allegorize the national way through alternative representations of its built forms. As Balshaw and Kennedy note, the city—and I would add built forms of the nation more generally—"clearly persists . . . as an imaginary totality which compellingly symbolizes generalised desires and anxieties—often, those configured around the meanings of nationhood, citizenship, urbanity and justice" (6). The contested view of the use and meanings of such apparatuses is thus nothing less than a contestation over the direction and content of the postcolonial national project.

Finally, we can translate our understanding of statist development back into Lefebvrian terms. In his sustained account of the gradual historical rise and domination of capitalist spatial relations, he describes the concept of *abstract space*. A more totalizing version of *representations of space*, it tends toward homogenization, the logic of visualization, and phallic orientation (Lefebvre, 285–87) and can be thought of as the spatial equivalent of Cheah's *techne:* "As a product of violence and war, [abstract space] is political; instituted by a state" (285). If social space is always polyvalent and contested, abstract space dissimulates an illusory coherence determined by power, tending toward the "reduction of three-dimensional realities to two dimensions" (285). The developmental states we have been discussing employ such a strategy, instrumentalizing space as "a *stake,* the locus of projects and actions deployed as part of specific strategies, and hence also the object of *wagers* on the future—wagers which are articulated, if never completely" (142–43).

In each of the following three chapters, I interrogate the way modernizing built forms, and especially transport systems, function as the imaginary totalities or wagers on the future through which developmentalist nationalism operates. To do this, I analyze writings and speeches of the long-tenured, authoritarian leaders of the three states. Accompanying this, I examine selected literary and cinematic texts that equally invoke the roads, planning, and infrastructure of national modernization programs, but that do so in order to make radically different claims about the nation. In the next chapter, I consider discourses of Singapore's official nationalism as articulated by the inimitable Lee Kuan Yew and the responses to such ideas of nationhood by two prominent poets, Edwin Thumboo and Arthur Yap. I then move to Taiwanese New Cinema of the 1980s and the early works of Hou Hsiao-hsien as the cultural texts that, arguably, most directly grapple with the new city–country relationship taking shape during the consolidating decades of Kuomintang rule. In the final chapter, I examine the Korean *minjung* literature movement exemplified by proletarian writer Hwang Sŏk-yŏng, whose work simultaneously responds to the issues of aggressive industrialization, cold war divisions, and the repressive regime of Park Chung Hee. Acknowledging differences in genre and historical context, I choose these specific cultural forms for their provocative responses to statist nationalisms and not because they are somehow representative of that era or nation's cultural production. Their relevance lies in the specific (mis)use of the spatial grammar of official nationalist discourses: of Lee's way ahead, Chiang Kai-shek's bridge to mainland recovery, and Park Chung Hee's New Village rural industrialization. Narrating decidedly other experiences on the road, these works explore the way wider communities experience, and are reshaped by, railways, roads, and bus routes to provide alternative symbolic versions of developmental landscapes.

Thus, it is again my aim to complicate the story of the exception, or the good pupils of the third world, by examining the interlocking forms and narratives of postwar national development. In examining how the state-directed struggle for development is held up as the "fight for the liberation of the nation, that material keystone which makes the building of a culture possible" (Fanon, 233), we must reckon with a vastly different conception of the relationship between material practice and cultural unity than that imagined by Fanon or Cabral.

PART III

INDUSTRIALIZING
LANDSCAPES

5

The Way Ahead

*The Politics and Poetics of
Singapore's Developmental Landscape*

the road slices through two lives
which are the quick and, mainly, the quicker

—ARTHUR YAP, "open road"

STATE AND POETIC NARRATIVES OF
POSTCOLONIAL MODERNITY

In January 1964, senior minister Lee Kuan Yew undertook a whirlwind tour
of independent African states in order to win support for his new country,
Malaysia, which had incorporated Singapore, Sabah (British North Bor-
neo), and Sarawak into the Federation of Malaya in 1963. In this period
of emerging postcolonial statehood, recognition of Malaysia by African
states was an essential international PR exercise in the face of suspicion
and aggression from Sukarno's Indonesia. In his memoir, *The Singapore
Story,* Lee relates the experience of visiting seventeen African countries
in thirty-five days, and the varied levels of welcome given to the Malaysian contingent reflect the complicated national ideologies in currency
at the time.[1] Although Lee's diplomatic exercise was made moot by the
effective ejection of Singapore from Malaysia in 1965 just two years after
their merger, the trip was nevertheless important training for the leader
of the fledgling postcolonial city-state of Singapore. More than the varying levels of support garnered at the meetings with African heads of state,
Lee's memoirs describe his own reactions to the physical and spatial environments of these encounters. His brief and metonymic descriptions
read as a comparative architectural tour of Africa's new seats of postcolonial power, where the presidential personage, the built environment, and

the well-being of the nation are strictly correlative. Approximately ten years after Lee's trip—the experience of which would deeply influence Singaporean national space—Edwin Thumboo, known as the father figure of Singaporean poetry, published the landmark collection *The Second Tongue: An Anthology of Poetry from Malaysia and Singapore.* Like Lee, the images most useful to his project have to do with the modernizing physical landscape. This chapter explores the way forms of a statist, developmental landscape are taken up in both Singaporean political and poetic discourses. Specifically, I examine the relationship of poetry to nation-statehood through the work of Thumboo and Arthur Yap, two prominent Anglophone poets early awarded literary cultural medallions by the Singapore government.

Before turning to the question of poetry, let us trace the genesis of Lee's understanding of rationalized, national space. For Lee, the African experience is most instructive regarding the varying material environments of different nations. In order to meet Ghana's Kwame Nkrumah at his refurbished Danish slave-trading post, for example, Lee is forced to "[walk] between Indian-style oil lamps, wicks floating in small brass bowls lining both sides of a red carpet" (*Singapore Story,* 531). This was only to be outdone by his encounter with Emperor Haile Selassie of Ethiopia, who was dressed in British-style military uniform and flanked by "two cheetahs lightly chained to posts" (536). Here, Lee points out that "in contrast to the sometimes handsome buildings around them, [the people] looked shabby and poor" (536).[2] But in Northern Rhodesia, soon to become Zambia, Lee notes approvingly, "we were put up at the Livingstone Hotel, an attractive, single-storey, rambling building, like a large inn in an English provincial town" (532). The governor's mansion at Lusaka, moreover, deserves praise for its well-maintained—but not luxurious—condition, evidence of the "one well-run system" put in place by the British. Recalling later visits to the Zambian capital, Lee remarks on the dilapidation of the once beautifully kept city: "I remembered the flowers, shrubs, trees and greenery at the side of the roads and at the roundabouts when I was driven in from the airport in 1964. Roses grew in abundance. Six years later, the roses had gone and weeds had taken over. Nine years after that, even the weeds had given up; the roundabouts were covered with tarmac" (538). The disappearance of the "well-run" British system is visibly evident in the physical deterioration of the landscape. Lee is clear about the insights that this trip afforded him:

> I had received an unforgettable lesson in decolonisation, on how crucial it was to have social cohesion and capable, effective government to take power from the colonial authority, especially in Africa.... When misguided policies based on half-digested theories of socialism and redistribution of wealth were compounded by less than competent government, societies formerly held together by colonial power splintered, with appalling consequences. (538–39)

One can read Lee's experience, of course, as justifying his own selective rejection of socialist and democratic principles, and as retrospectively casting doom on all those postcolonial states that took this path. The origins of Lee's own thirty-one-year (1959–90) authoritarian-style rule through the People's Action Party (PAP) may be discerned in his emphasis on "competent governments" and "social cohesion." The strongest impression, however, is the recognition that the control and care of national space, from the presidential mansion down to the roundabouts, is intimately tied to the nation's success—a recognition that would be embodied in Singapore's massive urban renewal programs under Lee's PAP government: no opulent mansions, red carpets, or cheetahs, but a national order literally built on the rational and efficient order of its structures.

The impact that Lee's lessons from Africa would have on Singaporean space would also be reflected in Singaporean poetry. As many critics have noted, Anglophone poetry in Singapore has occupied a peculiarly privileged place with regard to state building. Rajeev S. Patke writes, "The poet in Singapore bears an over-determined relation to the development of the state into nation, especially during the first few decades of the history of poetry in Singapore" ("Voice," 90). Similarly, Robbie B. H. Goh notes, "In a variety of ways . . . this [Anglophone] poetry echoed and in many cases articulated the macro-narratives of nationhood" (38). While these correspondences take several forms, I am most interested in how they operate through representations of national space. Goh accurately observes:

> The poetic treatment of space often becomes foregrounded . . . taking on a central symbolic role as the means of constructing a shared communal

and ultimately national space. In this sense Singapore's poetry of emergent nationalism once again reinforces, and is reinforced by, a kind of national ideology, in this instance the *symbolic control of space* enacted by the government's Housing Development Board (HDB) and similar agencies. (34, emphasis added)

To be sure, both symbolic and actual control of space was effected under Lee's PAP. As we saw briefly in chapter 3, after separating from Malaysia in 1965, among the most immediate problems for the Singaporean government were the question of a new hinterland and the problem of association of its majority Chinese population with communist China.[3] Eliminating union power, arresting leaders of the previously allied Barisan Socialists, and being ruthless toward anti-PAP (or antinational) opposition were all crucial to ensuring social stability and the construction of a new internationally oriented modernity. The government modeled its Economic and Development Board after Japan's Ministry of International Trade and Industry and reshaped the nation space to attract foreign manufacturing companies; Singapore eventually found its new economic hinterland in the large first world markets of the United States, Japan, and Europe. This required the construction of massive state-of-the-art industrial estates like the 9,000-acre one at Jurong, complete with "roads, sewers, drainage, power, gas, and water all laid out" (Lee, *From Third World,* 61), as well as HDB-built complexes that would eventually fill in most of the island. With the Economic and Development Board acting as a one-stop shop for foreign investors, the importance of presenting Singapore's modern infrastructure became the PAP's number one concern, to the delight of companies like General Electric and Hewlett-Packard. Thus, despite Lee's early career as an Oxford-educated, anticolonial activist and labor-union lawyer, he became the archetypal postcolonial developmentalist leader, happily arranging for the marriage of international capital and Singapore's cheap labor. As a 1973 *Newsweek* article quipped, his PAP party was one of the few ever "to ride the Red tiger to power and then successfully dismount" (qtd. in Yeo and Lau, 148).

As we know, Lee had imbibed the importance of first impressions from his trips to foreign states, and his first priority as prime minister was the presentation of a functioning and orderly Singapore. On his many official visits elsewhere,

> what impressed me was not the size of the buildings but the standard of their maintenance. I knew when a country and its administrators were demoralized from the way the buildings had been neglected—washbasins cracked, taps leaking, water closets not functioning properly, a general dilapidation, and, invariably, unkempt gardens. VIPs would judge Singapore the same way. (*From Third World*, 175)

If Lee concludes that a country's health can be read from its architecture and built environment, what does this imply for the poetic treatment of Singapore's national space? I argue that the new cityscape, rather than simply becoming incorporated into poetry, becomes the impetus for new poetic images and for thinking, reflecting, and critiquing the very logic of productive postcolonial states. In the exemplary national poetry of Thumboo, we will see how a poetic aesthetic might be forged in terms of the new cityscape's productive demands. In contrast, for Yap, who has been called the "most complex and intricate poet of the Singaporean city" (Haskell, 245), an equal investment in poetically reworking urban forms will show us other possibilities for thinking the Singapore nation.

Between graduating from the University of Singapore in 1955 and returning to do a Ph.D. in African literature in 1966, Thumboo (born 1933) worked for the Department of Inland Revenue and the Central Provident Fund Board for seven years. His early proximity to bureaucratic structures of the state may account for what Dudley De Souza calls a "transition from the poetry of powerlessness to . . . the poetry of power" (302) seen in the shift from the personal mode of his early poetry to the explicitly public poetry of his collections *Gods Can Die* and *Ulysses by the Merlion*, from 1977 and 1979, respectively. While Thumboo's mature poems are an attempt to come to terms with uneven societal power under the PAP and the smallness of Singapore, they undoubtedly also work to forge a national, literary identity based on the government's developmental path. These poems have often been considered ideologically at one with the PAP development described above. [4] Shirley Geok-lin Lim writes, "much of Thumboo's later poetry comes from an explicit desire to explain the ways of the Singaporean state to his readers, to participate in converting 'cultural tolerance to active cultural acceptance'" (118).

We see such a desire in the poem "Island" from *Ulysses by the Merlion* (1979), which narrates succinctly—almost simplistically—Singapore's startling transformation from tropical island to economic wonder. Initially, the virgin purity of the island's past is revealed through the frame of the speaker's memory that is at once personal and mythic:

Once
There was a quiet island,
With a name.
You must believe me
When I say that sunlight,
Impure but beautiful,
Broke upon the bay, silvered
The unrepentant, burning noon. (16)

The inhabitants of this paradise are generic Malay children, Aminah and Harun, "Too young to know the sea," "who followed crab and tide." The idyllic image is elaborated by the requisite "Mangrove and palm" and "Houses on stilts, boats drawn up," until these fanciful illustrations are brought to a halt with the accusing lines: "Romantic. Nostalgic. / But images change." The remainder of the poem narrates the replacement of every physical trace of the former way of life:

Nearby hills are pushed into the sea.
Tractors roar, lorries thrive
Till the ochre of the land
Scooped out day and night,
Crept upon the sand.
Aminah, Harun now reside in flats,
Go to school while father
Learns a trade.

Along Shipyard Road,
Not far from Bird Park,

A new song in the air:
Cranes and gantries rise;
Dynamo and diesel hum.
Men in overalls and helmets
Wield machines, consulting plans.

A welder's torch explodes
Into a rush of stars;
Rivets are hammered home till
Hulls of steel emerge.
Sophisticated, self-propelled,
The towering drillers look attractive:
This one bound for Norway;
The one before works by Antarctica. (16–17)

In contrast to the sleepy island and unworldly inhabitants, the tractors, lorries, cranes, drills, and boats testify to the immensely increased productive power of mechanized society. The previously unlocated island, floating alone as the word "Once" does, is now the mediating point between places as far off as Norway and Antarctica, marking not just a recognizable geography but the beginning of its history. The inhabitants, docile in comparison to the exploding torches and drills, now dutifully "reside in flats," attend schools, and learn trades. Women, unmentioned and presumably still limited to the domestic sphere, are apparently the only ones untouched by the modernizing process.

Yet even as this is presented as a world dominated by machines, Thumboo suggests that after a necessary time lag, the liberation of these productive powers will give rise to the formation of a new and collective identity:

In time images of power,
Our emergent selves,
Will be familiar
As, first, the body learns
This other song. (17)

For Thumboo, the potentially fearsome power of industrialized society is tempered by its status as simply "this other song," or perhaps the very song of poetry. In accordance with the developmental state's drive to moderniza-tion, top-down industrialization—the reshaping of the nation where "hills are pushed into the sea"—is simply necessary. At the same time, the people adapt to this new world and "the body learns," producing the first stage of Singaporean national identity. Although material development was actively desired by Singaporeans—recall from chapter 3 that the PAP was strongly supported for its development orientation—what Thumboo's poetry pro-vides is the necessary monumentalizing of its new forms into a national landscape. The process of material development is paralleled in the poetic production of "images of power," with which its citizens can identify.

Although Yap, whose work is often pitted by critics against Thumboo's, is less interested in national identities, he is no less interested in collectiv-ities.[5] Born in 1943 and therefore of a slightly younger generation than Thumboo, Yap received his education at the National University of Singa-pore and the University of Leeds. In contrast to Thumboo's emphatically public poetry, his work is paradigmatic of the kind of Singaporean poetry that deals with the everyday, the commonplace and the local. Regarding this literary strand of "emergent nationalism," Goh notes that

> apart from the sheer preponderance of poems directly or indirectly con-cerned with local places, the poetics of place involves a creation of "common-place" (to use the play on words which form the title of Yap's 1977 volume)—and idiom of references, experiences, personages and topics which might plausibly form the common currency of the Singapore people. (36)

If, for Thumboo, grand spatial transformations become poetic material in the service of national History, Yap's poetry heads in the opposite direction by taking on a small-scale but clear-eyed view of the changing industrial landscape. In "there is no future in nostalgia," originally published in *com-monplace,* Yap reworks the same narrative of urban transformation that was the subject of Thumboo's "Island." Whereas Thumboo's task was to harness the energies and forms of the developmental project toward an official, national past, we can read Yap as trading in terms of what Anne Brewster describes as the "additive and iterative nature of memory" (Intro-duction, xiii). Here, the replacement of human workers with machines is methodically recounted:

& certainly no nostalgia in the future of the past.
now, the corner cigarette-seller is gone, is perhaps dead.
no, definitely dead, he would not otherwise have gone.
he is replaced by a stamp-machine,
the old cook by a pressure-cooker,
the old trishaw-rider's stand by a fire hydrant,
the washer-woman by a spin-dryer (59)

Note two major contrasts to Thumboo's "Island." First, instead of the awe-inspiring technologies of modernization—roaring tractors and exploding torches—Yap chooses decidedly less impressive modern gadgets as poetic material: the stamp machine, the pressure cooker, the spin dryer. The replacement of former human characters—"the corner cigarette-seller" or "the old cook"—by such technologies renders the moment of modernity anticlimactic and bathetic rather than momentous or historical. Second, Yap's poem diverges from Thumboo's nationalist aesthetic in the refusal of any unifying consciousness that would wrap around and make nationalist sense of such changes. The poem ends simply and undramatically: "& it goes on / in various variations & permutations. / there is no future in nostalgia" (59). Yap neither aestheticizes the state-led modernization nor rues it for a previous time of authentic plenitude; his level-headed observer is simply content to note the changes and move on. Shirley Geok-lin Lim concludes that by "focusing on the particular situations of his community, [Yap] mocks them from an antagonistic position" (156) and defines his main poetic device as irony. Yet the distinction cannot be explained by the simple opposition between Thumboo as propagandist and Yap as ironist of state rhetoric. By understanding the complicated play of nationalist rhetoric, developmental landscapes, and poetic form, we can address deeper assumptions and possibilities concerning literature and the constitution of subjects, citizens, and collectivities.

We have seen how Lee Kuan Yew's nationalist rhetoric taps into and reveals the deeper logic behind the modernizing Singaporean landscape, a logic that might be contrasted to the more familiar culturally nationalist positions articulated in other areas of the third world and typified by Fanon and Cabral. Considering the case of Singapore, however, we need to ask the question I posed in the second Transition: how is the authoritarian production of a modernized national space narrated by such regimes as the country's future path to national freedom? Thumboo has written of Singapore that unlike postcolonial African states, "the anti-colonial movement had been mainly intellectual in origin and drive," such that the "dialectics of nationalism lacked a background of intense mass suffering" (Introduction, xiv). As noted above, independence for Singapore was not characterized by a violent anticolonial struggle: although the Malayan Emergency was significant, the island passed relatively peacefully into home rule in 1959. This, Thumboo recalls, along with the mixed racial makeup of colonial Singapore, made the forging of a nativist oppositional voice difficult. In such a context, the explosive theories of Cabral and Fanon would seem unsuited to a population simply craving "a development-oriented government" (Chua, *Political Legitimacy,* 160) and therefore more accepting of statist *techne,* the "parachuted-down" form of modernity.

Let us return to the extraordinary urban transformation undertaken by Lee's regime. We have already noted that images of authority in the New Asian City countries typically come less from prestigious symbols or icons and more from their physical imprint in highways, housing complexes, industrial zones, bridges, and airports. Indeed, we can see the postcolonial leader's desire to transform space as akin to the modernist desire to apply the revolutionary power of technology to all realms of life. In Fredric Jameson's terms, the latter finds expression in Le Corbusier's minimalist architecture, which would replace the

> diseased city fabric: the insalubrious, reeking, airless, sodden alleys of a dead inherited medieval city, the industrial slums of a modern agglomeration— best to do away with those streets altogether, to open all that to sun and fresh air by an act of joyous destruction, and to erect . . . exhilarating high-rises rearing off their ground on *pilotis* that stood as a symbol of defiance and refusal of, escape from, the old world, the old Europe, the nineteenth century. (*Seeds,* 142)

We might view developmental policies and documents as akin to that modernist genre of the manifesto: what both genres share is a desire for the new, where a change in the aesthetic form engineers a change in the social. Lee's disgust with the slums of Singapore that he encounters while canvassing for the 1955 domestic election seems entirely congruent with the attempt to escape from the rotting nineteenth century and open up—in Le Corbusian fashion—to sun and fresh air. Lee writes:

> Another scene of filth and dilapidation was presented by the rows of mean, broken-down shophouses in Narcis Street and the roads leading to it on the site where the Tanjong Pagar Plaza now stands. They had not been repaired for many years, and the drains were clogged with rubbish left by roadside hawkers, so that there was always a stink of decaying food. Enormous rats ran fearlessly in and out of these drains, ignoring the cats around. [. . .] I retched. (*Singapore Story,* 185)

Under Lee's direction, the Housing and Development Board did indeed decide it was "best to do away with those streets altogether" in the massive urban renewal projects that would eventually house almost 90 percent of the population and replace nearly all of Singapore's original building stock. Yet the impetus for this "joyous destruction" arises not from the desire to escape "the old Europe" and its congested industrialism, but rather to correct the backward conditions of the Asian colony and its lack of industrial capabilities. Moreover, the modernity and freedom envisioned here is directed not by any ideal of nonaligned independent development, as articulated at the historic 1955 Bandung Conference, but by the nation's very willingness to link to the international market. National culture is thus not the mass struggle to achieve independent modernity, but may simply be the by-product of its forms.

Retrospectively describing the remarkable ability of Singapore to attract major international investment and manufacturers, Lee confirms that the modernization of Singapore's space was the defining factor:

> I thought that the best way to convince [visiting CEOs to invest in Singapore] was to ensure that the roads from the airport to their hotel and to my office were neat and spruce, lined with shrubs and trees. When they drive into the Istana domain, they would see right into the heart of the city a green oasis, 90 acres of immaculate rolling lawns and woodlands. . . . Without a word being said, they would know that Singaporeans were competent, disciplined, and reliable, a people who would learn the skills they required soon

enough. American manufacturing investments soon overtook those of the British, Dutch and Japanese. (*From Third World,* 62)

Lee therefore envisions the modernity of Singapore against the background of other third world locations also competing for investments of transnational capital. His comments indicate the paradoxical position of forging a new economy for *national* survival by means of creating a comparative regional advantage which best serves the *international* interest. In contrast to other postcolonies, which may have followed the dire pronouncements of Fanon on neocolonialism, popular nationalist sentiment is reworked into forging an economic system that precisely capitalizes on Singapore's subordination in the international labor market. Thus, physical infrastructural improvements to attract foreign investment are synonymous with the national project. At the same time, the national scale of the built environment's reconstruction allows the PAP's commitment to the national project to be read symbolically and internalized by the

Prime Minister Lee Kuan Yew visiting an HDB housing project in 1965. Photograph by Larry Burrows/Time & Life Pictures/Getty Images.

population. Such powerful signs signify the path of Singapore's future through the assumption of consent, that is, the population's desire for freedom through material improvement. The road to Singapore's national future is thus not just the one from the airport, but the one that leads the population into its new factories, processing plants, and hotels.

Poetic Reinscriptions and Productions

Thumboo and Yap have been described by Shirley Geok-lin Lim as "both construct[ing] an imagined community called Singapore," one speaking for "social harmony," the other speaking against "social hypocricies" (156). More specifically, we can understand the differences between Thumboo and Yap in terms of their respective relationships to technology and the national landscape envisioned by Lee Kuan Yew. Part of the emphasis on Singapore's physical landscape has to do with the complex language politics in play. The brief effort to "assemble a synthetic language using English as a base with importations from Mandarin and Malay"—Engmalchin—was short-lived, rendering the language of colonial bureaucracy and postcolonial development the only available national literary language (Thumboo, Introduction, xvi).[6] For Thumboo, who is himself of mixed Chinese and Indian heritage, because the language that poets are obliged to use is no one's native language but everyone's second tongue, English carries less of an anticolonial national identity than Chinese, Tamil, or Malay. The solution to forging a national literature in English relies heavily on remaking the language "by adjusting the interior landscape of words in order to explore and mediate the permutations of another culture and environment" (Introduction, ix). That is, the task is to map the interior poetic and linguistic landscape onto an external one, differing from much other postcolonial writing in English, which marks specificity of place through nonstandard syntax or dialect. Thumboo admits that he has chosen the public form of poetry to carry the "pro-nationalist feeling," which was a natural sentiment for Singaporeans of his generation ("Interview," 269). The 1965 separation from Malaysia meant that whereas for Lee the task was to find an economic hinterland, the proper task for Singapore's poets is to construct a psychic hinterland. Thumboo explains, "We are busy constructing a common, shared culture out of the very diverse elements we have inherited, and therefore the creation of this hinterland is important because it

really is the base, upon which all writing ought to rest" ("Interview," 272).[7]
Thumboo's lyric poetry, therefore, attempts to narrativize a people's relationship to this metaphoric hinterland in a way analogous to the developmental revolution described above. If Lee saw the ability of the landscape
to narrate the nation's future, Thumboo uses it to invoke the nation's past.
As evidenced in "Island," Thumboo must refigure the nation diachroni-
cally through a narrative history of the city-state's development.

The consequence is that in his less reflective poems, Thumboo's voice
is almost at one with PAP national rhetoric. In "Catering for the People,"
Thumboo admonishes the "delinquent days" of Singapore's 1960s race riots
with the appropriate government reminder of a common task of national
arrival:

> *Bring the hill to the valley, level the place and build,*
> *And generally cater to the people . . .*
> Set all neatly down into Economy.
> There is little choice—
> We must make a people. (*Gods Can Die,* 56)

It is difficult to tell whether these lines are ironic parodies of PAP rhetoric or
not. He goes on to list, in Lee style, the marketable strengths of the emerging city-state: "We have a promising amalgam— / Youth, anger, a kind of will,
a style of politics, / And bargain hard, sell common and unlikely things."
The final stanza, moreover, reminds the reader of Singapore's geopolitical
precariousness, the most concrete of shared political motivations:

> We are flexible, small, a boil
> On the Melanesian face.
> If it grin or growl, we move—
> To corresponding place,
> Keeping sensitive to trends, adapting,
> To these delinquent days. (57)

Thumboo's free verse poems, with their succinct, pragmatic language, thus
align neatly with official national ideology—or, in Patke's words, "Thumboo . . . adopts the persona of a friend to the post-independence nation"

(*Postcolonial,* 75). In the logic of "Catering for the People," the insecurity over Singapore's immediate and potentially hostile neighbors (Malaysia and Indonesia) is to be countered by general education and a complete spatial reorganization of the domestic sphere: "*level the place and build.*" If Thumboo does not quite celebrate the political and economic direction of the nation, he accepts it out of his rational understanding of the nation's tenuous viability. In such poems, the sense of the national comes from an understanding of the realpolitik project of building (economic/political) stability.[8] The personal, poetic "I" thus slides seamlessly into the national-istic "we."

This is not to say that Thumboo's poems are always simply mouthpieces for the developmental state and its official historical narratives. His poem "The Way Ahead" questions the already decidedness of the use of the city. Appropriately for Singapore's premier poet, this is nothing less than a poetic rendition of a bureaucratic planning meeting:

> We were to speak, to chat,
> Involve our several minds on how
> To frame a City.
> We were asked, judiciously, to talk of beauty
> In a town, how the town would change,
> Turn supple, rugged, yet acceptable. (*Gods Can Die,* 58)

The speaker/poet is an interloper among the technocrats. Next to a "Pro-fessor," a "Senior Civil Servant who knew the way ahead," and "The Town Planner"—all with capitalized occupations—the poet is "The average man, the man-in-the-street / Feeling nervous." Invited to this think tank on the future of the city, the Professor and Town Planner argue over competing visions: a congested Chinatown—"The teeming interchange of word and gesture"—versus the Corbusian ideal of "A flat in the sun" and "regiments of flats." Despite their apparent differences, both versions actually rest on the same assumption that the city can be rationally determined by the right perspective or correct principles. Instead of advocating another com-peting view, our poet-turned-bureaucrat balks: "What could I say? Or think?" His tactic is to change the language of the discussion from rational town planning precepts to a poetics based on lived spatial experience:

A City smiles the way its people smile.
When you spit, that is the city too.
A City is for people, for living,
For walking between shadows of tall buildings
That leave some room, for living.
And though we rush to work, appointments,
To many other ends, there must be time to pause,
Loosen the grip of each working day,
To make amends, to hear the inner self
And keep our spirits solvent.
A City should be the reception we give ourselves,
What we prepare for our posterity. (59)

Thumboo affirms the nonrational aspect of the urban environment as the backdrop to the everyday and as the material counterpart to the collective "people's heart." Unlike the modernist emphasis on sun and fresh air as natural rights, he emphasizes the need "For walking between shadows of tall buildings." Instead of presenting a city teeming with life, Thumboo reminds us it is also what we leave behind on our death, "What we prepare for our posterity"; it is the very image of national heritage to be passed on. The "way ahead," Thumboo indicates, cannot be exhausted by the technocrat's national vision. At the same time that Thumboo recognizes in many of his poems the lack of choice for developing states, he is unwilling to leave the defining of the nation entirely to the state. He thus both participates in the language of the state (English, bureaucratic) and shows how it has set up immoveable terms of debate (where the nation equals Economy, Education, plus Town Planning). The question remains as to whether Thumboo, by bringing in the poetic, lived, and unquantifiable elements to the experience of the city, actually challenges PAP developmental logic or is merely the "voice of a propagandist mediating for 'active cultural acceptance'" (Lim, 118). My suspicion is that Thumboo's poetry offers the appropriate nationalist structure of feeling corresponding to the facts of political and economic developmentalism: poetic renderings naturalize and aestheticize the city as the proper image of "our emergent selves."

Thus, more interesting is the way that Thumboo accedes to a model of poetry that sees its role as mediating or reconciling the existing realities of the nation to its people. While the formal tone, public nature, and influence of canonical English poets have all been identified in his poetry, what remains unsaid is Thumboo's remarkable fidelity to the objects of the Singaporean landscape as his poetic material. Returning to the theory of reading I invoked in the Introduction, recall Macherey's insight that literature is not merely a reflection of some other reality, but "is an authentic *production* rather than a reproduction" (qtd. in Kavanagh, 36) that nevertheless uses existing social realities as its raw material. In terms of this approach, we see how Thumboo's poetry assumes that the only way to use those raw materials is as pregiven, self-evident social objects, which results aesthetically in the "effect of deliberate arrangement" and "expository constructions" (Lim, 114). Although the contours of mythic history or daily lived experiences add another dimension to the imposing forms of Singapore's new landscape, they do not, in the end, challenge their fundamental status as something to be accommodated. By accepting both the forms and terms of development, Thumboo's poetry participates precisely in the reinscription of material progress into cultural-national progress and history.

By contrast, Yap's poetry invokes what we might term "small m" memory (Yap's general aversion to capital letters will be discussed further) and is often characterized by a limited, singular perspective. In explicit opposition to Thumboo's wide-lensed, nationalist perspective, Brewster notes that "many of [Yap's] scenes are framed by a window" (Introduction, xvi) where the preferred point of view is often from within the narrow and intimate Housing and Development Board flat. The effect is to reverse the top-down view of the cityscape and undermine those official discourses of development. In "sunny day," for example, the window frame thoroughly domesticates even the sun's actions—"sunny day / comes through the window / and sits on the table" (5). In "june morning," originally published in Yap's 1974 collection *Five Takes,* the mundane viewpoint of an anonymous inhabitant actually seems to precede the existence of the landscape:

> think sharp:
> this scene is also very brittle,
> copes with the problem of the accidental

to make it come more fully to life.

you look up from your thick black diary,

frowning, lines fragile as little bones

and it is you who structure this scenery. (37)

What is given substantial reality in this poem is not the observed exterior world from any perspective—the "brittle" scene—but the reader's internal thought: "your thick black diary." Such a shift in scale and hierarchy is echoed at the linguistic level, where Yap differs starkly from Thumboo's standard, at times formal, English. Patke notes, "Yap at his best excels at projecting a voice that is uniquely personal, but capable of absorbing Singlish [Singapore's English dialect] into the dramatization of a wide range of local sensibilities and speech habits" (*Postcolonial,* 75). As Yap himself has stated, however, it is not merely a choice between standard English and the development of a local literary language:

> it is certainly not merely a question of "standardness" nor is it, on the other hand, a set of quaint terms and idiosyncratic structures.... It is the use of language where the notions of "standardness" and "non-standardness" are not external prescriptions and where, internal in the situation, the two terms are perhaps not so crucial after all. (Yap qtd. in Patke, "Voice," 92)

Yap's poetry does more than simply narrate an oppositional, personalized experience "from below" in vernacular and local idiom. It involves "a bigger clutch of parameters" (Yap qtd. in Patke, "Voice," 92) that questions the poet's very "fidelity" or responsibility to the raw materials of his or her society. I have been describing how the new technological landscapes of statist development—the prosthesis of *techne* in Cheah's analysis—may be poetically inscribed through a coherent, mediating nationalist poetic voice (Thumboo) and, in reverse, challenged by a local, bottom-up perspective (Yap). While Yap's work offers an alternate, grassroots version of Singaporean experience, more radically, it reveals and goes beyond the material logic and ideology of the new productive landscape, undermining poetry's ontological dependence on those very forms of modernization. Let me work through this claim in two parts. First, note that for Macherey the available materials and social conditions do not fully determine the form of the work: "A condition is not that which is initially given, a cause in the empirical sense; it is the principle of rationality which makes the work accessible to thought" (55–56). As James H. Kavanagh puts it, the special nature of literature's transformative labor is that it "'resumes,' elaborates, and displays the ideological in a peculiar way, endowing it with a *visibility* that it did not have before the literary work" (36).

Yap's poem "& the tide" (1977) performs precisely this labor that makes visible the rationality—and not merely the material forms—of urban renewal.

& the tide which is being urban-renewed
at bedok must go on its own tidy ways
without too much of a fuss,
coming in as riprap waves
met by the breakwaters
or going out sufficiently
for undisturbed analysis.
& the sum of their margin:
a littoral of slightly raised damp sand
& carefully arrayed litter.
out there where the waves curl,
the liquid is greenly uneven
in the sun's rays & the sky's
layers of noon darkness. (58)

The ostensible theme of the poem is nature, where the tide, waves, sand, and sun's rays compose something like a beach scene. Yet these untamable natural forces all succumb to the calculus of a Housing and Development Board bureaucrat. The tide becomes another controllable feature of the landscape, "going out sufficiently / for undisturbed analysis," showcasing Yap's ear for "the formal bureaucratic English used by the civil-service class" (Lim, 152). From the perspective of the productivity-driven planning tenets, curving waves and liquid are found lacking as "greenly uneven," the double stressed syllables of the phrase gently mocking the equilibrium and measure demanded. Yap's originality lies precisely in the absurd application of the logic of urban renewal onto that most romantic of poetic material, the natural landscape, such that every inch of sand and water is now subject to the tidy imperatives of the productive state. By taking this logic, which pushes "tide" into "tidy" and "littoral" into "litter," to its illogical extreme, the poem distills the peculiar ideology of the developmentalist landscape—its indiscriminate and constant renewal—offering a deeply parodic materialist critique. Commenting on the enigmatic final lines of the poem, "the renewal of a large imagination / may be rare, in a seascape" (Yap, 58), Dennis Haskell comments, "Yap's poem may suggest that curtailment of nature means curtailment of the imagination also" (246).

The second part of my claim—that Yap moves beyond a materialist ideology—deals with just this "renewal of a large imagination," and how it simultaneously offers an alternative image of expansion. A striking feature of Yap's urban poetry is its anthropomorphization of the landscape and its lack of poetic agents. In the early poem "expansion" (1971), for example, the poet contemplates how

> the skyline of houses
> grows with the sky
> and who can tell
> what is this completion (10)

The poem progresses by way of loose chiasmus, putting the sky and houses into a reversed relation with "sponginess":

> the line of sponge houses
> soaks in the sky
> as the sponge sky
> seeps into the houses.
> where once houses hung from sky
> they now are clutches.
> so one urban expansion

has to lean on another
or they die.

while the tree of night grows and grows (10)

Mysteriously, the expanding stretch of new dwellings is absorbed, sponge-like, into the darkening sky, where they take on a life-form of their own. Existing as hybrid creatures in "clutches," they must "lean on another" in order to survive. We might think of the poetic impulse here as the reverse of that in "& the tide." Instead of nature being controlled and directed by an absurdly rationalist logic of development, here the very principle of expansion is what gives life to usually inanimate objects. In this case, the logic of the natural world—the symbiotic connection between life-forms, the tendency for creatures to huddle together—takes over the man-made environment. The result is an oddly antihumanist but living landscape; not quite devoid of human evidence, it is still firmly rooted in the organic world.

We can further understand Yap's reworking of nature/technology/humanity in terms of Benjamin's study of the Paris arcades. As we saw earlier, for Benjamin, the new architectural technology inaugurated in the nineteenth-century arcades (iron and glass construction and mass production) functions as something like a text in which competing images are reflected. The shift from traditional masonry columns to iron strut construction, for example, elicits "images in the collective consciousness in which the old and the new interpenetrate" (4). To requote the most relevant portion of Benjamin's explanation, "These images are wish images; in them the collective seeks both to overcome and to transfigure the immaturity of the social product and the inadequacies in the social organization of production.... These tendencies deflect the imagination (which is given impetus by the new) back upon the primal past" (4–5). In the most provocative of Yap's poems, we see both the critiquing of the "inadequacies" of the developmentalist logic—the revealing of its absurd logic—and the "deflect[ing of] the imagination" that intertwines the new and the "primal past." Yap reveals how these new urban technologies give rise not only to the urge to historicize and order them into a national image à la Thumboo, but also to the impetus for radically reimagining a social landscape where buildings and sky are organically connected, animate houses huddle together, and large-scale renewal applies to the imagination. Thus, at the moment of the actual wiping out of communal *kampongs* (Malay villages) under the processes of urban renewal, the new landscape also enables emergent images of a primal, mythic collectivity. In other words, Yap's poems do not merely narrate a localized, culturally specific viewpoint to counter the top-down, parachuted *techne* of roads, urban redevelopment, or bridges. His poetry offers us a way beyond both Lee's statist projects and Fanon's and Cabral's commitment to the release of productive powers for the authentic national project: it delinks the logic of production from the productive landscape itself. To put it in Benjaminian terms, his work reflects on the inadequacy or "immaturity of the social product"—on the forms of the developmental landscape—in order to liberate the forces of thinking and the reimagining of a collective project.

To look more carefully at the formal means by which Yap achieves this, let us again contrast one of Thumboo's poems. Recall "The Way Ahead" and Thumboo's re-creation of a bureaucratic planning meeting. Despite his acknowledgment of the spaces and moments that escape rationalist planning principles, the City retains its capitalization and its stability as object throughout the poem. Similarly, despite the free verse form, for much of the poem, the line length and rhythm are roughly uniform throughout, with each capitalized line corresponding to a natural breath or phrase unit. In contrast, a poem like Yap's "would it have been" from *Down the Line* (1980) relishes in breaking as many poetic conventions as possible. The first part of the poem reads:

> would it have been different if it were not an apple
> but a bomb which bit the world into being
>
> &, whatever the conditionals, would it be different
> after the bite, the lingua franca of the world
> were sign language, metalanguage, antilanguage,
> argot, braille, ipso facto esperanto (82)

First, as with all Yap's poems, uppercase letters are completely eschewed, giving all words the same (lack of) formality. Second, the poem seems less interested in mediating a world out there than in playing with a grammatical structure, the conditional tense: "would it have been different." The structure of each line, moreover, demonstrates the extent to which Yap rejects phrase- or breath-based poetic form. The second stanza starts abruptly with two typographical symbols, "&," and continues with two instances of interruptive enjambment: "different / after the bite" and "world / were sign language." The poem concludes:

> houses were nests & people prefabricated
> soyabean sculptures,
>
> sunlight falling on a field burnt grass
> into terminal rainbows,
>
> cities held to ransom by their own devils
> or collective dream sequences
>
> : would it be very different if all these things
> have had being been untrue? (82)

Even in the three stanzas where the poem settles into a regular formal pattern of discrete scenic images—"houses," "sunlight," and "cities"—the content of these images moves us firmly into the world of unreality. As in the previous poems discussed, Yap disrupts or confuses our idea of natural versus man-made logic by proffering nest-houses, "prefabricated / soyabean sculptures" and cities plagued by "collective dream sequences." What is most striking is the poetic challenging of their status of unreality. We expect the final stanza to read "would it be very different if all these things / *had been true?*" only to discover that the question imagines the poem's content being *untrue*, or—better—it describes the very problem of constructing an appropriate grammatical tense ("have had being been") for their unstable ontological status. What Yap does, therefore, is offer a powerful way to reread what otherwise would merely be the signifying forms, or *techne,* of state progress—those prefab houses, planned cities, and reclaimed tracts of land. Like the moment of Benjamin's Paris arcades, the gleaming new forms of Singapore's modernity are also an opportunity to deflect the imagination into previously unthought "collective dream sequences." Yap's poems thus allow us an alternative, three-dimensional way to make sense of the remarkable spatiality of Singapore's development.

Let us leave Singapore's unique urbanscape and turn now to Taiwan and the quite different configuration of Kuomintang-directed reconstruction of that island. Unlike the limited spaces of Singapore's city-state territory, in the next two chapters, we must attend to the vexed questions of rural to urban migration and the processes, images, and logic of countrywide industrialization.

6

Mobility and Migration in Taiwanese New Cinema

Neither will the city save the country nor the country the city. Rather the long struggle within both will become a general struggle, as in a sense it has always been.

—RAYMOND WILLIAMS, *The Country and the City*

KUOMINTANG RECONSTRUCTION ON TAIWAN

Expressions of statist modernization ideology in Kuomintang (KMT)-controlled Taiwan parallel much of what we have seen in Singapore. However, the comparison to Lee Kuan Yew is complicated by the fact that Chiang Kai-shek's speeches and writings were almost entirely negative in focus: Edwin Winckler writes that the KMT's "main positive state cultural program was anti-communist propaganda" (30). Second, they were not primarily directed at a Taiwanese audience, but at Chinese mainlanders and overseas Chinese communities. A sampling of Chiang's speeches on a variety of occasions all bear the familiar refrains of "the outlaw Mao" and his "threat to world peace," the "false regime of the Communists," and, of course, the task of "national recovery" *(fuguo)* or "retaking the Mainland." Taiwan is figured as the "revolutionary base" where the material buildup of "military strength and economic prowess" allows for the spiritual command of "the hearts of our 700 million compatriots on the mainland as well as the patriotism of our 18 million anti-Communist compatriots living overseas" (Chiang, *Selected Speeches,* 46). For Chiang's more positive ideas on Chinese reconstruction, however, we can turn to his 1952 *Chapters on National Fecundity, Social Welfare, Education, and Health and Happiness.* These were written as supplements to the unfinished third section of Dr. Sun Yat-sen's *People's Three Principles,* or *San Min Chu I (San Min Zhu Yi),*[1] consisting of the Principle of Nationalism, the Principle of Democracy, and the Principle of People's Livelihood, or Minsen *(Min sheng)*.[2]

Chiang's detailed writings on the question of the People's Livelihood include meditations on welfare, educational aims, and especially population control. Although they are written primarily in regard to mainland China, we can trace trends in Taiwan's physical development back to the preoccupation of both Sun Yat-sen and Chiang with the successful transformation from agricultural to industrial societies. Regarding urbanization, Chiang follows Sun in recognizing the potential imbalances between urban and rural lifestyles. Echoing early European urban theorists, he writes that industrialization and city life bring a characteristic "tension which drives all persons on and on, ever hurrying and busy at their jobs," causing "problems in connection with [the urban dweller's] waking hours, his sleep, his work, and his free moments" (Chiang, *Chapters,* 72–73). Chiang notes that contrary to these perils, "in Taiwan there is not much difference between urban and rural life. Its cities are dotted with scenes characteristic of village life, and its villages are provided with public means of communication, electricity, and other facilities" (75).[3] On the mainland, equally, "we must achieve the ruralization of cities and the urbanization of villages before our people can live in a really healthy and happy environment" (75). Despite gestures toward Sun's (and Mao's) socialist-style welfare and reforms, Chiang ends his supplement with a curious explanation of the "Era of Minor Prosperity," the immediate forerunner to "The Great Commonwealth." Like Lee Kuan Yew's "Asian Democracy" and Park Chung Hee's concepts of "Presidential Guidance" and "Administrative Democracy" (or countless other euphemisms for postcolonial authoritarianism), for Chiang, democratic political systems and redistributive economic systems are understood to be possible only after a period of tutelage and the buildup of wealth.

In the Era of Minor Prosperity, following Sun Yat-sen's definitions, economics is "dictated by free enterprise," and social welfare is provided by families and the clan system. Drawing from Sun's description of the previous "Age of Absolute Monarchs," politics is a system in which "the supreme authority is vested in a ruling family and handed down from father to son, and the community protects itself against hostile attacks by building strong walls and digging deep trenches and moats" (Chiang, *Chapters,* 106). The goal, of course, is to move from the Era of Minor Prosperity to the Great Commonwealth, which will be a "free and secure society" in which all boys receive a state education and become "independent citizens enjoying all the rights of political suffrage, liberty and struggle" (106–7). Such a society is only reached, however, by way of "the Minsen [People's Livelihood] type of reconstruction [which] is a sort of bridge that serves to lead from one to the other" (106). In Chiang's logic, then, the Minsen principles are not the goal of the nation's development but rather its means: "In our efforts to carry out our task of revolutionary reconstruction, we should be able eventually to reach the . . . Great Commonwealth, if only we would go towards the bridge and march straight on" (106). We can conceive of the KMT's project on Taiwan as the geographic version of the Era of Minor Prosperity, a transitional system characterized by capitalistic relations, the clan-based social system, and the building of strong walls. Taiwan and its people are not merely the ex-Japanese territory that will be resinicized through development; it will become the very bridge to an eventual defeat of communism and Chinawide reconstruction. As with the analysis of Singapore, this chapter examines the symbolic logic of official nationalism and its metaphoric use of infrastructural development. While poetry was the most relevant medium for reinscriptions of such nationalism in Singapore, the early films of Hou Hsiao-hsien, the major figure of the Taiwanese New Cinema movement, have most provocatively recast elements of KMT-led development and modernity. The question of cinema in Taiwan—and cinematic development in our other two sites—will be considered later in the chapter.

The KMT's emphasis on developing light industry, mechanizing agriculture, and improving transport and infrastructure during the 1960s and 1970s intensified in proportion to the weakening of Taiwan's political standing. As in Singapore and South Korea, economic development came to be figured as coterminous with the nation's destiny. After the shock of Nixon's visit to China in 1972 and the loss of Taiwan's seat in the U.N. (and diplomatic recognition from many nations) to the People's Republic of China, economic development became the raison d'être of the increasingly alienated KMT regime. As Bérénice Reynaud remarks, "especially during the diplomatic isolation of the 1970s—it was a place you could not leave" (75). After Chiang Kai-shek's sudden death in 1975, the KMT government strove even harder to complete the task "of building Taiwan into a *San Min*

Chu I model province" (Hsieh, 2), a task that required the "accelerated development" of the island. Governor Hsieh Tung-min's 1976 report to the Taiwanese Assembly begins with pledges of faithfulness to both Chiang Kai-shek's and Sun Yat-sen's People's Three Principles. The practical program of the government, however, focuses exclusively on four major infrastructure projects: "construction of the Suao-Hualien section of the round-the-island chain of railways[,] . . . the Taichung Highway, electrification of the North–South Railway Line in the western part of Taiwan, and expansion of the Suao Harbor" (Hsieh, 5). Such grand-scale projects had begun as early as the late 1950s under the direction of Chiang's son and successor, Chiang Ching-kuo, and would continue apace through the latter's presidency (1978–88). In the assembly report, Hsieh describes how "political reconstruction" *(zhengzhi jianshe)* based on the Three Principles is to be effected through four fundamental economic principles: "that man's potential be fully exploited *[ren jin qi cai]*, that the resources of land be fully exploited *[di jin qi li]*, that all good things in life be turned to good account [*wu jin qi yong*, literally, that things be exhausted, or used to their utmost], and that the free flow of goods be facilitated *[huo chang qi liu]*" (Hsieh, 17). What occurs here, as in the other narratives of developmental states, is that potential discussion over the nation's direction, which the Three Principles ostensibly raises, is displaced into questions over the means for the full exploitation of labor and resources and the "free flow of goods." Regarding the latter principle, Governor Hsieh specifies:

> To facilitate the free flow of goods, the main points to be aimed at are to let no hindrances stand in the way of their transportation and their safe arrival at their destination so as to preserve their timely value and help to stabilize commodity prices. To attain these objectives, we should build and expand more railroads, highways, truckways and harbours and ports on the one hand and, what is still more important, develop a sound and efficient system of transportation and make an overall study for the rational improvement of transportation, on the other hand. (27)

Not only are rural areas now to be efficiently connected to cities, ports, and harbors by such a transportation revolution, but villages displaying irrational planning will be duly corrected:

In addition, in order to improve the rural environment and raise the farm-ers' standard of living, we are undertaking a program for the replotting of dwelling-houses in areas marked out for community development. The pro-gram calls for abandoning the old lanes and streets that are irregular in shape or narrow and small and dilapidated houses and replotting and rebuild-ing them into paved roads and orderly and splendid buildings with several storeys, and leaving sufficient open spaces in between to beautify the envi-ronment or to be used for productive purposes. (13)

What is most striking, of course, is the explicit desire for newness, regular-ity, and rationality of built forms, familiar to us from Lee Kuan Yew's writ-ings and—we will see in the next chapter—Park Chung Hee's prescriptions for modernizing Korean villages.

In Taiwan, such remarkable islandwide achievements in transport and communication were relatively successful in staving off the worst levels of urban–rural inequality and avoided overly concentrated industrialization in just one or two areas as seen, for example, in Korea's greater Seoul and southeast coastal areas. The highway and train system inherited from the Japanese was improved, especially the north–south route, and the estab-lishment of the Kaohsiung Export Processing Zone in 1966 in southern

A busy Kaohsiung highway in Hou Hsiao-hsien's *The Boys from Fengkuei* (1983).

Taiwan countered exclusive migration and development in the north of the island (Tsai, 218–19). Nevertheless, by the mid-1980s, half of Taiwan's population was residing in the four largest metropolises of Taipei, Taichung, Tainan, and Kaohsiung (Tsai, 229), indicating that the transport system had not facilitated the free flow of goods alone, but also of rural migrants to the urban centers.

Like the national spaces of South Korea and Singapore, the raison d'être of Taiwanese reconstruction lies not in itself but in a deferred future. And like divided Korea, this is a temporal *and* geographic future in which the unified national spirit and territory will be coterminously realized. In a reversal of the Fanonian formula for building national culture—where every citizen was to participate politically as well as physically—the nation's actualization is understood as the aftereffect of state-directed development, and is popular insofar as it calls for the entire nation's economic or military participation. Chiang's idea of reconstruction *(jianshe)* is thus the temporal and ideological link to a new future. Let us not forget, however, that all three leaders also had clear agendas for more conventional versions of cultural nationalism, as Lee Kuan Yew's interest in neo-Confucianism or Asian Values, Taiwan's Chinese revivalist architecture, and South Korea's historical nationalist discourses attest.[4] I contend, however, that what enables this structure of delayed national liberation is not the regime's ability to define the direction of national culture in such conventional terms. Nor is it simply the political repression of the masses combined with a canniness in assuming the bureaucratic forms of the colonial state, or what Chatterjee calls, after Gramsci, the "passive revolution" of "find[ing] for 'the nation' a place in the global order of capital" (*Nationalist Thought,* 168). What is important is the ability of the state to *narrate* this revolutionary future nation—both to other nations and to its own people—through the built forms of modernization. As we noted via Castells in the second Transition, there is something of the structure of revolutionary vanguardism in developmental states. Lee Kuan Yew's determination to make Singapore into a first world oasis through meticulously kept roads and golf courses had the effect of proclaiming this status in advance of the fact; similarly, we will see how Park Chung Hee's exhortation to replace dirt roads and thatched roofs with concrete is the material act that represents the raising of Korea in the ranks of the world. Equally, the KMT's economic rationalization of

Taiwanese space constitutes the "imagined totality" (Anderson), which is also the means to a recaptured and unified China.

Taiwanese Space in Literature and Film

We should not be surprised that nationalist discourses in postcolonial Taiwan have been complex. Of the major strands, one has revolved around the incorporation of Taiwan into a greater Chinese nationalism (a goal absolutely agreed on by the KMT and the People's Republic of China, but in opposing terms); the other stresses the idea of a distinct and separate Taiwanese consciousness based on the local experiences of early Chinese migration, Japanese colonialism, and the postwar development of the island. Coming out of the *hsiang-t'u* literary scene (discussed in chapter 3), there were two main nationalist ideological camps by the late 1970s: the mainland-oriented group affiliated with the San-san bookshop and journal, and the "neo-nativist movement that no longer espoused the *hsiang-t'u* literature of old but the more provocatively named Taiwanese indigenous literature *[taiwan ben-t'u wenxue]*" (Yip, 45). Certain members of the latter group, in pushing their claims for total independence from China, used only the Taiwanese language and even claimed that the Taiwanese were a different race from the Chinese (Yip, 46).[5] These two groups thus bring the logical binaries identified by the *hsiang-t'u* movement to their extremes and indicate the moment when the once-strident modernist versus nativist debate had effectively played itself out. In contrast to the previous decades, when the categories of "city" and "country" were at their most oppositional, by the 1980s, urban lifeways had become somewhat consolidated. Yang Chao explains: "Activist nativism in the 1970s makes the rural area a base for attacking the city and is therefore teeming with self-righteous words of fire and brimstone. In comparison, 1980s mainstream nativism takes the city as the central point of reference and often looks to rural villages and towns as wellsprings of spiritual energy" (101). Furthermore, because the energies of "the more radical Nativists . . . were increasingly channeled into direct political involvement" and the 1980s saw the rise of more popular and sentimental literary trends (Chang, "Modernism," 3), conditions were ripe for the emerging relevance of cinema. Before moving to the question of film, however, there is a significant voice in Taiwanese literature of the late 1970s and 1980s that deserves our attention: that of Ch'en Ying-chen.

Known as a committed leftist writer, he was charged with unspecified subversive activities by the KMT government and imprisoned from 1968 to 1975, when his ten-year sentence was commuted in an amnesty honoring the death of Chiang Kai-shek (Miller, 3). Like other Taiwanese of his generation, the works of mainland Chinese literature were proscribed to him, but thanks to a fortuitous encounter with Lu Xun's work, Ch'en's writings may be figured as part of the larger Chinese tradition rather than as a separatist Taiwanese writer (Miller, 22), making him unique in this period.

Ch'en's early works are often melancholy or satirical and deal with issues of nihilism, political idealism, and the experience of war, while his later stories deal more explicitly with the nature of Taiwan's heady development. After his release from prison, he wrote a series of stories known as the Washington Building stories (Huashengdun dalou gushi), which critique the new business world of Taiwan brought about by the advent of multinational firms. Miller gives the background to these stories:

> A number of western and Japanese multinational corporations and banks established branches in Taiwan and took advantage of cheap labor, favourable tax and trade incentives, and the general absence of environmental restrictions, labor unions, and safety regulations. . . . Within a decade, Taiwan became a consumer culture, a sometimes smugly superior second-world [*sic*] entity among the third-world community of other poorer Asian countries subject to the vagaries of the world economic climate and foreign investment as well as the failures of the local factory. (8)

In this context, Ch'en's stories certainly "tak[e] the city as the central point of reference," but rather than look to rural life for balancing "wellsprings of spiritual energy," he takes its new consumer culture to task on its own terms. His stories critique the insular world of corporate life in Taipei, the petty office politics of the American multinational firm, the English-speaking Taiwanese staff and their downtown condos. We might read Ch'en's work as a partial continuation of the literary strategies we saw in chapter 3, where urban forms are ciphers for much larger economic/social systems. The limitation of Ch'en's strategy, however, is that the sole focus on condemning this system attenuates the stories' critical power. Joseph S. M. Lau notes that in his postincarceration writing, he is "less concerned with dialectics than with the question of Chinese selfhood being sapped by the forces of modernization" ("Ch'en Ying-chen," 102).

In the story "One Day in the Life of a White Collar Worker," for example, we spend a day with Olive, an upwardly mobile Taiwanese who has worked for ten years for Taiwan Morrison, earning good money and leading an affluent, Americanized life. He works in "Morrison's spacious, elegant, and fully air-conditioned offices" in downtown Taipei (Ch'en, 176), takes taxis rather than walks, eats Western food at places like Harvey's, and enjoys a Taiwanese mistress by the name of Rose (who eventually leaves Taiwan to live in the United States with an American serviceman). The anchoring spatial figure of this story is the building that houses the Morrison offices: "In the white heat the Washington Building stood straight up, oblivious to all else" (185). Such a description echoes both the twenty-four-story hotel in Huang Chunming's "The Two Sign Painters" and the high-rise of Cho Se-hŭi's "A Little Ball." Yet the perspective is now that of its white-collar inhabitant, rather than migrant construction worker or slum dweller. The only instance that working-class Taiwanese enter the story is when Olive daydreams about one day returning to the filmmaking that he studied in college. In a moment of idleness, he imagines shooting a scene: "Start with the revolving wheel, then move to the lunch-box mounted behind the seat. Next, the most menial white-collar worker is seen riding the bicycle and disappearing down a street filled with private cars, taxis, and buses. At the end, the camera shifts to a shot of skyscrapers that look like a huge forest of building blocks" (178). From this worker's perspective, imagined by Olive, central Taipei and its office buildings take on the completely different aspect of "a huge forest of building blocks." Yet in Ch'en's story, the scene functions as a mere moment of indulgent reverie before Olive's attention returns to the real business of office politics. Although the author's critique of the hollow consumerism of this lifestyle is clear, there is no alternative position from which the dominance of the Washington Building culture is perceived. There is, moreover, no tension around the individual's development because Olive is a fully formed adult with little capacity to change—this is no bildungsroman tale of moral education. Finally, the actual transformations of the Taiwanese countryside and the grand infrastructural developments on which these corporate operations rely are completely blocked from view; all that can be summoned up is the clichéd figure of "the most menial white-collar worker." In a sense, Ch'en's stories reveal the way Taiwan's national development is lopsidedly interpreted as a completely urban phenomenon. It is at this moment, I argue, that the most urgent debates connecting the representation of islandwide development to national narratives emerge in cinema.

First, I want briefly to discuss the question of cinema in relation to what has until now been an engagement with urban form through literature. In general terms, the cinematic presentation of architecture and urbanism may seem to provide more transparent access to spatial realities as a result of its indexical relationship to them. Yet as the vast array of cinematic interpretive methods—including formal, narratological, psychoanalytic, Deleuzian, and reception-oriented, just to name a few—attests that the task of interpreting spaces in films is no more straightforward than in literature. Balshaw and Kennedy provide a good summary of the relationship of visual representation more broadly to urban form:

> Visual representation may be said to bring the city into focus: it frames recognition of urban forms (architectural syntax, street signage); it offers legibility through the reproduction of what is seen (in maps, plans, guides and images); it unites aesthetic and spatial apprehension of the urban scene (levels, planes, perspectives); it mediates scopophilic and voyeuristic desires (to look, to be seen); it technologises the act of seeing (the fusion of the eye and the camera lens). (7)

Among the many functions of visual representation, I am especially interested in Taiwanese New Cinema for what it can "bring . . . into focus" and make legible in contrast to the KMT perspective, which operates along the lines of Lefebvre's two-dimensional abstract space. Unlike the masterplan view of the island's smooth transit networks and flowing goods, Taiwanese New Cinema is able to "map transitions in physical and mental space, locating and dislocating the viewing subject's relation to the city as a space of representation" (Balshaw and Kennedy, 8). As with literary forms, I am interested less in the mimetic function of cinema—what the lens can simply capture of the city's landscape—than how the incorporation and arrangement of built figures reveal less visible contradictions and struggles occurring within them. Before exploring this, it is worth considering the trajectories of each country's film industries to fully appreciate the unusual development of Taiwanese New Cinema.

While all three countries now have established film industries—Korean and Taiwanese film in particular are now staples of international film festivals and art-house cinema showings—independent cinema in each location has a distinct history. Kenneth Paul Tan recounts the standard view of Singapore's film industry, which "begins with the 'golden age' of mostly Malay-language filmmaking by the Shaw and Cathay-Keris studios in the 1940s to 1960s, moves into the 'dark ages' when nothing of significance was produced in a newly independent nation obsessed with economic achievement, and then enters a government-induced rebirth in the 1990s" (42). While scholars have noted that this ignores the grassroots film- and video-making activities of the 1980s, the problem for film—in contrast to literature—is that it is highly subject to government production laws and censorship, meaning independent film is often later to emerge than its literary counterparts. In Singapore, the "new wave of filmmaking [that] emerged" in the 1990s (Tan, 41) was enabled by the government recognizing cinema's commercial prospects and encouraging its development as part of the culture of a world-class city. The year 1988 saw the simultaneous establishment of Singapore's Advisory Council on Culture and the Arts and the first mainstream film production company, Raintree Pictures, which began producing films by Singaporean directors Jack Neo, Eric Khoo, and Kelvin Tong in the early 1990s (Tan, 48–49). The last decade has seen a dramatic increase in the number of films produced, largely aimed at domestic audiences.

The Korean film industry under Park Chung Hee's rule (1961–79), while existent, was centrally controlled through draconian laws. Park's motion picture law of 1961 overnight "reduced the number of licensed film production companies from seventy-one to sixteen" by limiting licenses to companies with large-scale production facilities able to produce the minimum fifteen films per year each (Standish, 73). Although the quota system—which linked domestic production to foreign film importation—actually saw the number of domestic films increase, most were what were known as "quota quickies" of poor quality (Standish, 73). By the early 1970s, domestic film quality had dropped, and Park's *Yusin* reforms (to be discussed in the next chapter) "required film companies to produce films directly related to government policies" (Standish, 74). It wasn't until the mid- to late 1980s that, in tune with broader political liberalization, substantial amendments were made to filmmaking laws and the production field opened up again. In the two decades since this time, Korea has boasted a number of internationally recognized filmmakers, including Im Kwon-taek, Kim Ki-duk, and Park Chan-wook.

Taiwan's cinema history shares elements of both Singapore's and Korea's industries. A Taiwanese-language film industry had been allowed to develop under the Japanese and flourished in the early postwar period with more that 2,000 films made, rivaling Hong Kong's film industry at the time. These films were formulaic and filmed quickly (usually in seven to ten days) on locations in the Beitou area north of Taipei. By the end of the 1960s, however, Mandarin-language film had overtaken them in production levels as the KMT promoted Mandarin as the national language *(guoyu)*. The KMT-run Central Motion Picture Company announced "healthy realism" as their filmmaking policy, which ironically produced films that were not realistic at all: martial arts films and romances were the order of the day. During the 1960s and 1970s, the KMT effectively controlled Taiwan's film industry, with the result that Mandarin-language films came to wipe out the once thriving Taiwanese-language industry of the late colonial period and 1950s.[6] Unlike in Singapore and Korea, however, which had to wait until the late 1980s or early 1990s and formal political liberalization, events in Taiwan conspired to give room to independent film earlier. In Sung-Sheng Yvonne Chang's account, Taiwanese New Cinema arose "around 1982–83" and signaled "the coming of age of the baby boom generation of artists and the disintegration of the ruling Nationalist regime's ideological domination" ("Twentieth-Century," 141). This period also coincides with the tenure of Chiang Ching-kuo, who, while retaining a tight reign of the country (his name literally means "managing the country") is credited with initiating political liberalization.[7] The New Cinema also fortuitously benefited from the new policies of the Central Motion Picture Corporation, which "supported serious-minded young filmmakers as part of its desperate attempt to salvage Taiwan's bankrupting film industry" (Chang, "Twentieth-Century," 141). For Kuan-hsing Chen, this desire for a new locally based national cinema is also linked to the moment at which Taiwanese consumer society had matured:

With the so-called "Taiwan Miracle," a consumer society was to take shape in the late 1970s which had diversified and shifted the landscape of cultural tastes in the market. Hence, a new generation of moviegoers demanded something directly connected to their own experiences. . . . In short, the formation of the TNC was historically overdetermined by economic and political forces. ("Taiwanese New Cinema," 558)

What is unique, then, is that while martial law in Taiwan was not lifted until 1987, an unusual breathing space was given to independent filmmaking some years prior. While Taiwanese New Cinema, like Korean New Wave cinema of the 1990s and 2000s, has since flourished with the international success of Edward Yang and Tsai Ming-liang, it is the early films of founding figure Hou Hsiao-Hsien that are the focus of the remainder of this chapter. These films, I argue—like poetry in Singapore and *minjung* fiction in South Korea—grapple with the subject and forms of state-led modernization at a moment before political reforms and consumer benefits become the accepted teleology of industrialization. Although Hou's films are made at the cusp of this transition, several of them are explicitly interested in the pre-Ching-kuo KMT years of the 1960s and 1970s. Interestingly, several 1980s Taiwanese directors have sought to revisit these decades "as a world that hadn't, up to that point, been given any representation on film" (Yip, 64). Duan Chen-su writes:

We find that, in the eighties, when the New Taiwan Cinema Movement began, there came up different perspectives for reviewing the history of the sixties. With a critical spirit and a realistic style, film creators give a different representation of the details of ordinary people's life from before, through such manners of presentation as actors' unrefined performance, real-life setting, natural light source, long shots by deep-focused lens. (73)

The depictions of youth migrating from the countryside to the metropolis (or vice versa) in Hou's films *The Boys from Fengkuei* (1983), *Summer at Grandpa's* (1984), and *Dust in the Wind* (1986) recount a central reality of Taiwan's history; early Taiwanese New Cinema thus attempts to re-present a crucial, passed-over moment in Taiwanese national development. Not coincidentally, the period is that of Hou's individual, and Taiwan's industrial, development. Yip writes of Hou's migration films: "Adolescence, after all, is a difficult period of transition during which one experiences both a sentimental nostalgia for childhood and a desire to achieve adulthood. One might therefore describe the current period of transition from country to city as the adolescence of Taiwanese society" (210). As we saw in chapter 3, the trauma and trials of adolescent protagonists can be read as the trials of individuals against the entropic forces of the city. With the broader historical focus of Hou's cinematic lens, however, they become important for the national redefinitions of the 1980s. As Yip writes of Hou's autobiographical film *A Time to Live and a Time to Die:*

> Hou's luminous film transcends its personal coming of age story to become an examination of the origins of modern Taiwanese life, a graceful and elegiac tracing of Taiwan's history from the KMT government's exile to Taiwan in 1949 to its decades of quasi-colonial rule on the island and the gradual relinquishment of the dream of returning to the mainland. (61)

Thus, these bildungsroman narratives of Taiwanese New Cinema "[signal] the end of an era and the beginning of a new one: the move from an agricultural to an industrial society, from poor rural life to the urban centers, from political identification with China to that of Taiwan" (Chen, "Taiwanese New Cinema," 559).[8] Unlike Ch'en Ying-chen's caustic internal critique of urban consumer culture, Hou's narratives insist on seeing these shifts as more complex and dialectical processes and contribute to the construction of a new and syncretic Taiwanese consciousness.

Hou is best known for his Taiwan trilogy, comprising *City of Sadness* (1989), *The Puppetmaster* (1993), and *Good Men, Good Women* (1995). The three films, which address the 2/28 massacre, Japanese colonial rule, and the 1950s communist hunt known as the "white terror," respectively, were all groundbreaking in their treatment of previously taboo historical subjects as well as for their artistic innovations. Yip has read these films as expressions of a popular countermemory challenging the official KMT-centered history that excluded the realities, linguistic differences, and struggles of the Taiwanese. Following the path blazed by the *hsiang-t'u* writers, Taiwanese New Cinema directors "have dedicated themselves to challenging the narrow view of modern history institutionalized by schools and official culture by acknowledging the multiplicity of historically subordinated groups in Taiwanese society" (Yip, 73). More than just restoring balance to narratives of Taiwan's development, such works also create a new historical narrative mode: they represent political and public events in terms of the micro-level, everyday effects and events of individuals and families. In rewriting public events through common subjective experiences, such films figure national identity from, as it were, the bottom up, reminding us of Arthur Yap's poetic strategy in Singapore. In one of the most important films to launch the Taiwanese New Cinema, the portmanteau collection of adapted Huang Chunming stories *The Sandwich Man* (*Erzi de da wanou,* or His Son's Big Doll, 1983), Hou Hsiao-hsien insisted that his film's dialogue be in Taiwanese, rather than Mandarin—a radical move at the time.[9] Hou's films, however, do not simply assert Taiwanese language or culture against the official Mandarin one, or a transposed nativist aesthetic against a modernist one. His other films use a variety of Chinese dialects: Shanghainese features prominently in *City of Sadness,* Mandarin is dominant in *The Boys from Fengkuei,* and the autobiographical *A Time to Live, A Time to Die* features a mix of accented Mandarin, Cantonese, and Hokkien (Chris Berry, 42). It is precisely the ability of Hou's films to fold both modernist and nativist representative strategies into a unique cinematic spatiality that makes his work exemplary for this study.

By following individual routes of migration, Hou foregrounds the dialectical passage between rural and urban subjectivities—the physical and psychic journeys of getting from one place to another—accompanying Taiwan's general shift to modernized industrial society. Like the *hsiangt'u* writers, he is concerned with the specificity of Taiwanese land and Taiwanese placeness without their tendency for binary formations. Unlike the main *hsiang-t'u* proponents, who were all local Taiwanese, Hou, a second-generation mainlander, moves beyond simple dichotomies between country/city and Taiwanese/mainlander to a more nuanced framing of the nation based on concrete lived experiences in the developmental state. If the Taiwanese New Cinema has "brought its field of vision home to our native soil, to everyday realities, to the people and events that surround us" (Yip, 59), the accelerated reconstruction of Taiwan since the 1960s is the event that most affected people's everyday relationship to that soil. The new aesthetic visioning of the nation thus emerges not from an idealist, nativist conception of culture (as Fanon had indeed warned against), but from the forging of new subjectivities within new developmental spaces.

Hou's bildungsroman films depict a series of individual negotiations with the changing relationship between city and country. *Dust in the Wind (Lian lian feng chen)* follows the story of teenagers Wan and Huen, who, after completing middle school, leave their mountainside village to find work in Taipei. In this film set in the 1960s right on the cusp of Taiwan's economic takeoff, Taipei is visually presented almost exclusively in terms of cramped work spaces typical of the small, family-owned factories that were often subcontracted to larger Japanese or U.S. companies. For Wan, this means a noisy and grim printing factory, and for Huen a cagelike seamstress shop. Other scenes take place in the dilapidated back room of a cinema, where Wan finds lodging with some friends and, once or twice, the interior of a noisy pub. In the film's visual logic, the usual terms used to describe relative size do not obtain: the "big" city of Taipei is always cramped and claustrophobic, with no long shots or cityscapes at all. Conversely, the "tiny" hometown village is presented in wide and lingering establishing shots that take in treetops, sky, and the common courtyard the village households share (Yip, 205–6).[10] The technological and cinematic link between the bleak city and the lush village is the train; in the film's first image, the train emerges from a tunnel and careers through verdant mountainsides on the two teenagers' return from middle school in the city. The film alternates between a series of scenes at the village and in the city, connected by a repeated shot of the darkened train tunnel leading into or out of the village—the literal portal between the two worlds.

The scenes in the city are bracketed by a view of the Taipei train station clock indicating how "urban life . . . is measured in abstract time—divided into sequential units to be defined, counted and consumed" (Yip, 207). The first Taipei scene also conveys the city's new sociality though its distinct timing and shot composition. Wan, who has already been working in the printing factory for some time, goes to meet Huen at the station, where, he discovers, she has naively entrusted her bags to a stranger. As Wan confronts the stranger to retrieve the bags, an oddly undramatic struggle follows between Wan and the stranger, who refuses to give them up. Eventually, the bag—a gift of village-grown potatoes—is spilled all over the railway tracks, implying that the routes leading to opportunity and education are also the site of confusion and deceit. Even more significant is the scene's unusual framing. The struggle takes place in an extreme long shot, with no camera movement or soundtrack to direct our viewing. The result is that we are not quite sure what we are watching: who is the elderly stranger? And whose bags are they fighting over? The viewer is placed in the position of mere bystander, not quite close enough to the scene of action to fully understand it, let alone intervene. At a formal level, this corresponds to the city's very indifference to the trials of the newcomers and gestures toward the general alienated structure of urban society.

Recalling that Hou's narrative project is to open up "different perspectives for reviewing the history of the sixties," we see how the migrant's individual experiences occur on the very channels cleared by Chiang Ching-kuo and Governor Hsieh's policies for the free flow of goods described in the first section of this chapter. But unlike mere goods, the migrant is not guaranteed a "safe arrival" that preserves his or her "timely value." The experience of the city is found to be neither rational nor efficient, but full of contingencies and struggles. Wan splits his time between exhausting

Wan and Huen encounter a stranger at Taipei Station in *Dust in the Wind* (1986).

work for the printing company, visits to Huen (to whom he must speak through the barred windows of her workplace), and night school. Shortly after he finds a better job as a deliveryman, his moped is stolen while out shopping with Huen, forcing him to borrow money from her to repay the boss. Meanwhile, Huen suffers a burn while on the job, and we learn that another village boy working in the city is severely beaten by his boss. Most of these events take place offscreen and are therefore—like the distant, awkward struggle at the railway station—muted and undramatic; we hear of them in passing, just as the events themselves are unremarkable every-day occurrences to the city. The physical and psychological toll of such conditions are evident when Wan becomes seriously ill, yet they are only verbalized by one friend who is in the hospital after being beaten again by his boss. During a hospital visit, the friend begins to rant about his night-mare: "Billboards were falling from the sky . . . I couldn't escape . . . got hit all over." The city is precisely the space where the dead labor of exchange value takes precedent and haunts—or physically threatens—the living.

The logic of migration results in the formal exaggeration of movement and nonmovement in the film. In visual contrast to the numerous de-partures and arrivals of the film, we see Wan standing at work, locked in position by his repetitive movements at the printing machine, while Huen sits and sews behind bars. Unlike the mobility implicitly promised by the bridge imagined by Chiang Kai-shek to lead to the Great Commonwealth, migrating back and forth from the countryside requires long intervals of achingly fixed labor. The landscape of development is thus one alternat-ing between extreme movement and stillness. In an interview with Hou, Michael Berry comments on the frequency of "on-the-road" sequences in his films: "Whether it be cars, trains *(Dust in the Wind, City of Sadness),* motorcycles *(Goodbye South, Goodbye),* or simply walking, the whole issue of movement and the dialogic relationship between the country and the city is very important for your works" (702). When asked whether these things are "purely visual devices" or in service of a "larger allegorical read-ing," Hou compares the individual's desire to travel around a circum-scribed island to the nation's economic needs:

When I was young, transportation wasn't very developed, so we would have to take the train to get out of Fengshan. We would travel all around the island, from north to south, east to west. . . . This outward longing actually holds true not only for the individual, but for Taiwan as well. Whether it be economics, or what have you, Taiwan has always been forced to look outward because of its dense population and limited local resources. Living in a small, closed place it is only natural to look to the outside in order to develop. This longing for the outside seems to have, almost unconsciously, worked its way into my films in these road sequences. (Hou qtd. in Michael Berry, 702–3)

Hou's "longing for the outside," echoing the directionality of Taiwan's export-led industrialization, gets reworked formally in terms of the shifting spatiality between country and urban lifeways. Rather than plot or dramatic events, the film hinges on the spatial tension emerging from the desire for movement running up against the fixed and claustrophobic spaces of the city.

In Hou's films, the portrayal of stillness and drudgery versus the desire for movement and fluidity is resolved by what I call the sideliner aesthetic. Chris Berry explains how the quality of his long shots evoke the position of the "sidelined bystander": "Hou's camerawork . . . mimes this position, choosing long shots and minimal camera movement over any interventionist stylistic gestures such as the close-up or the shot–reverse-shot sequence" (44). According to the director himself, his fondness for long shots came fortuitously through filming master shots of dialogue scenes, which guide actors in shadow acting reverse-angle shots. "Often," Hou comments, "we found that the reverse-angle close-ups weren't needed at all, and so I developed a preference for continuous takes from one angle" (qtd. in Rayns, 164). Acknowledging Hou's claims that he was not deliberately "resisting Hollywood conventions or consciously trying to evolve a 'Chinese' style" (164), we can read this formal strategy as resulting from the particular organization of movement and stillness required of Taiwan's migrating labor force. Han resists the close-up, with all its references to individuality and personal agency, and his characters are more often than not simply defined by the spatial location they find themselves in. Exemplifying this is the scene in which Wan and his grandfather walk to the bus that will take Wan to military service on the island of Quemoy. After Wan leaves the scene, the grandfather lingers in the extreme distance, continuing to light firecrackers. The viewer, puzzling over this barely discernible activity for such a long time, can do nothing else but consider the relationship of the old man to the scene *around* him: the boundaries of the village, the not-quite-in-view road on which we presume the bus has just departed, and the distance growing between himself and Wan.

To be sure, then, Hou's films and their sideliner aesthetic resist presenting the countryside in unequivocally positive terms. As a counterpoint to the scenes of the city, country life is characterized by beauty but also by poverty and violence. The family dwelling is meager, and the adult men of the village labor for low wages in a dangerous coal mine, indicating the village has, in fact, long been incorporated into an industrialized economy. At the end of the film—after enduring three years of military service and losing Huen, who marries a postman—Wan returns to his village. The final scene is one of uncertain reconciliation with the land: in contrast to the muted city scenes, his loquacious grandfather expounds at length on potato farming against a background of lush mountainside. The scene is prefaced by another close shot of the train signal at the village station, which we now realize is a kind of mechanical face, observant yet oblivious to all human dramas. Throughout Wan's trips back and forth to his hometown, the "visual motif shots" (Reynaud, 73) of this signal, the railway

Wan bids farewell to his grandfather in one of *Dust in the Wind*'s extreme long shots.

tunnel, and the empty station platform have silently punctuated his move-ment. In the service of the developing economy and militarized state, Wan's experience of growing up reveals the other side to developmental-ism's obsession with free-flowing movement. While the economy com-pensates for the Taiwanese "outward longing" with export production and domestic spatial integration, the mobility required of its laborers thwarts real passage or progress.

I suggest that the profound muteness of the long shots is the defin-ing formal feature of not only this film but most of Hou's films (and has influenced other films of the Taiwanese New Cinema). Reynaud has de-scribed how Hou's technique of "decentring" scenes provokes the realiza-tion of how "*transitory* and *accidental* the human presence is" (74). She explains: "people are floating over the composition of the shot like un-necessary ghosts. The shot does not need them. And they do not need the shot either" (74). The result is an unsettling freedom in the spectator, as "his/her gaze is free to wander within the shot as well" (74).[11] Like the youths' lives, there is no sense of an overarching narrative or anchoring view. The viewer's perspective, like that of the average individual, is that of forced nonintervention: one has little choice but to stand by and watch the unfolding of developmentalist logic. The Taiwaneseness signified in this film (and registered by the Taiwanese New Cinema's enormous success) thus comes not from the viewer's identification with Taiwanese language or culture against mainlander—though it is not insignificant that we hear Mandarin only from the schoolteacher, postman, and military officers in the film. Rather, it comes from the paradoxical, shared experience of being motionless while on the road, the concrete experience of participating in, and being sidelined by, Taiwan's galloping development.

The Boys from Fengkuei (Fenggui lai de ren), set in the contemporary 1980s, loosely follows the same narrative of adolescence to maturity. Three loutish teenage friends from the depressed islands of Penghu migrate to the new industrial center of Kaohsiung, where they find jobs at an Amer-ican electronics factory. As in *Dust in the Wind,* the film hinges on the boys' comings and goings, but here we also witness traffic and movement within the city: in order to get by in the metropolis, the boys must puzzle over alien street signs and negotiate bus numbers and ferry routes. Along the way, we also see the disciplining and maturing of one of the boys,

Ching-ah, who takes his job stacking boxes in the factory seriously, tries to study Japanese through lessons broadcast over the radio, and becomes infatuated with Hsiao-Hsing, the older woman who lives across the court-yard with her boyfriend. In the end, however, the experience of migration means alienation from both the city and the country: his father dies, and Ching-ah returns to his hometown for the funeral, only to find himself even more at a distance from his family members. Emotionally, he becomes closest to Hsiao-Hsing, who has also migrated from the country, yet when things don't work out for her in Kaohsiung, her solution is simply to leave for Taipei (Yip, 204). Updating the farewell scene from the one at *Dust in the Wind*'s train station, Ching-ah accompanies Hsiao-Hsing to the crowded bus station, where he helplessly watches as her bus rapidly disappears into plumes of traffic exhaust.

In *Fengkuei,* the twin experiences of struggling to make it in the city and being drafted into the military define Taiwan of the 1980s as much as they did the 1960s. One of the three friends leaves factory work to sell music tapes at the local market but gets drafted before the business is established. The film's final scene poignantly posits the boys' tentative arrival at maturity within the limits of their circumstances: as shoppers walk blithely by them in the market, Ching-ah jumps atop a chair and begins to aggressively hawk the tapes to the crowd, yelling over and over, "Buy three for the price of one!" It is the most earnest and intense behavior of the film. The crowd, however, like the incongruous classical music soundtrack, seems oblivious to him and to the camera; the people simply continue their quotidian searches for cheap clothes and food. Like the struggle-over-the-potatoes moment and Wan's farewell to his grandfather in *Dust,* the scene is striking because it lasts much longer than seems visually required. The abundant energy displayed by Ching-ah is dialectically linked to the inter-spersed images of utterly disinterested shoppers and passersby. The lack of shot–reverse-shot continuity here—the reactions we see of the crowd members are not the ones we expect—prevents us from identifying with, cheering on, or sympathizing with the hero. Rather, we become more aware of the pointlessness of his efforts as the scene progresses.

The final scene is deeply ambivalent: there is no final return to pictur-esque Penghu island or even the partial reconciliation with nature via the grandpa's monologue as the end of *Dust in the Wind* suggests. Instead, there

Ching-ah does his best in the marketplace in the final scene of *The Boys from Fengkuei* (1983).

is simply a sense of uneasy determination about the future. Yip writes: "While the failure of Ah-jung's audiotape business suggests the difficulty— even the futility—of entrepreneurial endeavors in the crowded and competitive atmosphere of the city, the exuberance with which Ch'ing-ah and the boys hawk their wares in the final shots of the film demonstrates their determination to try their best to succeed" (204). The realization of the very temporariness of their time together—the military or another city could always whisk one of them away—motivates them to a new level of sobriety and solidarity, but a solidarity that is itself contingent. Despite the refusal to represent a unified ethnic idea of Taiwan, Yip claims that "all of [Hou's] films revolve around a central question: what does it mean to be not Chinese but a modern Taiwanese?" (76). What is national in Hou's films is precisely the refusal of both KMT-scripted historical discourses and the reassertion of a pure Taiwanese ethnicity initiated by the *hsiang-t'u* movement. *Dust in the Wind* and *The Boys from Fengkuei* examine the everyday life experience of rural migrants and question the rationality of Taiwan's economic leap by revealing its contradictions from their perspectives. No longer merely the "revolutionary base" of KMT-prescribed development, Taiwanese society arrives at a new level of critical consciousness through the material experiences of labor, migration, and military. Hou's cinematic rendering of the sideliner experience challenges the KMT's vision of Taiwan as a bridge to a greater Chinese nationalism and articulates a new kind of collective subject, one formed precisely through its dislocating journey.

While Sung-Sheng Yvonne Chang has noted a direct line of influence from "the nativist literary movement of the previous decade, which called upon artists to get out of the ivory tower and pay greater attention to contemporary Taiwanese sociopolitical reality" ("Twentieth-Century," 141), interestingly, she reads Taiwanese New Cinema as belonging to a tradition of artistic modernism. Hou's idiosyncratic auteur style and formal experimentation, for Chang, is evidence of a "modernist aestheticism in both the affirmation of art as possessing values beyond the mundane law and morality, and the attribution to the creative act of writing a quasi-religious redemptive power" (144). I argue, however, that what makes Hou's films simultaneously moving and arresting is less their participation in a modernist aesthetic than the result of a cinematic engagement with a unique set of spatial and social conditions. In the "desire to translate the Taiwanese space onto the silver screen" (Reynaud, 75), elliptical editing, discontinuous space, and muted long shots are the aesthetic correlatives to a lived experience of spatial transformation. What is redemptive, finally, is not the "quasi-religious" power of art, but simply the determined, incongruous exuberance shared by the characters in the final scene of *Fengkuei;* it is the characters themselves who must redeem their situation through tireless efforts to adapt to the changing industrial landscape of Taiwan. Let us nevertheless keep this question of redemption in mind for the final chapter, in which we examine literary strategies in the context of modernization under Korean dictator Park Chung Hee.

7

The Redemptive Realism of Korean *Minjung* Literature

I think
I have to stay on one road,
Though roads are open everywhere
No more attachments,
No more sideways.

—KIM CHI-HA, "No Sideways"

EXPRESSWAYS, EXPORTS, AND PARK CHUNG HEE'S NEW VILLAGE MOVEMENT

The growth of transport systems and the allure of movement is a powerful metaphor for several reasons, not least being the actual reduction in a nation's size. All three New Asian City nations, in fact, became unwilling islands between 1949 and 1965. Under the Kuomintang, Taiwan was contentiously severed (again) from the mainland, provoking to this day competing versions of One China and the specter of military attack from Beijing. As we saw in chapter 5, Singapore was disassociated from its hinterland, Malaya, rendering it a city-state, or "a heart without a body" (Lee, *Singapore Story,* 23) despite its continued practical linkages with the Malaysian peninsula. And the partition of the Korean peninsula, Bruce Cumings has remarked, turned the south into a virtual island and a decades-long antagonist toward its rival in the north.[1] Like other ex-colonies, these states contend not just with the distorted industries and societies left behind by colonialism, but also with the haphazard geographies and overly concentrated populations resulting from the process of decolonization. In such precarious and geographically limited contexts, the extraordinary development of roads and transport systems integrates the nation space with the demands of international capitalism and compensates for territories cut off from their adjacent regions. With no other way to survive, these nations—and perhaps most enthusiastically the Republic of Korea—chose to promote the free movement of their only available surplus resource: labor power. Focusing on South Korea in this chapter, I again argue that the forms of national infrastructure become the figures through which material and ideological debates are staged. If one of Fanon's greatest concerns regarding "the pitfalls of national consciousness" was the centralization of postcolonial power in capital cities to the neglect of the rural masses (185), Park Chung Hee's transportation systems symbolically (if not actually) achieve countrywide inclusion into the national project. Images of the country's newly built roads, freeways, and bridges both allegorize the future path of the nation and prescribe the correct use of national space.

Like the two previous regimes discussed, the presidency of Park Chung Hee (Pak Chŏng-hŭi)—from 1961 until his assassination in 1979—stressed the physical development of postcolonial South Korea in terms of a single national project. Numerous political and economic studies of Park's rule have traced his authoritarian style to his training in Manchurian, Japanese, and Korean military academies and note his service as a lieutenant in the Japanese Kwantung army. Despite being denounced as a communist in 1949 and almost sentenced to death in the military purges of the Syngman Rhee era (1948–60), he took advantage of the disorder that followed the April 19, 1960, student-led protests *(sa-il-gu)* that ended Rhee's reign. With his military allies, he staged a successful coup d'état in 1961 and quickly turned to restructuring the country. Park followed the Japanese model of a strong state-business alliance and export-oriented industrialization, but the incredible growth in productivity of the working masses cannot be explained by this strategy alone. Following Kim Hyung-A's analysis, I argue that Park was most successful in steering the country toward an efficient labor system (Kim, 55) in which the ideas of construction and reconstruction of the nation were mobilized simultaneously at physical, national, and psychic levels.

Kim Hyung-A describes how Park cannily tapped into the liberal public discourse that flourished in the year of civilian rule preceding the coup of 1961. Based on the apparently shameful history of Korean dependence (on the Chinese, the Japanese, and now the Americans) and the embarrassment of national division, the reconstruction of a new dynamic Korean nation became paramount. The evident dissatisfaction of the masses with Syngman Rhee's corrupt and inefficient leadership laid the groundwork for a results-oriented government, just as Singapore's resourceful People's Action Party enjoyed enormous success following British rule. Like Lee Kuan Yew, Park rechanneled desires for a new and independent nation into a state-led effort, characterized by both U.S.-backed anticommunism and the single-minded goal of developing Korean exports. Just a few of the achievements of his government's first years[2] include winning President Kennedy's support through his virulent anticommunist stance; purging the bureaucracy and filling top positions with handpicked technocrats; bringing the private sector under control by arresting illicit profiteers (who would be released on agreement to invest in state-chosen industries); and beginning the first wave of industrial construction based on "cement, synthetic fiber, electricity, fertilizer, and iron and oil refinery" industries (Kim, 82). The beginning of the 1970s consolidated the nation's successful entry into export production and also saw the intensification of North Korean aggression; Park's industrial plan consequently shifted to heavy and chemical industries that would include the capability to manufacture weapons and lessen reliance on U.S. forces. Such cold war competition was also based on the fact that, at independence in 1945, the Japanese had already partially industrialized the north with coal mining and power stations, while the south remained relatively lacking in industry. The main areas of Park's industrial push became: "(a) industrial machinery; (b) shipbuilding and transport machinery; (c) iron and steel; (d) chemicals; and (e) electronics" (Kim, 173). We can note the gendered dimensions of such a shift: the symbolic move from light industries centered on shoes and wigs (feminine, bodily accessories) to industries promoting ships, machine tools, and chemicals (masculine, national defense) is perceived as central to the nationalist project. As we saw in chapter 4, at the symbolic level, women are "marginalized in the community of male citizens" (Moon, 51) despite increasing expectations for them to participate in the national export economy as factory workers.

Park's prioritization of industrial development was presented as one with the project of national reconstruction. The system of *chaebol* ("conglomerate") investment, often funded by large U.S. and Japanese loans, fortuitously obscured the foreign nature of this development. The mediator between the domestic and international terms of his project was the total modernization of the built environment, which could be held up as an emblem of national progress. His New Village Movement, or Saemaŭl Undong, begun in 1970, was a perfect encapsulation of the belief that with hard work and basic building materials, a physically and spiritually new Korea could be achieved.[3] The New Village Movement was, in essence, a program of rural industrialization in which the government provided villages with quantities of cement and reinforcing bar and encouraged them to construct roads, bridges, and riverbanks. The ostensible aim was to "directly or indirectly contribute to increasing village income" (Park, 110). By 1973, this had become part of the broader *Yusin* ("revitalizing") reforms, a nationwide program of self-improvement built on Park's twin tenets of anticommunism and economic nationalism. Under these reforms, Park increased his power to that of a dictator: "The National Assembly became a mere rubber stamp; unions, universities, churches, and the media were put under surveillance by the Korean CIA, the riot police were used to control the students, and a network of spies infiltrated the population to control public opinion" (Standish, 68). Meanwhile, the many government slogans of the period stressed national unity and hard work, such as "construction on the one hand and national defense on the other" ("ilmyŏn kŏnsŏl, ilmyŏn kukbang") and "our national land with our strength" ("uri ŭi kukťo nŭn uri ŭi him ŭ ro"; Kim, 111). The national spirit was thus assumed to lie in the very acts of construction, which would build the economic and military viability of the country. In a 1972 speech, "The Saemaŭl Undong, A New Mind Movement," Park explicitly equates the modernization of houses and roads with the reconstruction of the Korean spirit:

> I think that the Saemaŭl Undong should begin, above all, with a fresh spirit.
>
> As the old straw roofs of our farmhouses are replaced, so should our hearts be renewed with a fresh community spirit of diligence, independence and cooperation.
>
> As our narrow country roads are expanded and repaired, so should our hearts be filled with a new determination to pave a smoother future for our own families and for our nation.

> The Saemaŭl Undong is a spiritual revolutionary movement intended to cure the malaise of idleness and complacency which sprouts under the shade of stability, and to eradicate luxury and extravagance which spread in the name of growth.
>
> The Saemaŭl Undong will provide impetus to achieve a consistent national consensus, which is required for the modernization of our fatherland. (Park, 175–76)

Underpinning this verbosity is the single most important metaphor for Park: the development of roads as the "future path for our families and our nation." As in Singapore and Taiwan's modernization, we witness something like the Le Corbusian desire to effect revolutionary social change through a change in the built environment. For Park, national defense was the other side of the coin to national industrialization. In another speech urging a "second liberation" (the first being from the Japanese in 1945), he directly links the maintenance of peace with "national power" in an equation where "peace can be maintained only when national power is nurtured; and the prospect of unification becomes brighter when peace is maintained" (53). Glossing over the exact logic of how military buildup leads to peace, Park concentrates on the concrete evidence of this power:

> Having expedited our progress in growth and construction thus far, we have just entered the stage of heavy and chemical industries. Functioning as the main artery linking all industrial complexes throughout the country, the expressways—symbol of our expanding national strength—are continuously pouring vitality into our effort for greater prosperity and development. (53)

In Park's logic, peace is not just a function of national strength but is also encouraged by a grand nationalized transport system as the country's "main artery."

Park's vision of a modernized Korea that "will be able to emerge as a great nation-state and a final victor, to join the main currents of world history" (41) thus does more than merge economic development with national destiny. It is predicated on the overlaying of national space with a complete transportation grid, a circulatory system for the national body facilitating the efficient combination of goods, materials, labor, and finished commodities to their final destination on the world market. While the development of transportation technology has usually signified increased movement and the modern freedoms or cosmopolitanism that accompanies it,[4] here, as in the Taiwanese migrations we saw in chapter 6, they signal a freedom of movement intended not for humans but for things. In one astonishing speech, Park predicts a glorious future in which "our products and our technical knowhow travel to the six continents across the five oceans" (86). In Park's fantasy, it is Korea's exports, rather than Koreans themselves, that allow for the nation "to join the main currents of world history," and their movement depends on the industrialization of villages and construction of roads. Indeed, Kim Hyung-A reports that "between 1967 and 1977, Korea constructed nine expressways throughout the country, while 44 percent of national roads were paved by 1975" (210). This construction frenzy complemented Park's heavy and chemical industrial push of the 1970s, incorporating the major Korean industries into the effective megafirm of "Korea Inc." (Kim, 208). In this sense, Park was both the nation's CEO and its on-site construction manager who urged ever greater productivity and higher export targets.[5] As basic infrastructure necessary for the nation's new massive industrial zones—such as the 39,900 hectares at Ch'angwǒn—expressways, state roads *(kukdo),* and ports functioned just as the elevators, forklifts, and loading bays do in any large factory.

Meanwhile, the extraction of disciplined labor for national reconstruction was achieved by levying production targets in the name of national competition for prosperity; Park openly invited North Korea to "participat[e] in a competition—a bona fide competition in development, in construction and creativity" (17). As noted in the first Transition, funding for Korea's military and much of its infrastructure was acquired through the looming presence of the communist north. Cumings points out that Japan, South Korea, and Taiwan were all advantaged by the cold war; they benefited "in the 1950s [from] a rare breathing space, an incubation period allowed to few other peoples in the world" (68).[6] Military buildup also added to the domestic economic capability of Korea by underwriting those powerful symbols of national strength: the expressways. Of the total $13 billion in U.S. economic and military aid received by South Korea between 1945 and 1979 (Cumings, 67), mention must be made of the South Korea–U.S. agreement that sent 300,000 Koreans to fight in the Vietnam War.

After Park initially agreed to send a light division in 1967, President Johnson countered with a deal pledging assistance for national security and the construction of the Seoul-to-Pusan (Kyŏngbu) expressway. In assuring Park of his support for the security and development of Korea, Johnson writes in a 1967 letter: "I am prepared to provide a special program . . . to assist you in the construction of . . . a major modern highway between . . . Seoul and Pusan" (Johnson qtd. in Kim, 104). The deal clearly equates U.S. infrastructural aid with Korean military troops in Vietnam; in other words, anticommunism is actualized in accelerated material development. The result is that Korea's role in the cold war "firmly placed it on the path of capitalist development, with all alternative possibilities written out of the decolonization bargains" (Namhee Lee, 3). Under Park's brutal modernization program, questions over the nature of postcolonial development are silenced by the unarguable logic of the president's oft-quoted mantra: "Let's get rich first." We could say, then, that in Park's Korea, the externalized forms of industrial development—Cheah's *techne*—have gone so far as to define and direct the nation's essence. In his Yusin measures, it is industry and infrastructure, after all, that require revitalization rather than the people, who may merely be reproduced biologically.

The Kyŏngbu (Seoul-to-Pusan) expressway, just after completion in 1970. Courtesy of the National Archives of Korea.

If we have discussed the national inscription of a transport system, what was actually occurring in individual towns and villages, where "old straw roofs of . . . farmhouses are replaced" (Park, 175–76)? While undoubtedly raising productive levels and incomes, the program of village reconstruction had the further effect of inculcating capitalist ideology. Kim notes how the "sink or swim" attitude that was used with business–government deals (involving protection, loans, and support for *chaebols* that had shown that they could meet production targets) was echoed at the village level. He describes how the Saemaŭl Undong "was shaped into a strictly goal-oriented top-down rural development program" (134). Villages were ranked according to three categories of basic villages, self-helping villages, and self-sufficient villages, where only the latter two were rewarded with further government assistance, and the former implicitly cast as lazy. The Saemaŭl Undong movement thus allowed for greater government control over rural management and actually widened instead of reduced the income gap (Kim, 136). Development was thus a double-edged sword and, in Namhee Lee's words, "brought feelings of immense achievement and of alienation among Koreans at large, giving rise to severe feelings of disconnectedness between past and present, between city and countryside, and between the emerging working and middle classes" (5).

A short story by Yi Mungu, perhaps Korea's best-known rural writer, succinctly represents the ambivalence and disconnectedness of the village industrialization program. His *Essays on Kwanch'on* (*Kwanch'on sup'il,* 1977), eight stories based on his native village in south Ch'ungch'ŏng-do province, give a sustained portrayal of rural change and dispossession. The "Ballad of Kalmŏri" concerns the predicament of a dull-witted farmer, Yong-mo, who is wrongfully arrested and charged with killing a pheasant, an animal now considered protected wildlife under the new rationalized logic of the government. The narrative shows what Park's rhetoric of New Village modernization does not: how small rural villages and their farmers are actually faring under the nation's big industrial push. The opening description of the town railway station is especially revealing: once the center of village activity, it is now a cold remnant of its former self from which the narrator is only too eager to depart. Even though the town is now full of the modern architecture, amenities, and bustling scenes that officially signify progress, the station building and accompanying square are home only to the ghosts of living labor that once animated them.

In one and a half decades a lot of things had been modernized as the town grew. This modernization was not prompted to develop the traditional virtues. . . . This place simply had adapted to the method of concrete construction and thereby undergone a metamorphosis of concrete. The outdoor waiting "room" on the wide paved square, the blaring public address system, the bus terminal opposite the taxi pool, the pay latrine, the shoeshine stall next to it, and the unbecoming clock tower built by the Rotary Club. The station had grown to a complex consisting of a six-story hotel furnished with a barbershop in the basement, a public bath, a coffee shop, and a teahouse; around it there were also five other separate teahouses, twelve houses, and nine inns all crammed in side by side.

But whatever gaudy, modern components had been thrown in, the station did not look right. There was something incongruous. It was not only that the natives had been pushed out by the outsiders who had proceeded to entrench themselves, but the whole thing seemed somehow sorrowful and barren [*ŏssŏlp'ŭgo ssŏllŏnghan ggol*] even to my native eyes. (369–70, translation modified)

We learn that Yong-mo's family is among those "natives" *(wŏnjumin)* pushed aside by the forces of agricultural modernization: their home and land fall prey to a new reservoir necessary for one of the government's land reclamation projects. With their meager compensation, they are forced to live in remote and impoverished Slow Village ("Nŭrŭmsae") where, at least, "life was bearable because no petty officials ever annoyed them" (376).

In such a narrative, we see the familiar dialectic between change and tradition mapped on to the new and old village forms: the loss of a native, organic, rural lifestyle is wiped out by development. (Although as a result of the Japanese rail system, the village had already been integrated into a larger, colonial economy and is not quite the repository of untouched traditional virtues.) On another level, however, the object of critique is the resulting sink-or-swim social effect arising from the uneven spread of modernizing logic. Narratively, both critiques are lucidly rendered in the mere description of the station complex, even before any action or drama begins. The station building is now fitted out with those generically modern amenities—the hotel, public bath, barber shop, teahouse, and inns—yet nevertheless is presented as desolate and unpopulated: "the whole thing seemed somehow sorrowful and barren." Park's simple logic of village growth through industrialization produces, in the end, something much less than the human labor that went into its construction. Again, we can think of Fanon's image of the bridge "parachuted down from above" (201), where industrial technology is used less for correcting imbalances in the underdeveloped country than for exacerbating them. For those who can "adapt to the method of concrete construction"—capitalist logic and "revitalized" village life—the shift to agribusiness and export industries becomes their ticket to prosperity. For a substantial segment of the population, however, it means being squeezed out of land and livelihood and relocating to places excluded from development like Slow Village. In the story's aesthetic logic, the catalyst for Yong-mo's material expropriation is precisely the "metamorphosis of concrete," the metonymic and symbolic indication of Yusin-mandated material development.

The *Minjung* Movement and Redemptive Realism

There is much more to be said about the literary forms that take up Park's extreme developmental logic. Broadly, the interpretive context through which to view them is the major oppositional movement, the *minjung undong*, which arose in response to the industrialization program and the division of the peninsula. The word *minjung* has been variously translated as "the people," "masses," "working classes," "folk," and "common people" and contains something of all these connotations. In Namhee Lee's exhaustive study of the subject, the *minjung* are most typically conceived as factory workers and farmers, but in the 1970s and 1980s, it came to include a broader alliance of workers, intellectuals, students, and artists. *Minjung* "was not conceived as a primordial opposition to modernity and modernization," but its practices "were seen as potential antidotes to the brutal pace and deleterious side effects of development. Minjung was thus the site of intense longing for a 'utopian horizon' by intellectuals and university students and of contestation with the state" (Namhee Lee, 6). Choi Hyun-moo writes of *minjung's* opposing view to government ideologies: "One is an official, formal nationalism based on anticommunist ideology; the other, an antiestablishment nationalism that arose under dictatorship and the process of industrialization. The gap between the two steadily became wider and wider" (169). In short, the *minjung* "came to signify those

who are oppressed in the sociopolitical system but who are capable of rising up against it" (Namhee Lee, 5). In cultural histories of the *minjung* of
the 1970s and 1980s, the emphasis is decidedly dual, on the one side class
struggle—pertaining to accelerated industrial development—and on the
other the national question—pertaining to anxiety over the divided Korean
nation.[7] Choi concedes that *minjung* literature differs from "people-oriented
or proletarian literature of the West" precisely in its "nationalistic character"
(172). Korean *minjung* nationalist ideology emerges as single counter-
narrative to both statist internal development and the geopolitical division of North and South Korea. We thus see how postcolonial nationalism
can operate simultaneously in multiple configurations: that of ethnonationalism (to unite North and South Korea) and proletarianism (critiquing
state-led industrialization and exploitation); antiauthoritarianism and pro-
democracy (opposing Park's regime); and neocolonialism (protesting the
division of the peninsular by superpowers Russia and the United States).

Wells's introduction to a volume on the *minjung* movement confirms
the multivalency of the movement:

> A very general understanding emerged that the minjung are Koreans,
> predominantly workers in agriculture and urban industries, who retained
> the values and sentiments of the Korean masses in the face of militaristic
> rule and cultural and economic systems imposed directly or otherwise by
> foreign governments or interests, along with those among intellectuals, writ-
> ers, politicians, and professionals who have supported their aspirations. (2)

Such complexity renders the term *minjung* easier to use as an adjective—
"minjung theology, literature, historiography and so on—than as a noun referring to any specific group of Koreans" (1). The flexibility of this adjectival
term means that *minjung* experience and *minjung* literature cannot be limited to a certain ideal subjectivity (the farmer, for example), nor a particular
political issue (dictatorship), but rather connects the diverse and contradictory forces that overdetermine South Korea. As Namhee Lee puts it,
"the very abstraction and elasticity of the term required a constant shoring
up of the counterimage of the forces considered to be inimical to minjung:
the military dictatorship, corporate conglomerates, and foreign powers" (6).
Unusually, the concept of *minjung* connects class-based grievances with

a larger, deeply rooted idea of ethnic solidarity; it is not merely an oppositional movement but a site of shared suffering and "intense longing" (Namhee Lee, 6). The emphasis on suffering has as its dialectical opposite the restoration or redemption of a common humanity, a tension that will be explored in the literary realism of Hwang Sŏk-yŏng. We should note first, however, that the *minjung* cultural movement—understood at its broadest as a popular nationalism—was by no means exclusively literary, but consisted of a vast spectrum of social practices including *minjung* historiography (which sought to trace the *minjung* as agent of social change since the late nineteenth century), oral traditions, religious practices, student and farmer alliances, people's folk theater *(maddanggŭk),* and, of course, the reunification movement. Nevertheless, as in the previous chapter, where I argued for film's unique role in reimagining Taiwan's development, in *Yusin* Korea, it is literature that most clearly articulates an oppositional *minjung* aesthetic. Hyun-moo Choi writes:

> Whereas national identity was the pursuit of the 1960s, consciousness as the creator of a new history and nationalism through literary practice were emphasized in the 1970s. There was a move to formalize, in accordance with literary realism, the essence of the minjung as that which fully experienced the contemporary pervasive historical contradictions. An attempt was also made to understand, comprehensively and cooperatively, in the spirit of Third World literary theory, Korea's political and economic national realities within the global capital structure. In this way there emerged in literature the analytic endeavor to group the people's place within the organic interconnections between individual and society, nation and the world. (173)

The problem with the analytic attempt to "group the people's place" in this nexus of forces is precisely the difficulty of identifying a single *minjung* "essence" conceived in opposition to the multiple realities of the period. Cho Se-hŭi's "A Little Ball Launched by a Dwarf," we recall, dealt with the conflict between big business *(chaebols)* and the individual in the specific struggle of urban renewal. The *minjung,* by definition, is of a broader conception—a "confederation of classes that hold certain crucial values and objectives in common" or a "cultural commonality" (Wells, 4)—

and spans the urban and the rural. The question that arises is: what unifies a continuous cultural outlook that incorporates both the struggles of the agricultural sphere and the new forms of exploitation in the urban sector? In other words,

> The dilemma for activists desirous of uniting theory with practice is that the *rural* minjung is where the most indigenous of the "nonofficial" (nonsinicized, nonwesternized, nonelite) Korean sources lie, whereas it is in relation to the *urban* minjung that issues of dramatic social change, modernity, and the impact of global capitalism arise most sharply. (Wells, 7)

The question might be rephrased as how to unify an opposition movement made up of both Cho's savvy urban slum dwellers and Slow Village's hapless Yong-mo. The dilemma points to the unavoidably syncretic nature of popular nationalism within a developmental state. As we saw above, Park Chung Hee invoked national destiny through the country's exports and expressways—"symbol of our expanding national power." Such transformation also has the unintended effect of making the nationwide modernizing landscape a common object of *minjung* experience where even Yi Mungu's small village is affected. With the idea that the *minjung* are, above all, sufferers (Wells, 12), the greater the suffering of either urban workers or farmers in these modernizing spaces, the more their status as *minjung* is confirmed. Thus, as with both Singapore and Taiwan, the production of a popular national consciousness arises not against (or somewhere supposedly outside) the forms and processes of official modernization and its infrastructure, but through them. In the following I discuss Hwang Sŏk-yŏng's unique redemptive realism, which reveals a social and aesthetic logic comparable to Hou's sideliner cinema of the previous chapter. Both are alternative narrative modes made possible by the very forms of national development. Where Hou's films visualize a collective adolescence through the presentation of migration, Hwang uses the concrete material transformations of the nation's rural sphere as the horizon of communal experience. In comparable ways, both the Taiwanese New Cinema and *minjung* literature use the landscape as the matrix of a new and fundamentally ambivalent national subject.

HWANG SŎK-YŎNG AND "THE ROAD TO SAMPO"

Hwang Sŏk-yŏng's writings have been identified as one of the anchors of early *minjung* literature. Yŏm Mu-wung speaks of "70s literature" and "the 70s writer"—catchwords that were used to refer to the zeitgeist of the day—and of the pivotal emerging writers in their thirties, including Yi Mungu, Cho Se-hǔi, Pak Tae-sun, and Yun Hǔng-gil. "In my mind," Yŏm continues, "it is precisely Hwang Sŏk-yŏng, with his keen sensibility of the typical realities of the period, who most prominently realizes the '70s writer'" (586, my translation).[8] Hwang himself is something of an exceptional figure in Korean letters: born in 1943 in Manchuria, he began publishing in 1962 with the short fiction "Ipsŏk pugǔn" ("Near Ipsŏk") and started fashioning his unrelenting realist aesthetic *(reŏllijǔm mihak).* Through his participation in the *madanggǔk* people's theater movement, he became known as a *minjung* cultural activist. In 1989 he visited North Korea—contravening South Korea's security laws—and was forced to live in exile in the United States and Germany until his return in 1993, when he was promptly jailed. He was released in 1998 only after the liberalization of the country had begun. Namhee Lee gives an account of the reemergence of realism as the preferred style for *minjung* writers and traces the genre back to the proletarian writers of the 1920s and 1930s and KAPF, or Korea Artista Proletaria Federacio (mentioned in chapter 2). The post-1945 "decimation of the labor movement and the subsequent rise of anticommunism obliterated proletariat literature" until the 1970s and the reappearance of the labor novel *(nodong sosŏl)* (Namhee Lee, 270–71). Lee defines *minjung* literature proper as novels and stories that deal with labor strikes, student worker activism, and wage struggles, and dates its emergence to the late 1980s, the climax of South Korea's democratization movement spurred by the 1987 mass protests against the presidential candidacy of General Roh Tae-woo. In the view of one critic of the day, such literature was to portray representative prototypical individuals and situations, achieved when the "author's subjective choice converged with the present society's objective needs" (Kim Myŏngin, 1989, qtd. in Namhee Lee, 272). In Lee's account, the labor novel's pure form is not recognizable until it exhibits the thematic concerns of the strike or class struggle. In contrast to this definition and periodization, I am interested in Hwang Sŏk-yŏng's work from the 1970s, the moment when the changing social landscape first becomes available to the literary consciousness, provoking the "move to formalize . . . the essence of the minjung as that which fully experienced the contemporary pervasive historical contradictions" (Choi, 173). The vehicle for this move has most often been theorized along the lines of a social realism. According to Marshall R. Pihl, "Growing numbers of writers, critics, and activists came to conceive of 'the people' as the principal element in society, as consumers of literature, and also as a power base. Emerging out of literary nationalism in the 1970s, populism gradually developed into a distinct literary theory with its own theoretical framework" (213).[9] Most influential for this "distinct literary theory" was the work of Georg Lukács, whose Marxist validation of realist literature was attractive to Korean writers (as to many other third world writers) attempting to make aesthetic sense of social realities. Pihl notes that "in Korea, his [Lukács's] concepts of 'totality,' 'typicality,' and 'concreteness' gained currency in the 1970s" (211).

Recall that for Lukács, realism is that objective aesthetic providing "a three-dimensionality, an all-roundness" (*Studies,* 6) by which authors "inexorably depict the true essence of reality as they see it" (13). What makes Lukács's theory so appealing is not simply the descriptive power of realism, but the power of the individual story to tap into truths of the social totality. Crucial is the role of "type, a peculiar synthesis which organically binds together the general and the particular both in characters and situations" (6). In the later—often autobiographically inspired—*minjung* literature depicting labor activism, we can readily delineate the function of these general but particular types. Like Lukács's account of Balzac's realism, this fiction relies on "the particular individual traits of each of his characters on the one hand and the traits which are typical of them as representatives of a class on the other" (43). Such a view accords a higher, humanistic purpose to literature, which Lukács confidently describes "could play the leading part . . . in the democratic rebirth of nations" (19).

Hwang's fiction certainly incorporates both the typical and concrete conditions of Korean society while detailing a particular experience. Some of Hwang's work has engaged directly with the major struggles of the day: workers' rights are center stage in the short story "Far from Home" ("Gaekji"), set on a construction site, while imperialism and the unsavory sources of Korea's economic buildup are detailed in the Vietnam War saga

The Shadow of Arms (Mugi ŭi kŭnŭl), a novel populated by such representative types as Vietcong militia members and Korean opportunists. However, the truth content of his fictional representations lies less, I argue, in
the Lukácsian presentation of types, totalities, and class struggles than in
the profound depiction of individuals in relation to the dynamic forces
reshaping Korea's landscape. A version of Lukács's "three-dimensionality"
or "all-roundess" is achieved not through the exemplarity of the workers'
lives presented, but through the relationships figured in and by the spaces
they inhabit. We may think of this in terms of the competing meanings
between Lefebvre's statist, homogenizing abstract space and literature's
polyvalent representational space. Along with the straightforwardly socialist
realist works mentioned above, Hwang has written of the less dramatic but
profound consequences of national division and industrialization in countless short fictions. Among his many important works, I choose his 1975
"Road to Sampo" ("Samp'o kanŭn kil") for its realist description not of
labor struggles, "representative prototypical individuals," or capitalist development as a totality, but of the new figures populating and traversing the
national landscape.[10] In juxtaposing Hwang's work with the poetic and
filmic productions of the previous two chapters, I trace yet another distinct
aesthetic construction emerging from the contradictions of developmental nationalism. Reflecting the different political, historical, and material
conditions of Korea, however, this formal strategy refigures the developmental landscape in terms of the redeeming and ongoing production of
new forms of community, of *minjung* on the move.

In the 1970s, one of the consequences of Park Chung Hee's New Village Movement was the creation of a new class of laborers by "foster[ing]
a building boom in the provinces. Many of the construction projects depended for manpower on day labor, and once a project was finished the
workers had to journey elsewhere for work" (Fulton, "Hwang Sŏk-yŏng,"
715). "The Road to Sampo" is important for its narration of a new *minjung*
subject through the marginal and contingent experience of migrant laborers—those who, like Hou Hsiao-hsien's protagonists, construct and occupy
the new industrializing landscape, yet lack the status of recognizable class
or political actors. The story narrates one particularly laborious "journey
elsewhere for work." Yŏngdal, a machinist, has just left his temporary
winter job at a chophouse *(bapjip)* after being caught in bed with his boss's

wife. Leaving the village at which he had arrived four months earlier in search of construction work, he meets Chŏng, a slightly older tradesman and probable ex-convict, who plans to return to his hometown after an absence of nearly ten years. Despite complaining that the small island of Sampo would offer little in the way of construction work—"Such an out-of-the-way place *[byŏkji]*. Especially in winter like this" (179)—Yŏngdal decides to join him.[11] In this brief narrative, Hwang skillfully weaves together the material, physical, and social aspects of the journey, such that one register implicitly informs the others. In an aesthetic that I call "redemptive realism," the questions of rural versus urban, authentic *minjung* or class subjects, are overshadowed by the slowly revealed process of how shared suffering on a journey posits and forges new communal forms.

After the two men's initial, slightly awkward meeting, they "turned on to the roadway [*ch'ado,* literally "vehicle-way"]. It was now easier to walk as the road was covered with gravel and clay" (181). Paralleling the better road conditions, their relationship begins to thaw. As they make their way though the frozen landscape in sparse conversation, their friendship deepens with the concrete descriptions of the physical surroundings. Hwang's impeccable realism informs us of every detail of the men's physical relationship to the countryside they traverse, including the very tilt of their bodies—"the uphill road became a downhill road" (187)—the traction of their feet, the feel of the wind. The crossing of a frozen stream is presented in visceral detail: "The ice was rough and not slippery, the water having frozen over several times after repeated freezing and melting. The wind picked up loose bits of ice and slapped them harder into the faces of the two men" (182). In this way, the story connects the physical reality of their journey to the sociality that forms between the characters: the deeper their difficult material, shared experience—and more accurate its description— the stronger their bond.

Making their way to the mountain village of Ch'ansaem, described as an "insignificant appendage" (183) to a fenced-in military station ("ch'ŏlch'aek ŭi kkŭťe kansinhi maeŏdallyŏ ittnŭn kŏt kaťattda") (399), they stop for a meager meal at Seoul Restaurant. Inside, the owner and several guests are in disarray over a young bargirl/prostitute who has stolen money and run away that morning. After Chŏng and Yŏngdal mention their own travel plans, the scurrilous owner of the restaurant offers them 10,000 won if they catch and return the girl. After jokingly agreeing to this, the two return to the road, where they wade through a thick snowstorm that "blanket[s] them with a soft, downy feeling" (187). The snowstorm, rather than a descriptive device to stress nature's power over the man-made world, allows for even more detailed descriptions of the conditions of the roads and villages they pass. The two travelers stop to tie some old straw rope on their shoes:

> Now the two men could walk with surer treads. They turned into the lower road. It soon became narrower but stayed wide enough to let an ox-cart pass. A stream with gravel borders *[kaech'ŏn kwa chagalbat]* ran by the road. There was a thin sheet of snow on the stream. The two men kept on walking, leaving behind their footpaths in the snow.
>
> They entered a village, and passed among the village children and dogs which were scampering about in the snow-covered fields. The frost was thick on the window of the village shops. People were talking behind the windows. (188–89)

Resisting picturesque depictions of pastoral life in the snow-covered village, the narrative persistently attends to the constructed aspects of the landscape, such that "The Road to Sampo" emphasizes the physical journey in all possible social detail. Rather than dwelling on Chŏng and Yŏngdal's personal histories and motivations or position them in terms of class analysis, the short, factual sentences do not allow access to the characters' interior thoughts, but simply and plainly describe their passage through the physical surroundings: "[They] could walk with surer treads"; "They turned"; "The two men kept on walking." In a sense, the story is less about the two men and their journey and more a narrative that uses the two characters as a device to register each physical, subtle change of the landscape. Note that the stream, like many in Korea, is bordered by gravel beds *(chagalbat)* and is thus already a product of industrial "improvement" of the landscape. Hwang hints at the substantial transformation of even this remote mountain area through the bar owner's question to the men, "Are you taking the big road?" (186), and mention of a "newly-constructed road" *(sinjakno)* linking the villages. Furthermore, the travelers' brief rest stop at an abandoned, half-collapsed farmhouse indicates local population changes: "the farmer and his family must have departed for some other place" (194). If these are quintessential *minjung* subjects, it is not because they are representative types of their class or have access to a privileged, indigenous Korean folk culture. Rather, the characters shuffle along the country's modernizing contours such that the realist description of their exhausting journey itself becomes a profound account of the *minjung* experience.

It is helpful here to briefly compare other notions of realism in relation to the *minjung* cultural movement. Isolde Standish has written of the New Wave Korean cinema that emerged in the late 1980s and sought—somewhat similarly to Taiwanese New Cinema with regard to nativism—to "represent the shift into mainstream popular culture of the formerly suppressed underground philosophies of the *Minjung* Movement" (65). Key to her analysis is the way that these films, in an industry only released from political censorship in the 1985 reforms, "placed the working man/woman at the center of the narrative, hence the use of the term 'new realism' in describing them" (76). Certainly the 1970s *minjung* literature on which these films draw was partially defined by the shift in focus to previously unrepresented subjects, locations, and issues: the working classes and dispossessed farmers, factories and slums, labor struggles and urbanization. Standish describes what constitutes the realism of one of the most important films of this genre, Pak Chong-wŏn's *Kuro Arirang* (1989, adapted from a short story by Yi Mun-yŏl): "it is often the factory or the dormitory sites, rather than the action of the characters, which demands spectator attention. . . . the factory and the dormitory in *Kuro arirang* are accredited with an autonomy of their own outside the narrative, authenticating the film's claim to realism" (80). Despite the attention to spaces and built form, Standish's account of *minjung* realism—here in the cinematic mode—is not the way I conceive of realism in Hwang's fiction. What I am calling Hwang's redemptive realism is less about a simple shift of narrative focus to throw light on previously excluded settings or characters than about the way these new environments encrypt a *social process* that then is the ground for shared experiences and eventually solidarity. In other words, it is not merely their inclusion that is notable, but the careful presentations of roads, streams, and train stations that operate as the matrix of Hwang's characters' simultaneous abjection and growing solidarity. As Williams has described, realism's special power is its access to reality "not as static *appearance* but as the movement of . . . social or physical forces" (*Keywords,* 261). We can think of this narrative mode as redemptive not in a religious sense, but in terms of a new sociality that arises in response to material depravity, which redeems not sin or evil but suffering. It is an experience that connects the most downcast of society's members to each other as well as to its readers. Hwang's *minjung* realism is thus produced neither by the formal inclusion of new settings or the centrality of proletarian actors, nor by reference to an ethnos transcending the effects of industrialization, but to the most unflinching experience of its alienating landscape.

As the reader expects, Yŏngdal and Chŏng meet Paekhwa, the escaped bargirl, first spotting her urinating at the edge of some woods. Instead of turning her in, and with no debate, all three simply continue walking together to their common destination—the railway station at Kamch'ŏn. Paekhwa (literally "white flower") is, after two years of bargirl–prostitute work serving military stations, attempting once again to return to her village and family in the south. The very act of walking with Yŏngdal and Chŏng seems to prompt her to reveal her history to the two men: "The more they walked, the more talkative Paekhwa became; she often fell behind. She talked of her time when she was popular in several cities. But her conclusion was that love in the world of whorehouses, aside from making and spending money, was all mere trickery" (*Sampo kanŭn kil,* 408, my translation). Their winter journey by foot is by no means easy, and while the snow symbolizes the general hardships of their lives, each step— rather than explicit formations of class or national consciousness—contributes to their contingent but growing solidarity. Paekhwa, still wearing her work shoes (high heels), predictably falls into a hole hidden by the snow and twists her ankle. From there on, Yŏngdal carries her on his back, but "far from feeling weighed down with the burden, he felt more light-footed (197; "ŏjjŏnji kappunhan nŭkkimiŏttda," *Sampo kanŭn kil,* 413). At Kamch'ŏn station, Paekhwa waits for the Chŏlla line while Chŏng and Yŏngdal prepare to take the Honam line toward Sampo. Before parting, Yŏngdal uses what is close to his last penny to buy Paekhwa food and a train ticket so she will not have to ride (for free) in the soldiers' car. In return, she tells them her real name, Yi Chŏmnye. Such intimacy is used sparingly by Hwang, yet we understand the significance of the characters' small but redeeming actions by the way they are indexed to their degree of suffering.

The story reveals how, in a dialectical fashion, the itinerant life of construction and sex workers produces the most unlikely of outcomes: community among strangers who share different struggles, experiences, and goals. Yet Yŏm Mu-wung explains the way this dialectic of material hardship is redeemed through a communion of sorts:

A day laborer looking for work, a vagabond without a hometown to return to, a bargirl fleeing after stealing money—what did the writer see in these characters, characters set adrift in industrial society, from whom nothing more can be taken, and for whom the future holds no hope or security? Through their journey together, they come to realize their fundamental commonality and thereby come to share the noblest humane sympathy and purest solidarity. That is, in this society with its specific realities of lost hometowns, social inequality, merciless competition and severe labor exploitation, they face up to the period's contradictions and achieve a union through solidarity. (594, my translation)

This "noblest humane sympathy and purest solidarity" are not products of the characters' virtues or achieved insight, nor the subjective conditions meeting the objective in ideal Lukácsian style. Rather, such qualities simply emerge out of the intimate experience of the landscape, the modernization of which has literally set all three adrift. Thus, the truth content to Hwang's realism arises from the presentation of, and engagement with, the changing material and social effects of development—effects most keenly experienced on the road that brings the three characters together. And as with Hou's films, Hwang does not allow Chŏng and Paekhwa's desire to return home to provide a moral conclusion to the story; he refuses to suggest an original space untouched by the processes of industrialization. Just as we are uncertain about Wan's future at the end of *Dust in the Wind,* we doubt Paekhwa's ability to make it home after her previous failed attempts because for both, it is not simply a matter of returning to an unchanged home. "The Road to Sampo" ultimately tells us that there is no pristine space outside the violent transformations of modernization—those "metamorphoses of concrete," in Yi Mungu's phrase. Hwang's alienated characters "from whom nothing more can be taken" are precisely the subjects who hold the redemptive possibilities of *minjung* experience; they are the ones who most fully experience "the contemporary historical contradictions" (Choi, 173) and whose struggle to survive indicates a surpassing of their objectification. The new lives and connections created on modernization's road therefore signify a contingent "cultural commonality" (Wells, 4) as well as the double-edged nature of modernity in Park Chung Hee's Yusin period. People are both objects of the state's developmentalism and potential subjects of ever-forming oppositional communities.

Waiting at Kamchŏn station for their train, Chŏng chats with an old man and learns, after their long journey, that Sampo is no longer the idyllic, peaceful island of rich soil and good fishing he has described to Yŏngdal. Horrified, Chŏng hears how one of the country's many land reclamation projects, involving countless trucks "carrying tons and tons of rocks and gravel and dumping them into the sea" (200), has turned Sampo into part of the mainland. His small village is now "full of construction people" who plan to build a tourist hotel and a "road right over the sea" (200). Having joked that Yŏngdal, a nonnative (*t'agwan,* or "outsider"), wouldn't be welcome in his hometown, Chŏng is galled to find that his own status as "native" now means nothing with the virtual destruction of his hometown: he himself is "in the same situation *[ttok k'at'ŭn ipjang]* as Youngdal" (201). Indeed, this same position with regard to the changing industrial landscape is precisely what has been achieved through their shared journey. The final snowy scene of the train pulling out of the station is, like the final scenes in Hou's films, deeply ambivalent: while the two men are now on their way to certain employment, it has also been a journey of loss for Chŏng. Ultimately, the story suggests that with even the most remote villages transforming and modernizing beyond recognition, the road itself is the place to find community and meaning, however brief and difficult to maintain such relationships might be. As Paekhwa points out on one part of their journey, "When I first went on the road [into prostitution], I too had a life-and-death love" (195). The story therefore reconciles the dilemma of locating the "authentic" Korean, indigenous experience in the rural sphere against the assumption that the greatest political and economic impacts are in the urban: through the distinctive redemptive realism of shared spatial experience, the road is where the two sides come together as the site of *minjung* experience.

What the great variety of *minjung* narratives—from Sin Kyŏng-nim's farmer's poetry, Yi Mungu's rural tales, and Hwang's fiction to the New Wave cinema—collectively do is refigure the significance of Park Chung Hee's New Village movement and Yusin programs. In various ways, they counter the state's representation of space with imaginative representational space. What is unique to Hwang's work, however, is that he narrates the unevenness of industrialization's footprint via the very footsteps of its most marginalized workers, contrasting human and mechanical technologies. The symbolism of Park's national expressways as glorious arteries of the country, enabling national productivity and defense buildup, is effectively defused by the attention to the raw bodily experience of such a landscape.

To close this chapter, I want to make brief mention of another of Hwang's short stories, "Longing for the North, a Far and Desolate Place" ("Pungmang, mŏlgodo kojŏkhan kot") from 1973. Here, Hwang describes with gloomy precision the plight of a young man who tries to fulfill his mother's dying wish to be buried with his father. After he arrives unannounced in a small, desolate village, his goal is to find an elderly man who had been a friend of his parents. Using an extreme form of gritty realism, Hwang provides the bare bones of a narrative in which much remains unsaid. We surmise that the young man's parents had moved down from the north and his father was captured and killed in ambiguous circumstances by "the ones who had guns" during or immediately after the Korean War. While his mother fled with her infant son (the protagonist), his parents' friend managed to hurriedly bury the father in a nearby mountain valley. While the village setting seems like another economically excluded Slow Village, on closer examination, the desolation is actually a legacy of the three-year civil war. Presumably located near the border of North and South Korea, the village was all but devastated in the fighting and turned into a mere *sukbat,* or "wasteland." After tracking down the old man who had assisted his parents, the two spend an evening and day together. Looking across at the still-scarred valley, the old man comments, "You just can't cut a mountain's vein like that" (299, my translation).

After a harrowing episode in which they exhume the father's still-decomposing corpse and move it to a dryer, more suitable location, we discover that the ramen box the youth has been carrying on his back all along in fact contains the remains of his mother. At length, the father's and mother's bodies are combined in a new grave so that "soon you couldn't distinguish the white bone in amongst the black bone" (305). Having fulfilled his mother's dying wish and performed the filial mortuary rights *(sŏngmyo),* the exhausted youth and the old man sit next to the freshly covered grave.

> Staring piercingly at something, the old man mumbled:
> "Do you know, young man, what this is? It is that thing called *han.* . . . If it had a color, it would have exactly this appearance."
> The youth raised his head and looked across. With the clear blue sky as background, the ridge that ran along the opposite side had been cut off obliquely by a landslide. Like a mouthful of red peach, the light from the cliff shone all the more intensely. (306, my translation)

This story perfectly encapsulates the concept of *han*—a Korean term meaning "unfulfilled longing," "regret," or "pain"—and is another way of understanding the communal and redemptive nature of *minjung*.[12] Despite such grim subject matter of poverty, the legacy of war, the inability to go home, dead bodies, and burials, *han* is both the painful recognition of this common suffering *and* the desire for the intense, peach-flavored light. Note that nowhere in the story is North Korea mentioned except for in the title; the "Longing for the North" is thus an unstated affect implied only, perhaps, by the relocation of the father's grave. Yet by foregrounding the material landscape, Hwang's story again describes a specific *minjung* experience, one that counters Park Chung Hee's interpretation of national division: not simply the impetus for economic competition and anticommunist defense, it is the historical precondition of that development written into the very landscape, as well as a continued cause of shared suffering. "Longing for the North" highlights the way the battle scars of a war twenty years prior constitute the material and psychical background to the heady days of the South Korean miracle. Landscapes—both man-made and natural, war-ravaged and developmental—continue to speak.

CONCLUSION

Too Late, Too Soon

Globalization and New Asian Cities

Asia is not a place, yet the name is laden with history and cultural politics.

—GAYATRI CHAKRAVORTY SPIVAK, *Other Asias*

The year 1987 saw the first democratic elections in South Korea, paving the way for the election of the first civilian president Kim Young-Sam in 1993. In Taiwan, the island's first nonmainlander leader, Lee Teng-hui, was elected president in 1988, a year after the end of nearly forty years of martial law, and in 2000 the first non-Kuomintang leader, Chen Shui-bian, was elected. Lee Kuan Yew's long tenure as Singaporean prime minister finally came to an end in 1990. Although the People's Action Party has remained in power since 1959 to this day, and the South Korean and Taiwanese governments are still locked in various struggles with North Korea and China, respectively, the era of cold war authoritarian rule in the three nations appears to be over. Economically, the stellar rise engineered by this earlier generation of leaders came to an resounding halt in 1997 when, starting with the collapse of Thailand's baht, the Asian financial crisis swept through most of East and Southeast Asia: South Korea, Hong Kong, Thailand, and Indonesia were the hardest hit. The crisis ushered in an era of IMF- and World Bank–imposed fiscal measures and—after a decade of disintegrating socialist regimes—seemed to confirm the shift to a fundamentally new, globalized system of interlinked national economies. In the same period, globally consumed cultural productions from the Asia Pacific were on the rise, including the new generation of Hong Kong auteur films (Wong Kar Wai, Ann Hui); the now well-recognized Taiwanese New Cinema directors Hou Hsiao-hsien, Edward Yang, and Tsai Ming-liang and blockbuster-producing Ang Lee; the Asia-wide phenomenon of Korean film and television dramas (the Korean Wave, or *halyu*) broadcast to audiences from Beijing to Hanoi; and developments in Singaporean theater and art that have challenged stereotypes of the country's cultural desert. It would seem, then, that across the political, economic, and cultural spheres, a definitive break occurred around 1987–90, from which moment the paradigm of globalization has been the predominant lens through which we see this part of the world. Many literary and cultural studies, both from within and outside Asia, have been absorbed by this post-1990 period and the transnational cultural flows correlating with our current globalized age. In contrast to these assumptions, however, this book has argued for a longer memory in examining cultural production from this region. In order to understand the present, we need to revisit the cultural texts and urban spaces of an earlier moment, a period when the Asian Tigers were celebrated only—if misguidedly—for their manufactured goods and incredible rates of productivity.

From the field of American studies, critic Michael Denning has studied the three decades prior to 1989 in *Culture in the Age of Three Worlds,* in which he describes how this period is defined retroactively by globalization as the "name of the end . . . of the historical moment of the age of three worlds" (11). The "established tale" of this age—recalling Amin's account in the first Transition—that Denning both relies on and challenges follows:

> The long boom of U.S., Japanese, and German Keynesian capital that created a global Fordist mass culture characterized by sex, drugs and rock and roll; the long and uneven struggle between the Stalinist bureaucracy and the forces of "thaw" and *glasnost* in the apparently separate world of centrally-planned people's democracies; and the rapid decolonization of the Third World followed by various forms of state-led development and modernization, whether through capitalist import-substitution or Soviet-style central planning. What the three worlds, and these three stories, shared, Eric Hobsbawm has argued, was a commitment to secularism, planning, equal rights, education and modernization. (27)

Denning's project recovers a transnational history of the period and demands a more complicated view of contemporary globalization than simply the atrophying of nation-states and homogenization of culture; in short, he attempts a prehistory of globalized culture. At stake in acknowledging the inherited structures of today's empire is the question of unequal access to, and uneven development of, forms of modernity across the globe. Denning's project is a bold attempt at an interlinked history of what he calls "the asymmetrical three—West, East, and South . . . [before] the East gave way, and the South divided into rich and poor with the emergence first of the oil states and then of the NICs (the Newly Industrializing Countries of East Asia)" (26–27). Broadly, my task in this book has been to investigate one region of the South—the "NICs of East Asia"—at the very moment of its differentiation from the rest of the postcolonial world. *The New Asian City* has explored how the forces of export-oriented industries, domestic authoritarianism, and postcolonial nationalist desires interact in unexpected ways within the cities and landscapes of capitalism, neocolonialism, and the cold war. The modernization success of these Asian Tigers must be seen as the profound product of the age of three worlds, even as it is often thought of as exception to it. My analysis has shown how the unfinished business of developmental nationalism is irrevocably linked to today's globalized condition. That is, the development of these Asia Pacific nations marks the uneasy intersection between third world industrialization and first world post-Fordism, and the creation of new capitalist powers. By following the evolving development of and responses to urban form from the colonial era to the late 1980s, we do away with the sudden temporal break to globalization and its "winners" and understand that New Asian Cities have been colonial, postcolonial, modern, and global all along.

My choice to focus on three sites from within postcolonial Asia fulfils another goal of this project. Spivak has evoked the concept of "Other Asias" and written of the need for "expanding versions of postcolonial theory . . . to 'pluralize' Asia, rather than singularize it so that is was nothing but one's own region" (*Other Asias,* 8). In his recent book *Asia as Method,* Kuan-hsing Chen advances a similar methodology as antidote to the "unnecessary obsession with the question of the West" (215) and asks, "Why are such comparative analyses within the third world so rare—perhaps even non-existent?" (225). Following the work of several postcolonial thinkers, he writes, "there is an urgent need to do comparative studies, or inter-reference studies, of modernity as it is experienced in third-world spaces" (225).

My own personal and intellectual trajectories have brought me to attempt such a study. By considering the material histories and narratives of these three countries in light of each other, rather than against the master term of the West, I hope to deactivate the progress/backwardness and modern/unmodern binaries for a more horizontal, and more useful, comparison. At the same time, I suggest that postcolonial studies can build upon its sophisticated analyses of transcultural formations by the comparative attention to the distinct spatiality of modernity and nationhood.

Chen specifies in his study that Asia is not a unitary, fixed object; rather, he suggests that "using the idea of Asia as an imaginary anchoring point, societies in Asia can become each other's points of reference, so that the understanding of the self may be transformed, and subjectivity rebuilt" (212). For Spivak, it is precisely the loose signifier of "Asia" that holds potential as both a regionalizing and pluralizing concept that will undo the bilateralism between the West and non-West (*Other Asias,* 214). It is in this spirit that I have used the terms "Asia" and "Asia Pacific" in this book—not as a static region, but as a possible and comparative idea. This is not to say that examining Western cultural, political, and technological forms has not been a central task of *The New Asian City.* Indeed, part of the point has been to trace the assimilation of these forms in a comparative context. Chen reminds us:

> In the form of fragmented pieces, the West has entered our history and become part of it, but not in a totalizing manner. The task for Asia as method is to multiply frames of reference in our subjectivity and world-view, so that our anxiety over the West can be diluted, and productive critical work can move forward. (223)

A main purpose of this book has therefore been both to recognize the historical influence of the West and to open up more space for inter-Asian, or south–south, analyses of modernity that no longer need the West for validation.

Finally, through my focus on urban transformation and its fictional textualization, I have shown that city spaces and built forms are among the richest narrative and poetic objects for such analysis. In examining the real and symbolic spaces of certain cities, *The New Asian City* complicates dominant regional accounts by modernization studies and awestruck architectural critics alike. These two unsatisfactory approaches—teleological modernization studies and architectural bewilderment—point to two conflicting (but ultimately compatible) temporal views of the New Asian City. One is that it can never catch up to the West's industrial modernity, begun some 200 years earlier; the other is that it has not only caught up, but (skipping some stages) supersedes it and therefore resides in the future. The New Asian City is thus both an urban form too late (too traditional, too backward to have "normal" development) and too soon (too premature, too capricious to be taken seriously). Such views only make sense, of course, from the assumption of a single narrative of development and modernity. By performing a spatial history of the city as object of desires, fantasies, and competing images, I have attempted to fill in the broader movement of capitalist modernity with a region's local discourses, practices, and struggles. Against standard ideas of Western influence, reproduction, or belated imitation, all which imply a sense of the underdeveloped "poor or colonial or ex-colonial societies as places in which already established ideas of development must be applied" (Williams, *Keywords,* 103), the New Asian City becomes a vital and contested component of global modernity. We may think, then, of the struggles of postcolonial modernizing states in terms of the demand to translate the various forms enshrined by Western modernity—the nation-state, industrial production, citizenship, individual rights—into spatially embedded processes in which these sites have *already* played a fundamental, if subordinate, role. As we have learned from Lefebvre and other philosophers of space, such processes of translation are always ongoing, partial, and uneven. They must be also understood as multiply productive: of new spaces and literatures of work and home, country and city; of new configurations of power; but also of new subjectivities, modes of social connectivity, and collective imaginings.

In the two chapters comprising part 1, "Colonial Cities," we saw how these urban sites were not simply blank slates for postwar development but have long been contested terrains for the implementation of colonial orders and debates over modernity. In the second part, "Postwar Urbanism" we saw how the reproduction of society is predicated on new labor and architectural patterns, themselves entwined with local spatial histories, subjective formations, and power relations. The various fictional genres I examined there demonstrate anxiety over the individual's place in these expanding spaces in terms of both content and form, revealing the often contradictory logic of New Asian City expansion. In part 3, "Industrializing Landscapes," I argued that evidence of state-led growth and development is symbolically located in the landscape with its rationalized architectural forms, expressways, export zones, and rail systems, prompting the articulation of nationalisms and counternationalisms in spatial terms. The last three chapters point to the need to look more carefully at fictional texts that reflect on new infrastructure, those built forms that give rise to wholly new ways of conceiving the social landscape, communities, and indeed futurity itself. I stress here the importance of addressing the psychic and symbolic energies that adhere to material forms of development. These fictional texts thus show us that the 1960s–1980s New Asian City is not merely a temporary, derivative, or anomalous modernity (developmentalism, compressed modernity, or Kipnis's "beyond history"). Rather, the three-dimensional reinscriptions of urban forms allow us access to a spatial logic in which are deposited the residues of colonialism, forces of global capitalism, and dialectics of nationalist desires. Paradoxically, we discover that the New Asian City is not so new after all.

Although this book has examined just three locations, it also aims—somewhat immodestly—to contribute to the larger collective project of rethinking what cultural texts can tell us about colonialism, globalization, modernity, and urban history, for these can and must be studied from new vantage points. To quote Chen again, "the purpose of a renewed understanding of the world is to perceive ourselves differently in relation to our new vision of the world" (253). This study, I hope, will open up new analytic paths in which to examine the most recent of Asian miracles: the rising megastates of China and India. Rather than see their emergence as economic powers in terms of simple neoliberal or evolutionary development, they too must be examined in terms of their colonial histories, postcolonial desires, and enduring local forms of settlement and migration alongside their new global and regional economic roles. Their own narratives of the great ongoing battle between country and city must be excavated and retold, which will simultaneously require readjustment of our previous narratives. At the very least, we shall have to trace further trajectories of such development, its struggles and achievements, in order to avoid the simple judgment of an inherently narrow and conformist idea of Asian modernity.

Acknowledgments

It is a pleasure to thank the many people and institutions that have made this book possible. The original research and first version was written while at Duke University, and I am deeply indebted to the fine teaching and intellectual environment of the graduate program in literature. My tireless dissertation director, Ranjana Khanna, introduced me to the rigors of feminist and postcolonial thinking while guiding me throughout the (sometimes bumpy) working out of this project. She was, and still is, my role model in theoretical sophistication, intellectual generosity, and professional grace. My other exceptional teachers at Duke, including Leo Ching, Fredric Jameson, and Ken Surin, inspired me to make connections across postcolonial Asia, architectural theory, and materialist philosophy and gave me the intellectual training needed to formulate this work. I am also indebted to my peers who read and commented on sections of the work in progress, including Monique Allewaert, Amy Carroll, Lauren Coates, Nihad Farooq, Jaya Kasibhatla, Vin Nardizzi, and Eden Osucha. I also owe much to the generosity of Haeyoung Kim, Seonmin Kim, Yoonkyung Lee, and Hun Lee for language training, translation help, and many heartening Korean–Chinese meals.

Much of the book was written and revised while teaching at New York University, where many generous people read and commented on the manuscript. The friendship and daily comradeship of Toral Gajarawala was particularly sustaining. Elaine Freedgood, Martin Harries, and Rajeswari Sunder Rajan read portions of the project and helped shape the final version, while Robert J. C. Young read the entire book and gave indispensable advice. I am also grateful to members of writing groups I was involved with during this time, including Haytham Bahoora, Michael Ralph, Sonali Perera, and Naomi Schiller. NYU and the Department of English enabled this project in a number of ways, including the Goddard Fellowship, which allowed me to enjoy the hospitality of the University of Melbourne's School of Culture and Communication in 2009, and the Abraham and Rebecca Stein Fund, which supported this publication.

Rob Wilson, Ackbar Abbas, and one anonymous reader gave thoughtful and constructive feedback that helped make this a stronger work, and I am truly grateful for their encouragement. At the University of Minnesota Press, Jason Weidemann and Danielle Kasprzak provided helpful and patient guidance and were enormously supportive throughout the process. In the final stages of this project, I was grateful for the meticulous assistance of Durba Basu and Sharon Wu, as well as the invaluable detective work of Youngon Choi. Lili Hsieh sent feedback from Taiwan, while Alex Galloway extended a hand at just the right moment. Bryce de Reynier offered a fresh perspective, technical assistance, and the best kind of encouragement.

There are, of course, many other sustaining relations that do not make it into the acknowledgments. I have been fortunate to find the company of inspiring friends, teachers, and peers throughout my life in Australia, South Korea, and the United States, and it is thanks to them that I have felt grounded despite my travels. Finally, my deepest gratitude goes to my family: to my parents, Taisoo Kim and Keith Watson, who instilled in me curiosity and the confidence to take my chances and study abroad, and to my brother, Tori, for his reliable humor and down-to-earthness. My mother, in particular, has been an anchor of support and guidance throughout the years it took to write this book. Without her, I certainly could not have done so, and I owe her my greatest admiration and thanks.

Notes

1. Jeffrey Kipnis has published essays on postmodern and deconstructivist architecture and teaches in the School of Architecture at Ohio State University.

2. I borrow Raymond Williams's phrase from his discussion of the changing physical shape of London as a result of the Industrial Revolution: "But it was only late in the century that a physical contrast, which had been long developing, became generally available as an interpretive image. By the 1880s everyone, it seemed, could see the East End and the West End, and in the contrast between them see the dramatic shape of the new society that had been quite nationally and generally created" (*Country,* 220).

3. Testifying to the "Speed and Dominance" described by Kipnis is the fact that many of the recent tallest buildings in the world have been in Asian cities: the Petronas twin towers in Kuala Lumpur, which was superseded by a Taipei sky-scraper, "Taiwan 101," itself competing with the Shanghai World Finance Center. All are overtaken, however, by the 2010 completion of the Burj Khalifa in Dubai, United Arab Emirates.

4. Gayatri Chakravorty Spivak has recently noted the influence of Singapore's urban development on five major cities in India: "The Indian vision of the mega-city was . . . the city-state of Singapore" (*Other Asias,* 169).

5. The discipline of postcolonial studies, having taken root primarily in English departments, has emphasized European—and specifically British and French—imperialism, colonies, and languages. This has resulted in the relative oversight of non-English-language postcolonial texts, as well as the non-Western colonizer Japan, which, according to Duus, by the 1940s boasted some 400 million subjects and colonial territories three-quarters the size of the British empire's (xii). I am not, however, interested in merely righting an imbalance within the field, but rather am interested in how examining these locations opens up new questions and paradigms for postcolonial thinking.

6. For more details on the separation of Singapore and Malaysia, see Kim Wah Yeo and Albert Lau.

7. Tani E. Barlow further maintains that most postcolonial theorizations are insufficient when dealing with the case of partial or "semicolonization" of China by multiple European powers and Japan (5).

8. Paik describes this as "certainly a legacy of colonial rule and even more a direct product of neocolonial intervention . . . that has taken on a systematic nature of its own with self-reproducing antidemocratic structures on both sides of the dividing line" ("Nations and Literatures," 227). See also his important discussion on the division system and modernity in "Coloniality in Korea."

9. Although Singapore has English alongside Malay (designated the national language), Mandarin Chinese, and Tamil, neither Korea nor Taiwan has retained the Japanese language.

10. See Frübel, Heinrichs, and Kreye.

11. Wade's broad argument is that the standard neoliberal, free-market explanation of successful third world economies must be rethought when considering East Asian newly industrializing countries. Acknowledging the postcolonial dimension of this development, he shows how they exhibit "governed markets" consisting of strong state intervention in industry, selected exposure to international competition, and corporatist authoritarianism (27). Crucial to his analysis is the role of Japan as both former colonial power for Taiwan and Korea and as regional economic leader and model in the postwar period (73–75), as well as the key role of the United States in guiding investment. Other factors include the strategic use of import substitution policies alongside export promotion; the nurturing of technocrats; anticommunism; and the militarization of society. Like this study, Wade also considers Hong Kong "too special to be put alongside the others as an equivalent unit" (331), because its industrialization was built up by "British-linked trading companies" and "lifetime expatriates who largely run the government" (331).

12. Similarly, in Terry Eagleton's account of the career of "culture" in the humanities, he notes the relatively new correlation between justice for political minorities and culture (17).

13. Even the project of destabilizing or problematizing cultures and identities, best exemplified by Homi Bhabha's work on hybridity, still leaves the critical focus and object of study as culture and identity. As Pheng Cheah has recently suggested, Bhabha's emphasis on linguistic freedom and ambivalence "exaggerates the role of signification and cultural representation in the functioning of sociopolitical life and its institutions" (*Inhuman Conditions,* 90).

14. For a detailed account of the vicissitudes of Pacific Rim discourse, see also Christopher Connery's "Pacific Rim Discourse." Here, he ruminates not only on the way such discourses are overdetermined by Orientalism, modernization theory, Confucian essentialism, and "residual American frontierism," but also on the spatial topology of a rim: "A rim unites—it unites across oceans, across ethnic and racial divides. . . . A rim is thin. It is stable but precarious. One can fall off a rim. A rim is a horizon: the horizon of capital, of history, of space and time" (41).

15. Nuttall's own study of recent South African urban literature works in a such a fashion, first zooming in on the specific "figures" of Johannesburg—migrant worker, angry white man, illegal immigrant, hustler—and, second, on the locations that constitute "writerly, metropolitan maps" (200)—the street, café, suburb, and campus.

16. Kristin Ross's work on Rimbaud and the Paris Commune is an influential example of an analysis that, drawing on Lefebvre, acknowledges the simultaneity of built form as concrete reality and social relation. *The Emergence of Social Space* reads the experimental social space of the 1871 Paris Commune at work in Arthur Rimbaud's poetry, and the poetic forms within the space of the Commune. In the latter, Ross notes, "street" fighting took place inside houses, and adjoining houses were "lateral[ly] pierced" (37), turning closed interiors into corridors. Equally, Rimbaud's poems confound interior and exterior, personal and political spheres. In Ross's dual-level analytic—the spatial and the literary—similarities are tapped and placed into mutual relationships, with neither level the determining factor of the other.

17. Architectural theorist Anthony Vidler, in both *The Architectural Uncanny* and *Warped Space,* performs a further upturning of assumed spatial hierarchies from a psychoanalytic perspective. By asking whether or not certain architecture and spaces might be constitutive of modern subjectivities at the same time that they are a formal response to them, he challenges the very ontology of the modern subject and the purity of the interior/exterior division.

18. Mandel explains this as a result of declining profits in raw materials industries, the general drop in prices after the Korean War (64), and a third technological revolution, where new technologies of communication and transportation allow for the first time the internationalization of production. See his chapter 17, "Late Capitalism as a Whole."

19. To acknowledge Mandel is not to exclude the uneven domestic and regional effects of this shift seen, for example, in the role played by companies such as Korea's now multinational Samsung or Hyundai in Southeast Asia, or the many Taiwanese manufacturing companies now operating in mainland China.

20. Connery is referring here, of course, to the notorious Japanese euphemism of imperialism as the "Greater East Asia Co-Prosperity Sphere."

21. My approach to the region is indebted to that in Wilson and Dirlik's 1995 edited volume, *Asia/Pacific as Space of Cultural Production.* Challenging the way the discourse of Asia/Pacific and Pacific Rim (I use the terms interchangeably) has been saturated by cold war geoimaginaries and the "futurology" of successful flows of transnational capital, the authors attempt to address this regional conceptualization with "a more critical orientation toward area studies that transcends individual countries/islands/states and that ties in with world-system analysis in noncategorical ways" (12). For them, to trace the dynamics of "global interactive space" is to consider the formation of "alternative subjectivities and of heteroglossic communities" (12).

22. I am thinking here of nativist movements such as Négritude, which posited a moment of precolonial plenitude and harmony before the arrival of colonialists.

On the provocative theorization of postcolonial modernities as alternative modernities, see Dilip Parameshwar Gaonkar's edited collection.

1. Imagining the Colonial City

1. For theories of imageability with regard to urban spaces, see Kevin Lynch.

2. Raymond Williams's *The Country and the City* is one of the most elegant (and literary) accounts of this differentiation, tracing the gradual subjection of English spaces to "improvement" and progress.

3. In addition to the work of Smith, Lefebvre, Harvey, Williams, and Luxemburg, other important works broadly in this tradition are Kristin Ross, *The Emergence of Social Space,* and Edward W. Soja, *Postmodern Geographies.*

4. In 1895 Cecil Rhodes gave one of the most concise accounts of the role the colonies would play as this "spatial fix" outside the system: "I was in the East End of London [in a working-class quarter] yesterday and attended a meeting of the unemployed. I listened to the wild speeches, which were just a cry for 'bread! bread!' and on my way home I pondered over the scene and I became more than ever convinced of the importance of imperialism. . . . My cherished idea is a solution for the social problem, i.e., in order to save the 40,000,000 inhabitants of the United Kingdom from a bloody civil war, we colonial statesmen must acquire new lands to settle the surplus population, to provide new markets for the goods produced in the factories and mines. The Empire, as I have always said, is a bread and butter question. If you want to avoid civil war, you must become imperialists" (Rhodes qtd. in Lenin, 1:737).

5. Lenin traces the historical development of capital to its monopolistic and imperialistic stage, characterized by the period of finance capital. At this stage, rentier (rather than productive) systems of profit prevail, and the export of capital to "backward countries" is necessary to relieve the domestic problems of overpopulation, excess capital, and unemployment at home. Colonialism is simply the subsequent political form in which the major capitalist countries—which can be best thought of as big business operations—first divide up the materials for production, and then the world's populations and territories, between themselves. Thus, "colonial possession alone gives the monopolies complete guarantee against all contingencies in the struggle against competitors" (Lenin, 1:740).

6. For numerous excellent essays on comparative urban colonialisms, see Nezar AlSayyad's edited collection, *Forms of Dominance.*

7. See my article, "Imperial Mimicry," on the question of Western-styled imperialism in Japan.

8. See Paul Rabinow's *French Modern* for the way colonial Morocco became France's laboratory for urban planning experiments. The colonial power "to expropriate property for the public good, to control speculation, and to retain for the collectivity profits from improvements" (292) could never be realized in France. Note that here, too, the separation of the "medina" and the European town was an integral feature of Morocco's urban planning.

9. Manuel Castells has similarly stressed the need to analyze metropolitan and postcolonial (or, in his language, "dependent") urbanization as separate components of a single unified structure. He proposes a distinct theory of postcolonial urbanization to avoid Eurocentrist urban planning concepts often applied to the non-West, where terms such as "overurbanization," "premature metropolises," and "underdevelopment" all take as their norm the development patterns of the first world. Hitherto separated "factors" of analysis thus unite to form a coherent "structural theory of space" (*Urban Question,* 125). In Castells's program of "extend[ing] in the field of the analysis of space, the fundamental concepts of historical materialism" (125), the common concept of "underdevelopment" is preferably rendered "exploited and dominated, with a deformed economy" (Charles Bettelheim qtd. in Castells, 43).

10. See "The Origin of the Work of Art" for Heidegger's discussion of a Van Gogh painting and Greek temple as prime illustrations.

11. The competing systems of "worlding" undertaken by the imperial powers leads, unsurprisingly, to clashing versions of spatiality and, eventually, war. Contrast the British vision of linked trade territories to Japan's total and hierarchical conception of East Asia: "the focus of the Japanese colonial geopolitical structure was the hinterland of Japan. The sub-circle included Hokaitou and Ryukyu. An outer circle is Korea and Taiwan and then Manchu and China, while the outermost circle, the edge of the empire, comprised south-east Asia and the islands of the Pacific Ocean" (Hsia, 9).

2. Orphans of Asia

1. *"Manse"* (literally "hooray") is usually translated as the "March 1st Movement" ("Samil Undong"), as Yŏm's novel is a depiction of the colonial society leading up to the 1919 resistance movement. The movement was directly inspired by President Woodrow Wilson's 1919 proclamation of the right of small nations to self-determination at the Paris Peace Conference. A mass protest, apparently led by students studying in Japan, converged in Seoul, where a Korean Declaration of Independence was read. It was brutally put down by the Japanese police, to little international attention.

2. Unless otherwise noted, all translations of *Mansejŏn* are my own.

3. There is little colonial period Singaporean or Malayan literature aside from that published in literary supplements to some newspapers. Wong Yoon Wah has written of this paucity: "Chinese literature prior to the post-WWII period is small in quantity, and with few exceptions, inferior in quality. The writing can be divided into two groups: those written for readers in China and those intended for the local Chinese themselves. But both writings are primarily utilitarian and political" (15). The output in English by the non-British population during the colonial period was also minimal.

4. In a literal sense, European modernities were built on the wealth of colonial materials, trade, and labor—or, as Walter Mignolo summarizes, "There is no modernity without coloniality" (43). In this chapter I am indebted to Mignolo's

formulation of "modernity/coloniality." Ryan Bishop et al. confirm this dual concept by noting the transfer of new technologies from the colonies back to the metropole, in such forms as dictionaries, fingerprinting, penal systems, telegraph links, and medical research (24). In comparison to the older European empires, the case of imperial Japan makes even more explicit the simultaneity of metropolitan and colonial modernities in that Japan's first colonial possession (Taiwan, in 1895) closely followed the beginning of the Meiji Restoration's modernizing push (1868).

5. Literature in classical Chinese was considered the most prestigious literary form until the breakdown of the class-based system in the reform era, which ended the civil service examination and the scholar-bureaucrat profession. See Kim Hŭng-gyu, "Chosŏn Fiction in Chinese," for more details. Vernacular Korean fiction (literature written in the phonetic alphabet of *hangŭl*) had been gaining popularity from the seventeenth century onward, but largely as a literary form associated with women's lowbrow reading. At the beginning of the twentieth century, "Chinese literary influence declined, [and] various literary forms using the Korean language expanded to the masses through newspapers such as the Independent *(Tongnip shinmun),* Korea Daily News *(Taehan maeil shinbo),*" and many others (Kwŏn Yŏngmin, "Early Twentieth Century Fiction," 390). After *Tears of Blood,* Yi Kwangsu's *The Heartless (Mujŏng)* of 1917 is usually designated in national literary histories—such as Kim Hunggyu's *Understanding Korean Literature*—as the next most important modern literary accomplishment, in which a modern sense of interiority or individual subjectivity finds expression. For this reason, the beginning of modern Korean literature is often dated to 1917, with the preceding years of active experimentation considered a transition period.

6. The school of realist Korean writers educated in Japan were influenced by translated works of Zola, Maupassant, Tolstoy, Turgenev, Dostoevsky, and Wilde.

7. Prime examples of this kind of literary realism are "Potato" ("Kamja") by Kim Tong-in and "A Lucky Day" ("Unsu choŭn nal") by Hyŏn Ching-ŏn.

8. Kim Tong-in's story of a miserable couple living in urban poverty, "Potato," has famously described this environment. The story begins with: "Strife, adultery, murder, theft, begging, imprisonment—the slums outside P'yŏngyang's Ch'ilsŏng Gate were a breeding ground for all the tragedy and violence of this world. Until Pok-nyŏ and her husband moved there, they had been farmers, the second of the four classes (scholars, farmers, artisans, and merchants) of society" (16). Moral degradation is understood as inhering within these spaces: "The main occupation of the slum's inhabitants was begging, and their secondary pursuits were thieving and whoring among themselves.... Pok-nyŏ began begging with the rest" (17–18).

9. A traditional Korean system of heated floor.

10. Two other fascinating Taiwanese colonial-era texts are Yang Kui's "Paperboy" (1932) and Chu Tien-Jen's 1936 short story "Autumn Note" ("Qiu xin"). "Paperboy" concerns another Taiwanese student studying in Tokyo, where he becomes politicized through understanding the larger contradictions of capitalist modernity via the hardships of his job as a paperboy. The gleaming Japanese

modernity he first finds in Tokyo reveals its cracks in the pathetic condition of the unemployed and underpaid struggling to survive in the city. "Autumn Note" fol lows an elderly Chinese farmer living in the south of Taiwan who visits Taipei's "Exhibit," the Japanese-sponsored trade expo held to celebrate 40 years of Japanese rule. On visiting the capital, Master Tou-wen finds himself unable to speak the new language or negotiate the much-changed city. Here, modern urban planning and the installation of the exhibit literally replace the previous spatial order of the Chinese city; Master Tou-wen notes with disappointment that the Taipei streets "were no longer under their old names" (27). The city is turned into the show-case of industrialized, imperial Japan, while the countryside, through the web of advertising and railways, is interpellated into the colonial audience for this new metropolitan space. The story's affective despondency at the end arises from the understanding that the hegemony of exchange value also requires the violent re-placement of Taiwanese/Chinese identity for Taiwanese productivity.

11. All English quotations are taken from Ioannis Mentzas's translation.

12. According to Jane Parish Yang's study, the Taiwanese semimonthly *Taiwan minbao* was the organ of the Taiwanese vernacular movement, much influenced by the literature of the May Fourth Movement. Lai Ho (Lai He) was the most impor-tant Taiwanese writer to popularize writing in the vernacular. See Yang's account of the literary milieu of the day.

13. In Kleeman's detailed study of Taiwanese colonial literature, she describes three general attitudes of language choice coming out of these contestations: "During the early years of the occupation, when ties with China were still strong and the colonial government had not yet implemented an aggressive policy of lan-guage assimilation, the linguistic preference of most intellectuals was for some form of Chinese. Gradually, as ties to the continent weakened with the advance of colonization, they began to wrestle with the choice between Taiwanese, which reinforced a newly localized, indigenous ethnic identity, and Japanese, the lan-guage of the colonizers, which promised participation in a rising empire. The sec-ond generation of Taiwanese writers, men such as Yang Kui, Zhang Wenhuan, and Lü Heruo, came of age just at this juncture, and their literature reflects the prevail-ing ambivalence regarding these linguistic paths. In the latter half of the occupa-tion, a new breed of writer, the 'imperial-subject *[kominka]* writer,' emerged. To most of these authors, China was but a distant and irrelevant memory of their grandfathers and they had only limited familiarity with written Chinese" (123). The enormous success of the Japanese education system can be gauged by the fact that in 1941 "57 percent of the total population was being or had been educated in Japanese" (142).

14. Compare the following description in Wu Zhuoliu's 1968 memoirs *The Fig Tree (Wu Hua Guo),* in which not only industrial products are on display, but aboriginal culture and the Japanese army royal family are equally spectacles of an architecturally ordered nature: "That year [1916] was the twentieth anniversary of the incorporation of Taiwan into the Japanese empire and an industrial promotion fair had been organized to celebrate the event. . . . When her imperial highness, the

wife of Prince Kitishirakawa, arrived from Keelung, the welcoming ceremonies surpassed themselves in splendour. Shots rang out in a deafening crackle, then came the resounding brass of a military band and behind it, mounted on magnificent chargers, the splendidly attired generals of the Imperial Army. Following them in perfect formation, column after column of infantrymen paraded past and then, in a pitter-patter of hooves, the two-horse carriage of her imperial highness led by the governor-general himself on a single mount" (89).

15. A secondary exodus of workers followed promises of work in the larger imperial labor market in Manchuria and Japan.

16. Unless otherwise noted, all quotations are from the translation by Jung-hyo Ahn and James B. Lee.

17. See chapter 4 for a more detailed discussion on gendered space and domestic planning.

18. See Benjamin on the prostitute and her relationship to the commodity in "Prostitution, Gambling" (Convolute O): "Love for the prostitute is the apotheosis of empathy with the commodity" (511).

19. Jason C. Kuo writes of the similar function of colonial fairs in Japan's colonies: "Like the industrial exhibitions and world expositions held in other parts of the world since the second half of the nineteenth century and early twentieth century, the colonial government's 1935 Exhibition in Commemoration of the Fortieth Anniversary of the Inauguration of Rule in Taiwan was a classic example of imperialism in its conception and construction. It displayed the material culture of an industrial and commercial empire (Japan), with an emphasis on manufactured goods derived from raw materials from the colony" (24).

20. We should note here how often the suicidal plot device recurs in the New Asian City literature analyzed in this book. See chapter 3 for suicides from a factory smokestack and tall hotel, and chapter 4 for a suicide from high-rise housing blocks.

21. An interesting comparison is James A. Fujii's account of Japanese Natsume Soseki's seminal modernist text of 1914, *Kokoro,* in which Fujii attends to the "imperial dimension of Japan's modernity" (200). Fujii parallels the text's self-conscious textuality with the Japanese recreation of itself from its "dead" past though imperial power: "As surely as a helpless silence and death would fuel and encourage narrative activity in *Kokoro,* confrontation with Japan's own mordant history would lead Japan to emulate the imperialist trajectories of the Western powers and to narrate its own history of coercion onto the map" (217).

TRANSITION. EXPORT PRODUCTION AND THE BLANK SLATE

1. Hong Kong too, though beyond the scope of this study, also owes its unique post-1949 development to its position as a British capitalist outpost on the edge of communist China.

2. In fact, Frank finds that it is the areas most closely linked to imperialist development—British Bengal or Spanish Santo Domingo, for example—that later become the most underdeveloped.

3. See, for example, Frederic D. Deyo, John Lie, Lawrence J. Lau, and James M. Livingstone.

4. We can also think here of the deal between President Lyndon Johnson and President Park Chung Hee, which sent 300,000 South Korea soldiers to fight in the Vietnam War in exchange for infrastructure and military aid. See chapter 7 for details.

5. I am grateful to Ackbar Abbas for suggesting this phrase.

3. Narratives of Human Growth versus Urban Renewal

1. Anthony D. King early made the point that "much of what was previously accepted as 'universally applicable urban theory' has been based on an ahistorical Western ethnocentricism" and that such models and theories "do not fit the majority of cities in the non-Western world" (14). Similarly, Beng-huat Chua rightly points out with regard to Singapore that cities on the periphery are "inextricably tied to global capitalism" and are therefore equally a product of the "cultural modernity of capitalism" ("World Cities," 985).

2. See, for example, Jon Woronoff.

3. We must also take into consideration the role that national divisions—the cold war partition between North and South Korea, the KMT's loss on the mainland to the Communist Party, and the 1965 ejection of Singapore from Malaysia—played in the antilabor approach to productivity.

4. In his essay "Singapore Songlines: Portrait of a Potemkin Metropolis or Thirty Years of Tabula Rasa," Koolhaas also notes other Westerners have reacted to Singapore's "stunning overdose of newness" (1019) with suspicion, including William Gibson, who termed it "Disneyland with the death penalty" (Gibson qtd. in Koolhaas, 1013).

5. For more on the multilingual literary landscape of Singapore, see Wong Yoon Wah, Liaw Yock Fang, and Arthur Yap et al.

6. In Pinyin, *xiangtu wenxue.*

7. Even in Henry-Russell Hitchcock and Philip Johnson's seminal treatise, *The International Style: Architecture since 1922,* and despite the establishment of skyscraper building technologies by this time, the authors confirm that "horizontality . . . is the most conspicuous characteristic of the international style as judged in terms of affect" (65–66).

8. This rationalization of space is also linked to the late nineteenth century's fascination for the newly defined category of *landscape.* Kristen Ross describes how Vidal de la Blache led the development of the university discipline of geography—the "science of landscapism" (85)—which coincided with the bourgeois quantification and rationalization of industry and the global expansion of European commercial interests. In her words, "Western, Christian colonialism demands a certain construction of space that Vidalian, academic geography was to help provide: natural, which is to say, nonhistorical—and one where all alterity is absent" (87). See also W. J. T. Mitchell's important study *Landscape and Power.*

9. While Korea's colonizer, Japan, did not undergo the same urbanization and industrialization process as Europe, the Meiji period (1868–1912) saw the

importation of technological, economic, cultural, and architectural forms from Europe. Its colonies were similarly crucial for its development and modernization. See chapter 1 for details.

10. All English citations refer to Bruce and Ju-chan Fulton's translation.

11. For a more in-depth discussion of *chaebols,* see chapter 7.

12. My thanks to Ranjana Khanna for pointing out this striking image.

13. This was, of course, standard colonial urban practice from British Delhi to Dutch Batavia. See the discussion of Singapore and other colonial cities in chapter 1.

14. This is not to say that Singapore, before urban renewal, was an intact village society; it was always urban and a society of migrants, such that the term "traditional Singapore" is something of an oxymoron.

15. See chapter 6 for a discussion of Ch'en's "Washington Building" stories.

16. Wu Zhuoliu, the author of *The Orphan of Asia* discussed in chapter 2, could similarly maintain (in 1971) that addressing the social reality of Taiwan was a means of participating in both Chinese and literary universality (Hsiau, 82).

17. Li notes: "after the end of the Second World War, the Chinese government (the Nationalists) took over (from the Japanese colonial government) the administration of the transportation and communication systems, major financial institutions, and other monopoly businesses like sugar refining, paper, cement, and electrical power" (24).

18. This is not to say that city governments did not desire the greater rationality of modern forms, cleaner streets, and organized road systems. A 1978 publication on urban renewal projects by the Taipei City Government states typical modernist aims such as: "Eliminate the buildings with undesirable conditions" and "eliminate narrow, winding and shabby streets and construct a modern, safe and convenient street system" (2). See chapter 6 for more details.

19. The plot of Huang's "The Two Sign Painters" was loosely adopted in Korean Pak Kwang-su's 1988 film *Chil-su wa Man-su,* which also ends with the police and crowds precipitating a fall/suicide from one sign painter.

4. The Disappearing Woman, Interiority, and Private Space

1. Being "not event-based, but character-based" (Yi Nam-ho, 254), the novel is indebted to the literary achievements of Korean women writers in the 1970s. These earlier writers discarded linear narrative structures for "eventless associations, the unfolding of events through dialogue, or the use of an open structure without conclusion" (Ch'oe Yun, 487).

2. My thanks to Lili Hsieh for this translation. Other important works by Su include *Leaving Tongfang* (1996) and *The Island of Silence* (1994).

3. Virginia Woolf is representative of a kind of Western liberal feminism that may arise through the development of individualized space. In *A Room of One's Own,* Woolf favorably characterizes the spaces of solitary, intellectual reflection, epitomized by the college library to which she is denied access. Looking over the

exterior of college towers, she writes: "I thought, too, of the admirable smoke and drink and the deep armchairs and the pleasant carpets: of the urbanity, the genial ity, the dignity which are the offspring of luxury and privacy and space" (23). She precisely wants access to those spaces of individual education and reflection rather than a rethinking of them—a move that New Asian City feminism cannot simply replicate.

4. See Stefan Tanaka for how this Japanese formulation came to dominance by the mid-nineteenth century as "Eastern ethics as base, Western technology as means," or *"toyo dotoku, seiyo gei"* (4).

5. In Singapore the percentage of women in the paid workforce rose from 29.5 percent in 1970 to 44.3 percent in 1980 and 50.3 percent in 1990 (Jasmine Chan, 41). Between 1960 and 1995, Korean women's economic activity rose from 26.8 percent to 47.6 percent (Hampson, 176). The development of light industry in Taiwan in the 1970s similarly "brought a massive migration of young women from rural locations to urban industrialised suburban areas and to export processing zones" (Lan-Hung Nora Chiang, 235). The 1980s saw a shift from factory work to more white-collar jobs for women in all three locations.

6. Lan-Hung Nora Chiang writes that Taiwan's first-wave feminist movement of the 1970s was "almost a one-woman crusade" led by Harvard-educated Lu Hsiu-lien, who has since served as Taiwan's vice president.

7. One indication of the apparent belatedness of South Korean feminism is the achievement of women's legal equality within the family. Only in 1991 was the family law changed, which had given legal order of succession of household leadership to male members only and made custody of children after divorce an automatic paternal right (Moon, 53).

8. Young is here quoting a paper on "The Contribution of Women to the Development of the Pan African World" given by a Guyanese delegation at the 1974 Sixth Pan-African Congress. See his chapter on "Women, Gender and Anti-Colonialism" for a summary of the vicissitudes of women's struggles in postcolonialism.

9. We must also make mention of the expansive feminist discourse in the West, which also productively challenges the assumptions of liberal feminism, often under the name of "women of color feminism." See bell hooks and Angela Davis for two early and seminal texts.

10. The figure of the prostitute in literature has special significance in this region. In the cases of Korea and Taiwan, where neocolonial power structures were a fact of everyday reality in the form of direct or indirect U.S. military hegemony, the gendered relationship between states is often rewritten onto the body of the prostitute and her U.S. soldier/customer. Thus, we find the anxieties of an incomplete postcolonial modernity played out through the implicit allegorization of women as nation in fictional accounts of military prostitution camptowns (Kang's "Days and Dreams," Ch'oe In-hoon's "The End of the State Road"), military sex tourism (Huang Chunming's "Sayonara/Zaijian," Wang Chen-ho's *Rose Rose I Love You*), and the abortion clinic serving military prostitutes (Pak Wan-sŏ's "Three

Days in That Autumn"). Attention to the figure of the prostitute highlights the myriad of contradictions of doubly colonized postcolonial women, often forced into such work by local patriarchal societies that reserve resources and education for men and demonize unchasteness. They also explore how such camp towns and tourist sites are spaces both internal and external to the nation, and both public (as places of work and business) and private (as places of sexual activity). Yet as several critics point out, the focus on the postcolonial woman as prostitute to foreign occupiers or military forces tends to erase the particular and material struggles—including against local patriarchies—of women for an obsession with the nation as the unit of analysis. See especially Hyun Sook Kim.

11. The first generation of postwar women writers would include Kim Chi-wŏn, O Chŏng-hui, Pak Kyŏng-ni, and Pak Wan-sŏ.

12. Sang-hae Lee addresses the division of spaces according to gender and the multipurpose function of rooms: "Each man, woman and child slept on the floor of whichever room he or she used during the day. As for meals, the head of the household ate in the *sarangbang* and other members of the family in the *anbang* or wooden-floored *maru*. Today these customs are changing, but Koreans' fundamental use of space reflects the traditional hierarchy based on seniority and the strict division between the sexes" (383).

13. The flexibility of the sleeping mat *(yo)*, which was usually rolled away during the day, also renders the very idea of permanent, separate bedrooms as something new.

14. Lefebvre writes that the modern interior kills Eros for mere genital sex and false intimacy: "the interior, where Eros dies, is also invested with value—albeit in a mystifying and mystified way. Heavy curtains allow inside to be isolated from outside, the balcony to be separated from the drawing-room, and hence for 'intimacy' to be preserved and signified" (315).

15. See Robin Evans's remarkable history of the sixteenth-century emergence of private rooms via the technology of the corridor. According to sixteenth-century theorists, one of the expediencies for the shift away from interconnected rooms is the deplorable "mixing of servant and family, the racket of children and the prattle of women" (50).

16. There is no surprise that Poe, with his uncanny tales set in ordinary spaces, is not only the inventor of the first mystery story, but also the "first physiognomist of the domestic interior" (Benjamin, 9).

17. Through the 1970s, light industries produced most of Korean exports, and female workers comprised more than half of the work force in the important electronics, textile, and rubber footwear industries (Seung-kyung Kim, 3).

18. "If a woman missed attendance call three times, she was reprimanded by the matron and punished by being assigned to clean the bathroom for a month. If a woman stayed out more than three times without getting prior permission, she was asked to leave the dormitory. By keeping such a strict code of behavior, the matron of the dormitory could thus 'vouch' for good behavior to prospective husbands and in-laws" (Seung-kyung Kim, 26)

19. Remarkably, in this context, further education may actually decrease work opportunities. Because of the predominantly blue-collar nature of women's work, "Korea faces the peculiar situation where the more educated a woman is the less likely she is to work" (Hampson, 180). Recent studies of women's roles in Korea confirm that women engaged in paid work are still often regarded as lower status than housewives. As late as 1991, only 3.9 percent of Korean female workers were college educated, while 65.2 percent had only middle school or lower education (Hampson, 180).

20. We may compare this scene to that in Yi Sang's *The Wings* (discussed in chapter 2), in which the protagonist gains sustained delight in examining his absent wife's cosmetics.

21. Knapp further notes: "The room is symbolic of unity and continuity—a significance heightened by the placement of a long table facing the door upon which are placed ancestral tablets, images of gods and goddesses, family mementos, and ceremonial paraphernalia. Most households have such a high table, but not every household displays all these items. The centrality of the common room, the ritual heart of a house, acknowledges patrilineal descent" (43–44).

22. After divorce a woman may, for example, strengthen ties with her natal family or emphasize her role as mother. In Lu's words: "Their efforts to 'position' themselves within a web of relationships lead to their ambivalence toward Western feminism. Because this web of relationships always includes their intimate male kin— their fathers and brothers—their criticism of men is primarily directed toward their husbands, rather than to all men. It is this feature, I maintain, that makes Taiwanese women's feminist experiences differ from those of Western feminism" (239).

23. Lim's own education at a Catholic convent in Malaysia before studying literature at the National University of Singapore would seem to be another major determinant of the narrative's setting.

24. *Rice Bowl* makes no pretensions to realistically represent either local or immigrant female factory workers. For a fascinating account of women factory workers in Malaysia, see Aihwa Ong.

TRANSITION. ROADS, RAILWAYS, AND BRIDGES

1. Pheng Cheah has also commented on Anderson's provocative metaphor. See *Spectral Nationality* (226–27).

5. THE WAY AHEAD

1. On the one hand, because of its defense and economic ties with Britain and the pro-Western attitude of the Malaysian leader, the Tunku Abdul Rahman, some interpreted the new Malaysia as betraying the spirit of the independent struggles and the nonalignment movement. On the other hand, Indonesia's Konfrontasi, a low-level war against Malaysia, could be viewed as a large country attempting to absorb another sovereign state, bringing sympathy for the latter.

2. We find that Lee most favorably judges the postcolonial leaders perceived to be most British in manner—that is, with a taste for quality and propriety rather

than ostentation. Thus, Nigeria is praised over Ghana because there "The ceremony was totally British" and "many of the public buildings [in Lagos] looked identical with those in Malaya and Singapore" (*Singapore Story,* 532). Julius Nyerere of Tanzania (then Tanganyika) hosts the entourage in the presidential mansion formerly used by both the British governor and the German administrator, but Nyerere himself displays British restraint in "prefer[ing] to live in a small house nearby" (533).

3. Singapore maintained a military alliance with the U.K. after their withdrawal and forged new strategic partnerships with Australia, New Zealand, and the United States. Lee secured military expertise and advice from Israel (another nation with troubled boundaries), and thanks to a quiet agreement made with Chiang Kai-shek's son, Chiang Ching-kuo, in 1974, he gained the space to train Singapore's troops in Taiwan; it currently trains part of its army in Australia. For a history of Singapore's postindependence politics, see Heng Chee Chan.

4. There have been many studies of Thumboo's poetry, as well as several comparisons between his work and Yap's. Significant works in addition to Lim, Patke, Goh, and Brewster cited in this chapter include Kirpal Singh and Ooi Boo Eng's "The Poetry of Edwin Thumboo" on the poet's early to mature poetic stages, and Anne Brewster's *Towards a Semiotic of Post-Colonial Discourse*, a monograph on the early experiments of Anglophone Singaporean and Malayan writers.

5. Another important poet often read in relation to Thumboo is Lee Tzu Pheng, whose 1976 "My Country and My People" reads something like counternationalist poem and includes this memorable description of HDB flats: "They built milli-mini-flats / for a multi-mini-society."

6. We should note, however, that before the 1980s, English was the language of instruction for only about 10 percent of the population, and a dialect of Chinese (and not the official Chinese language of Mandarin) was the mother tongue of most Singaporeans.

7. This is not to ignore the actual continuing and functional relationship between Singapore and Malaysia. Singapore draws many of its resources from the larger country, and Singaporean Chinese may properly regard Malaysia's Chinese population as a cultural hinterland. In terms of the nationalist symbolic renderings of the island nation, acknowledging this presence of a hinterland is useful to neither Lee nor Thumboo.

8. Such a desire is reflected in overtly national/political poems in *Gods Can Die,* "9th of August—I" and "9th of August—II," which deal with the day that Singapore was thrown out of Malaysia and uneasily embarked on independence. See also "The Exile," "The Interview," and "A Quiet Evening," the last of which seems to be about a dinner with Lee Kuan Yew.

6. Mobility and Migration in Taiwanese New Cinema

1. For nonproper nouns, I have included pinyin translations where appropriate.

2. For Sun Yat-sen's interesting definition of *Min sheng,* which he distinguishes from the related Marxist notion of socialism, see Lecture 1 in "The Principle of

Livelihood." Sun was, of course, extremely interested in Marxism, especially in his concern for redistribution and preventing a dominant capitalist class forming in China. It was perhaps fortunate for Chiang that the task bequeathed to him was finishing the section on livelihood, with its concern for material welfare and public order, rather than on the section on people's democracy or nationalism.

3. This was indeed one of the characteristics of Taiwan's early urbanization. Castells notes that Taiwan's flexible industrial structure of small family-run firms subcontracted to larger foreign companies allowed, until the 1960s, urban workers to sometimes work in both factories and agricultural plots that remained in the city (Castells, "Four Asian Tigers," 43). See also chapter 3's discussion of *hsiang-t'u* literature.

4. On Singapore and the invention of "Asian Values," see C. J. W.-L. Wee. For architecture and its role in resinicizing Taiwan after retrocession, see Jason C. Kuo's chapter "Colonialism and Decolonization." For an overview of Korean nationalist historiography and its influence on historical fiction, refer to JaHyun Kim Haboush.

5. The renaming of the Minnan-hua dialect spoken by the majority of non-mainlainders as Taiwanese *(Taiyu)* is evidence of the construction of a new Taiwanese ethnicity. This oppositional identity, however, tends to occlude the presence of the Hakka-speaking minority as well as the plight of the aboriginal peoples of Taiwan, to whom the mainlander *(wai-sheng,* or "outside province") versus *ben-sheng* difference is of little importance.

6. For more on Taiwan's film history, see Chen Ruxiu's volume.

7. Under Chiang Ching-kuo's leadership, for example, native Taiwanese Lee Teng-hui rose to the position of vice president and would become the first native Taiwanese president in 1988. My thanks to Lili Hsieh for the translation of his name.

8. Chen Kuan-hsing goes on to examine the function of the Taiwanese New Cinema in terms of the state's need for local signification as a way to secure global recognition. He discusses the way Taiwanese film travels the global festival circuit and participates in "the commodification of the implicit dialectic between nationalism and transnationalism" (557).

9. Considering that linguistic differences among Taiwanese are largely unrepresentable in written form, film (and the convenience of subtitles) is ideal for representing local dialects and identities.

10. See also Yip's discussion on the significance of the visual city–rural contrasts (205–6).

11. Reynaud summarizes the "recognisable" tropes of Hou's mise-en-scène: "One-shot sequences that explore both duration and the depth of space; elliptic editing and compositions that function as tableaux, or, even better, 'blocks' of discontinuous time/space; 180° reverse-angle cuts; the recurrence of empty spaces; a fondness for putting the camera at a distance—especially for scenes of violence, represented in extreme long shots. Human activity is not what commands the framing" (72).

7. The Redemptive Realism of Korean *Minjung* Literature

1. Cumings made this point at a lecture at Duke University in the early 2000s.

2. For the first few years, Park operated under the Supreme Council for National Reconstruction before running as a civilian in the 1963 presidential elections—and winning. While many have claimed these elections to be rigged, Kim Hyung-A's scholarship reports that it was probably not.

3. The idea came to him when visiting some flood-damaged areas of Kyŏngsangnam province, where one village caught Park's attention: "Despite the flood, this village had not only recovered from the devastation, but had also constructed a noticeably better standard of infra-structure and living conditions. There were wider roads and each house had a tidy roof and walls. Park learned that the villages had achieved this outcome mainly by volunteering their time and labor for the community" (Kim Hyung-A, 134).

4. For background, see Stephen Kern for multiple studies on how the invention of each new technology—from the electric bulb to the bicycle to the automobile—brought with it new modes of experiencing, thinking, and producing art.

5. A former engineer of the Seoul-Pusan (Kyŏngbu) expressway recalled his experience of Park as literal on-site superintendent: "Mr Park is not an easy man at the best of times, and he certainly was far from that during our project. But after a while, I found myself thinking of him as a sort of conductor of an orchestra—with a helicopter as his baton. Up and down he would go, this time with a team of geologists to figure out what was wrong with some mountainside that had crumbled on our tunnel-makers, the next time with a couple of United Nations hydrologists to figure out how our surveyors had got some water table wrong. If he didn't have the answer on Tuesday, Mr Park was back with it on Thursday" (qtd. in Kim, 156).

6. We should also not forget that Singapore achieved major economic acceleration during the Vietnam War, through supplying the U.S. military.

7. The term *minjung* should be distinguished from *minjok,* which translates more directly as "nation" (and *minjokjuŭi* as "nationalism") and can include a racial or ethnic meaning.

8. In choosing just one of the important 1970s writers to focus on, I am inevitably omitting the centrality of works by Yi Mungu and the others, as well as the influential poets Sin Kyŏng-nim (*Nongmu,* or *Farmers Dance*) and Kim Chi-ha (*Five Thieves,* or *Ojok).* While these are important evocations of the changing *minjung* rural experience, I chose Hwang Sŏk-yŏng for his more focused literary examination of the new person inhabiting the industrializing rural landscape.

9. Note that Pihl translates *minjungnon* (literally, "theory of *minjung"*) as "populism."

10. This story was also immediately made into a feature film of the same title by Lee Man-hŭi in the same year, 1975. Unlike the story, however, the film version is highly melodramatic.

11. Unless otherwise noted, all English translations refer to Kim Uchang's translation.

12. Rob Wilson has attributed the melodramatic tendency in 1980s Korean film to two factors, one being the colonial factor resulting from a "subaltern history" under Japanese colonialism, division, civil war and neo-colonialism, and the other being the "*han* factor" (99–100). The latter he describes, quoting Ahn Byung-sup, as a "sensibility of resentment, longing, envy, spite or a 'frame of mind characterized by a sorrowful lament' and sense of tragic resignation that has long been associated with the Korean national character by Koreans themselves" (99). Standish more simply describes *han* as a "bitter feeling," "hatred," and "unsatisfied desire"—primarily a result of Korea's numerous invasions and tyrannies (86–87n3). The term is important in the *minjung* context because the concept includes both the logic of collectively experienced suffering and ethnonationalism and a historical sensibility of its contingency.

Bibliography

Adorno, Theodor W. *Kierkegaard: Construction of the Aesthetic.* Translated by Robert Hullot-Kentor. Minneapolis: University of Minnesota Press, 1989.

Ahmad, Aijaz. *In Theory: Classes, Nations, Literatures.* London: Verso, 1992.

AlSayyad, Nezar, ed. *Forms of Dominance: On the Architecture and Urbanism of the Colonial Enterprise.* Aldershot: Avebury, 1992.

———. "Urbanism and the Dominance Equation: Reflections on Colonialism and National Identity." In *Forms of Dominance: On the Architecture and Urbanism of the Colonial Enterprise,* edited by Nezar AlSayyad, 1–26. Aldershot: Avebury, 1992.

Amin, Samir. *Re-Reading the Postwar Period: An Intellectual Itinerary.* Translated by Michael Wolfers. New York: Monthly Review Press, 1994.

An, Ji-na. "Mansejŏn ŭi singminjijŏk kŭndaesŏng yŏngu" [A study of colonial modernity in Mansejŏn]. *Han'guk Munhak Iron kwa Pip'yŏng* [Korean literary theory and criticism] 8, no. 1 (2004): 170–91.

Anderson, Benedict. *Imagined Communities: Reflections on the Origin and Spread of Nationalism.* 1983. Reprint, London: Verso, 1991.

Arrighi, Giovanni. "The Social and Political Economy of Global Turbulence." *New Left Review* 20 (2003): 5–71.

Balshaw, Maria, and Liam Kennedy. "Introduction: Urban Space and Representation." In *Urban Space and Representation,* edited by Maria Balshaw and Liam Kennedy, 1–21. Sterling, Va.: Pluto Press, 2000.

Barlow, Tani E. "Introduction: On 'Colonial Modernity.'" In *Formations of Colonial Modernity in East Asia,* edited by Tani E. Barlow, 1–20. Durham, N.C.: Duke University Press, 1997.

Barraclough, Ruth. "Tales of Seduction: Factory Girls in Korean Proletarian Literature." *positions: east asia cultures critique* 14, no. 2 (2006): 345–71.

Baucom, Ian. *Out of Place: Englishness, Empire, and the Locations of Identity.* Princeton, N.J.: Princeton University Press, 1999.

———. "Township Modernism." In *Geomodernisms: Race, Modernism, Modernity,* edited by Laura Doyle and Laura Winkel, 227–44. Bloomington: Indiana University Press, 2005.

Benjamin, Walter. *The Arcades Project.* Translated by Howard Eiland and Kevin McLaughlin. Cambridge, Mass.: Belknap-Harvard, 1999.

Berman, Marshall. *All That Is Solid Melts into Air: The Experience of Modernity.* New York: Viking, 1982.

Berry, Chris. "A Nation T(W/O)O: Chinese Cinema(S) and Nationhood(S)." *East-West Film Journal* 7, no. 1 (1993): 24–51.

Berry, Michael. "Words and Images: A Conversation with Hou Hsiao-hsien and Chu T'ien-Wen." *positions: east asia cultures critique* 11, no. 3 (2003): 675–716.

Bishop, Ryan, John Phillips, and Wei Wei Yeo. "Perpetuating Cities: Excepting Globalization and the Southeast Asia Supplement." In *Postcolonial Urbanism: Southeast Asian Cities and Global Processes,* edited by Ryan Bishop, John Phillips, and Wei Wei Yeo, 1–34. New York: Routledge, 2003.

Brewster, Anne. Introduction to *The Space of City Trees: Selected Poems,* by Arthur Yap, xi–xxii. London: Skoob, 1999.

———. *Towards a Semiotic of Post-colonial Discourse: University Writing in Singapore and Malaysia, 1949–1965.* Singapore: National University of Singapore/ Heinemann Asia, 1989.

Cabral, Amilcar. "National Liberation and Culture." In *Colonial Discourse and Postcolonial Theory,* edited by Patrick Williams and Laura Chrisman, 53–65. New York: Columbia University Press, 1994.

Castells, Manuel. "Four Asian Tigers with a Dragon's Head: A Comparative Analysis of the State, Economy, and Society in the Asian Pacific Rim." In *States and Development in the Pacific Rim,* edited by Richard P. Appelbaum and Jeffrey Henderson, 30–70. Newbury Park, Calif.: Sage, 1992.

———. *The Urban Question: A Marxist Approach.* Translated by Alan Sheridan. Cambridge, Mass.: MIT Press, 1977.

Çelik, Zeynap. *Urban Forms and Colonial Confrontations: Algiers under French Rule.* Berkeley: University of California Press, 1997.

Chan, Heng Chee. "Political Developments, 1965–1979." In *A History of Singapore,* edited by Ernest C. T. Chew and Edwin Lee, 157–81. Oxford: Oxford University Press, 1991.

Chan, Jasmine. "The Status of Women in a Patriarchal State: The Case of Singapore." In Edwards and Roces, *Women in Asia,* 39–58.

Chang, Sung-Sheng Yvonne. *Modernism and the Nativist Resistance: Contemporary Chinese Fiction from Taiwan.* Durham, N.C.: Duke University Press, 1993.

———. "Twentieth-Century Chinese Modernism and Globalizing Modernity: Three Auteur Directors of Taiwan New Cinema." In *Geomodernisms: Race, Modernism, Modernity,* edited by Laura Doyle and Laura Winkel, 133–50. Bloomington: Indiana University Press, 2005.

Chatterjee, Partha. *The Nation and Its Fragments: Colonial and Postcolonial Histories.* Princeton, N.J.: Princeton University Press, 1993.

———. *Nationalist Thought and the Colonial World: A Derivative Discourse?* London: Zed Books, 1986.

Cheah, Pheng. *Inhuman Conditions: On Cosmopolitanism and Human Rights.* Cambridge, Mass.: Harvard University Press, 2006.

———. *Spectral Nationality: Passages of Freedom from Kant to Postcolonial Literatures of Liberation.* New York: Columbia University Press, 2003.

Chen, Kuan-hsing. *Asia as Method: Toward Deimperialization.* Durham, N.C.: Duke University Press, 2010.

———. "Taiwanese New Cinema." In *The Oxford Guide to Film Studies,* edited by John Hill and Patricia Church Gibson, 557–61. Oxford: Oxford University Press, 1998.

Chen, Ruxiu, ed. *Focus on Taipei through Cinema, 1950–1990.* Taibei: Wanxiang, 1995.

Ch'en, Ying-chen. *Exiles at Home: Short Stories by Ch'en Ying-chen.* Translated by Lucien Miller. Ann Arbor: Center for Chinese Studies, University of Michigan, 1986.

Chi, Pang-yuan. "Taiwan Literature, 1945–1999." In *Chinese Literature in the Second Half of a Modern Century: A Critical Survey,* edited by Pang-yuan Chi and David Der-wei Wang, 14–30. Bloomington: Indiana University Press, 2000.

Chiang, Kai-shek. *Chapters on National Fecundity, Social Welfare, Education, and Health and Happiness.* Translated by Durham S. F. Chen. Taipei: China Cultural Service, 1952.

———. *Selected Speeches and Messages in 1971.* Taipei: Government Information Office, 1972.

Chiang, Lan-Hung Nora. "Women in Taiwan: Linking Economic Prosperity and Women's Progress." In Edwards and Roces, *Women in Asia,* 229–46.

Chien, Ying-ying. "The Impact of American Feminism on Modern Taiwanese Fiction by Women." In *The Force of Vision: Visions of the Others,* edited by Margaret R. Higonnet and Sumie Jones, 2:631–36. Tokyo:, International Comparative Literature Association, 1995.

Ching, Leo. *Becoming "Japanese": Colonial Taiwan and the Politics of Identity Formation.* Berkeley: University of California Press, 2001.

Cho, Nam-Hyŏn. "1970–80 Nyŏndae Sosŏl kwa Yŏsŏng ŭisik" [1970s–80s fiction and feminist consciousness]. In *Hanguk Munhak kwa Yŏsŏng* [Korean literature and women], 163–82. Tongduk Taehakkyo Korean Literature Research Center. Seoul: Asea Munhaksa, 2000.

Cho, Nam-Hyun [Cho, Nam-Hyŏn]. "Trends in Korean Fiction since WWII," translated by Ji-moon Suh. In *Understanding Modern Korean Literature,* 32–50. Seoul: Korean Culture and Arts Foundation, 1991.

Cho, Se-hŭi. "A Little Ball Tossed Up by a Dwarf." Translated by Bruce and Ju-chan Fulton. *Korean Literature Today* 3, no. 3 (1998): 126–69.

———. *Nanjangi Ka Soaollin Chagŭn Kong* [A little ball launched by a dwarf]. Seoul: Munhak kwa Jisongsa, 1993.

Ch'oe, Yun. "Late Twentieth-Century Fiction by Women." In *A History of Korean Literature,* edited by Peter H. Lee, 481–96. Cambridge: Cambridge University Press, 2003.

Choi, Hyun-moo. "Contemporary Korean Literature: From Victimization to Minjung Nationalism," translated by Carolyn U. So. In *South Korea's Minjung Movement: The Culture and Politics of Dissidence,* edited by Kenneth M. Wells, 167–78. Honolulu: University of Hawai'i Press, 1995.

Choi, Won-shik. "Seoul, Tokyo, New York: Modern Korean Literature Seen through Yi Sang's 'Lost Flowers.'" *Korea Journal* 39, no. 4 (1999): 118–43.

Chu, Tien-Jen. "Autumn Note," translated by James C. T. Shu. In *The Unbroken Chain: An Anthology of Taiwan Fiction since 1926,* edited by Joseph S. M. Lau, 24–32. Bloomington: Indiana University Press, 1983.

Chua, Beng-huat. *Political Legitimacy and Housing: Stakeholding in Singapore.* London: Routledge, 1997.

———. "World Cities: Globalisation and the Spread of Consumerism: A View from Singapore." *Urban Studies* 35, no. 5/6 (1998): 981–1000.

Coaldrake, William H. *Architecture and Authority in Japan.* London: Routledge, 1996.

Colomina, Beatriz. *Privacy and Publicity: Modern Architecture as Mass Media.* Cambridge, Mass.: MIT Press, 1994.

Connery, Christopher L. "Pacific Rim Discourse: The U.S. Global Imaginary in the Late Cold War Years." In *Asia/Pacific as Space of Cultural Production,* edited by Rob Wilson and Arif Dirlik, 30–56. Durham, N.C.: Duke University Press 1995.

Cumings, Bruce, "The Origins and Developments of the Northeast Asian Political Economy: Industrial Sectors, Product Cycles and Political Consequences." In *The Political Economy of the New Asian Industrialism,* edited by Frederic D. Deyo, 44–83. Ithaca, N.Y.: Cornell University Press, 1987.

Dal Co, Francesco. *Figures of Architectural Thought: German Architectural Culture, 1880–1920.* New York: Rizzoli, 1990.

Dale, Johan Ole. *Urban Planning in Singapore: The Transformation of a City.* Oxford: Oxford University Press, 1999.

Davis, Angela. *Women, Race, and Class.* New York: Random House, 1981.

Denning, Michael. *Culture in the Age of Three Worlds.* London: Verso, 2004.

Denton, Kirk A. "Historical Overview." In Mostow, *Columbia Companion,* 287–306.

De Souza, Dudley. "*Gods Can Die*: The Writer and Moral or Social Responsibility." In Quayum and Wicks, *Singaporean Literature in English,* 299–307.

Deyo, Frederic D., ed. *The Political Economy of the New Asian Industrialism.* Ithaca, N.Y.: Cornell University Press, 1987.

Duan, Chen-su. "Sisyphus: A Sociological Study of Taipei through Films, 1960–1990." In *Focus on Taipei through Cinema, 1950–1990,* edited by Ruxiu Chen, 72–77. Taibei: Wanxiang, 1995.

Duus, Peter. "Introduction: Japan's Wartime Empire: Problems and Issues." In *The Japanese Wartime Empire, 1931–1945,* edited by Peter Duus, Ramon H. Myers, and Mark R. Peattie, xi–xlvii. Princeton, N.J.: Princeton University Press, 1996.

Eagleton, Terry. *The Idea of Culture.* Oxford: Blackwell, 2000.

Edwards, Louise, and Mina Roces, eds. *Women in Asia: Tradition, Modernity and Globalisation.* Ann Arbor: University of Michigan Press, 2000.

Elden, Stuart. "Between Marx and Heidegger: Politics, Philosophy and Lefebvre's *The Production of Space.*" *Antipode* 36, no. 1 (2004): 86–105.

Evans, Robin. "Figures, Doors and Passages." In *Center: Vol. 9: Regarding the Proper,* edited by Kevin Alter and Elizabeth Danze, 42–57. Austin: University of Texas Press, 1985.

Fanon, Frantz. *The Wretched of the Earth.* Translated by Constance Farrington. New York: Grove Press Weidenfield, 1963.

Faurot, Jeannette L. Introduction to *Chinese Fiction from Taiwan: Critical Perspectives,* edited by Jeannette L. Faurot, 1–5. Bloomington: Indiana University Press, 1980.

Foucault, Michel. "Space, Knowledge and Power (Interview conducted with Paul Rabinow)." In *Rethinking Architecture: A Reader in Cultural Theory,* edited by Neil Leach, 367–79. New York: Routledge, 1997.

Frank, Andre Gunder. *Crisis: In the Third World.* New York: Holmes and Meier, 1981.

———. "The Development of Underdevelopment." In *Dependence and Underdevelopment: Latin America's Political Economy,* by James D. Cockcroft, Andre Gunder Frank, and Dale L. Johnson, 3–17. New York: Anchor, 1972.

Frübel, Folker, Jürgen Heinrichs, and Otto Kreye. *The New International Division of Labour: Structural Unemployment in Industrialised Countries and Industrialisation in Developing Countries.* Translated by Pete Burgess. Cambridge: Cambridge University Press, 1980.

Fujii, James A. "Writing Out Asia: Modernity, Canon and Natsume Soseki's *Kokoro.*" *positions: east asia cultures critique* 1, no. 1 (1993): 194–223.

Fulton, Bruce. "Historical Overview." In Mostow, *Columbia Companion,* 619–29.

———. "Hwang Sŏgyŏng." In Mostow, *Columbia Companion,* 713–17.

Gandhi, Leela. *Postcolonial Theory: An Introduction.* New York: Columbia University Press, 1998.

Gaonkar, Dilip Parameshwar, ed. *Alternative Modernities.* Durham, N.C.: Duke University Press, 2001.

Goh, Poh Seng. *If We Dream Too Long.* Singapore: Island Press, 1972.

Goh, Robbie B. H. "Imagining the Nation: The Role of Singapore Poetry in English in 'Emergent Nationalism.'" *Journal of Commonwealth Literature* 41 (2006): 21–41.

Gottdiener, M. "A Marx for Our Time: Henri Lefebvre and *The Production of Space.*" *Sociological Theory* 11, no. 1 (1993): 129–34.

Gramsci, Antonio. *Selections from the Prison Notebooks.* Edited and translated by Quintin Hoare and Geoffrey Nowell Smith. New York: International, 1971.

Grosz, Elizabeth. "Bodies-Cities." In *Sexuality and Space,* edited by Beatriz Colomina, 241–53. Princeton, N.J.: Princeton Architectural Press, 1992.

Gupta, Akhil, and James Ferguson. "Beyond 'Culture': Space, Identity and the Politics of Difference." In *Culture, Power, Place: Explorations in Critical Anthropology,* edited by Akhil Gupta and James Ferguson, 33–51. Durham, N.C.: Duke University Press, 1997.

Haboush, JaHyun Kim. "In Search of HISTORY in Democratic Korea: The Discourse of Modernity in Contemporary Historical Fiction." In *Constructing Nationhood in Modern East Asia,* edited by Kai-wing Chow et al., 33–51. Ann Arbor: University of Michigan Press, 2001.

Hallward, Peter. *Absolutely Postcolonial: Writing between the Singular and the Specific.* Manchester: Manchester University Press, 2001.

Hampson, Sasha. "Rhetoric or Reality? Contesting Definitions of Women in Korea." In Edwards and Roces, *Women in Asia,* 170–87.

Harootunian, Harry D. *History's Disquiet: Modernity, Cultural Practice, and the Questions of Everyday Life.* New York: Columbia University Press, 2000.

Harvey, David. *The Limits to Capital.* Chicago: University of Chicago Press, 1982.

Haskell, Dennis. "'People, Traffic and Concrete': Perceptions of the City in Modern Singaporean Poetry." In *Perceiving Other Worlds,* edited by Edwin Thumboo, 237–49. Singapore: Times Academic, 1991.

Heidegger, Martin. *Basic Writings.* Edited by David Farrell Krell. New York: Harper and Row, 1976.

Heng, Geraldine, and Janadas Devan. "State Fatherhood: The Politics of Nationalism, Sexuality, and Race in Singapore." In *Nationalisms and Sexualities,* edited by Andrew Parker et al., 343–64. London: Routledge, 1996.

Hitchcock, Henry-Russell, and Philip Johnson. *The International Style: Architecture since 1922.* New York: W. W. Norton, 1932.

Ho, Kong Chong. "From Port City to City-State: Forces Shaping Singapore's Built Environment." In *Culture and the City in East Asia,* edited by Won Bae Kim et al., 212–33. Oxford: Clarendon, 1997.

hooks, bell. *Ain't I a Woman: Black Women and Feminism.* Boston, Mass.: South End Press, 1981.

Hou, Hsiao-hsien, dir. *Fenggui Lai de Ren* [The boys from Fengkuei]. 1983. Film.

———, dir. *Lian Lian Feng Chen* [Dust in the wind]. 1986. Film.

Hsia, Chu-Joe. "Theorizing Colonial Architecture and Urbanism: Building Colonial Modernity in Taiwan." *Inter-Asia Cultural Studies* 3, no. 1 (2002): 7–23.

Hsiau, A-chin. *Contemporary Taiwanese Cultural Nationalism.* London: Routledge, 2000.

Hsieh, Tung-min. *Implementing the Four Major Objectives of Political Reconstruction.* Republic of China: Department of Information, 1976.

Huang, Chunming. *The Taste of Apples.* Translated by Howard Goldblatt. New York: Columbia University Press, 2001.

Hwang, Sŏk-yŏng. "Pungmang, Mŏlgodo Kojŏkhan Kot." [Longing for the north, a far and desolate place.] In *Sampʻo kanŭn kil* [The road to Sampo], 293–306. Seoul: Changbi, 2000.

———. "The Road to Sampo," translated by Uchang Kim. In *Modern Korean Short Stories,* edited by Chong-wha Chung, 176–201. Hong Kong: Heinemann Educational, 1980.

———. *Sampʻo kanŭn kil* [The road to Sampo]. Seoul: Tonga, 1995.

Im, Hŏn-yŏng. "The Meaning of the City in Korean Literature." *Korea Journal* 27, no. 5 (1987): 24–36.

ILO [International Labour Organisation]. *Economic and Social Effects of Multinational Enterprises in Export Processing Zones.* Geneva: International Labour Organisation, 1988.

Jacobs, Jane M. *Edge of Empire: Postcolonialism and the City.* London: Routledge, 1996.

Jameson, Fredric. *Marxism and Form.* Princeton, N.J.: Princeton University Press, 1971.

——. "Modernism and Imperialism." In *Nationalism, Colonialism, and Literature,* edited by Fredric Jameson, Terry Eagleton, and Edward Said, 43–66. Minneapolis: University of Minnesota Press, 1990.

——. *The Political Unconscious: Narrative as a Socially Symbolic Act.* Ithaca, N.Y.: Cornell University Press, 1981.

——. *Postmodernism, or, The Cultural Logic of Late Capitalism.* Durham, N.C.: Duke University Press, 1991.

——. *The Seeds of Time.* New York: Columbia University Press, 1994.

Jayawardena, Kumari. *Feminism and Nationalism in the Third World.* London: Zed Books, 1986.

Kang, Sŏk-kyŏng. "A Room in the Woods," translated by Bruce and Ju-chan Fulton. In *Words of Farewell: Stories by Korean Women Writers,* 28–147. Seattle: Seal, 1989.

——. *Supsok ŭi Pang* [A room in the woods]. Seoul: Minŭmsa, 1986.

Kapur, Basant K., ed. *Singapore Studies: Critical Surveys of the Humanities and Social Sciences.* Singapore: Singapore University Press, 1986.

Kavanagh, James H. "Marxism's Althusser: Toward a Politics of Literary Theory." *Diacritics* 12, no. 1 (1982): 25–45.

Kern, Stephen. *The Culture of Time and Space: 1880–1918.* Cambridge, Mass.: Harvard University Press, 1983.

Khanna, Ranjana. *Dark Continents: Psychoanalysis and Colonialism.* Durham, N.C.: Duke University Press, 2003.

——. "Post-Palliative: Coloniality's Affective Dissonance." *Postcolonial Text* 2, no. 1 (2006). http://postcolonial.org/index.php/pct/article/view/385/815.

Kim, Byŏng-ik. "Taeryŏp Segyegwan kwa Mihak" [Oppositional worldview and aesthetic]. In *Nanjangi Ka Ssoaollin Chagŭn Kong* [A little ball launched by a dwarf], by Cho Se-hŭi, 277–94. Seoul: Munhak kwa Jisongsa, 1993.

Kim, Elaine H., and Chungmoo Choi, eds. *Dangerous Women: Gender and Korean Nationalism.* New York: Routledge, 1998.

——. Introduction to Kim and Choi, *Dangerous Women,* 1–8.

Kim, Hŭng-gyu. "Chosŏn Fiction in Chinese." In *A History of Korean Literature,* edited by Peter H. Lee, 273–87. Cambridge: Cambridge University Press, 2003.

——. *Understanding Korean Literature.* Translated by Robert J. Fouser. Armonk, N.Y.: M. E. Sharpe, 1997.

Kim, Hyung-A. *Korea's Development under Park Chung Hee: Rapid Industrialization, 1961–79.* London: Routledge Curzon, 2004.

Kim, Hyun Sook. "Yanggongju as an Allegory of the Nation: The Representation of Working-Class Women in Popular and Radical Texts." In Kim and Choi, *Dangerous Women,* 175–202.

Kim, Joochul, and Sang-Chuel Choe. *Seoul: The Making of a Metropolis.* Chichester: Wiley, 1997.

Kim, Seung-kyung. *Class Struggle or Family Struggle? The Lives of Women Factory Workers in South Korea.* Cambridge: Cambridge University Press, 1997.

Kim, Tong-in. "Potato," translated by Charles Rosenberg and Peter H. Lee. In *Modern Korean Literature: An Anthology,* edited by Peter H. Lee, 16–23. Honolulu: University of Hawaii Press, 1990.

Kim, Yoon-shik. *Understanding Modern Korean Literature.* Translated by Jang Gyung-ryul. Seoul: Jipmoondang, 1998.

King, Anthony D. *Colonial Urban Development: Culture, Social Power and Environment.* London: Routledge and Kegan Paul, 1976.

Kipnis, Jeffrey. "Beijing 'n Seoul." In *Anywise,* edited by Cynthia C. Davidson, 168–74. New York: Anyone Corporation, 1996.

Kleeman, Faye Yuan. *Under an Imperial Sun: Japanese Colonial Literature of Taiwan and the South.* Honolulu: University of Hawai'i Press, 2003.

Knapp, Ronald G. *China's Vernacular Architecture.* Honolulu: University of Hawai'i Press, 1989.

Koh, Tai Ann. "Intertextual Selves: Fiction Makers in Two 'Singapore' Novels." In *Tropic Crucible: Self and Theory in Language and Literature,* edited by Colin Nicholson and Ranjit Chatterjee, 163–91. Singapore: Singapore University Press, 1984.

———. "Self, Family and the State: Social Mythology in the Singapore Novel in English." *Journal of Southeast Asian Studies* 20, no. 2 (1989): 273–87.

———. "Telling Stories, Expressing Values: The Singapore Novel in English." In *Skoob Pacifica Anthology No. 2: The Pen Is Mightier Than the Sword,* edited by C. Y. Loh and I. K. Ong, 129–45. London: Skoob, 1994.

Koolhaas, Rem. "Singapore Songlines: Portrait of a Potemkin Metropolis or Thirty Years of Tabula Rasa." In *S, M, L, XL,* edited by Rem Koolhaas et al., 1008–89. New York: Montacelli, 1995.

Kuo, Jason C. *Art and Cultural Politics in Postwar Taiwan.* Seattle: University of Washington Press, 2000.

Kusno, Abidin. *Behind the Postcolonial: Architecture, Urban Space, and Political Cultures in Indonesia.* London: Routledge, 2000.

Kwŏn, T'aek-yŏng. "Yŏksŏl kwa Muŭiji ŭi Arŭmdaum" [The beauty of paradox and weakness]. In *Uri Sidae ŭi Sosŏlga: Cho Song-Ki; Kang Sŏk-kyŏng,* 586–98. Seoul: Donga, 1995.

Kwŏn, Yŏng-min. "Early Twentieth Century Fiction by Men." In *A History of Korean Literature,* edited by Peter H. Lee, 390–405. Cambridge: Cambridge University Press, 2003.

Lau, Joseph S. M. "Ch'en Ying-chen." In *The Unbroken Chain: An Anthology of Taiwan Fiction since 1926,* edited by Joseph S. M. Lau, 102–3. Bloomington: Indiana University Press, 1983.

———. ed. *The Unbroken Chain: An Anthology of Taiwan Fiction since 1926.* Bloomington: Indiana University Press, 1983.

Lau, Lawrence J., ed. *Models of Development: A Comparative Study of Economic Growth in South Korea and Taiwan.* San Francisco: ICS Press, 1986.

Le Corbusier. *Essential Le Corbusier: L'esprit Nouveau Articles.* Oxford: Architectural Press, 1998.

Lee, Anru. "Between Filial Daughter and Loyal Sister: Global Economy and Family Politics in Taiwan." In *Women in the New Taiwan: Gender Roles and Gender Consiousness in a Changing Society,* edited by Catherine Farris, Anru Lee, and Murray Rubinstein, 101–19. Armonk, N.Y.: M. E. Sharpe, 2004.

Lee, Chulwoo. "Modernity, Legality, and Power in Korea under Japanese Rule." In *Colonial Modernity in Korea,* edited by Gi-wook Shin and Michael Robinson, 21–51. Cambridge, Mass.: Harvard University Asia Center, 1999.

Lee, Kuan Yew. *From Third World to First: The Singapore Story, 1965–2000.* New York: HarperCollins, 2000.

———. *The Singapore Story: Memoirs of Lee Kuan Yew.* Singapore: Prentice Hall, 1998.

Lee, Namhee. *The Making of Minjung: Democracy and the Politics of Representation in South Korea.* Ithaca, N.Y.: Cornell University Press, 2007.

Lee, Sang-hae. "Traditional Korean Settlements and Dwellings." In *Asia's Old Dwellings: Tradition, Resilience, and Change,* edited by Ronald G. Knapp, 373–89. Oxford: Oxford University Press, 2003.

Lee, Tzu Pheng. Foreword to *Gods Can Die,* by Edwin Thumboo, viii–xiii. Singapore: Heinemann Educational, 1977.

———. "My Country and My People." In *The Second Tongue: An Anthology of Poetry from Malaysia and Singapore,* by Edwin Thumboo, 162. Singapore: Heinemann Educational, 1977.

Lefebvre, Henri. *The Production of Space.* Translated by Donald Nicholson-Smith. Oxford: Blackwell, 1991.

Lenin, V. I. *Selected Works.* Vols. 1 and 2. New York: International, 1967.

Li, William D. H. *Housing in Taiwan: Agency and Structure?* Brookfield: Ashgate, 1998.

Liao, Ping-hui. "Postcolonial Studies in Taiwan: Issues in Critical Debates." *Postcolonial Studies* 2, no. 2 (1999): 199–211.

———. "Travel in Early-Twentieth-Century Asia: On Wu Zhouliu's 'Nanking Journals' and His Notion of Taiwan's Alternative Modernity." In *Writing Taiwan: A New Literary History,* edited by David Der-wei Wang and Carlos Rojas, 285–300. Durham, N.C.: Duke University Press, 2007.

Liaw, Yock Fang. "Malay Language and Literature in Singapore." In *Singapore Studies: Critical Surveys of the Humanities and Social Sciences,* edited by Basant K. Kapur, 323–36. Singapore: Singapore University Press, 1986.

Lie, John. *Han Unbound: The Political Economy of South Korea.* Stanford, Calif.: Stanford University Press, 1998.

Lim, Shirley Geok-lin. "Edwin Thumboo: A Study of Influence on the Literary History of Singapore." In Quayum and Wicks, *Singaporean Literature in English,* 282–89.

———. *Nationalism and Literature: English-Language Writing from the Philippines and Singapore.* Quezon City: New Day Publishers, 1993.

Lim, Su-chen Christine. *Rice Bowl.* Singapore: Times Books International, 1984.

Lim, William S. *Asian New Urbanism and Other Papers.* Singapore: Select, 1998.

Livingstone, James M. *The Contenders: The Rise of the Pacific Powers.* London: Cassell, 1998.

Lu, Hwei-Syin. "Transcribing Feminism: Taiwanese Women's Experiences." In *Women in the New Taiwan: Gender Roles and Gender Consciousness in a Changing Society,* edited by Catherine Farris, Anru Lee, and Murray Rubinstein, 223–43. Armonk, N.Y.: M. E. Sharpe, 2004.

Lukács, Gyürgy [Georg]. *Studies in European Realism: A Sociological Survey of the Writings of Balzac, Stendhal, Zola, Tolstoy, Gorki and Others.* Translated by Edith Bone. London: Hillway, 1950.

———. *The Theory of the Novel: A Historico-Philosophical Essay on the Forms of Great Epic Literature.* Translated by Anna Bostock. 1963. Reprint, London: Merlin, 1971.

Luxemburg, Rosa. *The Rosa Luxemburg Reader.* Edited by Peter Hudis and Kevin B. Anderson. New York: Monthly Review, 2004.

Lynch, Kevin. *The Image of the City.* Cambridge, Mass.: MIT Press, 1960.

Macherey, Pierre. *A Theory of Literary Production.* Translated by Geoffrey Wall. New York: Routledge, 2006.

Maeda, Ai. *Text and the City: Essays on Japanese Modernity.* Translated by James A. Fujii. Durham, N.C.: Duke University Press, 2004.

Mandel, Ernest. *Late Capitalism.* 1972. Translated by Joris De Bres. London: Verso, 1978.

Mbembe, Achille. *On the Postcolony.* Translated by A. M. Berret et al. Berkeley: University of California Press, 2001.

Mignolo, Walter. *Local Histories/Global Designs: Coloniality, Subaltern Knowledges, and Border Thinking.* Princeton, N.J.: Princeton University Press, 2000.

Miller, Lucien. Introduction to *Exiles at Home: Short Stories by Ch'en Ying-chen,* 1–26. Translated by Lucien Miller. Ann Arbor: Center for Chinese Studies, University of Michigan, 1986.

Mitchell, W. J. Thomas. *Landscape and Power.* Chicago: University of Chicago Press, 2002.

Moon, Seungsook. "Begetting the Nation: The Andocentric Discourse of National History and Tradition in South Korea." In Kim and Choi, *Dangerous Women,* 33–66.

Moretti, Franco. *Signs Taken for Wonders: On the Sociology of Literary Forms.* London: Verso, 1983.

———. *Way of the World: The Bildungsroman in European Culture.* London: Verso, 1987.

Morse, Ruth. "A Case of (Mis)Taken Identity: Politics and Aesthetics in Some Recent Singaporean Novels." In *Asian Voices in English,* edited by Mimi Chan and Roy Harris, 131–45. Hong Kong: Hong Kong University Press, 1991.

———. "Novels of National Identity and Inter-National Interpretation." *College Literature* 19–20 (1992–93): 60–77.

Mostow, Joshua S., ed. *Columbia Companion to Modern East Asian Literature.* New York: Columbia University Press, 2003.

Mumford, Lewis. *The Culture of Cities.* New York: Harcourt Brace, 1938.

Nuttall, Sarah. "Literary City." In *Johannesburg: The Elusive Metropolis,* edited by Sarah Nuttall and Achille Mbembe, 195–218. Durham, N.C.: Duke University Press, 2008.

Nuttall, Sarah, and Achille Mbembe. "Introduction: Afropolis." In *Johannesburg: The Elusive Metropolis,* edited by Sarah Nuttall and Achille Mbembe, 1–33. Durham, N.C.: Duke University Press, 2008.

Ong, Aihwa. *Spirits of Resistance and Capitalist Discipline: Factory Women in Malaysia.* Albany: State University of New York Press, 1987.

O'Rourke, Kevin. "Realism in Early Modern Fiction." In Mostow, *Columbia Companion,* 651–53.

Paik, Nak-chung. "Coloniality in South Korea and a South Korean Project for Overcoming Modernity." *Interventions: International Journal of Postcolonial Studies* 2, no. 1 (2000): 73–86.

———. "Nations and Literatures in the Age of Globalization." In *Cultures of Globalization,* edited by Fredric Jameson and Masao Miyoshi, 218–29. Durham, N.C.: Duke University Press, 1998.

Park, Chung Hee. *Major Speeches by President Park Chung Hee, Republic of Korea.* Seoul: Samhwa, 1973.

Park, Soon-won. "Colonial Industrial Growth and the Emergence of the Korean Working Class." In *Colonial Modernity in Korea,* edited by Gi-wook Shin and Michael Robinson, 128–60. Cambridge, Mass.: Harvard University Asia Center, 1999.

Patke, Rajeev S. *Postcolonial Poetry in English.* Oxford: Oxford University Press, 2006.

———. "Voice and Authority in English Poetry from Singapore." *Interlogue II: Studies in Singapore Literature, Vol. 2: Poetry.* Edited by Kirpal Singh. Singapore: Ethos Books, 1998: 85–103.

Pensky, Max. *Melancholy Dialectics: Walter Benjamin and the Play of Mourning.* Amherst: University of Massachusetts Press, 1993.

Pihl, Marshall R. "The Nation, the People, and a Small Ball: Literary Nationalism and Literary Populism in Contemporary Korea." In *South Korea's Minjung Movement: The Culture and Politics of Dissidence,* edited by Kenneth M. Wells, 209–20. Honolulu: University of Hawai'i Press, 1995.

Quayum, Mohammad, and Peter Wicks, eds. *Singaporean Literature in English: A Critical Reader.* Serdang: Universiti Putra Malaysia Press, 2002.

Rabinow, Paul. *French Modern: Norms and Forms of the Social Environment.* Cambridge, Mass.: MIT Press, 1989.

Ranchod-Nilsson, Sita, and Mary Ann Tetreault. "Gender and Nationalism." In *Women, States and Nationalism: At Home in the Nation?*, edited by Sita Ranchod-Nilsson and Mary Ann Tetreault, 1–17. London: Routledge, 2000.

Rayns, Tony. "Between Taiwan and the Mainland, between the Real and the Surreal: Tony Rayns Talks to Hou Xiaoxian." *Monthly Film Bulletin* 55, no. 653 (1988): 163–64.

Rendell, Jane. "Introduction: 'Gender, Space.'" In *Gender Space Architecture: An Interdisciplinary Introduction*, edited by Jane Rendell, Barbara Penner, and Iain Borden, 101–11. London: Routledge, 2000.

———. "Ramblers and Cyprians: Mobility, Visuality and the Gendering of Architectural Space." In *Gender and Architecture: History, Interpretation and Practice*, edited by Louise Durning and Richard Wigley, 135–54. Chichester: Wiley, 2000.

Reynaud, Bérénice. *A City of Sadness*. London: British Film Institute, 2002.

Richard, Nelly. *Masculine/Feminine: Practices of Difference(s)*. Translated by Silvia R. Tandeciarz and Alice A. Nelson. Durham, N.C.: Duke University Press, 2004.

Robinson, Jennifer. *Ordinary Cities: Between Modernity and Development*. London: Routledge, 2006.

Rosner, Victoria. *Modernism and the Architecture of Private Life*. New York: Columbia University Press, 2005.

Ross, Kristin. *The Emergence of Social Space: Rimbaud and the Paris Commune*. Minneapolis: University of Minnesota Press, 1988.

Said, Edward. *Culture and Imperialism*. New York: Vintage, 1993.

Selya, Roger Mark. *Taipei*. Chichester: Wiley, 1995.

Shin, Gi-wook, and Michael Robinson. "Introduction: Rethinking Colonial Korea." In *Colonial Modernity in Korea*, edited by Gi-wook Shin and Michael Robinson, 1–18. Cambridge, Mass.: Harvard University Asia Center, 1999.

Simmel, Georg. "The Metropolis and Mental Life." In *Rethinking Architecture: A Reader in Cultural Theory*, edited by Neil Leach, 69–79. New York: Routledge, 1997.

Singh, Kirpal, and Ooi Boo Eng. "The Poetry of Edwin Thumboo: A Study in Development." *World Literature Written in English* 24 (1985): 454–59.

Smith, Neil. *Uneven Development: Nature, Capital, and the Production of Space*. New York: Blackwell, 1984.

Soja, Edward W. *Postmodern Geographies: The Reassertion of Space in Critical Social Theory*. London: Verso, 1989.

———. "The Socio-Spatial Dialectic." *Annals of the Association of American Geographers* 70, no. 2 (1980): 207–25.

Spengler, Oswald. "The Soul of the City." In *Classic Essays in the Culture of the City*, edited by Richard Sennett, 61–88. New York: Meredith, 1969.

Spivak, Gayatri Chakravorty. *In Other Worlds: Essays in Cultural Politics*. New York: Routledge, 1988.

———. *Other Asias*. Malden, Mass.: Blackwell, 2008.

———. "The Politics of Translation." In *The Translation Studies Reader*, edited by Lawrence Venuti, 397–416. London: Routledge, 2000.

———. "The Rani of Sirmur: An Essay in Reading the Archives." *History and Theory* 24, no. 3 (1985): 247–72.

Standish, Isolde. "Korean Cinema and the New Realism: Text and Context." In *Colonialism and Nationalism in Asian Cinema,* edited by Wimal Dissanayake, 65–89. Bloomington: Indiana University Press, 1994.

Su, Weizhen. "Missing." Translated by Agnes Tang and Eva Hung. In *Contemporary Women Writers: Hong Kong and Taiwan,* edited by Eva Hung, 91–112. Hong Kong: Renditions, 1990.

Sun, Yat-sen. *The Three Principles of the People: San Min Chu I.* With two supplementary chapters by President Chiang Kai-shek. Taipei: China Publishing, [1989?].

Tafuri, Manfredo. *Architecture and Utopia: Design and Capitalist Development.* Translated by Barbara Luigia La Penta. Cambridge, Mass.: MIT Press, 1976.

Taipei City Government. *Urban Renewal in Taipei City.* Taipei: Taipei City Government, 1978.

Tan, Kenneth Paul. *Cinema and Television in Singapore: Resistance in One Dimension.* Leiden: Brill, 2008.

Tanaka, Stefan. *Japan's Orient: Rendering Pasts into History.* Berkeley: University of California Press, 1993.

Thumboo, Edwin. *Gods Can Die.* Singapore: Heinemann Educational, 1977.

———. "An Interview with Edwin Thumboo," conducted by Peter Nazareth. In Quayum and Wicks, *Singaporean Literature in English,* 266–81.

———. Introduction to *The Second Tongue: An Anthology of Poetry from Malaysia and Singapore,* edited by Edwin Thumboo, vii–xxxv. Singapore: Heinemann Educational, 1976.

———. *Ulysses by the Merlion.* Singapore: Heinemann Educational, 1979.

Tsai, Hsung-hsiung. "Population Decentralization Policies: The Experience of Taiwan." In *Urbanization and Urban Policies in Pacific Asia,* edited by Roland J. Fuchs et al., 214–29. Boulder, Colo.: Westview, 1987.

Utrecht, Ernest. "Gains and Losses in 25 Years of Export-Oriented Industrialization in South and Southeast Asia." In *Transnational Corporations and Export-Oriented Industrialization,* edited by Ernst Utrecht, 139–58. Sydney: Transnational Corporations Research Project/University of Sydney, 1985.

Vidler, Anthony. *The Architectural Uncanny: Essays in the Modern Unhomely.* Cambridge, Mass.: MIT Press, 1992.

———. *Warped Space: Art, Architecture and Anxiety in Modern Culture.* Cambridge, Mass.: MIT Press, 2000.

Wade, Robert. *Governing the Market: Economic Theory and the Role of Government in East Asian Industrialization.* 1990. Reprint, Princeton, N.J.: Princeton University Press, 2004.

Wang, Jing. "Taiwan *Hsiang-t'u* Literature: Perspectives in the Evolution of Literary Movement." In *Chinese Fiction from Taiwan: Critical Perspectives,* edited by Jeannette L. Faurot, 43–70. Bloomington: Indiana University Press, 1980.

Watson, Jini Kim. "Imperial Mimicry, Modernisation Theory and the Contradictions of Postcolonial South Korea." *Postcolonial Studies* 10, no. 2 (2007): 171–90.

Weber, Max. "The Nature of the City." In *Classic Essays in the Culture of the City*, edited by Richard Sennett, 23–46. New York: Meredith, 1969.

Wee, C. J. W.-L. "Capitalism and Ethnicity: Creating 'Local Culture' in Singapore." *Inter-Asia Cultural Studies* 1, no. 1 (2000): 129–43.

Wells, Kenneth M. Introduction to *South Korea's Minjung Movement: The Culture and Politics of Dissidence*, edited by Kenneth M. Wells, 1–10. Honolulu: University of Hawai'i Press, 1995.

Williams, Raymond. *The Country and the City*. Oxford: Oxford University Press, 1973.

———. *Keywords: A Vocabulary of Culture and Society*. Rev. ed. New York: Oxford University Press, 1983.

Wilson, Rob. "Melodramas of Korean National Identity: From *Mandala* to *Black Republic*." In *Colonialism and Nationalism in Asian Cinema*, edited by Wimal Dissanayake, 90–104. Bloomington: Indiana University Press, 1994.

Wilson, Rob, and Arif Dirlik. Introduction to *Asia/Pacific as Space of Cultural Production*, edited by Rob Wilson and Arif Dirlik, 1–14. Durham, N.C.: Duke University Press, 1995.

Winckler, Edwin A. "Cultural Policy on Postwar Taiwan." In *Cultural Change in Postwar Taiwan*, edited by Steven Harrell and Chung-chieh Huang, 22–46. Taipei: Westview and SMC, 1994.

Wong, Yoon Wah. *Post-Colonial Chinese Literatures in Singapore and Malaysia*. Singapore: National University of Singapore; River Edge, N.J.: Global, 2002.

Woolf, Virginia. *A Room of One's Own*. 1929. Reprint, San Diego: Harcourt Brace Jovanovich, 1989.

Woronoff, Jon. *Asia's "Miracle" Economies*. Armonk, N.Y.: M. E. Sharpe, 1986.

Wu, Zhuoliu. "The Fig Tree" [Wu hua guo]. Translated by Duncan B. Hunter. *Renditions* 38 (1992): 84–95.

———. *Orphan of Asia*. Translated by Ioannis Mentzas. New York: Columbia University Press, 2006.

Xu, Yinong. *The Chinese City in Space and Time: The Development of Urban Form in Suzhou*. Honolulu: University of Hawai'i Press, 2000.

Yang, Chao. "Beyond 'Nativist Realism': Taiwan Fiction in the 1970s and 1980s." Translated by Carlos G. Tee. In *Chinese Literature in the Second Half of a Modern Century: A Critical Survey*, edited by Pang-yuan Chi and David Der-wei Wang, 96–109. Bloomington: Indiana University Press, 2000.

Yang, Jane Parish. "The Evolution of the Taiwanese New Literature Movement from 1920 to 1940." *Jen Studies: Literature and Linguistics* 15 (1982): 1–18.

Yang, Kui. "Paperboy." Translated by Rosemary Haddon. *Renditions* 43 (1995): 25–57.

Yap, Arthur. *The Space of City Trees: Selected Poems*. London: Skoob, 1999.

Yap, Arthur, et al. "Singapore Literature in English I: A Survey of Criticisms on Singapore Poetry in English." In *Singapore Studies: Critical Surveys of the Humanities and Social Sciences,* edited by Basant K. Kapur, 459–86. Singapore: Singapore University Press, 1986.

Yeo, Kim Wah, and Albert Lau. "From Colonialism to Independence, 1945–196⬥." In Ernest C. T. Chew and Edwin Lee, eds., *A History of Singapore,* 117–53. Oxford: Oxford University Press, 1991.

Yeoh, Brenda S. A. *Contesting Space: Power Relations and the Urban Built Environment in Colonial Singapore.* Kuala Lumpur: Oxford University Press, 1996.

Yi, In-jik. *Hyŏl ŭi Nu; Solchungmae; Ŭn Segye.* [Tears of blood; Plum wine; Silver world]. Seoul: Chongumsa, 1955.

Yi, Mungu. "The Ballad of Kalmŏri." Translated by Ahn Junghyo. In *Modern Korean Literature: An Anthology,* edited by Peter H. Lee, 368–91. Honolulu: University of Hawai'i Press, 1990.

Yi, Nam-ho. "Hoesaek Chidae ŭi Chinsil" [Truth's gray area]. In *Supsok ŭi Pang,* 251–70. Seoul, 1986.

Yi, Sang. *Nalgae* [The wings]. Seoul: Munhak kwa Jisongsa, 2001.

———. "Tokyo," translated by Michael D. Shin. *Muae: A Journal of Transcultural Production* 1 (1995): 96–101.

———. "Tongkyong" [Tokyo]. In *Yi Sang Chŏnjip, Vol. 3: Sup'il* [Essays], edited by Yoon-sik Kim, 95–100. Seoul: Munhak Sasang, 1993.

———. *The Wings.* Translated by Jung-hyo Ahn and James B. Lee. Seoul: Jimoondang, 2001.

Yip, June. *Envisioning Taiwan: Fiction, Cinema, and the Nation in the Cultural Imaginary.* Durham, N.C.: Duke University Press, 2004.

Yŏm, Mu-wung. "Minjung ŭi Hyŏnsil kwa Sosŏlga ŭi Unmyŏng" [Reality of the masses and the fiction writer's destiny]. In *Samp'o Kanŭn Kil,* by Hwang Sŏkyŏng, 585–606. Seoul: Tonga, 1995.

Yŏm, Sang-sŏp. *Mansejŏn* [Before the March 1st movement]. Seoul: Ilsisŏjŏk, 1997.

Young, Robert J. C. *Postcolonialism: An Historical Introduction.* Oxford: Blackwell, 2001.

Zhu, Ying. "The Role of Export Processing Zones in East Asian Development: South Korea, Taiwan, China and Thailand." Ph.D. diss., University of Melbourne, 1992.

Index

Page references in italics refer to illustrations

Adorno, Theodor, 146; on inwardness, 141, 142
Africa, postcolonial, 179–81
Ahmad, Aijaz, 7, 129
Ahn, Byung-sup, 275n12
Akutagawa, Ryunosuke, 65
Algiers, colonial: urban space of, 29
AlSayyad, Nezar, 34
Althusser, Louis, 14
Amin, Samir, 1, 88–89; on U.S. aid, 92–93
An, Ji-na, 60
anbangs (master bedrooms), 139–40
Anderson, Benedict: *Imagined Communities,* 171; on national identities, 171–72
architecture: Chinese revivalist, 208; colonial Japanese, 38–40, 44, 45, 66, 69, 80; in colonial power, 29, 71; dissimulation of corruption, 126; geomantic principles of, 40; in Huang's works, 122, 124; the human and, 105, 107; as indication of national health, 183; in "If We Dream Too Long," 118–19; in "A Little Ball Launched by a Dwarf," 107, 111; in *Mansejŏn,* 59, 60, 84; Meiji, 38–39; and nationalism, 67; in

The Orphan of Asia, 66–67, 69, 84; in postcolonial literature, 105, 134; private space in, 139–40; role in private subjectivities, 138; in "A Room in the Woods," 143; Second Empire, 39, 199, 201; in *The Wings,* 78–79, 80; wish images of, 19. *See also* buildings, high-rise; built forms
Arrighi, Giovanni, 93
Asian cities: center and periphery in, 36, 38; feudal Korean, 36; as production platforms, 2; public spaces of, 42. *See also* New Asian City
Asian Tiger nations: economies of, 1; export production of, 91–93; gendered subjectivities of, 167; in modernization theory, 90; productivity of, 167, 252; urbanization of, 87; urban space of, 4–5. *See also* postcolonial nations
Asia Pacific region: cultural productions from, 251; discourse of, 260n14; financial crisis in, 251; global capitalism in, 16–17; material progress in, 168; repressive governments of, 173; sociospatial dialectic of, 18. *See also* East Asia
Austen, Jane: *Pride and Prejudice,* 114

293

Balshaw, Maria, 174
Balzac, Honoré: realism of, 241; urban
    life in, 11
Barisan Socialists (Singapore), 182
Barlow, Tani E., 54, 260n7
Baucom, Ian, 50–51; *Out of Place,* 29
Baudelaire, Charles: depiction of
    modernity, 19, 54, 82
Benjamin, Walter, 146; *The Arcades
    Project,* 18–19, 199, 201; on
    Baudelaire, 19; *flâneurs* of, 61; on
    interior space, 142, 143
Berlin Conference (1884), 104
Berman, Marshall, 75, 77, 82; on
    modern beauty, 85
Berry, Chris, 221
Berry, Michael, 220
Bhabha, Homi, 42; on hybridity,
    260n13
bildungsroman: contradictory aspects
    of, 100; Huang's use of, 121; individ-
    ual growth in, 112; interiority in,
    114; "A Little Ball Launched by a
    Dwarf" as, 107; mobility in, 114; in
    New Asian City fiction, 95, 99; in
    postcolonial literature, 130; of
    Taiwanese New Cinema, 216
bourgeoisie, postcolonial, 169–70
bourgeoisie, Western: condemnation
    of, 148; interiors of, 141, 165
Brewster, Anne, 186, 195
British East India Company, 45
buildings, high-rise, 259n3, 267n7; in
    New Asian City literature, 130, 211;
    in *Rice Bowl,* 159; symbolism of, 22;
    in "The Two Sign Painters," 125–26
built environments: human desire in,
    20, 21; modern dimensionality of,
    104; narrative elements of, 14; of
    postcolonial nations, 174; social
    change through, 231
built forms: global processes affecting,
    16; importance to state, 38; in liter-
    ary texts, 21; of New Asian City,

130–31, 188; in *Orphan of Asia,* 68;
    relations of production in, 18; as
    social relations, 261n15; sociopoliti-
    cal forces in, 20–21; technological
    advances in, 19; as wagers on future,
    175. *See also* architecture

Cabral, Amilcar, 168, 200; on cultural
    nationalism, 187; on productive
    forces, 174
capitalism: center and periphery in, 16,
    17, 33–34, 35; centralizing aspects
    of, 31–32; cultural modernity of,
    267n1; in European cities, 37;
    geographical organization of, 32;
    modernizing logic of, 166; nativism
    and, 166; in New Asian City, 17, 93,
    171; nineteenth-century, 18–19;
    primitive accumulation in, 33;
    productive forces of, 47; relationship
    to noncapitalist world, 33–34; role
    in development, 16–17; spatial
    relations of, 32, 43, 175; stages of,
    16; and underdevelopment, 32–33;
    universalizing tendency of, 32
capitalism, colonial, 16, 31–33, 262n5;
    in cities, 29, 31
capitalism, global: in Asia Pacific
    region, 16–17; competition in,
    190; complementary processes of,
    17; neocolonial, 93; postcolonial
    cities in, 267n1; and spatial differen-
    tiation, 6; territorialization of, 85; in
    third world, 190; in urban form,
    256. *See also* globalization
capitalism, late, 17; and postcolonial
    modernity, 15–21
capitalism, postcolonial, 90; of India, 7;
    in Korea, 111; in Singapore, 162; in
    Taiwan, 122–23
capitals, colonial: Manichaean spaces
    of, 22. *See also* colonial cities
Castells, Manuel, 40, 208; on colonial
    cities, 35; on colonial industries, 41;

on developmental state, 173, 174; on urbanization, 72, 263n9

Çelik, Zeynap, 29

chaebols (Korean conglomerates), 109, 130, 234, 238; individuals versus, 112; role in reconstruction, 229–30

Chang, Sung-Sheng Yvonne, 120, 214, 226

Chatterjee, Partha, 135, 208

Cheah, Pheng, 170, 171, 175, 271n1; on hybridity theory, 260n13

Chen, Hsin-chu, 39

Chen, Kuan-hsing, 214–15, 256, 273n8; *Asia as Method*, 253

Ch'en, Ying-chen, 120, 209; in Chinese tradition, 210; imprisonment of, 210; national development in, 212; "One Day in the Life of a White Collar Worker," 211–12; Washington Building stories, 210

Chiang, Ching-kuo, 206, 219; agreement with Singapore, 272n3; liberalization under, 214

Chiang, Kai-shek, 3, 87, 88, 176; anti-communism of, 205; authoritarianism of, 204; death of, 205; development under, 168; Great Commonwealth Program of, 204, 205, 220; idea of reconstruction, 208; People's Livelihood program, 204, 205; on reconstruction, 203–5; Three Principles of, 206; urbanization under, 204

Chiang, Lan-Hung Nora, 269n6

Chien, Ying-ying, 151

China, People's Republic of: economic emergence of, 256; nationalism of, 209; U.N. seat of, 205

China, Republic of, 3; Taiwan under, 87

China, semicolonization of, 260n7

Ching, Leo, 62, 68

Cho, Nam-hyun, 106, 136

Cho, Se-hŭi, 22; "City of Machines," 106; class differences in, 109–11;

Dongin Literary Award of, 106; "Mobius Strip," 106; themes of, 113

Cho, Se-hŭi, "A Little Ball Launched by a Dwarf," 8–9, 106–12, 117, 239; architecture in, 107, 111, 124, 211; bildungsroman aspects of, 107; growth in, 118; industrialization in, 107–9; narrative structure of, 106–7; oppositions in, 112; redevelopment in, 101; shrinkage imagery in, 111–12; urban imagery in, 21, 110–11; urban space in, 107; youth in, 112

Choe, Sang-Chuel, 101, 107

Choi, Hyun-moo, 236, 238

Choi, Won-shik, 75, 80–81

Chosen. *See* Korea

Chu, Tien-Jen: "Autumn Note," 264n10

Chua, Beng-huat, 130, 267n1

cinema: Korean, 214–15, 252, 275n12; Singaporean, 213; Taiwanese vernacular, 214; as urban representation, 212. *See also* New Cinema, Taiwanese

cities: aesthetic modernism of, 82; alienation in, 82; Asian versus Western, 36; built environment of, 11; capitalistic relations in, 82; center and periphery of, 36–37; as cognitive objects, 10; consumer, 105; decline of civilization in, 104; domination of countryside, 122; everydayness of, 77; in experience of modernity, 77; foreigners in, 103–4, 105, 117; lived experiences of, 11; producer, 81, 105; spatial histories of, 27; as world, 122; as worldview, 125. *See also* Asian cities; colonial cities; Western cities

city planning: colonial, 29, 41, 262n8; Eurocentrist, 263n9; experiments in, 262n8; poetic rendering of, 193–94; in postcolonial Singapore, 102, 157, 193

Colomina, Beatriz, 138

colonial cities, 21–22; administrative, 35–43, 44, 50; capital accumulation in, 31; capitalist-colonial relations of, 29; in circulation of commodities, 76–77; as crouching village, 80; the discrepant in, 71, 77, 83, 99–100; dualism of, 27–28, 29, 30–31, 40, 49, 54, 72, 82; ecosystems of, 79–80; gateway, 35, 36, 43–50; in global imperialism, 94; hybridity of, 42; interrelationships of, 77; Manicheanism of, 27, 29, 50, 83; misrecognition of, 49–50; modernity of, 54–55, 77, 83, 85, 255; as node of modernity/coloniality, 30, 50; as perceptual lenses, 84; postcolonial perspectives on, 22; power relations in, 35, 42, 80; public sphere of, 42; reconstruction of, 38, 44; representational space of, 71; spatiality of, 27, 85; trading ports, 35–36, 44–45, 50; types of, 35; urban planning experiments in, 262n8; worlded form of, 44. *See also* capitals, colonial; New Asian City; urbanism, colonial

colonialism: center and periphery in, 38; contradictions within, 68; cultural texts of, 256; economic dependence in, 81–82; effect on natural economies, 44; effect on urban forms, 34; ethnic categorization in, 115, 172, 268n13; French, 262n8; global, 43, 94, 104; Manicheanism of, 22, 27, 29, 50, 83; maps of, 172; Marxist analysis of, 31–32, 33; money economy of, 76; monuments of, 172; national forms of, 34; presence in postcolonial state, 171–72, 256; proletariat of, 33; spatial logics of, 30; territorial boundaries in, 172; third cultures of, 42; transition from, 87; urban forms of, 253; worlding in, 43, 94. *See also*

capitals, colonial; colonial cities; imperialism

colonialism, Japanese, 259n5; architecture of, 38–40, 44, 45, 69, 80; Colonial Fairs of, 266n19; end of, 88; geopolitical structure of, 263n11; literature of, 266n21; military, 72; resistance to, 62; spatial planning in, 40; Taiwanese consciousness under, 209; urban space of, 38–42

colonial literature: modernity in, 54–55, 72, 83; realist, 54, 56–57, 71, 72; Singaporean, 263n3; urban space in, 50. *See also* Korean literature, colonial; Taiwanese literature, colonial

colonial modernity, 264n4; characteristics of, 62; of cities, 30, 50, 54–55, 77, 83, 85; dislocation in, 77; Korean, 85; in literature, 54–55, 83; in *Mansejŏn,* 71; spatial realities of, 85

colonial space: contradictions in, 50; as external territory, 35; global, 104; ideological production in, 31; interpenetrations of, 43; in *Mansejŏn,* 58–59, 71, 84; of metropolitan industrial system, 71; in *The Orphans of Asia,* 66, 68, 70, 84; as phantasmic earth, 43; policing of, 29, 30; political production in, 31; racial discrepancies of, 48; representation of social relations, 30; role in European forms, 37; role in imperialism, 30–35; struggles over, 30; textualization of, 30; Western forms of, 41; worlding of, 43

Connery, Christopher, 260n14, 261n20

consumerism: of colonial Seoul, 81, 83; in "A Room in the Woods," 143; Taiwanese, 210; in *The Wings,* 75, 78, 84

cultural nationalism, 167; of Singapore, 187, 191–92; Taiwanese, 121, 208. *See also* national culture

cultural production: as identity, 7; in postcolonial nations, 23
Cumings, Bruce, 227, 232, 274n1

Dal Co, Francesco, 103, 104
Dale, Johan Ole, 45
Dante, the architectural in, 84
decolonization, 87–89, 169; concentrated populations of, 227; development following, 1, 22, 89–91; and industrial production, 16–17, 261n18; Lee on African, 181; in Manichean city, 29
de la Blache, Vidal, 267n8
Delhi, colonial, 40–41, 42; divisions of, 49
Denning, Michael: *Culture in the Age of Three Worlds*, 252–53
Denton, Kirk, 63
department stores, 81, 82
De Souza, Dudley, 183
Devan, Janadas, 161, 166
developmental space: form of, 5; in Hou's films, 217; logic of, 5; role of poetry in, 180; texts of, 5, 168
developmental state: civil societies of, 174; cultural histories of, 1; industrialization in, 185; lack of choice for, 194; movement in, 223; narratives of, 176, 206, 208; nationalism of, 167; revolutionary, 208; spatial histories of, 1; spatial strategies of, 175; technological landscapes of, 196; unevenness in, 7, 253. *See also* New Asian City; postcolonial nations
difference, production of, 5, 6
Dirlik, Arif, 17, 261n21
division of labor: gendered, 136; international, 31, 100, 129; New International, 4; racial, 45
domestic space, 94, 134; Chinese, 153–54, 271n21; definition through family, 154; femininity and, 150–66, 158; and kinship relations, 143; Korean, 139–40; of nations, 166;

Poe's, 270n16; postcolonial, 94, 134; and public sphere, 151; in *Rice Bowl*, 159, 162; Singaporean women in, 185; Western, 153. *See also* interior space
Dostoevsky, Fyodor: *Notes from the Underground*, 73
Duus, Peter, 259n5

Eagleton, Terry, 260n12
East Asia: NICs of, 17, 253; in postcolonial studies, 4; in postwar era, 87–90; urban development in, 35, 94; U.S. hegemony in, 89, 269n10. *See also* Asian Tiger nations; Asia Pacific region
Engmalchin (synthetic language), 191
Export Production Zones (EPZs), 91–95; blank slate character of, 93–94; in development strategies, 94; versus import substitution, 92, 93; political aspects of, 92; spatial logic of, 93, 94
exports, postcolonial, 90–95; from cities, 22, 105; of New Asian City, 105, 131, 171; of Singapore, 113, 117; South Korean, 228, 232; Taiwanese, 92, 123, 207, 221. *See also* import substitution

factory dormitories, women's, 144, 270n18. *See also* industrialization, postcolonial: women in
Fanon, Frantz, 72, 200; on constitution of nations, 170; on cultural nationalism, 187; on postcolonial bourgeoisie, 169–70; *The Wretched of the Earth*, 10, 27–28, 30, 80
femininity: and domestic space, 150–66, 158; kinship-organized, 155–56; in postcolonial states, 166; in *Rice Bowl*, 163
feminism: idea of accessibility, 151; of New Asian City, 269n3; postcolonial, 136–37, 147, 153, 269n3, 269n7, 271n22; South Korean,

269n7; spatial issues in, 153;
Taiwanese, 155, 271n22; Western,
136–37, 151, 268n3
fengshui, 40
Fordism, 100; mass culture of, 252–53;
post-, 253
Formosa (political magazine), 120
Foucault, Michel: on cities, 36, 44; on
utopian space, 147
Frank, Andre Gunder, 89, 266n2; on
export production, 93–94
Frankfurt School, 141
Free Trade Zones. *See* Export
Production Zones
Frübel, Folker, 4
Fujii, James A., 266n21

gender relations: in colonial Korea,
60, 75; in postcolonial modernity,
135–37
globalization: anticommunism and,
167; cultural texts of, 256; New
Asian City in, 131; signifiers of, 1;
urban studies of, 10
Goh, Poh Seng, 22; education of, 113
Goh, Poh Seng, *If We Dream Too Long*,
112–19; anomie in, 116–18; body
and building in, 119; functional
space in, 115; the individual in, 114,
117, 118; modernization in, 102;
modern subject in, 114; postcolonial
sensibility of, 113; seriality in, 116,
117, 118, 119; spatial alienation in,
115; urban space in, 116, 118, 119
Goh, Robbie B. H., 181–82, 186
Gottdiener, M., 13
Grosz, Elizabeth, 135

Hakka people (Taiwan), 4, 273n5
Hallwood, Peter, 6
han (unfulfilled longing), 250, 275n12
hangŭl script, 56
Hartoonian, Harry D., 77, 82
Harvey, David, 32, 34

Haskell, Dennis, 198
Heidegger, Martin: "Building,
Dwelling, Thinking," 43, 44
Heng, Geraldine, 161, 166
Hitchcock, Henry-Russell, 267n7
Hong Kong: auteur films of, 251;
economy of, 5, 35, 260n11; postcolonial, 5, 266n1
Hou, Hsiao-Hsien, 23, 175, 251–52;
auteur style of, 226; camerawork of,
221, 273n11; decentering scenes of,
221, 223; depiction of countryside,
222; developmental state in, 217;
early films of, 205, 215; languages
used by, 217; long shots of, 223,
273n11; migration films of, 215–16,
217, 219, 239; organization of movement, 221; on outward longing,
220–21; sideliner aesthetic of, 218–
26, 239; Taiwanese ethnicity in, 225
Hou, Hsiao-Hsien, *The Boys from
Fengkuei*, 207, 215, 223–26, 225;
camerawork of, 224; coming of age
in, 223, 224; *Good Men, Good
Women*, 216; movement in, 223; *The
Puppetmaster*, 216; redemption in,
226; *Summer at Grandpa's*, 215;
urban migrants in, 225; use of
Mandarin, 217
Hou, Hsiao-Hsien, *City of Sadness*,
216; Shangainese in, 217
Hou, Hsiao-Hsien, *Dust in the Wind*,
138, 215, *219*, 221–23, 247; long
shots of, 219, 221–22, 222; migration
in, 218, 219–21, 225; movement and
nonmovement in, 220; space in, 218,
221–22
Hou, Hsiao-Hsien, *A Time to Live and
a Time to Die*, 216; languages of, 217
Hsia, Chu-Joe, 40, 42
hsiang-t'u literature (Taiwan), 103,
119–29, 216; city and village in, 121;
modes of production in, 121;
nativism of, 120, 226; origins of, 119;

response to neocolonialism, 121; themes of, 121
Hsiau, A-chin, 120, 121
Hsieh, Tung-min, 206–7, 219
Huang, Chunming, 22; architectural themes of, 122, 124; bildungsroman themes of, 121; education of, 121; *His Son's Big Doll*, 121–22; in *hsiangt'u* movement, 103, 121; modes of production in, 124; *The Sandwich Man*, 217; *Sayonara, Goodbye*, 122; *The Taste of Apples*, 124; themes of, 120
Huang, Chunming, "The Taste of Apples," 126–29; American wealth in, 128; architecture in, 129; body/building relationship in, 126–27, 128; built forms in, 126; modes of production in, 126; spatiality in, 128
Huang, Chunming, "The Two Sign Painters," 124–26, 211, 268n19; architecture in, 124; body/building relationship in, 125–26
Hwang, Sŏk-yŏng, 175; depiction of individuals, 242; exile of, 240; industrializing landscape of, 274n8; redemptive realism of, 239, 240, 243, 245–46, 248; rural settings of, 239; *The Shadow of Arms*, 241–42; workers' literature of, 106
Hwang, Sŏk-yŏng, "Far from Home," Korean society in, 241
Hwang, Sŏk-yŏng, "Longing for the North, a Far and Desolate Place," 249–50; material landscape in, 250
Hwang, Sŏk-yŏng, "The Road to Sampo," 242–45, 246–48; film version of, 274n10; human solidarity in, 243, 246–47; industrializing landscape in, 242, 243, 244, 247, 248; rural development in, 248; rural versus urban in, 243; spatial experience in, 248; suffering in, 247
Hyŏn, Ching-ŏn, 56

Im, Hŏn-yŏng, 10
Im, Kwon-taek, 214
imperialism: effect on native industry, 16; postcolonial studies and, 6; role of colonial space, 30–35; role of literature in, 6; spatial policing in, 29, 30. *See also* colonialism
import substitution, 89–90, 260n11; versus EPZs, 92, 93
India, postcolonial: capitalism of, 7; economic emergence of, 256; urban development in, 259n4
individual, the: in bildungsroman, 112; versus family, 157; in *If We Dream Too Long*, 114, 117, 118; in "Missing," 154; in modernity, 142; in New Asian City literature, 100; in postcolonial literature, 94–95, 255–56; in postcolonial Singapore, 118; and production, 174; in *Rice Bowl*, 164; in "A Room in the Woods," 149
industrialization, 1; effect on colonial urbanization, 41; Western, 165
industrialization, postcolonial: decolonization and, 16–17, 261n18; export-driven, 90–95; of Singapore, 113, 117, 189–90; South Korean, 9, 143–44, 176, 228, 229–30, 232, 248; of Taiwan, 204–5, 268n17; women in, 135, 144–45, 148, 150, 162, 269n5, 270n17, 271n19, 271n24
Industrial Revolution, effect on urban space, 259n1
infrastructure: expression of political power, 168–69; role in ideological debates, 228
infrastructure, postcolonial, 168–69, 174, 175; of New Asian City, 168–69; of Singapore, 182; South Korean, 228; of Taiwan, 206, 211
interior space, 142, 143; Eros in, 270n14; gendered division of, 270n12; interconnected, 270n15; of

New Asian City, 131. *See also*
domestic space
International Labour Organisation, 91,
94
Ishikawa, Kinichiro, 65

Jacobs, Jane M., 31
Jameson, Fredric, 188; on capitalism,
17; on metropole-periphery
relations, 83; on seriality, 116; *The
Political Unconscious,* 14–15
Japan: commodity culture of, 81;
economic imperialism of, 261n20;
labor market of, 266n15; modernity
of, 57, 58, 69, 267n9, 269n4; postwar
economy of, 90; postwar leadership
of, 260n11. *See also* colonialism,
Japanese
Japan, Meiji: architecture of, 38–39;
colonial territories of, 38; technology
in, 136
Jayawardena, Kumari, 135
Johnson, Philip, 267n7
justice, role of culture in, 260n12
Jyoti, Hosagrahar, 34

kampongs (Malay villages), eradication
of, 200
Kang, Sŏk-kyŏng, 22; "Days and
Dreams," 139; feminist themes of,
139; gender hierarchy in, 137
Kang, Sŏk-kyŏng, "A Room in the
Woods," 139–43, 145–50; architecture in, 143; consumerism in, 143;
democracy movement in, 147–48;
as detective story, 142, 143, 150,
152; female subjectivity in, 141–42;
feminism of, 139; gendered hierarchy in, 146, 148; individualism in,
149; interiority in, 134, 149–50;
kinship structures in, 143; narrative
construction of, 133; patriarchy
in, 146, 149; physical settings of,
146–47; placelessness in, 145;

private space in, 139, 140–41,
145–46
Kant, Immanuel, 170
Kaohsiung Export Processing Zone
(Taiwan), 207
KAPF (Korea Artista Proletaria
Federacio), 56, 240
Kavanagh, James H., 196
Keeling (Taiwan), 44–45
Kennedy, John F., 229
Kennedy, Liam, 174
Khanna, Ranjana, 29, 43
Khoo, Eric, 213
Kim, Hyung-A, 228, 234
Kim, Joochul, 101, 107
Kim, Ki-duk, 214
Kim, Seung-kyung, 148
Kim, Tong-in: European influences on,
56; "Potato," 264nn7–8
Kim, Young-Sam, 251
King, Anthony, 29, 42, 49, 267n1
Kipnis, Jeffrey, 2, 20, 256, 259n1
Kleeman, Faye Yuan, 63
Knapp, Ronald G., 271n21
Koh, Tai Ann, 114, 158
Kon, Stella: *The Scholar and the
Dragon,* 157
Koolhaas, Rem, 101, 117, 267n4; on
new density, 119
Korea: Chosŏn dynasty, 38–42;
division system in, 4, 260n8; feudal
cities of, 36; liberation from Japan,
88; partition of, 227
Korea, colonial: development of, 35;
domestic food production in, 72;
gender relations in, 60, 75; in
Mansejŏn, 53–54; modernity of, 85;
and outside world, 57; overseas
students of, 57; rural society of, 72;
social morbidity of, 54; urbanization
of, 71–72; women in, 59–60
Korea, postcolonial, 4; export economy
of, 9, 92; independence of, 85. *See
also* South Korea

Korean literature, colonial, 55–62; censorship of, 72; European influences on, 56; naturalism in, 56–57; of 1930s, 73; proletarian, 56; realism in, 56–57, 264n6; vernacular, 264n5

Korean literature, postcolonial, 106–12, 139–43, 145–50; nationalist, 241; proletarian, 106, 175; rural, 234; social realism of, 241; urban forms in, 9; vernacular, 113; women in, 139; women writers, 268n1, 270n11. *See also minjung* literature, Korean

Korean War, 88; in "Longing for the North," 249

Kuo, Jason C., 266n19

Kuomintang party (Taiwan), 3, 88, 103; anti-communist propaganda of, 203; economic policy of, 120; film industry under, 214; loss of China, 267n3; modernization under, 205–7; New Cinema challenges to, 216–17; organization law of, 137; rationalization of space, 208–9; reconstruction under, 202, 203–8; vision of Taiwan, 226

labor: absorption of, 92–93; export, 90–92; exports from Singapore, 92; productive power of, 169, 174; women's, 94, 135, 144–45, 148, 150, 162, 269n5, 270n17, 271n19, 271n24. *See also* division of labor

Lalande, Georg de, 40

landscapes: anthropomorphization of, 198; cinematic representation of, 212; developmentalist, 173–75, 198–99, 220; in *minjung* literature, 242; modernizing, 239; nineteenth-century concept of, 267n8; productive, 200; technological, 196

landscapes, industrializing, 21, 22–23, 247, 248; Hwang's, 274n8; of South Korea, 242, 243, 244; state-led growth in, 256

Lau, Joseph S. M., 210

Le Corbusier, 102, 188

Lee, Ang, 252

Lee, Kuan Yew, 88, 113, 190; African visits of, 179–81; on Asian families, 158; authoritarianism of, 181; developmentalism of, 182; foreign trips of, 179–83; on gender equality, 161; interest in neo-Confucianism, 208; modernization under, 168, 181; nationalism of, 175, 187; political discourse of, 23; on postcolonial leaders, 271n2; *The Singapore Story*, 179, 189; understanding of national space, 180; way ahead of, 176

Lee, Man-hŭi, 274n10

Lee, Namhee, 236, 237

Lee, Sang-hae, 270n12

Lee, Teng-hui, 251

Lee, Tzu Pheng: "My Country and My People," 272n5

Lefebvre, Henri: on abstract space, 175, 242; on bourgeois space, 165; on capitalist spatial relations, 175; on global space, 104; on modern interiors, 270n14; *The Production of Space*, 12–14; sociospatial dialectic of, 18; on spatial practice, 12; on urban space, 31, 95

Lenin, V. I., 262n5; "Imperialism, Highest Stage of Capitalism," 33

Li, Ang: *The Butcher's Wife*, 151

Li, William D. H., 268n17

Liao, Ping-hui, 4, 65

Lim, Catherine: *The Serpent's Tooth*, 157

Lim, Shirley Geok-lin, 183–84, 187, 191

Lim, Su-chen Christine, 22; education of, 271n23; gender hierarchy in, 137

Lim, Su-chen Christine, *Rice Bowl*, 156–65; ambivalent ending of, 164–65; binary polarities in, 157; Chinatown in, 159–60; didacticism of, 161; domestic space in, 159, 162; education in, 161; factory in, 134, 162; family in, 158, 162; the feminine in, 150, 158, 163; gendered issues in, 163; the individual in, 164; naming system in, 158; narrative space of, 163; national identity in, 157; patriarchy in, 157; public/private space in, 150, 158, 160–61; romantic aspects of, 164; Singaporean society in, 157–58; social institutions in, 158; women's interiority in, 164; women's roles in, 158, 166

Lim, William, 102, 115

literature: access to social world, 15; architectural construction of, 84; consciousness-raising function of, 56; expression of materiality, 15; as production, 195; role in imperialism, 6; role in national rebirth, 241; transformative, 196. *See also* texts, literary; three-dimensionality

Literature Quarterly (Taiwanese journal), 120, 121

London, urban space of, 259n2

Lu, Hsiu-lien, 137

Lu, Hwei-Syin, 155, 271n21

Lukács, Georg, 84, 241

Luxemburg, Rosa, 33, 34

Macherey, Pierre, 15, 195, 197

Maeda, Ai, 141

Malayan Emergency (1948–60), 88, 188

Malayan National Organization, 3

Malaysia, 88; conflict with Indonesia, 271n1; relations with Singapore, 272n7; separation from Singapore, 179, 191, 227, 267n3

Mandel, Ernest, 32, 261n18; *Late Capitalism,* 16

Mao, Dun, 63

March 1st movement (Korea), 56, 62, 263n1

Marx, Karl, 31–32, 33

materialism: historical, 18, 263n9; literature and, 12; and national culture, 168, 170–71, 176; postcolonial, 170; of space, 7, 13. *See also* consumerism

May Fourth Movement (China), 63

Mbembe, Achille, 10–11, 169

metropole-periphery relations, 18, 68, 103–4; in Asian cities, 36, 38; capitalist, 33–34, 35; colonial, 38, 93; commodities in, 76–77; complementary processes of, 17; cultural texts of, 175; flow of capital in, 89; in *hsiang-t'u* literature, 121; in New Asian Cities, 129; realities of, 83

metropoles: administrative cities' replication of, 50; repressed spatiality of, 83

Mignolo, Walter, 263n4

Miller, Lucien, 210

minjung literature, Korean, 23, 175, 215; class subjects in, 243; diversity of, 237, 249; landscape in, 242; nationalism of, 237; oppositional aesthetic of, 238; realism of, 245–46; themes of, 245. *See also* Korean literature, postcolonial

minjung movement, Korean, 236–39; class struggle in, 237–38, 240; composition of, 236; cultural aspects of, 238–39, 245; *han* in, 275n12; modernizing landscape in, 239; multivalency of, 237; nationalism in, 239; philosophies of, 245; suffering in, 238

Minnan people (Taiwan), 4, 273n5

Mitsukoshi department store (Seoul), 81, 82

modernity: and anticolonialism, 51; built environment in, 104; capitalist, 255, 267n1; colonial, 72, 255; comparative studies of, 253; cultural texts of, 256; discrepant forms of,

53–55, 71; individualism in, 142;
Japanese, 57, 58, 69, 267n9, 269n4;
local discourses of, 255; in *Orphan
of Asia*, 65; primal past of, 19, 20;
processes of, 18; realist descriptions
of, 54; spatiality of, 254, 255; as
system, 51; of Tokyo, 57, 59, 80,
265n10; urban, 9–10, 51, 54; urban
character of, 122. *See also* colonial
modernity; postcolonial modernity;
Western modernity
modernization theory, 90
Modern Literature (Taiwanese journal),
120
Moon, Seungsook, 137
Moretti, Franco, 11, 99; on bildungsroman narrative form, 100, 114
Morocco, colonial: urban planning in,
262n8
Morse, Ruth, 157–58, 161
Mumford, Lewis, 36

national culture: of colonial Taiwan,
65; of New Asian City, 167; postcolonial, 167; of postcolonial
nations, 170–71; role of modernity
in, 189; of Singapore, 113–14;
Taiwanese, 208. *See also* cultural
nationalism
nationalism, postcolonial: of developing nations of, 167, 253; discourses
of, 168; failures of, 170; leadership
styles of, 171; narratives of, 176; of
Singapore, 175, 187–88, 190; social
imaginary of, 172, 173; South
Korean, 208, 236, 237, 239; spatial
grammar of, 176; Taiwanese, 121,
203, 208–9; *techne* and, 171; women
in, 135
national space: authoritarian production of, 188; care of, 181, 182;
infrastructure of, 168; Lee's understanding of, 180; modernized, 167–
68; poetic representation of, 181–82;

productive, 23; transportation
systems of, 231–32
National Symposium of Art and
Literary Workers (Taiwan, 1971), 120
native societies, spatial forms of, 84
nativist movements, 261n22;
cinematic, 245; *hsiang-t'u,* 103, 121.
See also hsiang-t'u literature
Natsume, Soseki: *Kokoro,* 266n21
Neo, Jack, 213
New Asian City literature, 8, 22;
bildungsroman model of, 95, 99;
body and building in, 95, 131; built
forms in, 130–31; formation narratives in, 130; growth in, 100;
high-rise buildings in, 125–26, 130,
159, 211; the individual in, 100, 105;
social integration in, 114; space in,
21, 165; stability in, 100; suicide in,
266n20; youth in, 95, 99, 100, 130.
See also postcolonial literature
New Cinema, Taiwanese, 175, 205,
251–52; bildungsroman narratives
of, 216; challenges to KMT, 216–17;
modernism of, 226; modernization
in, 215; national identity in, 217;
nativism of, 245; origins of, 214, 215;
rural-urban migration in, 215–16;
space in, 212–13, 214–26; successes
of, 215, 223; Taiwanese development
in, 217
New Delhi, colonial, 34
New Village Movement (South Korea),
176, 207, 230, 242, 249
NICs (Newly Industrializing
Countries), 17, 253
Nixon, Richard: visit to China, 205
Nkrumah, Kwame, 180
Nomuru, Ichiro, 40
Nuttall, Sarah, 10–11, 261n17

Pacific Rim. *See* Asia Pacific region
Paik, Nak-chung, 4, 260n8
Pak, Chong-wŏn: *Kuro Arirang,* 245

Pak, Kwang-su: *Chil-su wa Man-su,* 268n19
Paris, Second Empire: architecture of, 39, 199, 201; New Asian City and, 19–20; technological change in, 18
Paris Peace Conference (1919), 263n1
Park, Chan-wook, 214
Park, Chung Hee: anticommunism of, 137, 229, 230; authoritarianism of, 228, 230; coup d'état of, 228; economic nationalism of, 230; export policy of, 232; industrialization under, 229, 232, 233; Korean film industry under, 214–15; modernization under, 226, 233; New Village Movement (Saemaŭl Undong) of, 176, 207, 230–31, 242, 249; onsite management by, 232, 274n5; repression under, 175; and Supreme Council for National Reconstruction, 274n2; Vietnam War commitment, 232–33, 267n4; *Yusin* reforms of, 106, 213–14, 230, 233
Patke, Rajeev S., 181; on Thumboo, 192–93; on Yap, 196
patriarchy: concepts associated with, 134–35; expectations for women, 137–38; in postcolonial Singapore, 166; relations of exchange in, 148; in *Rice Bowl,* 157; in "A Room in the Woods," 146, 149
People's Action Party (Singapore), 3, 88; authoritarianism of, 181; commitment to national project, 190–91; control of space, 182; developmentalism of, 186; material development under, 113; national rhetoric of, 192; societal power under, 183; successes of, 229; in twenty-first century, 251; urban renewal program of, 102, 115, 119, 181; vision of modernity, 117; Women's Charter (1961), 137. *See also* Singapore, postcolonial

Phil, Marshall R., 241
Philippines, Spanish: colonialism of, 34
Poe, Edgar Allan: domestic interiors of, 270n16
Pontecorvo, Gillo: *The Battle of Algiers,* 29
postcolonialism, 5–8; aesthetic production in, 8; African, 179–81; Asian versus African, 169; colonial ideologies of, 171–72, 256; cultural production in, 23; economic transformations of, 89; exports under, 90–95; nationalism of, 22; political power in, 168–69; production of difference in, 5; spatial processes of, 5, 6, 7, 8, 153; technological advances in, 19
postcolonial literature, 6, 7–8; architecture in, 105, 134; bildungsroman models for, 130; coming-of-age-stories in, 105; the individual in, 94–95, 255–56; interiority in, 138; spatial neologisms in, 134; women in, 134. *See also* Korean literature, postcolonial; New Asian City literature; Singaporean literature, postcolonial; Taiwanese literature, postcolonial
postcolonial modernity, 85, 262n22; asymmetries of, 130; gender relations in, 137; and late capitalism, 15–21; mobility in, 100; narratives of, 179–202; nation space in, 166; of New Asian City, 23, 99, 137, 165; poetry of, 179–202; prostitution in, 269n10; role in national culture, 189; subjectivities in, 166; third-world, 253; uneven development of, 7, 253; and Western modernity, 134
postcolonial nations: authoritarian, 101, 129, 175, 181, 228, 230; built environments of, 174; cultural production in, 23; demand for labor in, 129; democratization of, 251; development of, 1, 7, 168, 253;

femininity in, 166; globalized, 251, 252–53; interlinked economies of, 251; isolation of, 228; of late twentieth century, 252–53; legitimacy of, 173; material histories of, 254; material sphere of, 135–36; movement in, 227; national cultures of, 170–71; nationalism of, 89; public/private aspects of, 166; revolutionary, 168, 171, 173; social production of, 174; societal goals of, 173; spatiality of, 166, 176, 255; spiritual sphere of, 135–36; state-building activities of, 171–72; *techne* of, 170, 171, 175, 233; transport systems of, 227, 228; uneven development of, 7, 253. *See also* developmental state; New Asian City; third world

postcolonial studies: developmental theory in, 89; East Asia in, 4; migration in, 6; New Asian City and, 2–5; non-English texts in, 259n5; spatial metaphors of, 5; transcultural formations in, 254

postmodernism: French-inspired, 2; urban studies in, 10

power relations: in colonial cities, 35, 42, 80; in postwar urbanism, 255; state-versus-people, 166

production: aesthetic, 17; cultural, 7, 23; gap with consumption, 129–30; growth in, 100; liberation of, 174; means of, 15, 141; modes of, 15, 121, 124; national, 149, 174; relations of, 15, 18. *See also* social production; spatial production

prostitutes: as commodities, 266n18; Korean, 143; in literature, 269n10; postcolonial women as, 270n10

Pusan (Korea), 44–45

races: categories of, 172; in colonial space, 48; spatial division of, 45

Raffles, Stamford, 45
Rahman, Tunku Abdul, 271n1
Ranchod-Nilsson, Sita, 165
realism: in Asian literature, 54, 56; Balzac's, 241; Hwang Sŏk-yŏng's, 239, 240, 245–46, 248; in Korean colonial literature, 56–57, 264n6; of Korean postcolonial literature, 241; of *Mansejŏn*, 60, 72; of *Orphan of Asia*, 63–64, 69
Rendell, Jane, 135, 148
representational space, 12, 13–14, 60, 95, 140, 149–50, 154, 164–65; polyvalent, 242; and representations of space, 14
Reynaud, Bérénice, 205, 223, 273n11
Rhee, Syngman, 228
Rhodes, Cecil, 262n4
Richard, Nelly, 149, 163
Rimbaud, Arthur, 261n15
Robinson, Jennifer, 61
Roh, Tae-woo, 240
Rosner, Victoria, 138
Ross, Kristin, 77, 261n15; on discipline of geography, 267n8

Said, Edward: on discrepant experience, 54; *Orientalism*, 6
San-san bookshop (Taiwan), 209
sarabangs (male quarters), 140
Sartre, Jean-Paul: on seriality, 116
Selassie, Haile, 180
Seoul, colonial, 38; as administrative city, 35; architecture of, 38–40, 44; consumerism of, 81, 83; development of, 27; imperial power in, 40; industrialization of, 71–72; Mitsukoshi department store, 81, 82; modernity of, 54, 55; relationship to metropolis, 83; Seoul Station, 79; urban space of, 76, 79–80
Seoul, postcolonial: Chamsil district, 10; development of, 2, 23, 105, 119, 168, 174, 208, 236; housing in, 101,

108, 112; migration into, 101; urban
  aesthetic of, 99, 107–11; urban poor
  of, 107; urban renewal of, 9, 101,
  107, 109
seriality, in human relations, 116
Shanghai, colonial, 34
Simmel, Georg: depiction of modernity, 54; on money economy, 76
Singapore: migrant society of, 268n14;
  separation from Malaysia, 179, 191,
  227, 267n3; urban transformation
  in, 1
Singapore, colonial, 3, 45–48, 49;
  anti-colonial movement in, 188;
  British establishment of, 45; Chinese
  population of, 45, 46, 48, 49, 115;
  development of, 27; European
  community of, 46, 48, 50; government district, 47; living conditions
  in, 47, 49; racial makeup of, 188;
  riots (1850s), 46, 48; sectors of, 46;
  shophouse system, 46–47, 115; trade
  economy of, 35–36, 45, 46, 113;
  urban system of, 47–48; worlding
  of, 46
Singapore, postcolonial, 2–3; Advisory
  Council on Culture and the Arts,
  213; alliance with U.K., 272n3;
  anticommunism of, 167; authoritarianism in, 101, 181; capitalism in,
  162; Chinese population of, 159–60,
  182, 272n7; cultural nationalism
  of, 187, 191–92; culture of, 113;
  development of, 101, 115–16, 182,
  188–91, 193; displacement in, 115;
  EPZ of, 91; export industries of, 113,
  117; feminism in, 137; film industry
  of, 213; Great Marriage Debate in,
  161; Housing and Development
  Board, 113, 182, 195; housing in,
  102, 118; imagined community of,
  191; independence of, 3, 85, 88,
  188, 260n6; the individual in, 118;
  industrialization of, 189–90;

influence on urban development,
  259n4; infrastructure of, 182; in
  international labor market, 190;
  labor exports of, 92; languages of, 3,
  191, 196, 260n9, 267n5, 272n6;
  literary identity of, 183; material
  improvement in, 191; modernity of,
  117, 119, 130, 163, 182, 190; modernizing landscape of, 187, 192, 195;
  multinational corporations in, 122,
  157, 182, 189–90; national identity
  in, 113–14, 185; nationalism of, 175,
  190; patriarchy in, 166; poetic construction of, 191; race riots (1960s),
  192; racial divisions in, 172; role in
  Vietnam War, 274n6; slums of, 188–
  89; urban aesthetic of, 99, 188–89;
  urban forms of, 115; urban planning
  in, 102, 157; urban space of, 112–13,
  202; women's education in, 161;
  women's status in, 160; women
  workers in, 269n5. *See also* People's
  Action Party
Singaporean literature, postcolonial,
  112–19, 156–65; Chinese family in,
  158; English-language, 191; national
  identity in, 183
Singaporean poetry, 180–202; Anglophone, 181; nationalism in,
  181–82
Sin Kyŏng-nim, 274n8
sleeping mats (*yos*), 270n13
Smith, Neil, 34
social production: organization of, 19;
  of postcolonial nations, 174; role of
  space in, 13
social relations: in colonial space, 30;
  effect of aesthetic change on, 188;
  effect of urban forms on, 9; spatial
  form of, 80; in urban space, 31
South Africa, urban literature of,
  261n15
South Korea, 2; agricultural modernization in, 235, 236; antiauthoritarian

movement in, 237; anticommunism
of, 167; authoritarian government
of, 137, 147; democratic elections
(1987), 251; democratizing movements in, 133, 147–48, 240; developmental landscape of, 230–33, 250;
development of, 228; economy of,
106; EPZs of, 91; ethnonationalism
of, 237; export industrialization of,
228, 232; feminism in, 147, 269n7;
gender issues in, 137, 146, 148, 149,
229; government surveillance in,
230; industrialization of, 9, 143–44,
229–30; industrializing landscape
of, 242, 243, 244; Kyŏngbu expressway, 233; labor movement in, 148,
240, 241; labor power of, 228; late
capitalism in, 111; military buildup
in, 232–33; modernization of
villages, 130, 176, 207; movement in,
232; national consciousness of, 239;
nationalism of, 208, 236, 237, 239,
273n4; people's theater movement,
240; reconstruction of, 229; relations
with Japan, 90; role in cold war, 233;
rural industrialization in, 176, 248;
rural lifestyle of, 235; state-business
alliances in, 228; student protests in,
228; subaltern position of, 111;
Supreme Council for National
Reconstruction, 274n2; transit systems of, 231, 233, 234–35, 239, 249;
urban transformation in, 1; Western
architecture in, 140; womanhood in,
143–45; women workers in, 269n5,
270n17. *See also* Korean literature,
postcolonial; *minjung* movement,
Korean
Soviet Union, third world involvement
of, 89
space: abstract, 25, 175, 212, 242;
capitalist, 32, 43, 175; essential being
of, 44; feminist analysis of, 135–36;
gendered, 60, 131, 140, 149–50, 154,

164–65; geomantic conceptions of,
50; global, 104–5; in Hou's films,
217, 218, 221–22, 226; ideological
functioning of, 95; imageability of,
29, 262n1; intelligibility of, 95;
Lefebvre's theories of, 12–14;
Marxist approach to, 31–34; mask-
ing of power configurations, 95;
material functioning of, 95; misrecognition of, 30; philosophical, 12;
produced nature of, 44; productive
relationships of, 7; rationalization of,
22, 112, 115, 180, 208–9, 267n8;
relationship to power, 13; representations of, 12, 13–14, 95, 175, 249;
serial, 116; social relations of, 13;
state power over, 175; structural theory of, 263n9; in Taiwanese New
Cinema, 212–13, 214–26; textual
representations of, 13, 14; uneven
development of, 7, 31–32; utopian,
147. *See also* colonial space; developmental space; domestic space;
interior space; representational
space; urban space
spatial practice, Lefebvre on, 12
spatial production: cross-scalar nature
of, 18; in literary texts, 20; material,
13; in New Asian City, 20; in postcolonialism, 8; of postcolonial
women, 134
Spengler, Oswald, 122; "The Soul of
the City," 103–5
Spivak, Gayatri Chakravorty, 43, 254,
259n4; on "Other Asias," 253; on
textuality, 149
Standish, Isolde, 245
Su, Weizhen, 22; gender hierarchy in,
137; *The Island of Silence,* 268n2;
Leaving Tongfang, 268n2
Su, Weizhen, "Missing," 134, 150, 151–
56; the individual in, 154;
public/private space in, 151, 153,
156; women's subjectivity in, 156

subjects: bourgeois, 141–42; capitalist,
114; subaltern, 6
subjects, colonial: comprehension of
First World, 83; psychoaffective
dimensions of, 35
subjects, female: disappearing, 22;
postcolonial, 138, 146, 149, 156, 158
subjects, modern, 77; female, 146;
hyperinteriorized, 84
subjects, postcolonial: gendered, 167;
shrinkage of, 111–12; women, 138,
146, 149, 156, 158
Sun, Yat-sen, 204; interest in Marxism,
273n2; on *Min sheng,* 204, 272n2;
Three Principles of, 206

tabula rasa development, 93, 94, 167
Tafuri, Manfredo, 81, 82
Taipei, colonial, 38; as administrative
city, 35; architecture of, 38–40, 44;
civic spaces of, 42; development
of, 27; imperial power in, 40;
modernity of, 54; Public Hall, 42;
relationship to metropolis, 83;
Tobacco and Wine Monopoly
Building, *41*
Taipei, postcolonial: Chung-hwa Road,
123; corporate life in, 210; in *Dust in
the Wind,* 218
Taiwan: ethnicities of, 273n5; languages of, 63, 64, 214, 265n13,
273n9; Minnan-hua dialect, 273n5;
postcolonial theories concerning, 4;
urban transformation in, 1
Taiwan, colonial, 265nn13–14; architecture of, 66; censorship in, 64;
Colonial Fair (1935), 266n19;
consciousness of, 209; development
of, 35; Japanese language use in, 63,
64; national culture of, 65; orphan
imagery of, 62, 70
Taiwan, postcolonial, 2, 3–4, 87–89;
American wealth in, 128; anticommunism of, 167; Central

Motion Picture Corporation, 214;
Chinese revivalist architecture, 208;
city-country relationship in, 175,
204, 209, 217, 221; consumer culture
of, 210; cultural nationalism of, 121,
208; developmental narratives of,
203–5, 206; developmental spaces
of, 218, 220; economy of, 174; EPZs
of, 91, 207; Era of Minor Prosperity,
204–5; export production in, 92,
123, 207, 221; feminism in, 137;
foreign investment in, 122; gender
hierarchies in, 155; government-run
industries of, 268n17; housing in,
103, 123–24; independence of, 85;
industrialization of, 204–5; infrastructure of, 206, 211; Kaohsiung
incident (1979), 120; loss of U.N.
seat, 205; manufacturing economy
of, 122; martial law in, 215; migration into, 102–3, 221; modernization
of, 205–7; multinational corporations in, 210; national culture of,
121, 203, 208; nativism in, 209;
outward longing in, 221, 223;
reconstruction of, 203–8, 217,
268n17; resinicizing of, 273n2;
retrocession to ROC, 87; rural life
in, 204, 205, 211; rural-to-urban
migration in, 202, 208; shophouse
form in, 123; social system of, 205,
226; state-directed development of,
208; "2.28" massacre, 87–88, 120–21;
urban aesthetic of, 99, 124–26, 128–
29; urbanization of, 122, 204, 273n3;
women workers in, 155, 269n5. *See
also* New Cinema, Taiwanese
Taiwanese literature, colonial, 62–71,
264n10; characteristics of, 63;
language choice in, 265n13;
naturalism of, 63; vernacular, 63,
265nn12–13
Taiwanese literature, postcolonial,
103; countryside in, 120; feminist,

151–56; modernist, 120, 209; nco
nativist movement of, 209; space
in, 209–12; themes of, 120–21;
urban forms in, 210; vernacular,
209; Westernization in, 120. *See also*
hsiang-t'u literature
Taiwan Tobacco and Wine Monopoly
Bureau (Taipei), *41*
Tan, Kenneth Paul, 213
techne: of New Asian City, 171, 196,
201; of postcolonial nations, 170,
171, 175, 233
technology: architectural, 18–19,
20, 199; of developmental state,
196; effect on creativity, 274n4;
nineteenth-century, 18–19; textual
functions of, 19
Tetreault, Mary Ann, 165
texts, literary: built forms in, 21;
colonial space in, 30; developmental
space in, 5; of modernity, 256;
of postcolonial culture, 6, 7–8;
postcolonial development in, 8;
representational space of, 13, 14;
social forces in, 21; spatial production in, 20; spatial reality of, 13;
unified solutions in, 149, 155; urban
forms in, 2; urban processes in,
14–15, 21, 245; urban spaces in,
11–12. *See also* literature
Thailand, collapse of baht, 251
third world: authoritarianism in,
260n11; bourgeoisie of, 135;
comparative analyses within, 253;
corporate activities in, 90; differentiation within, 87, 93; in
global economy, 90–95, 190;
import substitution economy of,
89–90; modernity of, 253;
multinational enterprises in, 92;
neoliberalism in, 260n11; social
unrest in, 90; Soviet Union's
influence in, 89. *See also* postcolonial nations

three-dimensionality, 14, 150; and
fiction, 20–21, 118, 202, 256;
Lukácsian, 241–42; versus two-
dimensionality, 175
Thumboo, Edwin, 23, 175; on anticolonialism, 188; "Catering for the
People," 192–93; construction of
Singapore, 191; on cultural construction, 191–92; ethnicity of, 191;
free verse of, 192–93; *Gods Can Die*,
183, 272n8; government career of,
183; "Island," 184–86; literary criticism on, 272n4; material progress
in, 195; modernizing landscape in,
180, 192, 195; nationalism of, 183,
186, 187, 191, 192–94, 195; as
propagandist, 187; relationship to
technology, 191; *The Second Tongue*,
180; on Singaporean state, 184–86;
Ulysses by the Merlion, 183; use of
English, 191; "The Way Ahead,"
193–94, 200
Tokyo: cosmopolitan culture of, 81;
modernity of, 57, 59, 80, 265n10;
modernization of, 38–39, 40
Tong, Kelvin, 213
Tsai, Ming-liang, 215, 251

Underdevelopment, 89–90; capitalism
and, 32–33; following colonialism,
266n2
United Nations, Technical Assistance
Administration, 102
United States: aid to East Asia,
92–93; hegemony in East Asia, 89,
269n10; neocolonial relationships
of, 4
urban forms: aesthetic, 11; colonial,
21–22, 253; effect of colonialism
on, 34; effect on social relationships, 9; fictional texts of, 2; in
global capitalism, 256; of modernity, 9–10, 51; nationalist desires
in, 256; in *Orphan of Asia*, 70; and

psychological realities, 130;
theorizations of, 29–30
urbanism, colonial: imagery of, 35;
maintenance of imperialism, 87;
mediation of power, 71; models
of, 34, 262n6. *See also* colonial
cities
urbanism, normative Western, 35
urban space, 1; of Asian Tiger countries, 4–5; of colonial Algiers, 29; in
colonial literature, 50; of colonial
Seoul, 76, 79–80; Dickensian
aspects of, 11; effect of Industrial
Revolution on, 259n1; European, 37;
everydayness of, 79; fictional
accounts of, 11–12; Japanese
colonial, 38–42; of London, 259n2;
in *Mansejŏn,* 57, 58–59, 70–71;
modernity in, 54; of postcolonial
Singapore, 112–13, 202; of postcolonial Taiwan, 122–23; social relations in, 31; Western, 61; in *The
Wings,* 73–74, 75–76, 78, 80, 81, 82
Utrecht, Ernst, 90

Vidler, Anthony, 261n17

Wade, Robert, 4, 260n8; *Governing the
Market,* 5
Wang, Jing, 119, 121
Wang, T'o, 120
Weber, Max, 117; on market economy,
105; on modern city, 103
Wells, Kenneth M., 237
West, the: bourgeoisie of, 141, 148, 165;
domestic space of, 153; feminism in,
136–37, 151, 268n3; industrialization in, 165; models for postcolonial
cities in, 267n1; modernity of, 8,
134; versus the non-West, 254; in
Taiwanese postcolonial literature,
120; urbanism of, 35
Western cities: medieval, 36, 37; as
model for states, 37–38; productive

capabilities of, 33; reintegration with
country, 36
Western modernity, 19, 61, 82, 263n4;
New Asian City's translation of, 255;
and postcolonial modernity, 134;
theories of, 8
Williams, Raymond, 33, 105; *The
Country and the City,* 10, 262n2;
on realism, 245–46; on Western
urbanization, 129
Wilson, Rob, 17, 261n21, 275n12
Wilson, Woodrow, 263n1
women, bourgeois: in domestic space,
135; versus working-class, 165
women, postcolonial: colonized,
270n10; education of, 161, 271n19;
fictional representation of, 134; in
industrialization, 135, 144–45, 148,
150, 162, 269n5, 271n19, 271n24;
literary production of, 164; as
nation, 269n10; in New Asian City,
131; opportunities for, 136, 145; in
private sphere, 136; as prostitutes,
270n10; psychic spaces of, 146–47,
150; public/private roles of, 154;
in public realm, 161–62; role in
Taiwanese family, 155, 271n22;
Singaporean, 160, 185; South
Korean, 143–45, 229–30; spatial
production of, 134; subject position
of, 138, 146, 149, 156; in Taiwanese
work force, 155; textual production
of, 134; as trace, 139–50
Wong, Yoon Wah, 263n3
Woolf, Virginia, 151; *A Room of One's
Own,* 268n3
worlding, 43; of colonial Singapore, 46;
competing systems of, 263n11
Wu, Zhuoliu: European influences on,
63; *The Fig Tree,* 265n14; *Nanking
Chagan,* 65; on Taiwanese society,
268n16
Wu, Zhuoliu, *Orphan of Asia,* 22, 54,
62–71; architecture in, 66–67, 69,

84; built forms in, 68; colonial space in, 66, 68, 70, 84; composition of, 64; the discrepant in, 65, 70; Japanese influences in, 66–67, 68–69; metropolises in, 65; modernity in, 64, 66; movement in, 68; production of subjectivity in, 77; realism of, 63–64, 69; subjective development in, 69; Taiwanese passivity in, 70; triple consciousness of, 62; urban forms in, 70

Yang, Chao, 151, 209
Yang, Edward, 215, 251
Yang, Kui: "Paperboy," 63, 264n10
Yap, Arthur, 23, 175, 217; "& the tide," 196; bottom-up perspective of, 196; construction of Singapore, 191; depiction of nostalgia, 187; developmentalist landscape of, 198–99; on developmentalist logic, 199, 200; *Down the Line,* 200; education of, 186; the everyday in, 186, 187; evocation of unreality, 201, 202; "expansion," 198–99; *Five Takes,* 195; invocation of memory, 195; "june morning," 195–96; modernization in, 187; natural world in, 199; relationship to technology, 191; social landscape of, 199–200; urban forms in, 183; urban renewal in, 197–98; use of bureaucratic English, 197; use of irony, 187; use of lowercase, 200; use of Singlish, 196; verse forms of, 200–201; "would it have been," 200–201
Yeoh, Brenda S. A., 46–47, 50
Yi, Kwangsu: *The Heartless,* 264n5

Yi, Mungu, 247, 274n8; *Essays on Kwanch'ŏn,* 234
Yi, Mungu, "Ballad of Kalmŏri," 234–36; Slow Village of, 236, 239
Yi, Mun-yŏl, 245–46
Yi, Sang: architectural career of, 73; literary style of, 83; "Tokyo," 79; urban themes of, 75–76
Yi, Sang, *The Wings,* 22, 54, 71–79; architecture in, 78–79, 80; consumerism in, 75, 78, 84; discrepant city in, 71; the everyday in, 80; labor/money relationship in, 75, 76; materiality in, 77; modernism of, 75, 77, 81; modern subjectivity in, 74; relations of exchange in, 76–77; suicide in, 82; urban space in, 73–76, 78, 80–82
Yip, June, 216, 225
Yŏm, Mu-wung, 240, 247
Yŏm, Sang-sŏp: European influences on, 56
Yŏm, Sang-sŏp, *Mansejŏn,* 22, 57–62; anticolonial resistance in, 64, 263n1; architecture in, 59, 60, 84; coloniality in, 57; colonial Korea in, 53–54; colonial space in, 58–59, 71; the discrepant in, 61–62, 66; hybrid identity in, 59; Japanese influences in, 84; modernity in, 55, 60–62, 71; production of subjectivity in, 77; realism of, 60, 72; surveillance in, 57; urban space in, 57, 58–59, 70–71
Young, Robert J. C., 269n8
Yuan, Ch'iung-ch'iung: "A Sky of One's Own," 151

Zambia, postcolonial, 180–81

JINI KIM WATSON is assistant professor of English and comparative literature at New York University.